HELLISH NELL

LAST OF BRITAIN'S WITCHES

Also by Malcolm Gaskill

Crime and Mentalities in Early Modern England

HELLISH NELL

LAST OF BRITAIN'S WITCHES

MALCOLM GASKILL

FOURTH ESTATE • *London*

First published in Great Britain in 2001
by Fourth Estate
A Division of HarperCollins*Publishers*
77–85 Fulham Palace Road
London W6 8JB
www.4thestate.co.uk

1 3 5 7 9 10 8 6 4 2

A catalogue record for this book is available from the British Library.

ISBN 1-84115-109-2

Typeset by Palimpsest Book Production Limited,
Polmont, Stirlingshire
Printed in Great Britain by
Biddles Ltd, Guildford and King's Lynn

To S.P., with love,
for allowing me to put her second to another woman.

The belief that disembodied spirits may be permitted to revisit this world has its foundation upon that sublime hope of immortality which is at once the chief solace and greatest triumph of our reason.

CHARLES MACKAY,
*Extraordinary Popular Delusions
and the Madness of Crowds* (1841)

No testimony is sufficient to establish a miracle, unless the testimony be of such a kind that its falsity would be more miraculous than the fact which it endeavours to establish.

DAVID HUME,
*An Enquiry Concerning Human
Understanding* (1748)

Now don't, sir! Don't expose me! Just this once!
This was the first and only time, I'll swear –
Look at me – see, I kneel, the only time,
I swear, I ever cheated – yes, by the soul
Of her who hears (your sainted mother, sir!)
All, except this last accident, was truth.

ROBERT BROWNING,
'Mr Sludge, the Medium' (1864)

How much is written of pigmes, Fayries, Nymphs, Syrens, Apparitions, which tho not the tenth part true, yet could not spring of nothing?

ROBERT KIRK,
*The Secret Common-wealth and a Short
Treatise of Charms and Spells* (c. 1690)

CONTENTS

Picture credits   x
Preface   xi

Prologue: UNDER FIRE   1

PART I: HELEN VALORIZED

1. YOU'LL BE BURNED AS A WITCH!: The Child-Prophet of Perthshire   17
2. DEVELOPING GOD'S GIFT: Labour, Love and the Arrival of Henry   43
3. RADIANT EFFECTS: 'Albert' and the Spectacle of the Seances   71

PART II: HELEN VILIFIED

4. DARKNESS AND LIGHT: Research and the Search for Respectability   109
5. CHANGING FORTUNES: A Brush with the Law and the Coming of War   147
6. A KIND OF CONJURATION: Trial and Denial at the Old Bailey 1944   181

PART III: HELEN VINDICATED

7. SQUARING THE CIRCLE: Phenomena and Fraud at the Seances   223
8. MANY MANSIONS: Public Life and Prominent Men   263
9. NELLIE, KEEP YOUR CHIN UP!: The Path to Liberty   305

Epilogue: BEYOND THE VEIL   349

Notes   369
Index   387

Picture credits

PREFACE

The title requires advance explanation. Although Helen Duncan was not actually the last person to be tried under the Witchcraft Act of 1735, her case was the most famous and influential of a handful of prosecutions made before the law was changed in 1951. Historians and ethnographers may object that Helen Duncan was not a witch in any folkloric or theological sense; New Age pagans that witches are alive, well and busy in their work. My defence is simple. Most witches recorded in history were defined thus not because they were confessed cultists, nor even because they claimed magical powers, but because they had been judged to be witches by process of law. Helen was one of Britain's witches because it was a British court (and a British press) which branded her so. Finally, she is remembered today as 'Hellish Nell' in the Perthshire town where she was born, not so much because of her conviction under the Witchcraft Act, but because that is how she was known as a child. From her earliest years she was mischievous, rebellious even.

This is a biography of sorts: a life and times with the accent on the times. With no disrespect to her memory, Helen Duncan has not been chosen as a subject because her life fits snugly into the grand historical narratives of our time, but because it reflects a pale light upon less obvious areas of social consciousness, especially their chaotic intersections. Historical reality was kaleidoscopic; neat, singular perspectives on the past are unreliable. As the explanation of 'witch' given above suggests, my primary aim is to explore alternative and contrasting definitions of what too often we confidently call 'the truth'. To this extent this book concerns practical epistemology: how we know the things we know and the way that cultural boundaries surrounding that knowledge determine who we are, in our own time and throughout history. But that is about as theoretical as things get and you will scarcely be troubled with the idea again – at least, abstracted in such an explicit way.

It may also be useful to say what this book is not about. Recently, interest in Helen Duncan has grown with the campaign to clear her name; but I do not seek to exonerate her, any more than I am committed to a rationalist crusade against superstition. Furthermore, I neither advance the cause of Spiritualism or the occult, nor do I promote parapsychology or any other branch of psychical research. That said, no code, belief, or habit of mind is intentionally impugned, although I anticipate withering scorn from those with stronger convictions than myself. My emphasis rests squarely on free interpretation rather than dogma; indeed, in many ways this is a book *about* interpretation. As all biographers and historians should, moreover, I have done my best to vanish in the presence of my subjects.

Analysis aside, this is a true story driven forward by the curious and the dramatic, and deserves to be read as such. As a historian, I am more used to writing about the seventeenth century; here, however, my interest is invested in an enormous cast of characters whose mental worlds span generations and eras, and whose lives can be plotted along intricate lineages and linkages of attitude, thought and belief. What matters most to me is the cluster of ideas and values which has crystallized around the themes of witchcraft, spirits and the supernatural over a period of five hundred years, not least because of the way that the threads of the past inevitably become woven into the fabric of the present.

PREFACE

All authors know that more people deserve gratitude than can be remembered in a preface. The encouragement and advice of friends has meant much to me, among whom Sheena Peirse and Rosamond Roughton are pre-eminent, the former saintly in patience and understanding. Both read drafts of the book in full and made invaluable suggestions. Chris Jones helped with the proofreading. Donald West kindly read the prologue, casting his mind back fifty-six years to save me from errors. Like most of my projects, this book began with one of my father's postal dispatches of newspaper cuttings and for this, as well as his good instinct and perspicacity, I am deeply indebted. Mention also needs to be made of my agent, Felicity Bryan, who placed me in the hands of Clive Priddle, an editor who from the outset has grasped and enhanced my own sense of what I was trying to achieve. Mitzi Angel was a huge help with the pictures.

The staff of many archives and libraries were helpful, memorably at the Cambridge University Library, the Public Record Office at Kew, the British Library at Colindale, the University of London Library, the Island Archives Service on Guernsey, the Churchill Archives Centre and the College of Psychic Studies. I would also like to thank the record management departments of the Crown Prosecution Service and the Home Office, both of whom arranged for me to examine restricted files. Jenny Lee showed me round the old London Spiritualist Alliance and let me nose around in the archives cupboard. Arthur Oram arranged for me to see a medium: Helen Duncan allegedly communicated. In Scotland, Andy Thomson took me to the pubs of Callander and photocopied a rare book kept behind the bar at the Crown Hotel; Sheila Livingstone helped with sources relating to witches north of the border. Roger Caldwell at the Home Office and the Rt. Hon. Michael Ancram MP brought me up to speed on the pardon campaign.

One pleasure of writing about the recent past is that many of the central characters are still alive: more than once I returned home after a day spent learning about an individual in an archive, only to find that he or she had left a telephone message. I am particularly indebted to Sheila Downie and Ann Pooey for giving generously of their time, and for permission to draw upon their mother Gena Brealey's published and unpublished work. Others who shared memories include Bob and Georgina Brake, Tony Cornell, Alan Crossley, Jean Frost, Richard Howe, Denise Iredell, Lucian Landau, Harvey Lingwood, Dorothy Mahoney, June Moore, Chris Newberry, Eileen Philp, Diane White, Geoffrey Wilson and Stanley Worth. I am grateful to the BBC for permission to quote from *The Last Witchcraft Trial*, a documentary broadcast on Radio 4 in 1979 for which Maurice Barbanell, Gena Brealey, Henry Elam and Arthur West were interviewed. Thanks also to the repositories mentioned above for permission to quote from their archives and to the Crown with regard to copyright documents held at the Public Record Office.

No amount of gratitude to Helen Duncan's friends, family and seance-goers can conceal the plain fact that their accounts frequently disagree in detail and interpretation. I have tried hard not to privilege one version over another, partly to avoid less cordial messages appearing on my answering machine, but mostly in the interests of establishing multiple truths, and in defiance of the philosopher and historian R. G. Collingwood's 'one real world', an uncluttered understanding of which was for him the exclusive objective of both his disciplines. Collingwood's dictum that history should aim to be 'the re-enactment of past experience', however, I endorse without hesitation or reservation. I do not stand in judgement over Hellish Nell, last of Britain's witches; rather, I wish to restore the faded images and amplify the echoes that have survived the colourful period in which she lived.

PROLOGUE
UNDER FIRE

Towards the end of March 1944 Donald West, a nineteen-year-old medical student, boarded a train from Liverpool to London. News from the capital was bleak. At night the shelters, deserted for over a year, were full once more, the huddled masses escaping what people were already calling the 'Little Blitz'. Days earlier, Islington had been in flames and the previous month the theatres of the West End had emptied as the bombers returned in force. In wartime Britain a poster asked rail travellers if their journeys were really necessary. But Donald paid little heed to this, nor did he reflect much on the dangers of the air raids. For he had heard there was going to be a witch trial and was determined to see it.

Earlier in the war, Donald had become a member of the London-based Society for Psychical Research and now was invited by leading light Mollie Goldney to join her for this remarkable event. A society lady from a genteel part of Putney, flame-haired, once elegant but still formidable, Mrs Goldney was as indifferent to the *Luftwaffe* as to the protests of the fraudulent mediums she exposed, and the drone of the sirens made little impression on her as she journeyed across the metropolis to keep her appointment with young Donald. The Old Bailey, London's Central Criminal Court, was situated in an area from Cripplegate to the Thames burned and blasted when the devastation of 1666 was revisited upon the City. Nearby, St Paul's Cathedral had been spared, the majestic dome amid billowing smoke an unforgettable image of the war. The 'Bailey', as the barristers called it, had been severely damaged, but as in so many shops and offices across the capital, 'business as usual' was declared and the Clerk of the Court got on with his work.

A queue of people extending far down the street, many more than would fit inside, bore out Mollie Goldney's prediction that they would need to be at court early. Some were Spiritualists, but most just curious citizens, successors to the Londoners of Hogarth's day who had gathered there to follow the condemned to Tyburn, cheering, jeering and sharing the latest from the Grub Street presses. In a boarded-up, blacked-out city, people were drawn to any diversion, the terrifying exhilaration of the first Blitz having long faded into flat predictable tedium. Apart from the cinema, where *Gone with the Wind* – reliving passions from another war – had entered its fourth year, sensational crimes, although rare, were the best entertainment and Fleet Street reporters had only to stroll up Ludgate Hill to check the screens for forthcoming cases. This, however, was something altogether new.

Mrs Goldney, who ranked high in the Women's Voluntary Service (and had once typified the British Raj), was not a woman to be denied and jostled her way into Court No. 4, a wide-eyed Donald West in her wake. Never having been in such a place, the magisterial setting stirred in him an anticipation felt by many spectators now filing to their seats, some of whom had queued for hours. Space was limited, the bombed public gallery still closed and the front benches reserved for the gentlemen of the press. Ahead sat the Director of Public Prosecutions' representative, J. E. Robey – son of the 'Prime Minister of Mirth', Britain's best-loved comedian – and next to him the Clerk. To the right were the barristers, to the left the war jury of seven, alongside whom loomed the raised dock, as yet empty.

Three sharp taps, like the signal to raise the curtain in a French theatre, silenced the hubbub and everyone rose to face the Bench. A door opened and the aldermen and sheriffs emerged, followed by the Recorder of London, Sir Gerald Dodson, who took centre stage in wig and scarlet robes. The usher intoned an ancient proclamation, Dodson bowed to the aldermen, Clerk, counsel and jury in turn, and all were seated. Little had changed in two hundred years. Defendants were allowed counsel now and the courtroom no longer opened out to a public yard like a gigantic Punch and Judy show. Yet in style and substance the court was the same. Only since the start of war had pens replaced quills and the customary herbal mementoes of gaol fever been discontinued – the protective rue and other magical plants along the dock ledge, the dried flowers scattered on the judicial dais.

The Clerk alone remained standing. At his order that the prisoners be put up, footsteps ascended the stairs from the cells and Donald West caught his first glimpse of Helen Duncan, a massive woman in her mid-forties, with a bluish-red complexion, flashing dark eyes and the hair beneath her hat as black as the fur coat which enswathed her. Beside her stood a diffident-looking man in horn-rimmed spectacles rather like Donald's own, and next to him two other women, one Mrs Duncan's rival in build and also in furs, the other smaller in stature, almost birdlike. The Clerk raised a sheaf of papers tied with a pink ribbon and the accused confirmed their names. Then he read the charges:

Helen Duncan, Ernest Edward Hartland Homer, Elizabeth Anne Jones and Frances Brown, you four are charged upon an indictment which contains seven counts. In the first count that between 1 December 1943 and 19 January 1944 you conspired together and with other persons unknown to pretend to exercise or use a kind of conjuration, to wit, that through the agency of the said Helen Duncan spirits of deceased persons should appear to be present in fact in such place as the said Helen Duncan was then in, and that the said spirits were communicating with living persons then and there present contrary to Section 4 of the Witchcraft Act 1735.

Other charges followed: actual pretence to use conjuration, monetary fraud, and 'effecting a public mischief' – a catch-all charge recently used against the builders of shoddy air-raid shelters, but here intended to mean the exploitation of anxiety at a time of national crisis.

The accused pleaded not guilty – Mrs Duncan alone, her Scots brogue reduced to a croak, adding 'sir' as a deferential gesture – the Clerk swore in the jurors and legendary prosecuting counsel, John Maude KC took the floor. For forty minutes the defendants came under fire in a speech of such self-assured wit and poise that Maude's junior, Henry Elam, could only look on in awe, not least because Maude, the Eton-and-Oxford-educated son of an actor-manager, was simultaneously defending a man for murder in Court No. 1.

Maude's message was that the prosecution concerned common fraud alone. At the back of Donald West's mind was the bogus medium he himself had exposed in Liverpool in 1942, for which he was booed and hissed from the seance room. 'The whole thing was a most revolting episode,' West had noted, 'and that such frauds can flourish and be aided and abetted by the stupid credulity of provincial Spiritualists is no less than a public disgrace.' Similarly, as Maude emphasized, the Duncan case had nothing to do with religion, still less witchcraft, even though it was inevitable that using the largely forgotten Witchcraft Act would shape how it was seen by press and public. Mediums were usually just fined under the Vagrancy Act of 1824, in the same way that fortune tellers had been back when Wellington's demobilized army scratched a living. To most minds the Witchcraft Act meant witchcraft.

Maude's sole concern, however, was the opinion of the six men and one woman of the jury. 'In olden days', he informed them, 'it was almost a popular matter to chase poor deluded creatures who were thought to be witches, or indeed sometimes may themselves have believed themselves to be witches, and the mass of the public believed in that sort of thing being possible.' But by the reign of George II, Maude continued, witchcraft trials were thought ridiculous and an Act was passed to end them – a watershed in British beliefs and values.

So we reach a position in 1735 which would no doubt be welcomed by any person who may call himself today a Spiritualist; for those persons . . . would no doubt be the warmest supporters of any measure directed by the State against the fraudulent and deplorable activities of any persons who would be pretending anything such as the calling back of the dead into a room.

Mrs Duncan sipped her water, exchanging glances with her daughter Nan below, as Maude condemned the return of the war dead as a 'false and hollow lie' and a cruel entertainment. Maude knew well how weary indifference for the war civilians masked a gnawing anxiety for servicemen overseas and never worse than in the weeks before the invasion of Europe.

Maude sketched events leading up to the arrests. At a place known as the 'Master Temple Psychic Centre', a room above Ernest Homer's chemist's shop in Portsmouth, Stanley Worth, a naval lieutenant, had attended several feeble seances. In December 1943, however, Elizabeth Jones (the putative Mrs Homer) promised something more special: in the New Year a Mrs Duncan was coming, a wonderful medium able to materialize spirits from ectoplasm, a swirling, shining substance part-physical, part-spiritual, which surged back into her body with such vitality, Mrs Homer enthused, that it sucked up dust and litter such as cigarette ends and matches – just like a vacuum cleaner. The price of admission – 12s 6d (today equivalent to £20–25) – might have been reasonable, Maude suggested, 'if one were going to see the ghost of Napoleon or the Duke of Wellington, but not of much value if you were going to see a bogus conjuring trick.' Worth was intrigued, however, and had bought tickets for himself and a fellow naval officer.

The seance they attended was typical. Chairs stood in rows facing 'the cabinet', a corner sectioned off with a curtain. Here Mrs Duncan sat in a black gown, drawers and shoes examined by the sitters, which three women appointed to search her body had watched her put on. Blackout material covered the window, the only illumination a weak red bulb dimmed further with a handkerchief, and Mrs Homer – who had entertained troops in France during the previous war – led the circle first in prayer, then song, as Spiritualists used to say, to raise the vibrations. On this occasion it was the medium's favourite, 'South of the Border'. Entranced, head on one side and snoring softly, by some occult means Mrs Duncan began generating her ectoplasm, which crept sinuously from beneath the cabinet. Frances Brown, Mrs Duncan's Geordie travelling companion, watched carefully from the back row. When Worth was called to summon a spirit he asked if it was his aunt, even though all his aunts were alive. 'Yes,' came the husky reply. Worth's sister also appeared, even though she too was alive and well, and driving an ambulance in London.

Afterwards, Worth said that he had been amazed by the seance; but, like Donald West, the more he thought about it the more indignant he became, so much so that he went to the police. There, a Detective Inspector Ford asked him if he would attend another seance as a stooge. On the evening of 19 January 1944, Worth and War Reserve Constable Rupert Cross went to 301 Copnor Road, and the seance began as before. This time, however, Cross lunged at one of the spirit forms, while Worth shone a torch towards the cabinet and blew a whistle to summon policemen waiting outside. Of the ectoplasm, which Cross swore was butter muslin, there was no trace.

The magical power of Maude's account lay not just in solemnity but in parody. He spoke less of spirits than of *ghosts* and asked the jury to consider the afterlife of a cat: 'What the cat was doing before it was summoned to make its appearance in Portsmouth one can only imagine: whether it was hunting pink mice in the Elysian Fields one does not know. All one knows is that a miaow came from behind the curtains; so, I suppose, if one is a cat, one does not make much progress.'

A ripple of amusement spread across the public benches, leaving only the Spiritualists defiantly unmoved as Maude, similarly poker-faced, extended the menagerie: 'A parrot is alleged to have appeared, his name is Bronco. It came fluttering round from somewhere; it was called up . . . from some heavenly forest, and it appeared in Portsmouth. It was followed by a rabbit. We do not know its name; we know the parrot was called Bronco.'

As the first wave of laughter was reinforced by a second, the Recorder shifted in his chair. Maude pressed on, relating how a sitter's materialized father, a policeman in life, had nipped back to collect his helmet. 'No doubt all policemen', he suggested to the court,

> hope that, when they pass into the next world, they will not go on being policemen for ever . . . Can you imagine anything more disappointing than a policeman having passed through life and apparently not having risen as high as an Inspector, because he still had a helmet? Finding himself in the next world, not in plain clothes, not at ease in a shirt and a pair of plain trousers, but having to look for his helmet?

Now that they were under his spell, Maude asked the jurors to put all the insanity to one side, and to try to think of anything more thrilling than asking 'Is that you, Dad?' and receiving the answer that it was Dad. And with that deft switch between the masks of comedy and tragedy, Maude simply stole the moment.

For the Defence, the Spiritualists' National Union had appointed Charles Loseby, an ardent Spiritualist and veteran of the trenches. Mrs Duncan he would defend by the simple strategy of proving her a genuine medium, thereby precluding the possibility of fraud. Of 300 witnesses he claimed to have waiting in the wings, he called forty-five, some of whom had attended dozens of seances. And their stories were extraordinary. Conjured up and clothed in ectoplasm, the spirits of parents, siblings, uncles and *real* aunts had returned (sometimes as many as twenty at a sitting), spectral hands reaching out, their lips planting warm kisses on tear-streaked cheeks. The reporters scribbled as never before to capture the witnesses' words. Here is Alfred Dodd, a sane, sober amateur authority on Shakespeare's sonnets, remembering a seance in Liverpool in 1936 where he was fleetingly reunited with his first sweetheart, Helen. She had died in 1897 at the age of twenty-one:

> She stood there dressed in a white flowing robe, and over that white flowing robe was a fine curtain of net. I was so astonished that I stood up in my seat, which I ought not to have done, and I called out to my wife . . . 'Why it's Helen; it's Helen.' The girl did not come to me direct, she came right round the room from left to right, and she stood before me, a living, palpitating woman. The same hair that I knew so well, dark and ruddy; the same eyes, hazel; they shone with animation; her face, the same ivory pallor on her cheeks . . . Then I heard her speak and she spoke in the same soft Scotch accent that I knew so well.

As the testimony floated out into the courtroom, so the Spiritualists felt Maude's sting abate, not least Mrs Duncan who wept when Dodd described her as an 'absolutely straight materialization medium'. Each witness, invariably of good standing, clear-headed and articulate, added to a chorus which, by the fourth day, had begun to seem endless. And here lay Loseby's most basic mistake: far from being overwhelmed, the jurors were bored rigid, the press began to crave novelty and the Recorder was irritated. What for the Prosecution was a stage, too often became a pulpit for the Defence. Only the psychical researchers sustained their fascination and even they suppressed the odd yawn.

Most tantalizing to Donald West was Loseby's offer for Mrs Duncan to hold a special seance for the jury. A hush descended, followed by an excited stir. Mrs Duncan stared straight ahead and passed a hand across her waxy forehead as if she might faint. The cup of water offered by the wardress she motioned away without breaking her fixed gaze. But the reporters were to be disappointed: the jury declined the offer, the Recorder having expressed a desire that the court not be turned into a sideshow. But Dodson was no killjoy; indeed, as the co-author of a successful West End musical, he had something of a passion for popular theatre. Instead, he did merely what the Crown paid him to do: he applied the law. If no phenomena were to appear, he argued, Mrs Duncan would be condemned before trial, constituting 'a reversion to the Dark Ages and to something very akin to trial by ordeal'.

On the Friday – judgement day – demand for a seat was greater than on any previous day. Conditions in the chamber were so cramped, the atmosphere so charged, that when one of Mrs Goldney's SPR colleagues offered her his seat, the police took exception and ejected him. Once proceedings began, it was clear that Loseby's aura of optimism was evaporating into the ether. Apart from the odd plaintive sob, until this time Mrs Duncan had maintained a composure which, as Loseby racked up the witnesses, bordered on the cocksure. 'On one occasion', noted an astonished reporter, 'she came up from the cells as if to a reception. After smiling at people in court, she sat down with as much elegance as a woman of her size could muster. Shortly afterwards, she took a wrap from her shoulders and, with the manner of a queen, handed it to the wardress behind her.'

By contrast, as proceedings reached their climax, her emotions fell into disarray. The jury were discharged from reaching verdicts on all counts except that of the Witchcraft Act and retired close to teatime to consider the Recorder's lengthy summing-up. For twenty-three minutes the spectators waited patiently, speculating in low voices, before the jury returned and the foreman rose and cleared his throat. When Mrs Duncan heard that she and her co-defendants had all been found guilty, at first she was too shocked to feel anything other than a strange anaesthetized calmness.

Prior to sentencing, the Recorder called upon the Chief Constable of Portsmouth, Arthur West, to provide some background regarding the lives of the accused. The court heard how Mrs Duncan had in fact been fined at Edinburgh in 1933 for a similar offence, and had threatened and cursed the woman who exposed her. At this, as if emerging from a trance, Mrs Duncan suddenly snapped, 'I never did!' West (no relation to Donald) pressed on. Most intriguing was his fleeting reference to the principal defendant having breached security regulations in 1941 when she predicted the sinking of a warship before its loss had been announced – a solitary hint at what, beyond the smoke and shadow of the seance room, the trial might really be about. She was, in any case, 'an unmitigated humbug and pest', with no redeeming features the Chief Constable could think of.

At Loseby's request, the Recorder postponed sentencing until Monday and the court was adjourned. As Mrs Duncan was led down to the cells, she cried out something which Mollie Goldney failed to catch, but others reported as: 'I never heard sae mony lies in a' my life. I dinna ken why they should get away with thae lies!' And as her muffled noises-off faded from the courtroom, her followers closed their brimming eyes in disbelief. Nan Duncan screamed that prison would kill her mother, brushing off the police officers who came forward to pacify her.

The following Monday the Recorder sent Mrs Duncan to prison for nine months, a decision which she received with bewildered disbelief. She sobbed and groaned her innocence, then cried out, 'Oh God! Is there a God? I never done it, is there a God?' before swooning heavily to the floor of the dock, knocking over her chair. The warders, police officers and three other defendants, who had scarcely broken her fall, helped her up and handed her back her hat. As she was taken downstairs she continued to rail, the Recorder waiting for her cries to subside before resuming. Mr Homer and his supposed wife were bound over for two years. Thus martyred, Helen Duncan was escorted to a van waiting to return her to north London. Her supporters, who had begun to disperse from the court hall, flowers wilting at their sides, reassembled momentarily and, as Charles Loseby observed, 'cheered her as though to encourage her but not excitedly'.

The trial had been long, seven days in all. Indeed, so much was said that the appeal hearing for which Loseby applied was delayed while the shorthand writers finished their transcript. Meanwhile, upstaged by John Maude (who also won his murder case) and facing the wrath not just of the Spiritualists' National Union, but of the editor of *Psychic News*, the Duncan family and even Spiritualists within the SPR, a sallow-cheeked Loseby suddenly looked ten years older. In the eyes of his supporters, the guardians of British justice had denied what was demonstrably true about life and death – and the life beyond death – and had pilloried an innocent woman into the bargain. The psychical researchers took a more detached, clinical view. On the Saturday between verdict and sentencing, Mollie Goldney wrote to her good friend

Harry Price, Britain's foremost psychical researcher, to reassure
him that he had not really missed much:

> As you see, a verdict of guilty. The Judge's summing up was
> very feeble. He did not *comment*; he merely recapitulated,
> telling the Jury with every word that she was a fraud . . .
> The fanatical conviction of 50 or 60 witnesses is a most
> amazing psychological study; they all averred that no argu-
> ment, no alleged fact would shake them in their conviction
> that they had verily seen their relatives.

And yet the principal issue had been the guilt of the defendants
according to the arcane, archaic but dispassionate processes of
law, never the possibility of post-mortem survival or the fallacies
of human perception, however much anyone may have wished
for these matters to be hammered out in the public arena. As
the Recorder had unequivocally stated: 'Whether genuine manifestations . . . are possible, the verdict does not decide.'
   Donald West's impression was that although Helen Duncan
was a fraud, the Crown had failed to prove its case. Instead, the
authorities had resorted to a statute which made the four accused
guilty from the moment of indictment. And as the prosecution
wound down, so reporters, editors, compositors and printers
rushed to get the witch trial on to the front page and into the
waiting news vans. Of course Helen Duncan was not a witch,
but in terms of popular associations and public image, the law
had cast her in that role, earnest protestations of the Crown
notwithstanding. To borrow a term from the Middle Ages, Helen
had been branded *invocator spiritum* and, by that token alone, in
wartime London the days of old and the burning times were
recalled to mind even as the bombs fell from the skies.

PART I

HELEN VALORIZED

1
YOU'LL BE BURNED AS A WITCH!
The Child-Prophet of Perthshire

In 1697, two centuries before Helen Duncan's birth, a Dumfriesshire woman named Elspeth McEwen sat miserably in gaol awaiting trial. In the previous year her neighbours had complained to the kirk of Dalry that she was a witch who spirited milk from their cows and stopped the eggs in their hens. Duly summoned, she was carried to the kirk sessions on a horse (which, rumour had it, sweated blood) and after a summary hearing was imprisoned while the agonizingly slow wheels of superior justice were set in motion. That year, the devil had been busy in south-western Scotland. Other parishes, angry and

Nell MacFarlane, the enigmatic tomboy.

afraid, had identified witches and at Kerrick an evil spirit had made life intolerable for the Mackie family by pelting them with stones, peat and balls of fire which set the house alight. A little white hand and arm had been seen beating the walls and when they pulled a cloth from a mysterious figure, which materialized by the hearth, they found nothing underneath. Inspired by righteous anger, the local minister committed their tale to print in Edinburgh; and in due course the London presses brought out an edition, the Scots dialect anglicized to aid comprehension of what was, hellfire rhetoric aside, a saleable sensational news story.

It was not until April 1698 that Elspeth was examined by a commission of justiciary in the burgh of Kirkcudbright, before whom she confessed to forming a pact with the devil, evidence which guaranteed her conviction. With the local memory still fresh of the witches executed in the Renfrewshire town of Paisley, the chief commissioner, Sir John Maxwell, recommended that Elspeth be burned to death, and she was returned to gaol for five months pending sentence from the Privy Council, in which time she was so badly treated that she begged her tormentors to kill her. On 24 August she was carried in a cart to a public place in Kirkcudbright town, bound with ropes, and set in a barrel of tar stacked up with peat and coal. The Provost repeated the sentence, accompanied by a drummer beating a solemn rhythm, whereafter the executioner, an indigent old man primed with drink, throttled Elspeth until she was insensible, then kindled the fire. An exemplum of sound administration in the Calvinist lowlands, the burgh treasurer meticulously recorded the costs in his account book, from the tar barrel and coals down to the executioner's ale. A total of seven Scots pounds and nine shillings was spent on the death of Elspeth McEwen.

Quite what they got for their money now seems obscure

because the hopes and fears of our forebears have all but passed from view. Imagine, though, a mental world where witches were a real threat, their execution reassuring proof that a divinely ordained State was resisting the dominion of Satan. For the punishment of Elspeth McEwen and 60,000 Europeans like her (four-fifths of whom were women) did not constitute just random slaughter, nor was it motivated by the love of blindness and ignorance lamented by the Elizabethan poet Spenser. Rather, the witch-hunts were the result of rapidly changing religious, political and economic conditions in the sixteenth century, erupting along fault lines in relations between Church, State and people, and indeed among the people themselves. Across the Continent, competing faiths sharpened the definition of a moral universe poised between good and evil, and of a physical environment where wondrous manifestations of the supernatural were commonplace. Folly the prosecution of witches may have been but, taking our (comparatively recent) ancestors on their own terms, greater folly would have been to ignore the devil who surely stalked in their midst. And so it was that virtually every Scottish generation from the 1590s to the end of the seventeenth century experienced its own regional witch panic, each lasting no more than a year or so.

The fate of witches was determined by the law, the standardization and uniform enforcement of which were essential to godly state building. In accordance with the injunction from the Book of Exodus, 'Thou shalt not suffer a witch to live', in 1563 the Catholic Mary, Queen of Scots, and her Protestant English counterpart, Elizabeth I, both passed legislation against witchcraft, Mary's the more severe of the two. Her son, James, was a lonely boy-king whose academic interest in religion and the body politic quite properly embraced demonology – the study of that which threatened to undermine all order and authority. His interest peaked with the first of the Scottish witch-crazes, which began in 1590 after the ship carrying James and his new bride, Anne of Denmark, was imperilled by storms attributed to witches hostile to bonding between nascent Protestant states. The first to be accused was a maidservant whose name, curiously enough, was Geillie Duncan. She had acquired a reputation as a healer and was said to attend secret gatherings in North Berwick church with other witches, some people of substance whom she identified when her finger joints were crushed in the *pilliewinkis* and her head 'thrawed' in a twisted noose. Upon her throat they found the devil's mark, typically a blotch or excrescence into which it was customary to thrust pins to see if pain were felt or blood drawn.

James interrogated personally those named by Geillie Duncan, among them Agnes Sampson, a respectable matron who had healed a man by assuming his sickness into her own body and then attempting to transfer it to an animal. Sampson told James many things, most famously snippets of pillow talk from his wedding night, which James received with a mixture of scepticism and credulity, calling the witches 'extreme lyars' – like their master the devil. On the whole, though, he took the witches seriously because to insecure European states the acquisition of such information was not only wicked: it was potentially treasonable. James sat through the witches' tortures and approved their executions (Duncan and Sampson were both hanged), and in 1597 published a short, erudite, if somewhat derivative treatise entitled *Daemonologie*, into which he distilled his learning and experience. When he succeeded to the English throne in 1603, little time was lost bringing the two countries closer legislatively and, for good measure, the *Daemonologie* was republished in London. In James's honour, the capital's most famous playwright wrote a short play (the King was known to fidget) about a usurper whose destruction was due not so much to witchcraft itself as ambition fuelled by the false promises of witches:

> *And that distill'd by magic sleights*
> *Shall raise such artificial sprites*
> *As by the strength of their illusion*
> *Shall draw him on to his confusion.*

The manner in which Hecate's advice to the weird sisters concerning Macbeth's fate emphasizes diabolic delusion rather than diabolic possession would prove highly significant for the legislative history of witchcraft in the next century and beyond.

The Witchcraft Act of 1604 was distinguished from its predecessor by a clause prescribing death for invocation and conjuration of diabolic spirits alone. In England, James soon lost interest in witches (unless it was to save women so accused) and in his lifetime there was no craze south of the border to match that of his homeland. Yet his law remained and became the statutory basis for several hundred witch trials in England spanning more than a century, in which time the *Daemonologie* ran to numerous editions.

In Scotland, too, the social and legal idea of the witch persisted, graphic proof of which is provided by the executions at Kirkcudbright and Paisley. At the Paisley trial in 1697, James Hutchinson, minister of Kilallan, was appointed to preach to the commissioners and, choosing Exodus as his text, inveighed that witches were such as by diabolical compact achieved unnatural ends, adding that 'The man or woman that hath a familiar spirit . . . shall surely be put to death'. By this time, however, doubts which had dulled James's witch-hunting ardour were hardening into scepticism among the educated élite and it was as a reaction to this 'atheistical' trend that the minister of Kerrick wrote his pamphlet about the Mackies' pyromaniac spirit. Likewise, in the following year another Scottish minister, John Bell, spilt yet more ink at Glasgow with a published tract proving the existence of spirits from sacred and profane history, and, echoing Hutchinson, describing the marks by which their acolytes might be known.

The prosecution of witches owed as much to folk tradition as to learned demonology. Plebeian beliefs, stretching back long before written records, paid heed to ghosts, revenants, demons and fairies, which populated a dreamscape where nature met supernature, and the mundane and the miraculous were conjoined. Cunning folk, the doctors and shamans of the poor, diagnosed, healed and prognosticated, interpreting omens and resisting curses, thereby allowing the powerless in small ways to take control of their lives. Even inquisitorial trials rarely proceeded without the testimony of ordinary parishioners; had the farmers of Dalry not feared for their eggs and milk, Elspeth McEwen would never have ended up in a blazing tar barrel. In the courts, truths were fashioned which served the needs of community and society, and there too declining witch beliefs among the élite were mirrored until witchcraft became legally unsustainable. In 1736 both Scottish and English statutes were repealed, and were replaced with a single Act (dated 1735) that made the pretence to conjuration an offence, a measure which, according to one Edwardian Scots antiquarian, turned the witch into a cheat and impostor, and substituted the pillory for the stake.

But in the nineteenth century the same social class which ended the witch trials produced men fascinated by ancient superstitions. Like anthropologists in their own land, they discovered a collective memory of remarkable longevity. Early in Queen Victoria's reign, one inquirer recalled meeting an old man in Renfrewshire whose great-grandmother had watched the witches burn at Paisley in 1697 and shuddered whenever she remembered the smell of roasting flesh. The beliefs and customs enshrined in oral tradition, and in countless archives, libraries and parish chests, suggested to these men the existence of a mentality separate in space and time from their own. What most failed to appreciate was the extent to which such beliefs outlived the repeal of the witchcraft statutes, a blindness revealed whenever they dilated upon their thoughts and discoveries in public. In 1841 Charles Mackay, a journalist and lexicographer of lowland Scots, filled hundreds of pages with stories of prophecies, delusions, apparitions and devils, and a whole chapter on 'the witch mania', unaware of the living thread that stretched between the Dark Ages and the age of industry and empire.

Callander, with its proximity to the fast-flowing River Teith, and enclosure by high wooded crags and the Trossachs range beyond, was a place of strategic significance where lowlands met highlands: the Romans had built a fort there, and the barons of Linlithgow and Callander a castle. Traditionally, the vulgar tongue was Gaelic. A reforming minister resigned his living in 1596 because his parishioners had but 'a poor pennyworth of the English', a state of affairs which a visitor in 1724 found unchanged, although anglicization of speech advanced in the eighteenth century with the building of a new town, sequestrations of property after the Jacobite rebellions and the settling of veterans from the Seven Years War. Today, if you happen to be half an hour north of Glasgow, it is the sort of place you might drive through without paying it much attention, an unexceptional town where shops sell Celtic knotwork, certificates of clan membership and tartan clothing from the local woollen mills. Buildings constructed from the flecked granite natives call 'plum-pudding stone' flank Main Street, the principal thorough-fare along which cattle were once driven to the great lowland fairs or trysts. An older British generation may remember Callander as the 'Tannochbrae' of the BBC's drama *Dr Finlay's Casebook*, a nostalgic evocation of small-town Perthshire life, every frame and line of dialogue lamenting the encroachment of urban anonymity and soullessness.

Nostalgia needs to be separated from a more brutal reality, however, as should heritage from history. The truth was that time out of mind, generations of Callander people had toiled on farms and crofts out in the sour moors and water-logged fields, or hiked across the exhausting hill slopes, shepherding, chopping wood and longing to be home by the fire. Even men with trades grew vegetables or kept chickens and cows in the long, narrow gardens that stretched behind their cottages, and competed with pike to eke out their starchy diets with trout and salmon from the Teith. Life was, to paraphrase Hobbes, nasty, brutish and short, oppor-tunities for self-advancement few. True, by 1800 smelting and weaving had been added to the staple occupations of the town, and it was common for men to carry cartloads of bark, wool and wood down to the lowlands, and return with coal, tar, grease and small luxuries to sell on for a profit. But even the most powerful witch prowling on the blasted heath could scarcely have predicted that the town's industrial future would lie not in commerce and trade, nor in the building of dark satanic mills, but in poetry.

Callander weather forecasts from early in the twentieth century were neither subtle nor diverse: it was either 'exceptionally cold and wet', or 'phenomenally mild'. In the century before that the roads were forbidding, the facilities rudimentary, the people inscrutable and intractable. All in all, the Trossachs resembled the safe world broken open and exposed to the elements, and offered no obvious resorts to lovers of comfort. Sensitive souls of a poetic disposition, however, began to find inspiration in its savage beauty, the perfect antidote to the prissy correctness of classicism. In 1803 the Wordsworths arrived in Callander in elegiac mood and spent a rainy evening huddled round a fire in their hotel room learning about the town from a pamphlet by the minister, Dr James Robertson. More than anyone else, though, it was Sir Walter Scott who attracted visitors with his verse romance *The Lady of the Lake*, published in 1810, which conjured up a melancholic realm of heroes and heroines, of primitive dark hills and even darker passes, of myth, magic and the primordial contest between good and evil. For in the rawness and vastness of nature the poets had felt touched by the sublime and immanent force of the supernatural.

The impact on the world of letters was nothing compared with the effects on the local economy. Public and private coaches imported successive waves of tourists, to the extent that a Romantic poet could scarcely hear himself sigh. In 1818 Keats sniffed that the area was 'vexatiously full of visitors', of whom three steamer-loads per day were being ferried up and down the loch by the 1840s, and the Dreadnought Hotel and Callander's handful of other places to stay were packed out. The turning point, however, came a decade later with the building of the Oban railway, which brought in the urban working classes too, prompting this cynical appreciation of Scott's legacy from Robert Pearse Gillies: 'All the world, rich and poor, including crown-princes and noblesse, crowded to visit the scenery he had depicted. Instead of being, as usual, a dull, stupid village, whose inhabitants were all in a state of cabbageism, Callander of Menteith became a rallying point for all classes, a place wherein to study varieties of character. Truly that study was not very consolatory or edifying.'

Cabbages, perhaps; but busy cabbages. By 1870 there had been a dramatic expansion in the number and variety of shops and services at the disposal of visitors, for whom there was also now a choice between six hotels and sixty-six lodging houses. By the time Helen Duncan was born here in 1897, the Callander Recreation Company had invested in a bowling green and a nine-hole golf course, and tennis courts had been laid and a keeper employed to look after them. At a time when good working-class housing was scarce, houses were built specially for well-to-do families – the so-called 'carriage folk' – who rented them for themselves, their pets and servants for the entire summer. It was at refined consumers such as these that fashions like tweed suits and ladies' capes were being aimed by 1900; likewise the 'Women's Chat' column in the *Callander Advertiser*, which traded royal gossip and style tips: 'The handkerchief of the moment is white,' advised 'Madge', before moving effortlessly on to a distinctly proletarian-sounding recipe for Balmoral pudding.

By 1897, Helen Duncan's parents would have experienced an improved physical environment and broader mental horizons in Callander – an awakening from rural somnolence. And with economic growth came political maturity. Burgh status was conferred in 1866 and the provision of public amenities over-seen by a council of commissioners. Gaslighting was extended, kerbs and gutters laid, sewers rebuilt and shrubs planted to hide the ash pits. Ratepayers took these matters seriously and civic-minded businessmen sat on innumerable committees. Still, life remained a kaleidoscope of old and new. Street dung was used to grow hay sold for public funds. Newspaper advertisements for rabbits and sheep-dip stood alongside those for French millinery and women's pills to 'quickly correct all irregularities, remove all obstructions and relieve the distressing symptoms so prevalent with the sex'. Deaths in boiler explosions were reported and so was tubercular infection in milk. At the turn of the century,

English had not so much banished Gaelic as established bilingualism – a means to cooperate with, but also to resist, the dominant culture. In sum, these contrasts suggest a town where the middling ranks prospered disproportionately compared with labouring families dependent on seasonal wages, Christian charity and the Penny Bank, and also account for Queen Victoria's impression that Callander had 'a few good houses and many poor ones'. Even lesser artisans and tradesmen fretted about rates of 1s 8d in the pound (as they were in 1897). Petty thieves were frequently brought before the commission chairman (also chief magistrate) as were fraudsters – weavers who adulterated linen with cotton, for example. Occasionally there were suicides. It was only natural, then, that many young men and women were seduced by visions of the New World conjured up by the emigration agents who visited Callander to recruit farmworkers and domestic servants, offering passages to Canada and Australia for a small fee or in some cases for nothing.

Hopes were also pinned on religion, which offered eternal life in the hereafter and, until then, a sense of dignity in adversity. Faith in Callander was as pluralistic as in any Victorian town embracing, among others, Free and United Presbyterians, Catholics, Episcopalians and the Church of Scotland. Dominant was Protestantism of the most tight-lipped, straight-backed variety, an ethos which pervaded a range of clubs and societies. There was the Ben Ledi Masonic Lodge and the Fiery Cross Lodge. The magistrate, Colonel Robertson, presided over the Abstainers' Union, his wife the YWCA Bible class which met during the summer season in the Mission Hall, where Mrs Chenevix-Trench also held her Band of Hope meetings. Edification and education were the keys. In 1892 the Free Kirk School evolved into a high school named after the McLaren Trust, which had been established to promote 'the sound religious and moral training of the young in the parish and neighbour-hood of Callander', but offered adult evening classes in short-hand, book-keeping, drawing and mensuration. Public lectures advanced ideals of prohibition and self-improvement more directly – for example, condemning swearing, cheating, lying and smoking among youths to whom models of morality were held up: in December 1898, a YMCA talk about Mr Gladstone, illus-trated with magic-lantern slides, was well-attended despite the stormy weather. This was, therefore, a formative environment characterized as much by restriction as opportunity. When the Callander Literary Society, a focal point of the town's social and cultural life, met to debate the future enfranchisement of women, the motion was defeated thirty-four to eighteen. Traditional roles were firmly established.

Then there was the other side to this rational existence of civic discipline and muscular religion. When the Dreadnought Hotel was built in 1802 its owners, the McNabs, had the severed head of a rival clan chief carved in relief to commemorate his murder and set it into the gable wall, where it stands today. Doubtless his ghost has returned. According to locals, the hotel is certainly haunted by a mother who died giving birth to an illegitimate child; even now the window of her room is visibly blacked out. And to stray beyond Callander's main streets, to hike up the winding paths into the crags, is to enter an altogether more spell-binding world of bloody deeds and their spectral legacy, where the looming presence of Ben Ledi – the Hill of God – and the enveloping chill and mist transport the mind across time and place. This was, after all, the site where the Romantic poets found truth in folklore and imagination, and where cold reason became redundant. Here roamed Robert MacGregor, the eighteenth-century outlaw lionized by Sir Walter Scott, and here the novelist's senses were beguiled by the morbid and the supernatural. A generation before Rob Roy, the witch-hunt had been most intense in the lowlands where the Kirk was most zealous; but this tendency only helped to preserve the highland belief in curses, charms, sacred ponds, fairy hills, ghostly warriors, angels, hags, necromancers, werewolves and banshees – the Celtic spirits whose wailing portended a death. Had the Wordsworths had access to the *Proceedings of the Archaeological Society of Scotland*, they might have had occasion to read Rev. Dr Robertson on this subject as well.

The highlands were also home to second sight: the gift of prophecy. Dr Samuel Johnson, of whom his companion Boswell said 'he did not affirm anything positively upon a subject which it is the fashion of the times to laugh at as a matter of absurd credulity', returned from his tour of the Hebrides in the 1790s utterly convinced of its power. In the seventeenth century opinion was divided as to its source: the devil, or the 'good folk' – the tribal fairies who inhabited the mountains and who could blind humans but for some reason were afraid of iron. The authority on the subject had been Robert Kirk, minister of Aberfoyle, a parish five miles south-west of Callander. Until his death in 1692, Kirk took a keen interest in every kind of spiritual and magical belief which, like the ministers mentioned earlier, he encountered every day among his parishioners and defended in order to repel the perceived advancement of atheism. 'There is no more absurdity for a Spirit to inform an infantin Body of Air', he argued, 'than a Body composed of dull and drousie Earth', a dualism which he extended beyond the existence of spirits to a practical understanding of their agency. Evil spirits sucked witches' blood, leaving the devil's mark; benign spirits could be invoked for creative purposes. Recalling the sort of healing power which had sealed the fate of Agnes Sampson a century earlier, he noted that: 'There are words instituted for the transferring of the soul or sickness on other Persons, Beasts, Trees, Waters, Hills or Stones, according as the Charmer is pleased to name: and the effect follows wonderfully.' By the nineteenth century this was just the kind of superstition which fascinated journalist Charles Mackay, like Kirk a Perthshire man; and likewise Glasgow-born anthropologist Sir James Frazer whose objective conspectus of ancient customs, *The Golden Bough*, was completed in 1915. It is ironic that Frazer's work actually served to emphasize the endurance and current vibrancy of such beliefs – even to propagate them in a new generation of poets.

One icy Thursday evening in January 1908 the Callander Literary Society welcomed a visiting speaker, Dr McDiarmid, an authority on Gaelic and the folklore of Bredalbane. Clutching his notes, McDiarmid proceeded to enthral an unusually large local audience with a vivid evocation of the days of romance and cruelty, reclaiming long-dead rituals, observances and supernatural beliefs from a past as dark and mysterious as the mountains which enclosed their town or the moonless winter night. After he had finished speaking, the society's Chairman, primary schoolteacher Alexander Cumming, offered his appreciation of McDiarmid's evocation of the world they had lost and prompted a modest round of polite but sincere applause. Appearances were deceptive, however. If some present supposed that McDiarmid's superstitious arcana belonged entirely to legend, there were surely others who knew differently, not least Mr Cumming who at that time had rather an unusual, not to say disturbing, little girl in his class.

These were the cultural foundations in which Helen Duncan's life took root, her mental territory mapped by a timeless past and an improving present, the evangelical Presbyterianism of the streets, and the spirits and sprites of the Menteith Hills. Helen was born a MacFarlane, a clan deeply rooted in and around Callander, their graves scattered across the kirkyard at the neighbouring hamlet of Kilmahog. The wife of an ancestor killed at Waterloo, it is said, wore her widow's weeds for the rest of her lonely life. In the eighteenth century, an age when ties of kinship were the sinews of local power, the MacFarlanes had provided numerous men of influence, among them John MacFarlane of Kilmahog, a teacher respected at the parish school for over thirty years. Later, Norman MacFarlane had given his name to a salmon pool on the Teith. By the time of Helen's birth this prominence had declined somewhat, although the MacFarlanes still cropped up here and there: the town librarian, a secretary of the cycling club, a finalist in a YMCA draughts tournament. Archibald, Helen's father, was a slater and builder, the sort of upper-working-class skilled artisan who, though not recorded as a town councillor or magistrate (as his descendants claim), nonetheless worried about the rates, and was typically industrious, God-fearing and loyal to the Crown. Tradition has it that when his wife Isabella was a girl, an open coach en route to Balmoral was caught in murderous weather and her family were called upon to shelter the Queen from the elements. The tale, however improbable, was repeated a thousand times, the embossed letter of thanks, like the crest on a marmalade jar, somehow asserting that the family were 'by appointment'. It was a pride which Isabella brought with her bottom drawer when she married Archibald MacFarlane and set up home at 96 Main Street, a house rented from Daniel Melrose, an ironmonger of the town, for the respectable sum of £14 a year.

In June 1897, during Queen Victoria's Golden Jubilee celebrations, Isabella MacFarlane was three months pregnant with her fourth child. Across the nation glittering pageantry and ebullient festivities marked the height of British imperial pride and Callander did its bit, despite controversy over plans to spend good money planting commemorative trees in Main Street when, it was said, the town's water pipes needed an urgent overhaul. Isabella's baby was born on 25 November at three o'clock in the morning, a healthy baby girl whom she and Archie named Victoria Helen in honour of the Queen. They celebrated modestly, but did not make an announcement in the *Advertiser*. Christened into the Presbyterian Church, the story goes that Victoria slept through most of the ceremony, waking only for the naming and blessing when the minister was able to look into those deep, dark-brown eyes which her followers would remember long after her death. The birth details were lodged with the Registrar (who used the schoolhouse as his office) and the MacFarlane siblings started adjusting to the new arrival in the family home.

Today, as for two centuries, there are still MacFarlanes living in Bridgend, a road crossing the Teith and by tradition the oldest part of the town, and it was here that Archie and Isabella moved early in the new century, to a small whitewashed cottage with a slate roof, three front gables and sash windows. Some say Archie built it himself. Her first name perhaps too grand for daily use, the MacFarlanes' youngest was known by her middle name, Helen, and even that soon evolved into 'Nellie' or 'Nell'. She grew into a plump, sturdy child, more handsome than pretty, with her flashing eyes and hair so black it had a shimmer of blue. As in many households in Callander, her father's regime was loving but austere. Although not exactly poor, by the time Isabella's eighth child was born the MacFarlanes could not afford to be profligate even if profligacy had not been a sin. Christmas was celebrated with minimal ostentation and emphasis on the festival's religious aspects. Luxuries were few. Helen, however, had a sweet tooth and craved confection (then as now, the local delicacy was 'tablet', an extravagant brittle fudge made from sugar, cream and butter). Her rugged frame fitted her for boyish pursuits and she played hard with her brothers, forming a solid bond with Peter, and it may be significant that in possibly the only surviving photograph of her as a child she looks very much like a boy in her jacket, collar and tie. An enduring memory in Callander is of her scaling up a building to retrieve a ball, and standing on the roof in triumph soaking up the applause and cheering from the children below. It was for such tomboyish antics that she acquired the nickname by which she is still known in her home town today: 'Hellish Nell'.

Like her brothers, Helen spent her summers outside and could often be found playing down by the Teith where kingfishers swooped low over the water. The weather was invariably unsettled: when it was hot the river sank (spoiling the salmon fishing); then it rained and there were floods. She surely would have known the old Scots saying that when the sun shines through rain it means the fairies are baking; she may even have believed it. There were activities thought fit for girls, but one feels they would not have been quite to Helen's taste. In June 1908, when she was ten, the Scotch Girls Friendly Society visit to nearby Doune Castle was tersely reported thus: 'The weather was unfortunately wet and interfered with the enjoyment of the excursion.' Better to be somewhere you could shelter in a tree. Up in the hills the MacFarlane children hid among the oak and birch, or surveyed their land from the earthworks of Dunmore Fort where the kicked-up ground occasionally yielded Roman coins. Closer to home, on the site of the old parish church sprawled the disused graveyard with its watch-house built to deter 'resurrectionists' – the nineteenth-century body-snatchers who supplied novice surgeons. Rarely far from mischief, the children once released the coal from a freight wagon on to the railway track and were made to pick it up lump by lump. It seems, though, that the more Helen was chastised and restrained, the more she resisted and persisted in her hellish behaviour. The MacFarlanes had long cherished their reputation as champion swimmers, but even this outlet was forbidden her, Norman's Pool being considered unsafe for a child and disporting oneself in one's undergarments unseemly for a girl. She did it anyway.

Growing up in Callander, Helen would have known about 'pancakes' – a hiding-and-stalking game where an appointed 'witch' would steal children (the 'pancakes') from a 'mother', and a 'maid' had to try and stop her. Its symbolic origins – a harvest festival described by Sir James Frazer where witch, maid and mother were names for the last cornsheaf depending on when it was cut – illustrate well how early twentieth-century customs harked back to a more distant past, historical traces which are perhaps most evident in the way children understand the world before rationalism intrudes too far upon innocence. And when Helen reached the age of seven or thereabouts, her nascent sense of herself met with the belief in highland second sight. The trigger may have been no more than a fireside tale or a vagrant telling fortunes, but it gave meaning to her life nonetheless. One of the earliest signs was actually her suspicion that her mother was psychic on the grounds that she always knew when her wayward daughter had been swimming. Even when Helen discovered the truth – Isabella MacFarlane noticed whenever the child's petticoat had been laced up the front – she did not give up the idea that her mother had special powers and her own suspicions about herself intensified, especially once she started to see strange things.

The personal memoirs of many psychics tell of powers which emerged in childhood. The Hungarian medium Maria Irtzl discovered her gift at the age of twelve and resolved to persuade the world of the truth of post-mortem survival. Most children who spoke of such convictions were chastised or punished, such as the Londoner Elizabeth Hope whose experience of seeing 'shadow people' in the 1860s landed her in a mental asylum. No surprise, then, that when Helen described clairvoyantly seeing a soldier (long dead) and a man lost in a snowdrift (alive), her mother warned her that if she carried on like that she would gain a reputation as a 'glaikit' or even 'fey' child possessed by unnatural power, and for good measure added that she would be burned as a witch or thrown into Loch Sloy. 'Noo, dinna ye be sayin' these things ootside,' Helen recalled her mother saying. 'When ye have anything like that to say come to me with it and to no one else.' But Helen stubbornly thought her behaviour natural and, as such, refused to suppress or disguise it. Nor did she avoid the church, as might have been expected of a witch. In fact, she was rewarded for good attendance, an achievement only slightly marred by her guessing in advance what her prize would be – a copy of *Oliver Twist* – and her sanctimonious disdain for 'a book that tells you how to steal'. Family lore maintains that the minister was sufficiently alarmed and offended by what he called her 'dreams and visions' to condemn her prognostications during Sunday service. By contrast Dr Todd, the family doctor, thought her quite a remarkable child.

In 1908 Rev. William Morrison penned an introduction for a new collection of instances of second sight, a phenomenon he attributed to the 'racial genius' of highland people. Like Robert Kirk in the 1690s, he asserted that children were powerless to resist the gift which passed to them through the bloodline – a mixed blessing which 'is in every case regarded as troublesome to the possessor of it'. It is implausible that Helen was ever as knowledgeable as Morrison; but even so his insights provide curious parallels for her life and work, suggesting a psychology shaped by physical factors as much as cultural ones. He described how clairvoyant episodes might be preceded by 'nerve storms' during which the spiritual knowledge-givers sometimes became visible, ending traumatically with the utter prostration of the seer. In its mildest form, second sight was a raised sensitivity, enabling seers, in Kirk's words, to 'perceive things, that for their small- ness, or subtlety, and secrecy, are invisible to others'. And in her extraordinary perception Helen enclosed herself in a cocoon. Every day she passed a doorway above which the text of John 3:16 was set in stone, a daily reminder that God so loved the world that through his only begotten son he promised everlasting life to the faithful. Of this she had no doubt; but the wall between heaven and earth – the barrier which made necessary the leap of faith – had inevitably started to crumble as the traffic of spirits between life and afterlife shimmered into view.

Helen could not live in her cocoon all the time and here lay trouble. She attended the parish school in Craigard Road whose traditions prior to the appointment of Mr Cumming in 1879 were incompetent teaching, poor attendance and mismanage- ment by the School Board. Scholarly and sober, Cumming (nick- named 'Tiger') was a fitting successor to Helen's ancestor John MacFarlane, and was remembered with fondness and reverence by pupils spanning a quarter of a century. Attendance remained a problem, however, especially in May when girls prepared the houses of the carriage folk, and boys ran errands and delivered messages. Even a talented and committed teacher could only achieve so much, especially with a pupil like Helen whose own estimation of her psychic gifts came to compensate for, or at least excuse, her lack of academic aptitude. Feelings of disjunc- tion were compounded by the discovery that she was less popular with her peers when not retrieving balls from roofs. In the play- ground she encompassed their pasts and their futures, issuing stern advice and fearful warnings – and they didn't like it at all. One girl was told she would marry a chauffeur who, exotically, *would not be from Callander*; worse, a boy in a sailor suit was told he would end up at the bottom of the sea in the coming war. On these occasions Helen was treated with a mixture of respect, fear and contempt and, like Elspeth McEwen, she became the subject of constant rumours, which contrived to place her outside normal social intercourse. Perhaps the children played 'pancakes' without her – or maybe she was always the witch.

The child-prophet's ostracism was self-perpetuating. A curious memoir set down in 1933, of which Helen was supposedly the author (one detects the hand of her husband), rationalized the blessing of foresight using the benefit of hindsight:

> Strange sayings fell from my lips. I could not control my tongue. I simply had to express the thoughts that came to me. The result was that I was left pretty much to my own resources, but this was no hardship. On the contrary, it allowed me to develop my personality free from the influence of others, and I believe this was a factor in fostering my psychic gifts.

And yet it would not quite be true to say that she was at ease with herself and the world. Her character traits – a crippling diffidence, timidity and passivity, punctuated by sudden outbursts of hysterical rage – suggest that her personality was not developing as it should and today might earn her the label of 'passive-aggressive'. A few stories stand out. She was fond of recalling how she never needed to study because, unbidden, knowledge would filter into her head from an unseen source (she thought God) and that whenever she was asked a question, 'I would lift my downcast head and sing forth the answer.' Once, an astounded

Inspector of Schools, suspecting she was hiding a book, ordered her underwear to be searched by another girl. On another occasion, when the dates of four famous battles miraculously appeared on her slate during a history test – she had clasped it tightly to her chest and prayed for God's help – Tiger Cumming accused her of cheating. She denied this to the point where she suddenly snapped, hurled her inkwell at him and ran home. A variant of the tale maintains that with the date '1066' fixed in her head, she predicted Cumming's death and that he succumbed to a fatal heart attack during a lesson about the Battle of Hastings.* Similarly, she feared for Dr Todd shortly before he was killed in a car crash. Assuming these stories are true, had she been a more studious pupil she might have heeded a lesson from the seventeenth century, namely that those given to predicting the deaths of others risked suspicion that they themselves were the cause.

Like all children in Edwardian Callander, Helen struggled to reconcile the world according to her parents with the images of gracious living which swam before her eyes each summer: the sleek, chauffeur-driven cars, the young women draped in silks or furs, depending on the barometer reading. In their fashions and manners the rich visitors advertised an era of change. The Cockhill Fair in May, once a highlight of the year, declined after 1900 and the influx of private motor cars prompted the commissioners to impose a speed limit of ten miles per hour. Popular recreation was no longer solely determined by the agricultural calendar and even the YMCA's limelight lectures lost their appeal after the first visit from Frame's Vaudeville Company which, propitiously, included performances of the Anglo-American Bio-Tableau Cinematograph. Watching luminous images in the

---

* Yet another version maintains the teacher's name was Fulton, the battle Bannockburn, 1314.

darkness was like peering into a secret garden and glimpsing an intoxicating alternative reality. We know more about Helen Duncan in later life than about how she thought as a child, but reading her backwards we might suppose that something stirred within her in these years, a longing which she knew would carry her away from Callander and virtually everything that went with it. Just how this would come to pass she could not foresee, although probably she correctly pinned her hopes on love and marriage. Indirectly, though, for her, as for thousands of others, the crucible of change would be war.

In February 1914, sitting before an audience numbering almost a thousand, Sir Arthur Conan Doyle, creator of Sherlock Holmes and a committed Spiritualist, received this chilling prediction from an Australian medium, Mrs Foster Turner:

> Now, although there is not at present a whisper of a great European war at hand, yet I want to warn you that before this year, 1914, has run its course, Europe will be deluged in blood. Great Britain, our beloved nation, will be drawn into the most awful war the world has ever known. Germany will be the great antagonist, and will draw other nations in her train. Austria will totter to its ruin. Kings and kingdoms will fall. Millions of precious lives will be slaughtered, but Britain will finally triumph and emerge victorious.

Predictions of war were numerous and varied, some publicized before the outbreak of hostilities, others, less impressively, afterwards. In Germany rumours had circulated since the 1850s about Prince Wilhelm having met a gypsy who, Macbeth-style, hinted at his becoming the first Kaiser; but forecasts of imperial greatness soon gave way to more apocalyptic visions of the future. In a private sitting of 1909, a medium at Teddington in Middlesex saw poppies, waxed mystical about the reign of Mars and, like Mrs Foster Turner, warned of a blood-soaked world to come. At the more popular end of the market, *Old Moore's Almanac* did not get into the swing of things until 1916, upon which an Oxford don who studied such auguries commented: 'What can one expect for a penny?'

War broke out in the summer before Helen Duncan's seventeenth birthday. All over Britain, popular patriotism and jingoism exceeded the levels reached during the celebrations of 1897 and men who were either proud, bored or unemployed merrily queued down the street outside the recruiting stations as if, Philip Larkin reflected, it were all an August Bank Holiday lark. The average weekly wage of these men, if they had jobs, was £2. In Callander, as elsewhere, boys keen to escape the fields, factories and pits (where many earned less than 10s a week) arched their backs and tried to look the recruiting sergeant in the eye when they gave their age as nineteen. Not that most needed to fear rejection: the sergeant's per capita bonus saw to that. As the men of the town marched off to France with the Black Watch and the flags were put away until victory, so refugees arrived from Belgium; and by Christmas – when everyone had said it would all be over – the casualties began to fill the beds at the requisitioned mansion house of Inverleny, soon to acquire permanence as Callander Military Extension Hospital. Life was transformed in countless small ways. The woods beneath the crags where Helen had played as a child were cut down for timber and as an economy the *Callander Advertiser* shrank in size.

Archie MacFarlane, who also thought the war would be over in months, laughed when his doom-laden daughter said it would drag on for three or four years, killing many thousands of men, and he laughed even more when she described her vision of horseless war machines which moved on their bellies and smashed through houses. Helen alone saw the horror, she later recalled, and her prophecies were as abundant as they were reliable. News of the first casualties from Callander itself trickled in during 1915, one of the first being Private William Ferguson, a plumber, severely wounded in the neck by shrapnel. That was in April. By June the trickle of stories about soldiers wounded, gassed, captured and missing had become a steady stream. The first death was John Cameron of the 1/6th Black Watch, aged twenty-nine, on 11 August 1915; before the war he had been the keeper of the Callander tennis courts. Memorial cards went on sale in the Main Street shops, 'specially suited for our Fallen Heroes', and, like the rest of Callander, the MacFarlanes did what they could to keep the men fighting and to accept grief. A photograph dated April 1915, depicting a group of Callander schoolgirls raising money to buy an ambulance, contains three MacFarlanes. Their clan did not emerge unscathed. Like her Napoleonic forebear a century earlier, in April 1918 Mary MacFarlane of Kilmahog donned her widow's weeds when her husband was killed during the last great German push on the Western Front.

Not that any of this meant much to Hellish Nell, however, for even before the outbreak of war she had gone, banished from her family under the blackest of clouds, and so too from the community whose traditions had instilled in her a sense of the mysterious and the miraculous. As the war dragged on and Mrs Foster Turner's vision turned into ghastly reality, at night Helen was transported to the trenches in her dreams and there sowed the seeds of a future where the purpose of her life would lie not just in highland second sight, but in an ability to commune more directly with the spirits of the dead.

2
DEVELOPING GOD'S GIFT
Labour, Love and the Arrival of Henry

In 1966 a nightwatchman at Edinburgh University suffered a stroke and was admitted to the City Hospital. Traumatized by the death of his wife some years earlier and haunted by her memory, he had sold their big house in Rankeillor Street lock, stock and barrel (including the Chippendale furniture and first editions given as presents), married his cleaner Anna and moved into a two-bedroom flat. It was here that his granddaughter Sheila visited him during his convalescence and found him sitting in a dream, quite naked and unabashed, while indifferently Anna got ready for work. Notes, cuttings and photographs covered the

Mr and Mrs Henry Duncan, Dundee, 1920s.

floor, and he was reminiscing in a stream of semi-consciousness. Sheila had always known him as a firm and disciplined man, an old soldier who wore a stiff collar and tie, even at home with a cardigan with leather elbow patches. He drank moderately, read voraciously and, although his health had been poor since youth, he was a rock to all around him. And here he was, diminished, suspended somewhere between death and the life that was spread out in paper before him. 'He's not talking to me, Sheila,' Anna said peevishly. 'He's talking to *her*!' She meant, of course, his first wife: his precious Nell.

After Henry Duncan died the following year, his eldest son, Harry, who had emigrated to Australia to lay telephone cables, took his father's papers back home but lost most of them in a house fire. When Harry's sister Gena began writing their mother's biography, he returned what little survived to Scotland, including Henry's meticulous record of his wife's development as a medium. Gena's daughter Sheila (Henry's visitor after his stroke) remembers her mother tapping away at the typewriter for years, fashioning the story from childhood memories, family lore, remnants from the fire and, crucially, spirit guidance. A seventh child, Gena had professed psychic and spiritualistic powers from childhood, powers which gave her a unique insight into Helen's gift and which she, in turn, passed down the matrilineal line to Sheila.

Gena also bequeathed to posterity her book, which fixed the details of Helen Duncan's life, but shows, too, how every family's knowledge of itself is shot through with faults of memory, ellipses, elisions and elaborations, secrets and lies. Even her birth year has attracted conjecture. Formally registered as 1897, Helen herself sometimes said it was 1898; Gena thought it was 1895 and elsewhere 1896 is given. In the western world the family is the last main repository of the oral culture and, like the highland bards idealized by Sir Walter Scott, we inherit ancestral tales reworked by each generation to make their truth powerful rather than precise, moral rather than empirical. To muddy the waters further, nowadays postmodernism has divided historical truth into a multiplicity of equally valid perspectives, on the premiss that observation and representation, as twentieth-century physicists learned, lead inevitably to uncertainty. The curious thing is, however, that even if we possessed the means to establish absolute truths, most of us would not bother to do so. We didn't really need Wittgenstein to tell us that we believe what we want to believe, nor to understand that so long as family fictions persuade, reassure and entertain, they remain as true as most things ever are. Fictions convey powerful truths, Sir Philip Sidney once wrote, because they 'may be tuned to the highest key of passion'.

There is a myth that in the past girls married young and lived in extended families, whereas in reality most needed to find a man able to establish a separate household. When Nellie MacFarlane left school in her early teens, about 1911, marrying her off was clearly impossible; but even at sixteen the prospect might still have been remote. The scarcity of regular employment in Callander meant many men could not afford to marry and, as occurred all over the highlands, they migrated or emigrated – and in greater numbers than the women, among whom the average age of marriage in 1911 was twenty-six. Yet even if the MacFarlanes recognized the need to make provision for their daughter's future in the next decade, there is something fishy about Gena's account of the cheerful discussions about finding her a job in Dundee – hard, badly paid work associated with unskilled married women too poor to subsist on a husband's wage. What Gena could not say, even in 1985, was that in the early summer of 1914 Helen became pregnant and was most likely sent away for that reason. When her baby was born in

February 1915 in Dundee Maternity Hospital, Helen registered her home address as Ivy Cottage, Bridgend, Callander, and her occupation as hotel waitress. Beyond a single spurious meeting shortly before Helen's marriage, Gena does not mention the MacFarlane family again. In fact, young Nell was banished for good and may have returned to Callander only once when she stayed with her brother Peter, her protector since the days when, fresh from the forbidden pool, they had learned to lace up her vest at the back to avoid detection by their mother. Poignantly, it was Isabella MacFarlane after whom Helen was to name the baby she did not want but could not surrender.

Her new life in a women's hostel was not the adventure Gena made it out to be: a dormitory caper tinged with homesickness, meagre wages touchingly spent travelling home. Of Dundee's two principal occupations – the jam factories and the jute mills – Helen chose the latter and there befriended Jean Duncan, a girl a year her senior with whom she spent much of her free time, in winter ice-skating on the old quarry pond. After war was declared, the two girls sought work making munitions, doubtless attracted by the responsibility, camaraderie and higher wages, but Helen was rejected due to her fifteen-stone bulk, a tubercular lung, or perhaps because she was three months pregnant. It was a blessing in disguise. Not only was she spared the yellowing skin and sickness of the TNT-poisoned 'canaries' but, as Gena related, the sanatorium she entered instead rapidly restored her health and inspired her to care for others. Soon after Isabella was born, she was taken on as a Nursing Auxiliary at Dundee Royal Infirmary and perhaps was able to have Isabella looked after there while she was on duty. Gena's daughter Sheila maintains that Helen's experience of the psychiatric wing made a lasting impression on her, not least the frantic woman who ate sanitary towels when she menstruated and the epileptics whose fits convinced her for ever that their affliction was due to demonic possession. Working apart, Helen and Jean continued to see each other whenever they could, and on one visit to Helen's hospital digs Jean, who had doubtless already shared her friend's biggest secret, was entrusted with another.

What happened was this. In her dreams, Helen had been visiting the trenches of Flanders, extending her dull and dread-filled life into what Lord Byron once called 'a wide realm of wild reality'. Had Byron been born a century later, the chances are he would have found himself 'eye-deep in hell', as Ezra Pound put it, a world where the temporal and infernal were hideously juxtaposed, and the reality of dreams and the surrealism of life thrown into hellish confusion. There, Jean heard, Nellie had met a young private whose war-sick eyes told her at once that his soul would be joined with hers for ever. To bring Helen down to earth, Jean encouraged her to write to her brother Henry, a *real* soldier at the front and Helen's age, and this she did; but Helen's first reply served only to fuse the material and the spiritual, fulfilling her sleep-borne prophecy and satisfying a profound yearning to love and be loved. At this stage her interpretation of this experience was still shaped by highland traditions of ghosts and omens, and not by the conviction that personality survived death, that spirits necessarily communicated with the living, or that mediumship was a gift from God. These were the principles of Spiritualism, a religion of which she had heard but whose extravagant claim to have opened up the kingdom of heaven she regarded, as yet, with scepticism. As in the hearts of thousands, however, the war would change that.

Across Britain, mechanized slaughter on the Western Front and the vast unmastered grief it engendered dramatically raised the public profile of Spiritualism and demand for the services of mediums. Private readings and seances brought messages of comfort and hope from the war dead, and today dusty albums of spirit photographs show drained-looking women buttoned up in black, the placid faces of studio-posed servicemen hovering above them in a fuzzy aura. Like participation in the killing, and its attendant sorrows at home, interest in such phenomena knew no boundaries of class or education: when Rudyard Kipling, heartbroken by the loss of his teenage son at Loos in 1915, begged to know 'who shall return us our children?' to a growing army of mourners the answer seemed obvious. Kipling was not alone in juggling ambivalent feelings towards Spiritualism, sentiments which, in one poem, he expressed through the biblical story of Saul breaking God's law by visiting a witch at Endor in order to communicate with the spirit of Samuel. Spiritualism could seem irrational, or by Saul's example even sinful, and yet for many parents, widows and siblings the temptation to ease the pain of bereavement proved overwhelming.

As a movement, Spiritualism had its origins at Hydesville in upstate New York. In 1848 the teenage daughters of a poor Methodist farmer, J. D. Fox, heard strange rapping noises, which they deciphered as messages from the spirit of a murdered man whose bones were subsequently discovered in their cellar. As word spread, the Fox sisters attracted the attention of several investigative committees and a huge number of people wishing to sit with them. The movement swept across America, spawning 'spirit depots' and numerous periodicals, and attracting converts among academics, writers, politicians and industrialists, an expansion unchecked even by the girls' confession that they were hoaxers. Before long, the enterprising showman Phineas T. Barnum (speciality: freak shows) had secured their services and money began to change hands. By this fact a cynic may explain not just the striking number of the Foxes' sitters who became mediums themselves, but the diversification of spirit communication. Automatic slate-writing (of which young Nell MacFarlane may well have heard), levitating furniture, paraffin casts of spirit hands, direct speech through trance and the appearance of shadowy faces became standard. The Koons family, farmers in a remote Ohio township, laid on spirit shows in complete darkness, playing musical instruments, waving phosphorescent hands and calling through trumpets, thereby establishing the standard repertoire of physical mediums for a century to come.

If Spiritualism married religion and entertainment, equally it matched religion with science. In religion there were antecedents in the desire of the Catholic Apostolic Church to speak in tongues; in America, consider the ecstasies of the Shakers and, to some extent, the radical nonconformity of Mormonism and Adventism. In science Spiritualism owed most to hypnosis and the 'animal magnetism' developed as a healing procedure in pre-Revolutionary France by an Austrian doctor, Friedrich Mesmer. At his sittings – naturally enough, termed *séances* – patients and visitors joined hands to allow free passage of an invisible fluid which, according to Mesmer, exerted electrical attraction upon human bodies. By the mid-nineteenth century, mesmerism had inspired 'spiritism' which, under the direction of religious philosopher Allen Kardec, treated the quest for physical phenomena as a red herring, and preached reincarnation as the main link between this world and the next. Even earlier than Mesmer, Swedish mystic and polymath Emanuel Swedenborg had as a child entranced himself by holding his breath, and by the 1740s was venturing freely into the spirit world and conversing with its inhabitants. For his discovery of the direct continuity between life and death he is often hailed as the father of Spiritualism, although it is significant that he denied the possibility of earthly interaction between humans and spirits – a fact which the deterrent stodginess of his writings continues to conceal.

Of course, the idea that the living might communicate with the spirits of the dead was much older, and pervades the pagan folklore and shamanism of non-European and ancient civilizations and, as cave paintings suggest, of prehistory as well. Spiritual encounters occur throughout the Bible (the lives of the Old Testament prophets were *controlled* by spirits) and formed part of the thinking of the early Christian Church whose principal luminary, St Augustine, believed that 'the spirits of the dead can be sent to the living and can unveil to them the future which they themselves have learned from other spirits or from angels, or from divine revelation'. Protestant and Catholic dogmas alike drew upon Augustinian teaching in the sixteenth century and preached the reality of the spirit world, even though the former held that the age of miracles had passed. Queen Elizabeth I (who, remember, legislated against witches) employed an astrologer named John Dee who held conversations with angels through a medium, Edward Kelley, which Dee recorded in question-and-answer form like a twentieth-century psychical researcher at a seance. Spirits, some of whom manifested, prophesied various things, including the death of Mary, Queen of Scots and the attempted invasion by the Spanish Armada. In the next century, educated men continued to regard the spirit world as a corollary of the doctrine of immortality. It was Milton who (paraphrasing Hesiod) asserted that 'Millions of spiritual creatures walk the earth, Unseen, both when we wake and when we sleep', a reality drawn upon by other writers to repel deism, an intellectual tendency which ushered an interventionist God and devil from the cosmic stage, along with a supporting cast of angels, demons, ghosts and witches. In 1661 Joseph Glanvill, later Chaplain to Charles II, reacted strongly against the 'atheism' of his age in a treatise entitled *The Vanity of Dogmatizing*, which contemplated the 'secret Art of the Soul, which to us is utterly occult, and without the ken of our Intellects'. Dominating belief, however, were ambiguity and ambivalence. Even Glanvill was a progressive thinker who absorbed the dualistic philosophy of Descartes, and we forget that his contemporary, Isaac Newton, was as fascinated by angelic wisdom as by gravitating apples. In attitude, Glanvill and Newton were typical of the virtuosi whose interest in nature was inseparable from reverence for God's design, albeit an interest which, unknown to them, was nibbling away at the traditional world view from within.

Predictably, the sort of metaphysical universe discussed at the Royal Society found its most conservative proponents in the meanest households of the unlettered poor. Into the nineteenth century, many ordinary people encountered spirits who revealed secrets, issued warnings, accused the guilty and exonerated the innocent. For these were not historical ghosts – the lugubrious Elizabethan, head beneath arm; the pregnant maid sealed in a garret – rather these were the familiar dead, the spectral analogues of relatives, friends and neighbours, and they had something to say. Long before Charles Loseby put Helen Duncan's offer to a jury at the Old Bailey, stories of apparitions had found their way into English courts, adding moral rather than empirical truth to testimony. In the 1760s a murder trial was initiated by a female spirit who, as in the Fox household, communicated by raps, and attracted Londoners who paid to see the haunted house. 'Scratching Fanny', as she was known, demanded justice for her poisoner through an eleven-year-old girl whom Dr Johnson questioned, concluding 'that the child has some art of making or counterfeiting a particular noise, and that there is no agency of a higher cause'. Yet Johnson's wider feelings were more ambivalent. Not only was he impressed by highland second sight but, distraught after his wife's death, he prayed earnestly that she would revisit him 'by appearance, impulses, dreams, or in any other manner'. And such ambivalence continued to be a part of English middle-class beliefs and manners a hundred and fifty years after Johnson himself had paid his debt to nature.

The difference between Victorian Spiritualism and the primordial belief in spirits consisted mainly in cultural context. From the time the Fox sisters were rapping their way to fame, in Europe and America the growth of technology and industry was nurturing trust in material progress. This, in turn, surreptitiously challenged the social relevance of scripturally based faith, a decline which in 1867 Matthew Arnold, then in his last year as Professor of Poetry at Oxford, likened to the 'melancholy, long withdrawing roar' of the sea at Dover. As science poisoned the constitution of religion, however, in Spiritualism it also offered an antidote. Research into invisible impulses – light waves, magnetism and electricity – and popular clamour at the invention of the telegraph display obvious parallels with interest in thought transference and spiritual communication. We may even hear echoes of the providential tradition within which Newton had worked, investigating the natural and supernatural realms as a single entity, albeit in a way which actually jeopardized the validity of Newtonian physics. In the public sphere the dominant image was of a glorious dawn rising over a world darkened by secularism and disenchantment. 'It seems to me that a new era in the history of humanity has actually commenced,' Rev. S. B. Britain declared in the first ever public lecture on Spiritualism, delivered in New York City in 1850,

and that those tremendous and unexplained mysteries that we have called in the earliest ages 'Magic', in the Biblical dispensation 'Miracle', and in the Middle Ages 'Witchcraft' are now coming to the front as the work of human spirits, ever aiming to communicate with the earth-friends they have left behind, and ever striving to impart that knowledge of spiritual life and possibilities, of which mankind has been so lamentably ignorant.

Critics noted the irony that Spiritualism, far from routing materialism, had capitulated to it. Indeed, the replacement of faith with tangible truths was Spiritualism's unique selling point and explains its appeal to the English respectable working class, for whom it offered an alternative to the ecclesiastical dogma and authority which long had preserved their subordination. Spiritualism, Sir Arthur Conan Doyle promised, was 'a religion for those who find themselves outside all religions'. No surprise, then, that the Catholic Church viewed it as a lethal contagion and condemned mediums (many, admittedly, youths of little natural promise) as halfwits or whores prostituted to a wicked trade – even as witches.

No surprise, either, that, as a progressive and idealistic movement, Spiritualism joined hands with socialism, and thrived in the nonconformist halls and mechanics' institutes of northern industrial towns. The social reformer Robert Owen, for instance, lived long enough to see it nourish the ideals of freedom and working-class combination he held dear. As with the friendly societies and trades unions, and as had happened in America, the key to the spread of Spiritualism was the popular press. The first of many Spiritualist periodicals was published in 1853 by the husband of a visiting American medium, Mrs Hayden, who held seances at a guinea a head and counted Owen among her converts. In the same year the first English Spiritualist church opened its doors at Keighley in Yorkshire. And it was around this time that Emma Hardinge, a musical actress from the East End of London who as a child had seen visions of dead relatives, met the Fox sisters in America and a decade later returned home to perform as a trance speaker. A skilled publicist and orator – having campaigned for Abraham Lincoln – she herself developed a range of skills from levitation to healing which she took all over the world, before settling in Cheetham Hill, Manchester. There, in 1887, she used the text of Rev. Britain's New York lecture to launch the first edition of her weekly newspaper *Two Worlds*, the masthead of which depicted Truth perched atop the earth, exhorting the crouching figures of Science and Love to elevate themselves to her level. Printed discreetly at the back, Mrs Hardinge Britten (as she had become) included herself in a directory of mediums which spanned Bradford and Bayswater, Barnsley and Bloomsbury.

Significantly, half of this list were women. It is another irony of Spiritualism that in their passivity and their role as mothers, women were commonly perceived to be natural mediums, a role in which they could find themselves respected, rewarded and placed at the centre of attention. Class and education were no obstacles: the simpler the soul, the purer the results. In a social world hard-wired with patriarchal values, where the spaces women inhabited were routinely policed by men, liberation at seances might also be sexual. As if Victorian mores were not challenged enough by the liaison of young women with men in a charged emotional atmosphere – men with whom they *held hands* – most seances were also conducted in darkness. Light tended to inhibit the production of psychical phenomena. The earliest suggestion that more natural inhibitions might also be lifted by seance conditions animated satirists and moralizers alike. A humorous cartoon from the 1890s shows a male and a female sitter abandoning all decorum at the moment the lights go down; but to harbingers of 'moral degeneration' in decadent times,

Spiritualist seances were no laughing matter. What these traditionalists saw, of course, were women – mediums and sitters alike – seeking empowerment, crossing boundaries, and breaking rules of class and gender. And, if only as a symbol of what was to come in the next century, these incursions were important.

Seance-going could also be a perfectly proper pastime, even forming part of the afternoon tea ritual indulged in by society hostesses whose guests would be advised accordingly on their invitations. Less frivolously, women were also prominent among the literary and scientific intelligentsia whose ruminatory habits made them vulnerable to religious doubt and therefore curiosity about Spiritualism. George Eliot took an interest, as did Elizabeth Barrett Browning, although her husband Robert was more cautious. Dickens, Trollope, Thackeray and Tennyson all satisifed their curiosity at seances, among whom Tennyson was *the* Spiritualist poet:

> *The Ghost in Man, the Ghost that once was Man,*
> *But cannot wholly free itself from Man,*
> *Are calling to each other thro' a dawn*
> *Stranger than earth has ever seen; the veil*
> *Is rending, and the Voices of the day*
> *Are heard across the Voices of the dark.*

And yet the very fact of this spiritual renaissance suggests the extent of despair within the educated élite as convictions were evaporated by the heat of economic change, advances in biblical scholarship, revolutionary discoveries in physiology and the possibilities for reorganizing human relations offered by empirical philosophy. Darwin (who had a low opinion of both mesmerism and Spiritualism) didn't help matters either. Drifting from the severed moorings of their faith, three Fellows of Trinity College,

Cambridge – Professor of Moral Philosophy Henry Sidgwick, Frederick Myers and Edmund Gurney (on whom George Eliot had a crush) – graduated from participation in the University Ghost Club to the active investigation of paranormal phenomena. In this energetic work they wavered between various positions from open-mindedness to absolute credulity – a spectrum of opinion which characterized the Society for Psychical Research of which they, with Professor William Barrett, were founders in 1882. It was an eminently respectable society, drawing its members, Spiritualist and non-Spiritualist alike, from all walks of intellectual life in Cambridge and beyond. Far from being unstable cranks, Sidgwick and Myers in particular were extravagantly bearded frowning men of scruple, with impeccable credentials and the power to express themselves cogently and be taken seriously among their peers. All of which was also true of another avatar of psychic science and friend of Myers, the renowned physicist and pioneer of wireless telegraphy, Sir Oliver Lodge.

In May 1915 Lodge received a letter from Alta Piper, daughter of a well-respected Bostonian medium, Mrs Leonora Piper, who more than anyone else had persuaded him of the reality of human survival. Lamenting America's neutrality, Miss Piper related how the war in Europe filled their souls with horror and enclosed a script from an automatic-writing session in which the spirit of Myers, who had died in 1902, foresaw a better world emerging from the war, but warned that 'some of our earthly helpers must be sacrificed ere this struggle ends, we say not whom'. One can only imagine the chilling effect these words must have had on Lodge whose twenty-six-year-old son Raymond was a junior officer in the South Lancashire Regiment serving on the Western Front. In his desk Lodge kept a sheaf of letters from Raymond – four sent in that month alone – describing trench systems, messy meals of bacon and cheese, and the occasional ghastly shrapnel wound. A note dated 12 September 1915 was his last. Two days later Raymond was struck by a shell fragment during an attack on a hill and died within a few hours. A week or so later, as the family sat stupefied by the news, Lady Lodge received a letter of consolation from a fellow officer, Lieutenant G. R. A. Case, who, as custom prescribed, waxed lyrical about Raymond's popularity and his painless end. But the Lodges' suffering, and the sacrifices predicted by the spiritual Myers, were almost too great to bear. And even as Lady Lodge was trying to take in his words, Case himself was already dead and buried.

Like many others – including their friend Conan Doyle who lost a son, a brother and a brother-in-law – Sir Oliver and Lady Lodge endured their grief through their Spiritualist belief and its exercise in mediumship. Regular communications from Raymond received through one of England's best-known mediums, Gladys Osborne Leonard, were compiled by Lodge into a book, simply entitled *Raymond*, which was published in November 1916 and entered another three editions before the month was out. The message was clear: death needed to be viewed as a rebirth into another state; it was, according to Lodge, not an extinction and at worst amounted to exile in a world connected to this one by a bridge of love. It is not recorded whether Lodge was surprised to receive a letter from William Shakespeare in June 1918, whispered into the inner ear of American medium, Sarah Taylor Shatford, and typed up in a New York hotel room. The bard, apparently demented by the centuries, spoke fulsomely of his love of England and his striving to 'open the soft and thin partition which hides her sons outgone from those on her fertile and worshipped land'. Accompanying the letter were almost four hundred pages of patriotic doggerel purporting to be his work, of which even the first verse of the first offering – 'Peace After

War' – is probably more than most Renaissance scholars will be able to bear:

> *When wars have done and peace is come, and to a wounded*
> *world no longer torn,*
> *By cannonshell or doubts or fears, there comes sweet rest, new-*
> *born,*
> *To solace hearts and make men see how traitorous their*
> *itching greed,*
> *O what a World wherein to live, where each man shares his*
> *brother's need!*

Although here, and in other alleged spiritual communications, the idea that war would be banished by love and enlightened brotherhood tended to be stronger in affect than detailed proposals, these sentiments were precisely those of many ordinary men and women who had lived through the war. They were certainly those of Private Henry Duncan who, by the time Sarah Shatford was transcribing the voices in her head, was already a veteran of a world torn by cannon shell, doubts and fears, and was looking forward to a better life.

Henry Duncan's new life had first been sought in war. He had grown up in Dundee where, in 1914, aged sixteen and a half, he ducked out of an apprenticeship and headed for the recruiting depot of the 4th Battalion, Black Watch. Lying to a sergeant, he was kitted out in tam-o'-shanter and kilt and was sent off for ten weeks' basic training with many other Dundonian men – so many, in fact, that they called the 4th Battalion a 'city at war'. With them they took their body lice and sunken chests, but left behind tenements, factories and mills. Most felt they had nothing to lose. Henry's father, an iron driller in the shipyards, joined up too. A Presbyterian with Spiritualist leanings, in 1895 he had married Annie Mearns, a Catholic from Arbroath who as a girl had toiled as a herring gutter. They raised five children in a cramped tenement flat from which the spirits of the dead were never far. Even by contemporary standards the building was infused with a gloom which stirred violent urges in Henry senior. One day Henry junior, who had experienced a recurring nightmare about a menacing man in his bedroom, smelt gas and went out on to the landing to investigate. There he saw a wraithlike woman he did not recognize, but who, according to the landlord, was the wife of a bully who had gassed herself; the husband had been found hanged. The Duncans were moved to another property where they found tragedy of their own. Aged eight, Henry's brother disappeared and the police, who investigated a rumour that he had been abducted by gypsies, drew a blank. Contrary to the doctrines of her church and with the same ambivalent feelings that were to trouble Kipling in the coming war, Annie Duncan consulted a medium who saw water and ships, and correctly predicted that news would arrive within three weeks. Right on time, a ship in for repair at Victoria Rock weighed anchor to reveal a drowned boy between its hull and the quay. On hearing what had happened, a Fife man sent Annie one of his poems which began with the couplet:

> *There is just a thin veil we almost see through,*
> *And one whom we love is dimly in view.*

Originally written for Queen Alexandra on the occasion of Edward VII's death in 1910, it brought her some comfort. But in 1914 the memory of loss returned vividly to her with the fear that she was about to lose another son and a husband.

At war, the Black Watch honoured its reputation for ferocity and endurance, once serving seven weeks in the line unrelieved. Like all men at the front, Henry was confronted by scenes with which he coped as best he could but with little real comprehension. Once, the blast from a shell tore the uniform from a friend standing nearby, stripping him naked at the moment of death. Exhaustion brought sleep, which discomfort and distress would otherwise have prevented, and with it escape into the wild reality of dreams, recalling Sir Thomas Smith's dictum that 'we term sleep a death, and yet it is waking that kills us, and destroys those spirits which are the house of life'. In the trenches, many found their faith in God tested, an awareness of which perhaps inspired the National Bible Society of Scotland's mission to provide every Scottish soldier with a threepenny 'active service' New Testament. In others, however, religious belief flourished as a primal reaction to danger and disorder. Even atheists found themselves observing superstitions and repeating rumours of supernatural occurrences which, among men facing mortality, acquired a currency and solidity rarely experienced in civilian life. Lucky mascots and talismans were universal, as were tales of bullet-stopping watches, cigarette cases and pocket bibles of the sort distributed by the NBSS, the latter gaining the greatest magical significance. Stories heard or read would feed back into experience. Everyone knew of the 'Angels of Mons', the spectral archers from Agincourt who relieved the British Expeditionary Force in 1914; but the popular writer who invented them was a lone voice indeed among those soldiers who claimed to have *witnessed* the miracle. The moral truth of the fiction was unassailable.

Soldiers met the ghosts of the more recent dead, too, those men whose mangled bodies lay all around, re-exposed by shelling or when rain dissolved the trench walls into which they had been built. It was inevitable that Spiritualism would flourish here for, as one artillery officer reasoned in the *Occult Review* in 1918, 'in a world of Death one would expect to penetrate the veil when it hangs so constantly before one!' Most soldiers had heard of *Raymond*. A best-seller at home, it was read avidly at the front and many a parcel of socks, jam and cigarettes must have contained a copy, much to the consternation of orthodox chaplains. By the end of its first year, Methuen & Co. had brought out six editions, twice that many by 1919. Not that this was the only Spiritualist work to address the hopes and fears of the infantryman. The medium Elsa Barker's *Letters from a Living Dead Man*, first published in 1914, entered successive editions and was still in print in 1932. She also published a volume of war letters in 1916, in which year J. P. Smyth's *The Men Who Died in Battle* explored the same spiritual territory as *Raymond*. In the years 1918–19, Rev. Frederick Bligh Bond, an ecclesiastical architect, published various spiritual communications (including the vision of poppy fields from 1909), which appealed to a nation staggering beneath its emotional burden.

Almost as if fire had wished no trace of Henry Duncan, a German bombing raid in 1940 destroyed sixty per cent of the ordinary soldiers' service records from the First World War and damaged the remainder so badly as to render most unusable at the present time.* It is reasonable to suppose that Henry's war ended in 1915, a year in which so many of the 4th (City of Dundee) Battalion died that it was amalgamated with the 5th. Sickness was rife among poorly fed soldiers continually exposed to the elements. The novelist Eric Linklater – who like Henry lied about his sixteen and a half years to join the 4/5th Black

---

* Records do survive for Henry's father, Henry Duncan senior. He was discharged from the Black Watch in February 1915, probably without having seen service in France.

Watch – remembers a downpour so heavy that they marched bare-buttocked, wearing their kilts as capes. In such conditions Henry's joints swelled and ached until, withdrawing after a spell of sustained fighting, he collapsed and sank into a coma. The last thing he remembered was the sensation of lightness and of being lifted by unseen hands. He regained consciousness a week or so later, lying in a field hospital next to a man with no legs, and was told by a doctor that rheumatic fever had damaged a valve in his heart and that he would be going back to Blighty. Whether from febrility or the liberally dispensed morphia injections, in the hours that followed he slipped in and out of delirium, and saw with a marvellous clarity the round smiling face of a dark-haired girl, her deep-brown eyes reassuring him, leading him closer to home. Meanwhile, back in Dundee, Nellie MacFarlane's latest dream showed her soldier ailing but safe in hospital. Helen and Henry, the eternal soulmates, had met at last.

Shipped home, Henry was admitted to Craigleith Military Hospital, Edinburgh and after a period of recuperation was allowed to travel to Dundee at weekends. One afternoon he arrived at his mother's house to find the table laid for tea and was told that his sister Jean had invited a friend. Naturally, Annie Duncan thought it odd that she had never seen this Nellie of whom her daughter was so fond and looked forward to meeting her. But not as much as Henry who at once realized this would be the girl who had written to him. It is said that Helen and Henry just stared when they were introduced, recognizing each other from their dreams and he realizing intuitively that she was a natural psychic. At what point he discovered that she was also a mother it is impossible to say, except that his inheritance of another man's child seems to have given him few misgivings; although a cynic might feel that a man in his position, enfeebled by illness and lacking a trade, could not afford to be choosy. The existence of baby Isabella probably explains why Helen had been keeping herself hidden away. Walking her home after tea, Henry did ask why she had not been to the house before, to which she replied that she had spent nine months in a sanatorium with a spot on her lung, adding that she and Jean rarely saw each other these days, especially now that her hospital was busy with the influenza epidemic. Their daughter Gena made more of a point of this exchange than it would warrant if it were absolutely true (the influenza epidemic did not occur until 1918). Not that this is important, however, compared with the moment when Henry asked if she knew what a clairvoyant was, upon which she enquired with genuine concern whether that was what the doctors had said was wrong with him. And with that remark, unwittingly, she laid down a favourite family joke for years to come.

When Henry finally asked for her hand in marriage, Helen's answer, by normal courtship convention, was more funny peculiar than funny ha-ha. Instead of just 'yes', Gena records, she said: 'I'm sure it has already been arranged in heaven that we two will always be together.' But Henry believed this too and the engagement was on. When he was demobilized and removed the kilt he had worn for so long, Helen discovered that it was infested in the fine pleats and burned it, thereby also bringing his war to a symbolic close, however persistent the ghosts might prove. Helen moved to Edinburgh, where Henry was still receiving treatment, and took a job in a baker's shop; Henry, meanwhile, did what he could, finding work as a casual labourer here and there. With two soldiers from the Royal Scots as witnesses, they married on 27 May 1916 at the Bank Street Register Office (certified under the Sheriff's warrant as an 'irregular' marriage) and left their temporary accommodation in Easter Road for a small rented flat in Forrest Road. Their early married life was characterized by monotonous hardship punctuated by tragedy. In the first winter of their marriage Helen contracted pneumonia and teased death, Henry clasping her hand at the bedside until she returned from a coma. Without her income they had only Henry's nugatory army pension and, once Helen was back on her feet, they were forced to return to Dundee where an offer of an apprenticeship to a cabinetmaker awaited. Enterprising but enfeebled, in time Henry struggled to start a business in a tiny shop with a workshop to the rear, but progress was slow due to bouts of sickness and mental perturbation – the legacy of the trenches – exacerbated by the anxiety of commercial failure, which hung over him like a cloud. Bedridden, he devoured the books Helen brought him from the public library, mainly works devoted to psychical research and Spiritualism, ranging from the sensational and the sentimental to the serious and scholarly. Also available by this date were numerous cheap books based on the self-improving home education model, of which E. W. and M. H. Wallis's *How to Develop Mediumship* was broadly representative.

Henry Duncan is remembered as a man full of love, a love which he expressed to his wife in a very physical way for one so frail. Helen gave birth to eight children in all – above the Scottish average but not uncommon among her class – of whom only six survived childhood. The toll upon her body was great because of her own poor health. Obesity, partly due to oedema, was linked to hypertension; later she suffered from pleurisy, abdominal problems requiring surgery, a chronic kidney condition leading to albuminuria – the abnormal passing of proteins in her urine – and, from the early 1940s, diabetes. Pre-eclampsia caused fits in labour, which damaged the limbs of her daughters Henrietta (Etta) and Gena, Etta living little more than a year before she perished from pneumonia. In January 1923 the birth of a ten-pound son brought especial joy; Helen, now twenty-five, called him 'my Henry', but everyone else knew him as Harry. He was soon joined by the prematurely delivered Peter, named after Helen's beloved brother; at only three and a half pounds, he was reared in a cardboard box and fed with an eye-dropper. The death of their last child, Alex (from pneumonia they attributed to a damp baby-suit), reduced his parents to a state of grief-stricken automatism, leaving Nan, the first child of their marriage, to take charge of her siblings. Nan herself was a sickly girl – like her father, she contracted rheumatic fever which damaged her heart – but always assumed responsibility before her elder sister, the aloof and awkward Isabella (or Bella, as she was known). As she grew older, Bella's resentment at the secret of her true father's identity was compounded by anger at a disaster that befell her while Helen was in hospital giving birth to Lilian, four weeks after Etta's death. Bella had been taken to stay with friends who lived in a caravan in the country and, left unattended, she was attacked by a ferret which destroyed an eye and part of her nose. Deeply troubled by this, Helen was nonetheless strict with Bella, as short on praise for her as for all her 'bairns' whom she made grateful for what little they had. The family saying remained 'God is good to us', reflecting a belief that divine care would preserve them from hunger.

But times were hard. Henry's business was failing due to a combination of overgenerous credit, customers neglecting to collect ordered furniture (which had to be sold off at a loss) and general low productivity due to illness. Henry had a nervous breakdown and then one day, struck by a premonition, Helen found him slumped over his bench suffering a heart attack. Pregnant with Lilian, she had been trying to hurry the orders by stuffing upholstery in the workshop, her babies at her feet, but with Henry back in hospital bankruptcy was inevitable. Helen found work in the bleach fields, took in washing and mending, sold off the contents of the shop to pay creditors and moved the family to a smaller flat. Locked in a constant struggle to keep body and soul together, Helen was the last to bed and the first to rise. The bleach fields were a cruel environment where she endured deteriorating back pain and her overalls froze to her body. Her housework, an occupation unnoticed by the census enumerators, was almost as demanding. Lifting washing from the boiler one day, Helen collapsed and was treated in hospital for kidney paralysis. When Henry recovered some strength, he managed to get a job as a postman, but trudging door to door in the hard winter fell prey to another attack of rheumatic fever. And so he became what in Dundee was known as a 'kettle-boiler' – a man who stayed at home while his wife worked, although it seemed that Henry was often too sick even to boil a kettle. On one occasion, out of bed but out of work, he took Harry to hear an immaculate middle-class lady deliver an improving talk on how the unemployed could boil up soup from a cod's head. At the end, a plump man in the chair asked the threadbare audience if there were any questions. 'Aye,' shouted an old woman near the Duncans, 'never mind the heid, wha eats the body?'

Things became increasingly desperate and the family was forced to subsist on porridge, vegetable broth boiled with bones, 'stovies' (corned beef or sausages cooked with potatoes and onions) and what they called 'mealey pudding' – oatmeal, bacon scraps and onions served with turnip or swede. The children, who prized the peas from the broth, stayed in on Saturdays while their clothes dried, ready for church and Sunday school the next day. Most women living in Helen's area raised families in varying degrees of poverty, and developed robust strategies of mutual cooperation and collectivism to survive the vicissitudes of fortune: they looked after one another's children and shared hand-me-downs, and they donated food, especially for christenings, weddings and funerals, which otherwise would have been impossible. They even helped each other pay the rent. After Henry's heart attack, the Duncans moved and found a friend in their new neighbour Mrs MacLain who brought flowers and started watching out for them. Christmas was predictably lean: Henry, still sick in bed, made Harry a windmill with coloured paper sails, while Helen unravelled the wool from an old jumper to knit socks. Auntie Mac, as Mrs MacLain became known, made up stockings with rag dolls and sweets (and a bear for Harry). Already overwhelmed, on Christmas morning Henry and Helen opened a small box from the MacLains to find a ten-shilling note for them to buy something for themselves.

Not everyone was so kind. Later in life Harry remembered that the Duncans were thought of as 'loonies' by some locals, and not just because of Helen's pretensions to second sight, or because Henry the kettle-boiler spent his days in bed reading paranormal literature. Few who knew her remembered Helen as a bookworm, although she did like Henry to read to her, her favourites being Scotland's worst poet, William McGonagall, and McNib of the *Edinburgh Evening News*; and bedtime digests of accounts of spiritualistic phenomena were always forthcoming. At Henry's instigation, Helen was already developing her mediumship by giving clairvoyant readings at home and began to feel the unbidden dead moving closer to her. One night the Duncans heard a 'peculiar whistle' like a banshee. Helen tried to deny it, saying it was a hawk; but they both knew the truth. At three o'clock in the morning Henry suddenly realized that his father must be dying and jumped out of bed; but later that morning, before he could get to the hospital in Leith, an apparition of Henry Duncan senior took shape before Helen's eyes, telling her it was too late. The time of death was confirmed as just after three. These supernatural experiences she shared with her neighbours. On Auntie Mac's first visit, Helen had seen the spirit of her son, David, who had died of diphtheria a year earlier; he asked 'Mama Duncan' to allay his mother's fears for her daughter who lay sick at the time. Auntie Mac was overjoyed.

There can be little doubt that by this stage Helen was a spiritualist of sorts although, given the icon she was to become, she had failed to embrace Spiritualism per se for a bafflingly long time. It was Henry's father who first pointed out to Helen that her highland second sight and contact with the dead were 'one and the same thing'.

And that was it. 'I caught a glimmering of the truth,' said Helen, 'and from that day I ceased to be sceptical of Spiritualism.' But perhaps the real turning point had been her pneumonic coma. Regaining consciousness, she had described to Henry a vision bearing characteristics of the hypnotic states of native religions – colours, lights, tunnels, barren landscapes. A man in white flowing robes led her by the hand across a river to a paradise and there left her alone. A bright light preceded the sound of a voice calling her name, whereupon she was shown a book in which a record of her life to date had been wiped clean. The Christ-like guide reappeared and led her back across the water and, although she was reluctant to go back to the grey dirty world, she had been instructed to serve others. Just before Helen's return, she saw her mother-in-law's coffin (complete with a date on the lid); they had never seen eye to eye, perhaps because of Helen's illegitimate child. Henry, normally ready to see spiritual significance in the most mundane of occurrences, dismissed the prediction as a mere dream. But the night before Annie Mearns Duncan died – a poor fifty-something diabetic exhausted by a life of restless toil and motherhood – Helen and Henry were woken by an apparition of her hand tapping at their bedroom window, the lines of the scars from her herring-gutter's knife clearly visible across her palm.

These stories formed an important part of family and Spiritualist lore regarding the changing course of Helen Duncan's life, and help explain why her faith hardly wavered almost to the hour of her death. Taking Gena's book and other documentary fragments as a guide, Henry's record of these years must have resembled the edifying accounts penned by the newly enlightened in more godly days: men and women who, instead of setting down their experiences just as they happened, crafted generic narratives of religious conversion which were neither wholly true nor wholly false, but were nonetheless powerful as fictions – moral truths – tuned to the highest key of passion. Precise details aside, we can be sure that Helen's hour was imminent and, to quote from the war that would be her undoing, that this was the end of the beginning. And she knew it too. She was convinced of the reality of spirits and had discovered her ability to commune with them, and now she was all fired up by the mission with which she had been entrusted by God, a fire fuelled by a desire to put the past behind her. It would not be long before she was ushering back the dead in physical form, and her awed and astonished husband was recording visible effects of spectacular radiance.

3
RADIANT EFFECTS
'Albert' and the Spectacle of the Seances

magine the scene. It is 1958, a dark room in a house in Edinburgh, and two girls aged six and twelve are dancing and misbehaving with their school friends, the coal fire casting long shadows on the walls. Their mother is at the theatre and was promised before she went out that nothing of the sort would occur. Suddenly a serving hatch opens and through it emerges a plump, disembodied arm enveloped by a glowing aura, a reproachful finger wagging at the miscreants. The younger of the two sisters takes a poker from the fireplace and vainly swings at the apparition; the others run into the kitchen to find no one

A Dundee tenement slum, *c.* 1920.

there. The arm vanishes. Arriving home, the mother chides the children immediately, for at the theatre her own mother's spirit warned of their mischief. But the elder girl, Sheila, already knew it was her grandmother who had intervened due to her distinctive gold wristwatch, identical to the one inherited and now worn by her mother Gena. Had she seen the reverse of the spectral watch, doubtless it too would have been inscribed: 'Helen Duncan – Double Chance'. Back in 1925, when Helen's career as a medium was in its infancy, she had shared her spiritual vision of a double-yolked egg with one of Henry's acquaintances, a gentleman's outfitter soon to be bankrupt unless he turned his finances around. Pinning his hopes on Helen's augury, he placed all his remaining assets on a horse called Double Chance running in the Grand National. It won. The watch was her first but by no means last gift of gratitude. Henry received a 'Swallow' raincoat, the best of its kind at that time.

If Helen was driven by a desire to love and watch over others (even after death), Henry was motivated more by an abstract intellectual curiosity and perhaps the desire to extricate himself from the snare of poverty. A gold watch and a fine coat must have started him thinking; he may even have wished he had backed Double Chance himself. Whatever the spur, the objective was the development of his wife's mediumship to its fullest potential, and to that end he devoured and digested every relevant printed work he could find. In 1917, for example, for the price of a hot public bath (lower classes), one could send off for a pamphlet entitled *Psychic Science and Barbaric Legislation* by Dr Ellis T. Powell, a barrister who later (after his own death, in fact) became President of a Spiritualist group called the Society of Communion. As 'propaganda publication' no. 20, it was published by the Spiritualists' National Union, the leading English association established in 1891, and had originally appeared as an article in *Light*, the oldest Spiritualist weekly and organ of another prominent body, the London Spiritualist Alliance. The LSA was founded in 1884 by Oxford-educated William Stainton Moses, a country curate whose mediumistic career began in his schooldays when he came top of the class for an essay written in his sleep. Dr Powell expressed the concern of both SNU and LSA, namely that the Witchcraft and Vagrancy Acts outlawed Spiritualism and psychical research ('youngest of the sciences') – 'a shocking recital of ignorant floundering' by such people as 'would not be reconciled to psychic investigation even if it were demonstrably inspired and guided by an Archangel, or the third Person of the Trinity'. At the end, a notice on behalf of the SNU appealed for contributions to raise £3000 to pursue legal change in Parliament – a vast sum. But, as in all such publicity, the tone was optimistic; it was a rallying cry not a lament.

Henry Duncan needed rallying. One of 26,000 rheumatics invalided out of the war, he received just eight shillings a week plus a small supplement for each of his children. As the post-war world piled on disappointment – too few homes for heroes – so he found hope in the things he read, and although there was little money for books, pamphlets like Powell's, and J. Arthur Findlay's short study of John Sloan, a Glasgow warehouse packer and medium, were more within his means. Periodicals too. In 1926 the first edition of *The Medium* was published in Scotland, a sixpenny miscellany of short articles, thoughts and quotations, for which its Dundonian editor composed a tribute to angels and a profile of Swedenborg, which admitted the narcoleptic effect of the great man's works. There was advice on dealing with jealousies among developing mediums, censure of the BBC for broadcasting 'creed-bound theology in an age that has outgrown creeds' and news of how unemployed miners in the coalfields of South Wales were discovering their 'latent psychic gifts'. Such

73

works, most of which lasted just a few issues, bound the home circles, small churches and incorporated societies into a common Spiritualist culture, establishing the identity of a defiant minority, and widening a world of knowledge and opportunity. Even before they had left Edinburgh, Henry Duncan was familiarizing himself with different types of mediumship. Reading in bed one night, he described to Helen how the soul could detach itself from the living body to travel great distances. When she next glanced over at him he had become very still with his book over his face and his skin was cold to the touch. In a panic, fearing another heart attack, Helen shook him and was about to call the doctor when suddenly he regained possession of himself, sat up and calmed her with a simple explanation of what had happened: he had just been to visit his sister Jean sixty-four miles away in Arbroath, a fact which Jean was later pleased to confirm.

Between leaving Edinburgh and settling in Dundee, the Duncans themselves resided temporarily in Arbroath and here took their first steps towards developing Helen's mediumship. Spiritualists today will tell you that we all have psychic power, but like any craft it needs to be nurtured with earnest and patient endeavour in an atmosphere of love and amity. Helen began with experiments in psychometry – divining information from vibrations inherent in inanimate objects – at first trinkets that Henry bought for her and of which she guessed the price; then graduating to personal possessions, usually rings, watches, brooches, cigarette cases and pocket knives. She discovered that she was able to sense the contents of sealed letters by running the envelope across her head and down her spine. She learned to read the luminous auras surrounding bodies and understood the golden cords connecting people, which indicated that they were related by blood. She showed real promise.

Gratified by success, Helen advanced to the next stage of her apprenticeship, Henry all the while puffing on a pipe, talking over matters with his friend Jim Murray – conversations which tended to exclude Helen – and scribbling his record for posterity. But Helen soon discovered that she needed more guidance than even her husband could give. We are told that during a discussion between Henry and Jim, a bored Helen fell into a trance – a feeling she described as rising into the air, not falling as if fainting – and began speaking in the deep voice of a 'Dr Williams', a spirit guide whose name was spelled in smoke from an extinguished candle. As with many Spiritualist experiences, the exchange that followed mixed the profound with the banal, the sublime with the ridiculous. The guide announced that important work lay ahead, which would require changes inside the medium's body and then, before his voice faded from Helen's lips, to show that he meant business, he materialized a distinctively bent tie-pin belonging to Jim Murray (who had recently trodden on it in his bedroom). Yet it was the very triviality of such things that gave Spiritualism its affinity with the signs and portents of Christian millenarianism, and from acorns of experience such as these would oaks of revelation grow. At any rate, Helen had secured the attention of the men, who now agreed it was time to start a home circle.

The idea of a circle for the development of mediumship had been crystallizing in Henry's mind since his father's death. Father and son had agreed a medieval-style death pact, that is, whoever died first would attempt to contact the other, and the night he died, after the ominous banshee wail, Henry junior had heard his father's distinctive double-knock at the door and decided this would be a good way for them to communicate. Just as Methodists were well-versed in the apostolic travels of John Wesley, and Mormons in Joseph Smith receiving the lost gospel from the angel Nephi, Henry knew the story of the Hydesville rappings and the ensuing craze for table turning. Like the Fox sisters, the Dundee circle – Henry, Helen, Jim Murray and his brother Frank – made a leap of faith and were rewarded with knocks upon the table, which they interpreted according to a code of their own devising. In due course, several friends joined the circle, among them Auntie Mac who had discovered her own psychic powers after Helen had revealed her dead son's presence. Seances were held every Thursday, interrupted only by Henry's spells of hospitalization, and times when Helen's kidneys were bad and Auntie Mac would care for the children and nurse her, bringing flowers and tempting her to eat. These domestic crises reminded Helen and Henry of their fragile existence and, like the premature deaths of Etta and Alex, spurred them on to seek consolation and meaning in God – and the guiding spirit of Dr Williams.

In the history of Spiritualism spirit guides – or 'controls' as they are sometimes known – illustrate the human need both to lead and be led, in that they act as servant and master simultaneously, an ambiguity which appealed to young people resentful of their elders and betters, but upon whom they relied and whom they had to obey. At the same time as he was forced to use Helen's voice-box to speak, Dr Williams had effectively taken her on as his student and perhaps, as the incident at the serving hatch suggests, as a spiritual heir destined to wield authority in the next life – a signal honour for a woman ostracized by her family and undervalued by society. Even prodigious mediums, however rapid their development, usually progressed only so far. Helen's achievements, by contrast, appeared to know no bounds, in her own mind confirming what her moribund excursion to the spiritual plain had taught her: that, like Joan of Arc ordered by the saints to liberate Paris, she was the chosen one. And as with St Joan, this was greatness thrust upon the low-born, a true purpose for a working woman otherwise denied one. It was power.

One of the oldest and most useful skills for which Helen displayed an aptitude was healing, specifically a tendency to take on the symptoms of any sick person. As a repercussion of being mauled by the ferret, Bella developed a swelling in her face from which Helen, like her sixteenth-century antecedents, sucked poison into her own body through prayer and touch, forming a dental abscess which required her to have a tooth extracted later that day. Even if Helen had accepted the reality of Spiritualism by this time, it would seem she still thought of her powers as natural rather than supernatural; she was a channel for psychic energies, not the factotum of the dead. Gradually, however, this changed as the spirits pressed themselves more forcefully upon her and, as it turned out, more threateningly. One evening Henry took Helen to a Spiritualist church to enjoy a demonstration of clairvoyance. There she saw something seen by no one else – a lumbering ape dangling a noose above the medium's head – and became hysterical. Later she tried to warn the medium's wife, but the woman dismissed the danger, until, that is, her husband was committed to an asylum, apparently suffering from paranoid schizophrenia. Someone – or something – he said, was trying to kill him. Helen visited the man, placed her hands on his head and prayed. Soon afterwards, Helen developed a blinding headache which, Henry surmised, must be due to her having assumed an evil spirit. Grabbing the family bible, he attempted an exorcism from where it fell open, Paul's Epistles to the Corinthians: 'Therefore, seeing we have this ministry, as we have received mercy we faint not; but have renounced the hidden things of dishonesty, not walking in craftiness, nor handling the word of God deceitfully; but by the manifestation of the truth commending ourselves to every man's conscience in the sight of God.'

At once the temperature in the room plummeted and a pause, pregnant with evil, was broken by something unseen seizing hold of Helen, causing her nose to spurt blood. Like a Catholic exorcist in the days when the devil still raged on earth, clutching his bible, Henry managed to stammer the words, 'The Lord is my shepherd, I shall not want' and continued the psalm until the malevolent presence exited with a loud bang. They discovered later that the start of Helen's nosebleed coincided with the moment when the medium who had been driven insane by the ape-spirit sank mercifully into death in the asylum.

The thought that this work should not be undertaken lightly or irreverently must have preyed on their minds as the spirits moved ever closer towards their intimate Thursday evening gatherings. Until this point they had communicated through rappings or, in Dr Williams's case, direct voice. But as the atmosphere of the seance room became more charged, the vibrations raised through the circle's conviction and concentration more intense, so hands, wispy and evanescent, began to appear through the crackling darkness and soon an occasional unrecognizable face. Love was the bridge, according to Sir Oliver Lodge, and that was the emotion Helen tried to push out into the void, dissolving her essential self even beyond the boundaries of the universe. But this was a bridge, too, which invited malevolent travellers to return. At one seance the circle gathered as usual, holding hands around a small table, an oil lamp at its centre, when Helen felt something grab hold of her leg. At first she thought it was a prank, but looking down, saw a hand that finished at the wrist. When the others looked too, they were petrified by the sight not just of the hand, but a severed head laughing at them. Like a child menaced by the night, Helen closed her eyes but found the spittle-lipped face still there when she opened them. The worst was yet to come, however, for Helen was about to be visited by the ape-spirit.

The claim by Matthew Hopkins, the infamous witch-finder of the 1640s, to have been pursued by a headless bear was just one example, admittedly an outrageous one, of an ancient belief that evil spirits took on the shapes of animals. Witnesses at Salem in 1692 described seeing the devil as a man-faced monkey, illustrating the way that apes, by way of their physical proximity to ourselves, were powerfully suggestive of debased or corrupted humanity – an association which gained more monstrous definition in the nineteenth century as a symbol of anti-Darwinism. Back in the 1590s the pamphlet story of *Dr Faustus* told how a servant, appointed by the eponymous scholar to be his apprentice in sorcery, conjured up a wicked ape which rampaged through the house. The cultural origins of Helen Duncan's ape, however, are more likely to lie in the manifestations mentioned by Robert Kirk a century later as part of Scottish highland belief. If this was a tradition that resurfaced from the past at the Dundee seances it was misunderstood, for Kirk's apes were not simian creatures but *doppelgängers* – spiritual replicants which *aped* the appearance and behaviour of real people, often in the role of guardian angels. And here the old idea was perhaps doubly misunderstood, for Helen's ape offered no such protection.

Henry recorded that earlier in the day Helen had complained of feeling tense and, unusually, put baby Gena in her cot upstairs before the seance began. She might have cancelled; but Henry, ever keen to discover more, dismissed her foreboding and in any case she never liked to disappoint her sitters. An hour before they were due to begin Helen, panting softly, rested her bulk in a chair to gather psychic energy. As the visitors started to arrive, she helped Henry prepare the room, then they all sat at the table and joined hands in the usual way. As had happened before, the room became eerily cold and then, in a scene reminiscent of the disturbances in the Mackie household in 1697, furniture and other objects began to move, some hurled across the room. The Singer sewing machine flew through the air, Henry's books were catapulted from the bookcase, a bed levitated, the curtains were ripped down and the iron grate wrenched from the fireplace. As the brick dust settled they waited in their seats, listening to the sound of a creature stalking them, which in the semi-darkness appeared to be half-man, half-animal – some species of ape, which ran a cold, clammy, hairy hand down their necks. 'Good Heavens! What's that on my head? Who's touching me?' cried two men present, probably Jim and Frank Murray and, if so, their last words before they fled. After the ape had retreated and the gaslight had been relit, Henry saw his darling Nell's pale face, her raven-black hair dulled from the dust, the only brightness her terrified eyes and a vivid scarlet streak of blood between nose and lips. Henry comforted her briefly, tidied the room a little, then with feverish excitement began writing an account in his journal, quizzing the Murray brothers once they had dared to return. When one of them said he thought there must be evil spirits at large, a briar pipe flew from its rack on the mantelpiece and rapped him on the bridge of his nose.

Helen's feelings were mixed. If before she had wondered what good their work would come to, now she saw the devil at play, her orthodox Presbyterian sensibilities rising against the idea that such manifestations were just the souls of the dead in various states of moral distinction or dereliction – traditional Catholic eschatology in other words. At the same time another part of her remained convinced that people they had known and loved could communicate from the other side – a belief lent weight by messages from Henry's father and drowned brother. But to proceed they would need protection and guidance. Henry made a small wooden cross mounted on a plinth and gave it a lick of luminous paint, and the circle resolved always to say a prayer or read from the Bible before a seance, and to sing a hymn, which also helped to raise the vibrations. At the first meeting after the ape manifestation they said the Lord's Prayer and sang the twenty-third Psalm, following which Dr Williams offered reassurance and advised them to make a cabinet – not a task requiring Henry's joinery skills as he first imagined, merely a curtain suspended across a corner of the room to create a private space where a medium could muster psychic strength. Instead of candles Dr Williams recommended a lamp radiating a dim red light, bright enough for sitters to witness phenomena, but not so bright as to cause harm to a medium in trance. Henry laid his hands on an old railwayman's paraffin lamp, which reeked but satisfied Dr Williams. To save Helen unnecessary strain a new guide, 'Matthew Douglas', a deceased gentleman of Kirkcaldy, advised the circle to invest in a trumpet, a sort of megaphone, and typically a narrow tin cone with luminous markings. Theirs, constructed from two telescopic sections, floated around the room bringing messages, and was such a hit that a second one was acquired. After Matthew Douglas came the spirit of 'Donald', a controlling intelligence they all found unbearably lewd, not least Henry, who complained that the man speaking through his wife was too dominant, the last straw being his flirtation with one of Auntie Mac's guests. In the end Dr Williams recalled Donald (for meddling with Helen's kidney medicine) and replaced him with the man who would serve her for the next three decades, standing by her in the darkness of which – it is worth mentioning – Helen was afraid.

As Dr Williams had predicted, in 1926 the Duncans moved the sixteen miles or so back to Dundee, closer to most of their fellow sitters. Henry found a terraced house in Ferry Road, near to where his parents used to live, and although at 12s 6d per week the rent was more than they could afford, its electricity supply plus the extra space for their expanding family made it irresistible. With labour and love the seances resumed. Henry built a wooden box fitted with a bulb and a sliding red glass lid over which a cloth could be draped to dim the light further, the effect being to throw a dull glow up rather than out, allowing sitters to pick out shapes if they focused hard. The new control was 'Albert Stewart' – a spirit of dignity and good sense a world away from disgraceful Donald, and eminently able both to direct proceedings and protect the interests of the woman he always respected as 'Mrs Duncan'. Like many of the young men of Helen's youth, Albert was a Scots émigré to Australia who had been apprenticed as a pattern maker but drowned in 1913 at the age of thirty-three. Given to making cryptic comments, often of a vaguely reassuring kind such as 'If your love is as big as yourselves then I should like to have it', his voice was a peculiar hybrid: not merely Scots inflected with Australian, but what sitters most commonly described as an 'Oxford' accent, or into the 1930s a 'BBC' accent – pronunciation which most British people associated with authority and wisdom. To one woman from York he was 'the nicest spoken man I have ever met'. But Albert alone did not set the tone, for his patrician reserve would in due course be tempered by the mischievous charm of a small Scots girl – Peggy Hazeldine – whom he was training to be a spirit guide and whom he allowed to stand in for him whenever he was called away on urgent spirit business. Peggy's mother Lena attended a seance and was convinced.

From this point in her development there was really only one place Helen could go. By now, clairvoyance and clairaudience were second nature to her, witnesses reported remarkable powers of levitation and apportation (transporting small objects into the seance room), and her psychometrical insights, it was said, were infallible. In the preceding years, as we have seen, there had been occasional visible manifestations, but these tended to be either faint, silent and meaningless, or vivid, violent and uncontrollable.

Now, however, Albert was ready to lend his patience and expertise to help Helen reach what Dr Williams had promised would be her destiny: the perfection of a skill which would eclipse anything she had achieved to date. And like a witch from the burning days – Elspeth McEwen perhaps – an otherwise impotent woman to whom others attributed special powers, she would rise to meet expectations; or like St Paul she would renounce hidden things and manifest the truth. In short, she would join the proud tradition of a rare breed: the materialization mediums able to summon the dead from the vasty deep and in radiance parade them before those who had loved them in life and now mourned their absence.

In the later 1870s a series of seances funded by a Manchester Spiritualist named Charles Blackburn were held at the Bloomsbury headquarters of the British National Association of Spiritualists, forerunner of the London Spiritualist Alliance. One of the first mediums engaged was William Eglinton who as a boy had mocked his father's home circle, pinning a sign on the seance room door which read: 'There are lunatics confined here; they will be shortly let loose.' A decade later, this account written by H. W. Seton-Karr, a visitor to one of the Blackburn seances, suggests how far his opinions had changed: 'There were about sixty people present and the large room was lit by three or four gas jets, making a brilliant light. A small curtain was suspended on a rod across one corner of the room farthest from the door, and Mr Eglinton's feet were visible under the lower edge as he sat behind, breathing heavily in trance.'

Seton-Karr, sitting a yard from the curtain, was astonished by a sequence of spiritual forms which appeared to build up inside the cabinet. When the last of them, a tall black man in white robes, waved a substantial fire-screen above his head to show his strength, he accidently demolished the cabinet, exposing the unconscious medium. 'As I gazed,' recalled Seton-Karr, 'the figure melted into a white cloud which slowly entered Mr Eglinton's body', after which he regained consciousness and staggered to his feet. The *Western Morning News* reported in 1876 that if Eglinton was a conjuror he was one of the best there had ever been, and certainly better than Maskelyne and Cook who, styling themselves 'illusionists and antispiritualists', packed out the Egyptian Hall on Piccadilly twice a day and challenged any medium to perform a feat they could not reproduce. The way these public seances bridged the devotional and the diverting is encapsulated perfectly by an escapology routine performed in Boston by a Mr Fay and remembered in 1911 by Sir Hiram Maxim, pioneer of the modern machine-gun. On successive evenings, Spiritualists who took Fay's act to be the most marvellous evidence of spiritual power feared that he would explain his trick – as he repeatedly promised to do – but when at last he did they were jubilant. His secret? The old pro divulged that he drew upon the 'spirits of the departed'.

Another of Spiritualism's bridges stretched between the Church of England and the people for whom it was losing its relevance. Formally, the Church had to adopt a hostile stance, but at grass-roots level showed considerably more interest in the way Spiritualist beliefs reactivated and sustained Christian faith. Rev. Stainton Moses, by becoming a medium himself, was the epitome of this tendency. For many the greatest problem was not proving Spiritualism, but distinguishing genuine mediumship from fraud. Thomas Colley, an Anglican clergyman who served the Church for over thirty years (becoming an archdeacon) and made no secret of his Spiritualist leanings, believed passionately that a former Baptist minister called Francis Ward Monck was a medium able to manifest spirits from a white fibrous vapour which billowed from his side like steam from a kettle. When Monck was imprisoned in 1876 under the Vagrancy Act, Colley hurried to his defence, despite the fact that 'conjuring apparatus' had been discovered in his room. Eglinton, by contrast, did not pass muster with Colley who once edged towards one of his spirit forms in the darkness and snipped off cloth and facial hair, which were later found to match muslin and a false beard hidden in Eglinton's trunk.

In some quarters the cold water poured over the claims of materialization mediums by academics was less influential than the academic endorsement such claims received. 'A living being, or living matter, formed under our own eyes . . . is surely the climax of marvels!' declared Dr Charles Richet, Professor of Physiology at the Faculty of Medicine in Paris. 'Nevertheless, it is a fact!' Richet, who cited Einstein in his speculations that mechanical energy could be projected in a similar way to light, became convinced of the reality of materialization in 1905 at the house of a French general in Algiers. After General Noël's son Maurice died serving in the Congo, Madame Noël had discovered that his fiancée, Marthe Béraud, herself an officer's daughter, possessed remarkable mediumistic gifts. Specifically she was able to materialize spirits, most famously her guide 'Bien Boa', a sixteenth-century brahmin of impeccable manners. Professor Richet applied vigorous tests at the Villa Carmen but remained sure about the things he saw (during which time Marthe was always visible), especially because of the social status of the participants. He took some remarkable photographs. An ex-servant's allegation that he had been forced to impersonate Bien Boa, Richet put down to Arab mendacity, and even reports of Marthe's confession he attributed to press sensationalism and the acknowledged mental instability of mediums. His photographs allow us to make up our own minds. The hard truth is that it is difficult to see Bien Boa as anything other than a man in a sheet wearing a silver helmet and a luxuriant beard stuck to his face. He resembles not so much an Indian sage as Kaiser Wilhelm II in a lacy white frock (attire to which, it must be said, the German emperor was not entirely averse).

In 1923 Richet published a book translated as *Thirty Years of Psychical Research*, which he dedicated to Frederick Myers and the recently deceased physicist Sir William Crookes OM, discoverer of the element thallium, inventor of the radiometer and pioneer of electric lighting. Crookes was also a committed psychical researcher whose open mind led to a curious relationship with a comely teenage medium from Hackney called Florence Cook whose full-form materializations were causing a sensation in Spiritualist circles. Her spirit guide (and *doppelgänger*), 'Katie King', was also the object of Crookes's attentions and, even though he took pains to identify differences between the two girls (only one was a nail-biter, he said), photographs lead one to suppose that they were one and the same. Of this fact Sir George Sitwell – who rarely lived up to his name at seances – was quite positive when in 1880 he leapt up and seized 'Katie', only to find himself holding Florence whose clothes lay in a pile in the cabinet. It is easy to let such frolics obscure the stature of men like Richet and Crookes in their conventional academic pursuits; Crookes's colleagues in the Royal Society certainly did, even though in 1913 they still elected him as President, the same year that Richet was awarded the Nobel prize for medicine.

Distinct camps of opinion can be identified, but to understand the life of Helen Duncan, above all the way she was regarded by others, one also has to appreciate the subtle shades forming a generation before her birth. Sidgwick was free-thinking but cautious, Myers almost recklessly credulous. Richet believed implicitly in materialization but not that this proved human survival; and even though he found certain cases puzzling (among them that of Raymond Lodge) he preferred to think that beings of higher intelligence were the cause. Crookes, who so admired Florence Cook, initially struggled to come to terms with the most famous physical medium of the Victorian era, Daniel Dunglas Home, but only because of the revolutionary implications he bore for Newtonian physics. Home's origins may sound familiar. Born in the Scottish highlands in 1833, he was a nervous child who inherited the gift of second sight and experienced visions, one accurately predicting his mother's death. Taken to America, in 1850 he attracted rappings to his aunt's house and she, aware of events in Hydesville NY, arranged exorcisms, then threw him out when they failed. Arriving in England in 1855, Home rapidly entered polite society as a medium of staggering talent, famously floating gracefully out of a window at Ashley House in the presence of, among others, Lord Adare and Lord Lindsay, and feeding the press stories throughout the 1860s. Most notoriously, he was banished from Rome for sorcery, a charge for which more than one attempt was made on his life. In 1871 the secretaries of the Royal Society, whose faith in Newton remained unshaken, declined on Crookes's behalf an invitation to attend one of his seances, but there were many other opportunities and Crookes came to regard Home as the world's most remarkable medium. Himself a harsh critic of charlatans in sheets, Home was investigated many times but never exposed despite rumours, among them that he used police intelligence, carried a secret monkey and drew magnetic power from cats. For some, however, seeing was disbelieving. Once, when Empress Eugénie of France claimed she had been touched by the spirit of a dead child, an onlooker swore he had seen Home extending his naked foot. Famously, Robert Browning was so disgusted with Home's fraudulence (and silliness: a wreath of flowers was 'levitated' on to the poet's head) that he penned his vitriolic satire 'Mr Sludge, the Medium' and with it condemned Spiritualism *tout court*. His wife Elizabeth, by contrast, clung to her fond hopes despite her estimation that Home's seances were 'twaddle'.

Here's a dream. Sir Oliver Lodge and Frederick Myers are roaming a deserted island in their pyjamas, Charles Richet has stayed behind to fish for food. At night, they sit in a darkened room watching strange lights and disembodied hands dance in the air. Sidgwick and his wife arrive and, instead of their usual scepticism, they are utterly convinced by the reality of the phenomena, which include an enormous floating melon. Except this wasn't a dream: it is precisely what occurred in 1894 on the Ile Roubard, Richet's private island off the South of France. Lodge and Myers wore pyjamas because of the heat, an indignity they endured in order to spend time with the medium Eusapia Palladino – a middle-aged, rotund, illiterate Neapolitan peasant woman. In the following year she was entertained at Myers's serene and leafy Cambridge home where, even though she was taken shopping and allowed to win at croquet, she remained unhappy with the food, the weather and the starchy social conventions. The unadorned and uninhibited earthiness for which the ladies detested Eusapia proved magnetic to their husbands; Sidgwick even had her photographed wearing his academical gown. Although suspicions about her accumulated with every seance she held there, the phenomena were nonetheless remarkable, the oddest being lumpy protruberances, some of which elongated into supernumerary arms extending from her back. Lodge and Myers were convinced; the Sidgwicks less so now. For his part, Richet had found her phenomena 'absurd and unsatisfactory' . . . but still he thought this insufficient grounds for crying foul.

Here we have the best illustration of the irony that Spiritualism relied on materialism for its anti-materialism; or, put another way, the ability to perceive materialized spirits depended on their material not their spiritual nature. And this begs a question. If, as Richet believed, materializations were mechanical projections, what exactly was being projected? The half-answer was 'ecto-plasm', organic matter already familiar to cell biologists as the complement of endoplasm, but appropriated to the language and culture of Spiritualism and psychical research by Richet and his followers. Like Monck with his steam-like discharge, William Eglinton was said to clothe his summoned spirits with ectoplasm (elsewhere 'teleplasm', 'psychoplasm' or 'plasma'), in the words of his biographer 'a dingy white-looking substance' which poured from his body, and pulsated on the floor as the shape of a spirit coalesced and rose to imitate life. Investigating Marthe Béraud, Richet noticed how

A kind of liquid or pasty jelly emerges from the mouth or the breast of Marthe which organizes itself by degrees, acquiring the shape of a face or a limb. Under very good conditions of visibility, I have seen this paste spread on my knees, and slowly take form so as to show the rudiment of the radius, the cuvitus, or metacarpal bone whose increasing pressure I could feel on my knee.

Its physical properties were those of gases, liquids or solids, depending on how spiritual intelligence directed it; but, Spiritualists and scientists never agreed quite what it was, or what it was not in composition. Undoubtedly there was something seminal and ovarian about it. Sitters were sometimes advised to uncross their legs so as not to impede the imperceptible flow of reproductive matter joining the stream emanating from the medium's body, usually from some orifice: the mouth, nose, ear, navel or genitals – an act which might produce the signs of orgasm or labour in the medium. Some believed that ectoplasm picked up dust and fibres in the seance room, either by accident or to increase its substance. But the type and quality varied, depending on the medium. The banged-up child visionary, Elizabeth Hope, better known in adult life as 'Madame d'Espérance', described it as a 'faintly luminous hazy material', which grew denser until fully visible:

> Sometimes this is of a greyish-white colour, sometimes of a dead whiteness, sometimes slightly luminous, becoming more so as it appears to condense, till it sheds a faint radiance on surrounding objects. To the touch it at first appears of a light fleecy character, resembling combed, finely drawn cotton wool, but quickly, even under the fingers, it seems to assume the character of a textile fabric.

A medium noted more for her looks than her phenomena, Hope rarely produced anything so fine. And in the same year that Florence Cook was exposed, someone grabbed her spirit guide 'Yolande' to reveal poor Lizzie standing there, blushing in her underclothes. Victorian bloomers could conceal several metres of tightly packed diaphanous cloth; but there were some places which were closed to investigation even in the name of science. After 1900, however, it seems that by shifting proceedings from the salon to the laboratory, etiquette and common decency could be cast aside and a colder empirical eye cast over the transmutations happening within and without these women's bodies.

Indeed, in the published research of the new era it is women's bodies that one finds depicted. Instead of sensuous, artfully draped teenagers, we see women in poses of entranced abandon, straining, ecstatic, as ectoplasmic effluvia snake from beneath their skirts, pictures which speak less of sexual repression than liberation, or at least submission as male investigators flashed their cameras in the darkness. To be fair, not all investigators took this direction, but a work by one who did became the bible of physical medium-ship for years to come. Baron Albert von Schrenck-Notzing was a Bavarian psychiatrist whose interests, rooted in somnambulism and hypnotherapy, led him to renounce materialism (though not to embrace Spiritualism), give up medicine (he married into money) and devote all his time to psychical research. One of his earliest ventures was to join the pyjamaed men of science on Richet's island to see Eusapia Palladino, whereafter he followed her across Europe. In 1909 his attentions turned to a Parisian medium called Eva Carrière, a woman in her early twenties who operated under a patron, a sculptor named Juliette Bisson, much as Marthe Béraud had done under Madame Noël. Although few knew it at the time, Eva Carrière *was* Marthe Béraud, who had escaped adverse publicity in Algiers and pseudonymously formed an intimate relationship with Bisson, who took many of the photo-graphs for Schrenck-Notzing's *Materialisationsphänomene*, publi-shed in 1913. Bisson was Eva's Svengali, her influence (as Madame Noël's had been) literally hypnotic, and Schrenck-Notzing was struck by the medium's passivity, the most memorable evidence of which were physical examinations *per rectum et vaginam* (to use Richet's discreet term) to check for concealed materials. Schrenck-Notzing watched as Bisson probed Eva's vagina; but he himself consented to feel her body only through her leotard. Like Eusapia, Eva moaned, her muscles racked with spasms of sexual or obstetric climax.

A famous photograph shows a tangle of gauzy matter suspended from Eva's bare breasts, alleged ectoplasm from which she moulded visible faces and body parts; another from 1913 shows her wearing nothing but a pained expression as she manifests a shrouded gentleman whose flat face some felt bore a striking resemblance to the King of Bulgaria. This theory was strengthened after the camera caught her head at an odd angle to reveal the back of a two-dimensional face bearing the word 'MIRO': part of the masthead of *Le Miroir* from which several faces were taken including the French and American presidents – and the Bulgarian monarch. Since paranormalist reasoning tends to be more sophist than Socratic, this evidence did not prove that Eva was a fraud; rather it implied that *some* of her phenomena were not genuine. Schrenck-Notzing even speculated that these images were 'ideoplasts' – sharply recalled images (a habit of hysterical women, he argued) projected externally. More plausibly, she regurgitated her props, suggested two German researchers of extreme sobriety (one of whom later married Erich Ludendorff, the walrus-faced general who helped Hitler to power). The celebrated escapologist Harry Houdini agreed, after he himself observed how the appearance of Eva's papery images was consistent with partial digestion. That Eva sometimes bled from the mouth added weight to the idea. All this was refuted by Richet: 'How can masses of mobile substance, organized as hands, faces and drawings be made to emerge from the oesophagus or the stomach? No physiologist would admit such power to contract those organs at will in this manner.' Schrenck-Notzing took a more empirical approach by administering an emetic after Eva had sucked back her ectoplasm, and making her drink bilberry syrup before seances. No result. And yet the regurgitation theory lingered and was raised again by the London Society for Psychical Research when Eva held a series of seances there in 1920.

That summer a letter was received by the editor of *Light* from Dr William J. Crawford, a thirty-nine-year-old mechanical engineering lecturer at Belfast Municipal Technical Institute with whom he had corresponded during the war. Convinced by Eva Carrière, Crawford, a neat, intense man with waxed moustache and rimless spectacles, won the trust of a working-class family in Belfast, the Golighers, who claimed to have developed psychic powers in their home circle, most of all the teenaged Kathleen. Crawford was to spend many hours in a small room above a shop on the Ormeau Road, the gaslight flickering dimly behind a pane of red glass, listening to spiritual raps and straining to see the feats of levitation. The theory he developed was that ectoplasmic rods – termed by him 'psychical structures' – levered up the table, a process which decreased the body weight of the medium by as much as 50 pounds. Fascinated by Kathleen, Crawford studied every aspect of her mediumship until depression weighed too heavy in his heart and he could not go on. 'I have been struck down mentally,' he confessed in the letter. 'It is not the psychic work. I enjoyed it too well.' The letter was a suicide note and, soon after it was written, having made what peace he could with his family and the world, Crawford drowned himself.

Although Crawford was discreet about specifying where the ectoplasm originated, it is clear that it was supposed to have come from her vagina and was variously as solid as iron, or 'as soft as the flesh of a baby's arm'. In a typical experiment, recorded by Crawford with clinical precision, Kathleen was made to wear clean knickers, stockings and shoes upon which coloured dyes were applied to track the 'plasma':

It was found that the methylene blue had been drawn downwards towards the foot of the knickers, and had also gone up nearly to the join of the legs. On the inside of the back of the knickers the blue dye had gone up between the legs as far as the base of the spine, and it had also gone between

93

the buttocks and had spread under them to some extent and over the seat of the knickers.

Crawford was also an avid photographer of the phenomena, but took advice from the spirit guides – or 'operators' – on how best to proceed: 'The chief difficulty seemed to be in preventing injury to the medium. The operators said it was necessary gradually to work her up to withstand the shock of the flashlight upon the plasma; nor is this to be much wondered at when it is considered the plasma is part of her body exteriorised in space.'

A selection of his pictures were used to illustrate the three books of his findings (one published posthumously), a body of research upon which Schrenck-Notzing bestowed a ringing endorsement. But in some ways it is those that were not printed which are most revealing. In the Society for Psychical Research archives, in a basement of the Cambridge University Library, is a tatty album in which they survive, one of which – '3f' – shows Kathleen Goligher in a stick-back armchair wearing a crisp white blouse, her plaid skirt raised above her knees to display stocking tops and flesh beyond. What we do not see, but Crawford did, was the way she shuddered and writhed with each blinding flash of ignited magnesium.

In his suicide note Crawford wrote: 'I am thankful to say that the work will stand.' But his body had scarcely been pulled from the water when doubts set in. On the one occasion Houdini met Crawford at a dinner and discussed the Golighers for three hours, he thought him insane, especially when he saw Crawford's portfolio of photographs, which he tactfully described as 'remarkable'. Less tactfully, a cold-hearted obituary in the SPR's *Proceedings* voiced rumours of fraudulence. In 1921 the SPR sent Sir William Crookes's biographer, Dr E. E. Fournier d'Albe, to Belfast where in twenty sittings with the Golighers he detected nothing paranormal (but did see Kathleen lift a stool with her foot), concluding that the family were 'an alert, troublesome group of well-organized performers'. But all this only strengthened the convictions of the believers, among them Ernest Oaten, President of the Manchester-based Spiritualists' National Union to which over 300 local societies were affiliated, twice what there had been before the war. In October 1917, as the Allies prepared to advance on Passchendaele, Oaten had gone to a seance in Belfast, and was impressed by Kathleen's phenomena, including a floating trumpet attached to an ectoplasmic rod and intelligent spirits who were 'splendidly co-operative and courteous'. When Fournier d'Albe's findings were published in 1922, however, Kathleen Goligher withdrew from the limelight, pleading trouble with her nerves, although later she would privately entertain her husband, a prosperous shopkeeper seduced by the enigmatic power of the mediumship.

It was in 1922 that Schrenck-Notzing rented a room in the garrison town of Braunau-am-Inn, a crossing on the German–Austrian border not yet famous as the birthplace of Adolf Hitler but notable for the popularity of Spiritualism. There he began tests on a nineteen-year-old apprentice, Willi Schneider, who, having heard about soldiers dabbling, had discovered in himself the trance personality of an adolescent mistress of King Ludwig of Bavaria, and through her produced astounding telekinetic and ectoplasmic phenomena, often becoming sexually aroused in the process, sometimes ejaculating. His younger brother Rudi demonstrated similar skills, panting like a dog to sustain a trance, but for the time being at least was more interested in cars and football. Seeking work in Munich (like Hitler before him), Willi was close to Schrenck-Notzing's laboratory and held regular seances attended by men of science and letters, including the novelist Thomas Mann who, utterly convinced, was reminded how 'impure, obscene, spiteful, demonic' was nature. Six months earlier, the guests had been Harry Price and another English researcher, Dr Eric Dingwall – 'Ding' to his friends – a shrewd but fickle observer who despite earlier criticisms of the baron's methods was now impressed, and even though the red light was poor they considered many of his phenomena impossible to fake. Back in Britain, printed accounts of their experiences popularized the Schneiders, even though Dingwall remained prone to equivocation.

Through the Spiritualist grapevine and presses, the figure who probably made the greatest impression on Helen Duncan was 'Margery' – the *nom de séance* of Mina Crandon, the attractive Canadian wife of Dr L.R.G. Crandon, a surgeon at Harvard medical school and descendant of a *Mayflower* pilgrim (he said), whose burning interest in psychical research was kindled by a lecture by Sir Oliver Lodge and fuelled by Crawford's work on the Golighers. Successful experiments in table tilting were followed by the development of Margery's mediumship for which her husband became a tireless entrepreneur, messages filtering down to her courtesy of her brother Walter, whose early death she had experienced as a kind of apotheosis. In 1924 the Crandons made a bid for the $5000 the journal *Scientific American* had offered to anyone producing a 'visible psychic manifestation'; the investigative committee included William McDougall, Harvard University's Professor of Psychology, and Harry Houdini, by now at the height of his fame. The affair sparked an acrimonious debate, which divided opinion in the American SPR and at Harvard. Especially critical was Houdini, whose scathing *A Magician Among the Spirits* was published that year. Margery did have her champions. The peasant Eusapia she was not, nor even 'Eva C.' (as Eva Carrière now styled herself), and her social standing enhanced her credibility. She was also fortunate that her humour, looks and charm invoked chivalric outrage whenever she was impugned, not least in Houdini's friend Sir Arthur Conan Doyle who considered Margery 'charming, cultivated and heroic', and felt so strongly about suggestions of fraud from the Harvard sceptics that he got up on Christmas morning 1925 to write a piece in her defence for the *Boston Herald*, arguing in his quixotic and clownishly pompous way that 'there is no day so holy that one may not use it for the fight for truth'.

As with 'Eva C.', interest in Margery's mediumship was poised between public scientific observation and private sexual voyeurism. Stereokodak photographs taken in 1925 show her in a variety of poses: in one she sits deep in trance, her robe opened high up her thighs, one stocking pulled down, ectoplasm of solid organic appearance extending from her mouth. In another she is naked beneath an overcoat, legs parted, a cloth scarcely covering her pubic region and a rubbery hand resembling a bunch of overripe bananas emerging from her navel. That year 'Ding' Dingwall, as SPR Research Officer, finally agreed terms with Dr Crandon and set sail for Boston. At 8.57 p.m. on 8 January he heard a rustling as the medium slipped into trance, followed by the sound of snoring, upon which Walter invited Dingwall to feel the clammy substance on her left thigh, 'a round mass with knobbly prominences', which jerked at his touch. McDougall, who was also present, likened it to placental cord. An hour later Margery began to cough from a throat irritation, which continued until 10.20 p.m. when, as a finale, she vomited. On other occasions she was dragged into trance against her will by 'tireless and cheery Walter' (Dr Crandon's words), causing her to moan in agony or ecstasy. 'Pay no attention to her, let her groan,' instructed Walter icily. 'She must sit every night. Don't ask her how she feels.'

But Dingwall did ask and did not have much patience with Crandon's aphorism: 'You didn't make the universe; you must accept it.' In fact, he suspected that the flabby ectoplasm, the whistles, bells and levitating luminous doughnuts, all amounted to 'a huge hoax got up for the purpose of discrediting psychical research'. Dingwall alleged that animal organs were used and reintroduced the idea of regurgitation, to which Walter sneered that this practice was common across the Atlantic because 'the British have ectoplasm served with their tea'. He also ridiculed Dingwall for his comments about 'little old Margery lying there like a beautiful corpse with lung tissue coming out of her ears'. An American conjuror, Grant Code, went so far as to suggest that Crandon could have surgically enlarged the mouth of his wife's uterus, enabling her to produce fraudulent pseudopodia from what he memorably, but horribly, called her 'most convenient storage warehouse'. For his criticisms Houdini, fresh from an anti-Spiritualist lecture tour, was accused of trying to frame Margery and, for good measure, Walter made a joke about Houdini's baldness. But for all this, professional opinion remained fiercely divided. On 6 June 1928, having seen a boneless materialized hand which dissolved as he prepared to photograph it, Professor R. J. Tillyard FRS, the pre-eminent Australian entomologist, wrote to Sir Oliver Lodge to express the thoughts he would publish in *Nature* that August: 'Margery, in my opinion, is now the finest medium that ever lived. She would assuredly have been burnt as a witch if she had lived three centuries ago.' In the end, her fate was more modern. Desolate and despairing, like many a fading starlet and the Fox sisters before her, she sank into alcoholism and died in 1941 at the age of fifty-three. Such a tragedy no one would have foreseen in the late 1920s when she was riding the crest of a wave.

When the Crandons disembarked at Plymouth from the SS *Mauretania* in December 1929 the British press were waiting at the harbour. A reporter from the *Daily Sketch* was pleasantly surprised to find Mina Crandon 'a charming, vivacious little woman, who almost danced into the room, a dainty smiling brunette in black velvet'. Under a barrage of questions about her phenomena, she fingered her necklace, glanced at her husband and with childlike trustfulness said: 'He does all the talking for both of us.' For his part Dr Crandon quipped that the real phenomenon was the ability of the Cunard waitresses not to spill the cocktails during the stormy crossing. Margery was a sensation. Crowds clamoured to see her, Captain Clive Maskelyne offered to donate £1000 to a hospital if she could produce a message from his grandfather explaining the family tricks and Dr Bernard Hollander rubbished mediumship in public, asking why the ghosts of the murdered did not return to accuse the culprits. At the Crandons' London hotel the telephone did not stop ringing until 2 a.m. on their first day and their diary filled quickly around the sittings already fixed up with the SPR (at which 'Walter' left his thumbprints in dental wax). It was with only slight exaggeration that journalist Hannen Swaffer, flamboyant inventor of the gossip column and a keen Spiritualist, opined that half the inhabitants of London would attend a 'Margery' seance if they could. Indeed, it seemed that the news-addicted English, facing economic depression and political turmoil, were in need of a Margery of their own.

Like the spirits at their table, opportunity was knocking for the Duncans. What Helen lacked in Mina Crandon's social qualifications, she made up for in the quality of her phenomena. She fell quickly into trance – possibly helped by a nerve-steadying drink and the morphine in her kidney medicine – and by the late 1920s had mastered the production of ectoplasm. Gena Brealey takes up the story from the moment Dr Williams asked the circle, bathed in muted rosy light, whether they were ready to experience this domestic miracle:

> As he spoke, out through the curtain . . . came a substance not unlike cheesecloth or butter muslin. The material continued to flow until there seemed to the sitters to be at least ten yards in a soft pile . . . Through the opening of the curtains they could see Helen sitting in the hard-backed chair, and the ectoplasm flowing from her nose and ears . . . down the front of her dress on to her lap, then down on to the floor and out to the centre of the room.

A great task lay ahead. Every Thursday, and sometimes twice a week, Helen laboured for many months to shape the diaphanous ectoplasm around otherwise invisible spirits, so that their sprawling and wobbling forms gradually grew in size and definition, thereby perfecting a performance which had been merely impressive but now became absolutely startling. Invitations were extended to selected guests. On numerous occasions in 1928, amateur photographer Harvey Metcalfe visited and, convinced by what he saw, arranged with the spirit guide Albert to take the earliest known flash photographs of the materialized spirits. As Walter had done, Albert gave directions and would not allow pictures to be taken until the medium was ready. Of about fifty glass positives taken by Metcalfe, a handful survive showing Helen sturdily seated, wearing a velour dress and a protective blindfold as Kathleen Goligher had done when she faced Crawford's camera. Her hands are held fast by sitters, her ankles lashed with rope. From behind an old-fashioned plant stand emerges a spirit baby attached to Helen's nostrils by an ectoplasmic cord. In another frame a figure looms further back behind the cabinet curtains, an apple-cheeked flapper shrouded in white. This, then, was their proof.

Interest grew quickly in Dundee and beyond. In June 1929 Helen was introduced to James Souter, a local man who visited the circle with an open mind and left the same day with a head swimming with images of the dead and the implications they bore for science, religion and the meaning of existence. A subscriber to *Light*, Souter fired off a letter to the editor to announce the arrival of a new prodigy in mediumship: 'The forms build up clearly and distinctly (as many as fourteen have manifested at one sitting); they speak clearly, giving their names and other convincing particulars, answer satisfactorily all questions put to them, they handle objects both light and heavy, [and] play musical instruments.'

Naturally, the most important manifestation was Albert, whom Souter thought a typically canny and level-headed Scot, over six feet tall and modestly bearded. We get a sense of his classically idealized features from a bust entitled *A Disciple* by Frederick George, an Aberdonian sculptor who exhibited it at the Royal Scottish Academy, then donated it to the Edinburgh Psychic College and Library. Helen was presented with a framed photograph of the piece. Several photographs of the spirit himself exist: at his best he resembles a cadaverous revenant, stooped and shrouded like a funerary monument; at his worst a piece of rolled-up paper. During the 1930s witnesses were treated to the novelty of his ectoplasmic voice-box, described incomprehensibly by one as 'a kind of vertebra with a larynx at the top'. Walter, too, had exteriorized his voice-box for Margery, an organic lump which was connected to her nose and perched on her shoulder like a lifeless but familiar pet. By this time Peggy, too, benefited from Helen's aptitude and joined Albert centre-stage, sharing his duties and looking much more herself than she had when Helen had struggled even to make her appear like a dancing dishrag. Now a sitter was able to report having seen 'a little girl named Peggy who said in Scotch dialect "Hoo air yeall" and sang a ditty relating to her discovery of the Mystery of Life'. Winsomely mischievous as ever, she swung from the cabinet curtain until Albert told her to stop, answering back: 'Now, I ken my weight wudna pull the curtain doon.' She resembled no one so much as Shirley Temple, the screen moppet who in 1936 reached her cinematic peak aged eight; but there were many Spiritualist precedents too. In 1907 John Lobb, editor of the *Christian Age*, reported the appearance of 'Mischief' – 'a young lady of colour' – who was 'addicted to practical joking, often imparting a stimulus to those inclined to secrete articles just when they are wanted, and enjoying the fun when the search is going on'. This was Peggy down to a tee. 'Mischief' consented to be photographed, the grainy result of which Lobb printed: today all we see is a sinister grinning face of a girl, her tongue protruding obscenely.

Spiritual materializations, under the stewardship of Albert and Peggy, were witnessed by a growing number of men whose opinion mattered in the world of mediumship. J. B. McIndoe, Oaten's successor as President of the Spiritualists' National Union, attended a seance and was so impressed that he invited Helen to Glasgow to give sittings there. Montague Rust, a doctor from Newport in Fife and later a witness at the Old Bailey, also became a staunch supporter at this time and introduced Helen to Lena Hazeldine, mother of the spirit Peggy. It is said that in order to stem some curious controversy as to whether Albert was really male or female, Rust was invited to perform a perfunctory examination from which he was pleased to confirm that Albert was all man. Most visitors to the Dundee circle, however, saw themselves not as observers of a scientific demonstration, but participants in emotional family reunions. Possibly the first full materialization for a sitter was a woman's son who had died young. As he sang a hymn and threw his arms round her neck, she was certain he had returned, and before leaving 59 Ferry Road whispered to Helen: 'I am a new woman. I have now something to live for. I know now that my boy is not dead; he lives. How can I ever thank you for what you have done for me tonight?' But this was gratitude enough for, as Helen later said, only a mother could understand what it meant for such a wound to be healed.

Such moments, and there were to be many, mixed rapture with melancholy, recalling the bitterest grief in the act of its amelioration. Yet the theatrical context derived less from tragedy than from farce, burlesque and vaudeville. For all his spiritual gravitas, Albert was nothing if not a Master of Ceremonies, a description which crops up repeatedly in the sources. And Helen's children were thrilled, not afraid. Unable to contain his curiosity, one of the Duncan boys once grabbed an airborne trumpet, causing his entranced mother to utter a fearful groan; if he wasn't sorry then, he was when shown the burn on her left cheek. Formal seances alone give a rather lopsided picture of what was going on in the Duncan household. Helen hung her photograph of Albert's bust in her bedroom, as one might a family portrait, suggesting an intimate relationship with the man her children adored as 'Uncle Albert'. By day they sat at Albert's spectral feet, as they might before a party conjuror or seaside Punch and Judy booth, and listened to his wise saws and parables. A favourite was that of the moth flying into the flame, from which they learned to seek only the true light where they would find the Saviour. Albert also amazed them with tricks, on one occasion holding a chair over his head, a feat worthy of Tarzan of the Apes with whom the boys were obsessed. At night they prayed to him like a saint and thanked him for his spiritual care. Particularly fond of him was Gena, whose life he is reputed to have saved by warning her parents that she had contracted pneumonia in hospital while having the lymph oedema on her arm drained, an injury resulting from Helen suffering an eclamptic fit during labour. Aged only four days, Gena attended her first seance and by the age of three was a budding psychometrist. In later life she remembered the time she had started to 'talk funny' when Henry's brother Robert came to tea. Uncle Bob, who had served with the Royal Scots in India, hugged her, saying she was just like her mother; apparently, she had accurately described a man known to him who had been killed in a rebel skirmish, her account made more remarkable by the fact that it was in Hindustani. The Duncan children accepted psychic phenomena as a matter of course, therefore, including a table controlled by Henry's dead brother which, by means obscure, would participate in games of hide-and-seek. But it was the seances which they loved the most. Soon after they moved to Ferry Road, Harry, then almost five, got his first taste:

> We the children had been playing in the back yard and making a lot of noise. My parents were holding their weekly seance and we were brought into the house and taken into the seance room being told to sit still and be quiet. The room was dark but dimly lit by an aladdin lamp. I remember people dressed in white shimmering 'nightgowns' coming out of the curtains that were stretched across a bed recess and disappearing into the floor.

Addicted to the spectacle and mystery of it all, Harry attended many more seances in years to come, but never quite found the right words to convey what ectoplasm was like. 'The closest I can describe it', he wrote, 'is to liken it to driven snow with bright sunshine shining on it. It appeared to sparkle with a million sequins.'

Other observers, though impressed by what they saw, described Helen in action, warts and all. In March 1930 a sitter reported how Helen had undergone a coughing fit, her chair creaking dreadfully as she fought to give shape to Albert. He complained again about the light but, rather ambitiously, did offer to return as Adam – as in Eve's husband. In the end, however, he managed only to lift the apparently unconscious Mrs Duncan from her chair ('my word this takes some doing,' he croaked) and then stood upon it, the back steadied by Dr Rust who took the opportunity to feel the umbilicus connecting Albert to Helen's body – like fine muslin, he said. But all was not well, as the report made clear: 'The curtain was then lifted, and the lady was seen sitting on the floor. Albert then said, "Thank goodness I love her – she is a poor beggar." The medium had a very bad cough, which Albert explained was due to the tightening of the cord. Medium coughed again very badly and sounded as if she was vomiting.' If the bulk of the performance was derived from Margery, the end was pure D. D. Home: Albert, always eager to offer proof, placed his bare foot in a sitter's hands, which she was either disappointed or astonished to find felt exactly like a human foot with a thin ankle. Before the final curtain Albert showed everyone his umbilical cord and, in response to Henry asking if any of the ectoplasm had been drawn from the sitters, said: 'I get a certain amount, as I love you all.' This donation the sitters were delighted to make, although one imagines that the convivial mood soured slightly when the house lights went up to reveal Helen sitting dazed in the corner, blood and slime dripping from her chin.

Like Mina Crandon, by the end of the roaring twenties and the start of the hungry thirties, Helen Duncan realized she was on the verge of something greater than her humdrum workaday self. The craft at which she excelled was practised everywhere: mediums advertised in newspapers and theatre programmes, and even exhibited publicly at Wembley. Alive to the commercial possibilities, the Duncans began to charge visitors a small admittance fee to their seances and, for the first time in their married life, felt the bitter chill of poverty, sickness and loss thawed by the glow of fortune. In the spring of 1930 Helen took herself to a photographer in Dundee to have her portrait taken: she stares at us from a sepia-toned past – simple, unguarded in plain clothes, but with ebony eyes that are unmistakably purposeful. Someone, perhaps Henry, wrote on the back of this print: 'Mrs Victoria Helen Duncan, Aged 32^1/$_2$ years', the 'Helen' subsequently scored through as if she was undecided how she wished be known in the future. The one thing of which she was sure as she packed a suitcase for London, laying the photograph on top of her clothes, was that she was on her way up and out. The days of cod's head soup were at an end.

PART II

HELEN VILIFIED

4

DARKNESS AND LIGHT

Research and the Search for Respectability

Helen Duncan's reputation grew in the early 1930s as more people fell under the spell of Spiritualism and sought the kind of mediumship at which she excelled. Ena Bügg, whose life would later be transformed by a sitting with Helen, was a shy teenager from a working-class family in Gosport, Hampshire, when in 1931 she attended her first materialization seance with a Mrs Baylis. She was overwhelmed. Distant voices drifted through a floating trumpet and spirit faces – adults, children and babies – crowded into the dark nothingness of the room, mirroring the joyful expressions of the sitters. Ena's experience was not

Ethel Beenham, Harry Price's secretary, posing with cheesecloth, 1931.

especially unusual. Many people attended at least one of countless Spiritualist meetings held in churches, public halls, scout huts,
back rooms, cellars and attics, whether from deep conviction,
sudden conversion or, as in most cases, just casual curiosity. Later
they might justify 'going to the spooks' as a bit of fun, a fashion,
or a favour to a friend; few went alone. More seriously, a vivid
constituency of the dead – the war dead – still haunted hearts
and minds, and it has been remarked upon that Lawrence Binyon's
much-quoted lines from his elegy 'For the Fallen' – remembering
them at the going down of the sun and in the morning – were
more of a description than an exhortation. Writing on Armistice
Day 1927, Rev. Charles Drayton Thomas of the Society of
Communion encouraged his readers to think beyond the memory
of the fallen and towards their afterlives. It was appropriate, then,
that Mrs Baylis's spiritual Master of Ceremonies should be
'George', a soldier from the trenches, and his assistant, 'Curly', a
boy who had perished in a Zeppelin raid.

Memory and desire fused at seances, even among sitters
unconvinced at the end; the fact that so many *were* convinced
and joined Spiritualist churches only makes the events more
intriguing. By the mid-1930s the number of churches affiliated
to the Spiritualists' National Union had risen to over 500, to
which should be added independent groups. The total in Britain
may have exceeded 2000, serving as many as 250,000 members.
The principal means of worship was not the seance as such but
the service, where a clairvoyant might be present to give messages,
but not before hymns, prayers, readings and a collection had
taken place. The main departure from orthodox ceremonies was
that most Spiritualists rejected faith in Christ as the route to
salvation; the *British Spiritualists' Propaganda Hymn Book*
addresses God in many of its 171 hymns but Christ not once.
Spiritualists did respect Christ, but as a superlative medium –

reflected in popular works such as Rev. G. Maurice Elliott's *Psychic Life of Jesus* (1938) – and saw the Bible as a compendium of paranormal phenomena: trance, clairvoyance, clairaudience, apportation, lights, spirit-writing, veridical dreams and materialization. Spirit hands were first recorded in Daniel and Ezekiel; it had been rumoured that Jesus invoked the spirit of John the Baptist; and, most famous of all, there was Saul's seance with the Witch of Endor.

Churchmen were appalled by all this and by what they saw as a return to medieval superstition. Saul had been condemned for conjuration, they said, heaven and survival were not the same thing, and demonstration at seances was the antithesis of faith, a heresy which led man away from God and back to the contrivances of man. Worse, spirits might be devilish deceptions sent to foment error, an echo of the Reformation and an argument advanced most vociferously by the Catholic Church. In 1917 the Holy See banned communicants from attending seances, even as curious onlookers or researchers. Priest and historian Montague Summers, whose books were read widely, excoriated Spiritualism in 1926 as a revival of witchcraft fuelled by wartime bereavement, a demonic illusion 'most foul, most loathly, most dangerous, and most damnable'. Anglicanism was less dogmatic and, as had been the case before 1914, there was little shame in a secular age for ministers to explore experiences which suggested the truth of Christianity. Higher up the Anglican ladder, committees of enquiry set up in England and Scotland to investigate Spiritualism were more circumspect than hostile in their conclusions: the new faith may fill gaps in knowledge, they said, it may be part of God's design. Moreover, many felt that Spiritualism had the potential to revitalize religion. In addition it promised social and moral stability in an age of war, revolution and upheaval.

111

One area of upheaval was class. Victorian mediums had managed to reverse the flow of deference, interest and obedience central to codes of sex and station; but in an age of emancipation and enfranchisement, the tendency could only increase. Inter-war mediums were new moderns, symbols of social reorganization, and although often treated with hauteur, were nonetheless in demand by bourgeois seekers with disposable incomes. In this role, travelling to wherever they were needed, they bore out the Duke of Wellington's fearful prediction that the railway would only make the working classes move about. Among materialization mediums, Helen Duncan travelled best, that is, her results were impressive even away from home. As the guest of SNU President J.B. McIndoe she had astonished sitters in Glasgow and seances at the Edinburgh Psychic College and Library had followed. She invested in a small attaché case for her seance outfit of black dress, knickers and loose-fitting court shoes, and began keeping an autograph book of clients, one of whom wrote: 'With grateful thanks to my friend Mrs Duncan who has raised and taught me to keep within one's heart of hearts the beautiful ideal.' Under the patronage of Dr Montagu Rust, the next step was to achieve recognition by the SNU whose diploma would open the doors to Spiritualist gatherings nationwide. Only by these means would she gain full credibility as a medium – and earn a decent living.

Around this time, F.W. Fitzsimons, a psychical researcher and authority on snake venom, argued that women made fine mediums because they were sensitive and relatively untroubled by reason. But there were differentiating criteria. If a stereotype existed of the *clairvoyante*, it was of a middle-aged spinster with owlish spectacles and a light wave in her hair. Not so the materializers, who were physical mediums in every sense of the word. 'Vitality in a woman', George Bernard Shaw once observed, 'is a blind fury of creation' and so it was with those who gave rebirth to the dead, the super-mothers who, as a veteran seance-goer once put it, were 'sexually flush', an electric life force coursing through their bodies. The very best, Fitzsimons advised, were women of 'gross material nature', most especially those of what he called 'a lymphatic temperament'. All of which defined Helen Duncan, the obese mother of six, down to the ground. Even her fondest advocates rarely saw fit to mince their words. She was described as coarse, gross, 'fish-wifey' and, by a businessman whom she *amazed* in the early 1930s, thus: 'She was in a brown tight-fitting dress . . . a large ungainly woman who moved slowly as though she suffered from heart trouble or glandular affection and had not to hurry. She had by no means a magnetic personality . . . rather a repellent one that aroused one's critical faculties.'

Between the time she had failed her medical at the munitions factory and the start of the 1930s, her bulk increased by almost 30 pounds so that she weighed 17 stone 4 ounces but was only 5 feet 6 inches in height. As for her other vital statistics, she measured 47 inches under the arms, 53 inches around the shoulders, and her bust and hips were 57 inches and 54 inches respectively. Her weight is said to have escalated as high as 22 stone, or even, her family say, 25 stone, and at seances the Laurel-and-Hardy contrast with the six-foot Albert invited his quip about size: 'I have it one way and Mrs Duncan has it the other.' At one sitting in Dundee, held to find out whether her own son would survive an attack of measles, Helen levitated in her armchair and, although she did not quite slip out of the window like D. D. Home (the spirits got her a foot off the ground), everyone present was deeply impressed by this Herculean feat of strength, not least Helen herself. At home, she enjoyed her food – porridge, stew, eggs, bacon and chips – and was often to be found baking and pickling in the kitchen wearing an immense wraparound pinafore. When her children hugged her they tried to join their hands around her body; nestling on her lap listening to stories or boggling at tricks, they toyed with the loose flesh of her arms. Once they clamoured to take a flight between London and Scotland, but Henry explained firmly that with their mother on board the bottom might fall out of the aeroplane.

Helen's weight exacerbated her various ailments. Recoiling from baby Alex's death, she learned she was pregnant again, but was persuaded by doctors to have a termination and be sterilized, an operation which left her gravely ill. And then there were the pulmonary, renal, cardio-vascular, glandular, urinary and intestinal malfunctions for her ravaged body to contend with. Even when she was mobile, her lurching blood-sugar levels made fainting a fact of life and she was in any case prone to falls. In London she tumbled down the stairs, injuring her arm, and more than once appeared with a swollen leg shuffling towards the cabinet, a person on each side straining to support her. Travelling was at best uncomfortable. On journeys lasting half a day she fidgeted in railway carriages and at seances of two hours' duration the seat of convention was a hard, upright stick-back chair – if the organizers were sensible a sturdy carver or smoker's bow. Beforehand, she benefited from help in getting dressed, in particular putting on her shoes. Installed in the cabinet, her weight bore down on her bladder, muscles weakened by obstetric strain. Invariably, she visited the lavatory immediately before and after seances, but even then the mop and bucket were sometimes required. The relentless flow of tea served at these occasions did not help matters.

But love and work, work and love, and the memory of the Christ-like man seen as she had lain close to death, all spurred Helen on. To achieve her SNU diploma she decided she would engage with the institutions of metropolitan psychic science; it seemed like the fastest route. In any case she may have heard that an investigator from the British College of Psychic Science had been sniffing around her seances in Scotland and spreading rumours of fraud. Time for a change of scene, perhaps. In August 1930, to pre-empt suggestions that her ectoplasm was regurgitated matter, Dr Rust arranged for Helen to be X-rayed at Dundee Royal Infirmary, where staff knew her as a regular, and thereby received a written report certifying that her oesophagus and stomach were normal. In the autumn Rust arranged with the London Spiritualist Alliance for the Duncans to relocate to the capital to allow Helen to give a series of sittings, some for research, others for paying guests. In October the family boarded a ship at Leith harbour and, as news spread of their impending arrival, the respectable men and women of investigative London sat back and sharpened their senses and pencils.

Dr W. J. Crawford's album of Goligher photographs is just one of many weird artefacts in the archives of the Society for Psychical Research. One only has to flick through the typed handlist for phrases such as 'tapes of telepathic baby', 'the flying armchair' and 'Barbados coffin mystery' to leap out. But like a Renaissance cabinet of curiosities, beneath the eclecticism and eccentricity of the relics lies a more coherent exploratory purpose: the need to tackle unanswered questions about the natural world, a need rooted in the agnostic angst and intellectual élan of the Sidgwicks' circle in Cambridge.

By 1890 the SPR had lost many Spiritualists but had made gains elsewhere. In Lord Rayleigh and J. J. Thomson they boasted two future Nobel laureates, and in William Gladstone and A. J.

Balfour (Mrs Sidgwick's brother) a past and a future Prime Minister. Gladstone, indeed, believed the research of the SPR committees on mesmerism, haunted houses and so on to be 'the most important work which is being done in the world'. For example, a census of hallucinations taken from 17,000 answers to a questionnaire revealed that one in ten had experienced *something* inexplicable.

The fraudulence of Eusapia Palladino and the occultist mystic, Helena Blavatsky, marked a loss of patience, however. Madame Blavatsky, who founded the Theosophical Society to challenge the Christian monopoly of spiritual truth, was the daughter of a Russian officer who after a childhood of greed, tantrums and hallucinations never ceased to wallow in burning fantasies about sex, semen and the supernatural, which at her headquarters at Adhyar in India she stoked with hashish. Her seances were satirized in *Punch* as the ancient wisdom of the Mahatmas manifested in feeble tricks, which included the extrusion of ectoplasm and showers of roses, all of which her housekeeper asserted were fraudulent stunts. And so it was to the dignified Mrs Piper and the socially refined ex-actress Mrs Osborne Leonard that the SPR redirected its attentions. Between 1894 and 1923, they published no major paper on apparitions.

It would be wrong to say that interest in Spiritualism after the First World War brought physical phenomena back into the mainstream concerns of the SPR, but there was money to lavish on such mediums as boasted great powers, even if more of it now came from donations. By the time Helen Duncan arrived in London, however, the SPR was no longer the only solvent research organization and some members – notably the wilful Harry Price who founded his National Laboratory of Psychical Research (NLPR) in 1923 – had gone their own way, spending money like water. Sir Oliver Lodge noted with dismay a rumour spreading abroad that the British psychical research establishment had succumbed to 'a kind of insanity'. If so, it was insanity that Helen and Henry Duncan were ready to exploit.

The LSA premises were situated at 16 Queensberry Place, a fine South Kensington town house with four floors and a basement. Whether Helen was permitted to enter through its neoclassical porch, or whether she was ushered in through the tradesmen's entrance like other mediums, is not recorded, although it is likely that Dr Rust and his wife would have conferred sufficient respectability. Once inside, they were cordially received by the Secretary, Miss Mercy Phillimore, who showed them the seance room with its double doors, the innermost padded with green baize; in a far corner stood the cabinet, a plush curtain suspended a cautious distance beneath the ceiling, at the centre of which hung a wooden chandelier holding four red lamps. Outside, Helen may have noticed the lavatory reserved for ladies. Her attention was drawn to the seance rules intended to protect mediums: lights, smoking, striking watches, touching manifestations and so on were all forbidden, and on a point of honour all proceedings were confidential. A copy of this code was pasted inside a book every sitter was obliged to sign (ladies on the left of the page, gentlemen on the right). Helen was satisfied with everything she saw and heard that day, and was only concerned by malevolent vibrations she sensed from a tall, smartly suited gentleman in his late forties who happened to be climbing the stairs ahead of her on his way to the fourth-floor flat he rented from the LSA as a laboratory. That man was Harry Price.

The first spiritual communication by which Dr Rust sought to establish the psychical credentials of his protégée was an act of clairvoyance. On Saturday, 25 October a meeting was arranged at Queensberry Place to which he brought a wax-sealed envelope labelled 'The X Document, June 1910', explaining that it was a message given to him by a deceased friend, William Martin, and only to be opened after his death. Rust handed the envelope to Helen who ran it over her forehead and up her spine, silently staring out through the sitters and beyond. In an atmosphere of reverence they watched as her pencil hovered over a page torn from an exercise book, before she began to write laboriously in her best curvilinear hand. When she had finished, the envelope was opened and the messages compared. Even allowing for a certain predictability of content – Martin had said he would try to contact Dr Rust after his death – Helen did rather well, especially in the unusual way Rust was addressed as 'physician and friend'. It is surprising that she failed even to *guess* the year of his death – she said 1915, when in fact it was 1910, less than a month after the valedictory note was made – but the company were nonetheless impressed with this appetizer for her first proper seance and made encouraging noises.

The following evening, shortly before six, President of the LSA Dr Robert Fielding-Ould welcomed Helen into the spacious seance room where a handful of sitters, who had already inspected her black satin housecoat, knickers and stockings, were seated patiently in a crescent facing the corner cabinet. Ready by the gramophone, Henry smiled encouragingly as his wife strode silently and regally towards the open curtains, oblivious to the staring eyes and hushed whispers. The medium was helped into a black sack loosely tied at the neck, and tapes wrapped around her body and secured to the chair. Dr Fielding-Ould tugged at the knots, then sealed them with wax. As in a submarine preparing to dive, the white light was switched to red, raising an eerie pinkish luminescence barely sufficient to count seconds from a watch and to allow notes to be taken. At five past, trussed up like Houdini, Helen's eyes closed and the curtain was drawn. After a few minutes, the sound of heavy breathing was heard over the scratchy, jolly strains of the music, and Henry asked everyone to be as quiet as possible and not to touch anything. They waited and waited. Twenty minutes later, Miss Phillimore noticed a pale strand creeping from the cabinet, upon which Dr Rust asked: 'Is that Albert? Can you show us more of that psychoplasm, Albert?' There was a pause of bristling anticipation. 'I will show you some, my lad,' came the sonorous reply, followed by the sight of an expanding human form, rallied into life by Rust's encouraging words. And there stood the spirit guide, not quite in the flesh, who proceeded to invite sitters to sample the other-worldly matter pouring from Helen's body. Dazzling phosphorous-white against the blank blackness of the room, a trail of ectoplasm suspended loosely in the air gradually formed itself into a crude cross, which Fielding-Ould was encouraged to feel, reporting that it was soft like fine merino cloth. Albert also asked Fielding-Ould to smell the ectoplasm and made no effort to conceal his irritation when the LSA President detected nothing owing to the fact that he was a smoker. Others who approached the cabinet reported a pungent odour of something indefinable, which Miss Phillimore had noticed before at materialization seances – like old cloth, Henry suggested – but Albert protested it was much nicer than that.

The remainder of the seance set a pattern, which would be repeated many times over the coming weeks with only minor variations. A child's face appeared, causing Albert to complain feebly: 'If only I could get rid of the girl!' and was followed by several other shapes struggling to achieve definition, including a figure 'like a little baby in long clothes'. Rustling and banging from within the cabinet suggested that the medium was also struggling until, without warning and still entranced, she wandered out free from the sack and slumped down on a chair in the circle. As she was being helped back to the cabinet like a sleepwalking child, sitters had a chance to make a preliminary check that the sack was undamaged. It was. Shortly afterwards Helen re-emerged from the cabinet and stood directly in front of the light, twelve or thirteen feet of luminous matter streaming from her mouth to the floor, and then paraded left and right in a stately fashion, exercising obvious care not to step on the ectoplasm despite her apparently semi-conscious condition.

The dominant, spiritual Albert used the subordinate, corporeal Helen to put down the man who stood between them. Speculation as to how her escape had been achieved prompted Henry to propose 'an elongation of the medium' as the cause, to which Albert replied testily: 'Nonsense, you fool. You are a perfect ass with your theories.' Henry, meek as ever in the presence of the control, tried to lighten the atmosphere by suggesting that Albert was sometimes as good as George Robey; but this only made things worse, for Albert made him explain who Robey was – Britain's most famous comedian – and then took offence. Albert's characteristic shifts in mood and manner between clipped formality, burlesque levity, waspish sarcasm and pious solemnity were sustained to the end of the seance, at which point he drew attention to the way the ectoplasm, like a skein of wool, was withdrawn, saying, 'I want to let you see it go right down into the mouth.' Unable to resist a quip, playful or caustic, he picked Dr Rust up when he said they were looking forward to the next *séance*. 'Oh help! That is surely French!' Albert cried with mock horror, but when this was confirmed added only: 'The Lord be with you.' The lights went up at 7.25 p.m. Helen, shaking off her sleepy head, hurried out of the room with less ceremony than she had arrived and on returning found the LSA researchers deep in concentration re-examining the pristine seals. She lit a cigarette and watched them.

On rare occasions Helen needed smelling salts to leave her

trance, but more often than not her disorientation or catatonia eased once she had absorbed some nicotine and water or tea. Sometimes, as she readjusted to the world, she would make unsettling cryptic pronouncements. 'I ken ye,' strangers were told, or, 'I dinna ken ye, but I ken of ye.' Once, affecting the air of a highland seer perched on a crag, she revealed: 'I have been in a strange house, one that I have never visited before. It is a house with an unmade bed and under the mattress there are some papers.' But such informality was kept to a minimum in the auspicious surroundings of the LSA, at least until she got into her stride. Albert was quicker to assert himself, which for Helen was just as well since the boldness and intrusiveness of her hosts increased dramatically after the first performance. At the second sitting, on 30 October, Dr Fielding-Ould examined Helen's mouth, nostrils, ears and hair, and once the seance had begun there were protests about the restraints: 'I wish there were someone here to take this blinking bag off,' grumbled Albert as he laboured to deconstruct the perspiring medium atomically in order to extrude her through the 27-inch aperture. His efforts were in vain and the bag had to be removed, although ectoplasm did appear and was formed into hands, which grasped at the sitters before dissolving. There was more bickering with Henry, although this ended when Helen began to splutter and choke, a fearful sound, which her husband smothered with a happy tune from the gramophone.

The sittings continued every Tuesday and Friday throughout November and December. There were some changes and surprises: a woollen dress costing £1 4s was exchanged for a larger size; a sack made from airy mesh was introduced; and the medium's dentures were gently plopped into Miss Phillimore's hand for no apparent reason. Just as bafflingly, Albert talked about getting the medium's brain under his domination one minute, the next he was offering to play the bagpipes at Miss Phillimore's wedding. Splashing was heard from the cabinet, where the floor was sometimes found to be sticky. And yet throughout, the ectoplasm flowed, shimmering, numinous and pastel-tinged, and the manifestations were impressive, not least Peggy who bounced a ball, sang 'Baa, baa, black sheep', then waved 'ta-ta'. Sitters treated the spirits with an almost fawning respect, but followed Albert in his contempt for Henry and his innocuous interjections. Once Albert threatened to 'twist his blinking neck' after he proposed playing another record, and at the next seance called him an 'old fathead' and accused him of wanting to bring down the moon when he suggested they adjust the lighting. Albert's facetious offer to have the medium controlled by nailing her into a coffin was politely declined.

A loss of weight was recorded after seances, while pulse and blood pressure rose, and urine tests revealed 'an amazing amount of albumen'. From this scientific angle December saw two other key developments: the procuring of an ectoplasm sample and the making of a photographic record. On the 5th, Fielding-Ould brought a bowl of water as Albert had instructed and placed it inside the cabinet. At this sitting the researchers were experimenting with a new type of illumination when a painted glass shutter accidently slipped and exposed Albert to the full glare of the white light. 'Though behind the curtain and not directly exposed to it, the medium emitted a fearful groan, following as closely on the flash as if she had been shot, and Albert described the effect on him as resembling a horrible blow from a red-hot poker.'

Despite this setback, a piece of ectoplasm did reach the bowl; another larger fragment found on the chair was described as 'two inches square and rather more than an eighth of an inch thick, of a creamy white leathery-looking matter which floats readily on the water'. Meanwhile it was noticed that Helen's jaw was inflamed and a circular patch of skin the size of a sixpence had been excoriated as if burned. J. A. Stevenson, a sculptor, sat in on two seances at which, under Albert's supervision, he exposed seventeen photographic plates for use in a magic lantern. All showed the opaque white forms, although the fine folds and kid-like sheen were not well reproduced. After the second seance, however, Stevenson obtained an even better souvenir. While he and others were conversing with Mrs Duncan over a cup of tea, she complained of something icy cold under the seance suit into which she had been sewn. Wielding scissors, Miss Phillimore picked open the stitches to reveal a strip of ectoplasm stuck to her chest, which Fielding-Ould removed with forceps, dropped into a bottle of distilled water and later divided into several pieces. One portion was given to a Mr Montagu Scott from Hampshire and another went to Stevenson who made a lantern slide from a detailed sketch, recording it in his notes as a 'piece of substance resembling tissue – in parts apparently fibrous and in parts resembling fatty nodules'.

Almost from the start, sceptical notes had been creeping into the observations. Early in November a fleshy arm was seen beneath the spirit form of a child swaying in time to the music. Later in the month Helen stepped to one side of the cabinet, leaving a lifeless phantom there attached to her face by an ectoplasmic umbilicus which, as she turned to the light, appeared to be tied in a knot beneath her nose. To Stevenson, one manifestation appeared solid with cylindrical legs as if wrapped in cloth like a mummy. The swinging of another form created such an unrealistic effect that Albert was forced to explain that the medium was nervous. During the seances, some said the ectoplasm resembled muslin; afterwards, that the samples looked like a dishrag. The circular burns Mrs Duncan occasionally exhibited, and which were attributed to the sudden withdrawal of ectoplasm whenever it was disturbed, only ever seemed to appear after she had finished her post-seance cigarette. By the end of the sittings the LSA decided that at least a measure of fraud was involved but could not agree how much, especially since some members had attended more seances than others. All of which, however paradoxical, meant that the LSA felt they were on to something and wanted Helen to return to London in the New Year. But by the time the Duncans reached Dundee in the week before Christmas, she was feeling profoundly unhappy about the LSA and was open to new offers. Even from Britain's most sceptical psychical researcher, Harry Price.

Harry Price and Helen Duncan had more in common than they ever realized, their lives a tangle of fantasies and conflicting facts, ambition getting the better of them the more others took them seriously. Scientist and showman, Barrett and Barnum in equal measure, Price was primarily a ghost hunter and journalist, and used his expertise in both fields well, filling newspaper columns and popularizing the term 'poltergeist' in English. He was reviled by Spiritualists and psychical researchers alike, even though much of the time he aimed only to publicize the truth by circumventing the polite conventions of the SPR and LSA. 'Good mediums do exist,' he said, 'but they are so few and far between that the casual inquirer is not likely to come across them.' The Schneider brothers impressed him in 1922 and a year later he met a self-effacing nurse, Dorothy Stella Cranshaw, whom he nurtured as the physical medium 'Stella C.' and with whom he formed a friendship which she thought it proper to terminate when she married in 1928. An obsessive bibliophile, Price spent the inter-war period trying to foist his huge library upon any institution that would give it a home. The SPR stored the books for a while, they were moved to the NLPR, the LSA refused them (four times) and finally they were accepted by the University of London, but not before, it was said, he had offered them to Hitler. Today, the collection is both priceless and steeped in Price down to the bogus heraldic bookplates and the dubious provenances. His immaculate first edition of Reginald Scot's *Discoverie of Witchcraft* (1584) was just possibly the actual copy Shakespeare used to research *Macbeth*.

Price had an unerring eye for opportunity. Baron von Schrenck-Notzing died in February 1929 and within weeks Price had snapped up Rudi Schneider for a series of sessions from which a best-selling book emerged the following year. In October 1930 Price booked a clairvoyant of Irish birth, Eileen Garrett, who had brought messages from Captain Walter Hinchcliffe shortly after his aeroplane disappeared over the Atlantic in 1928. These were impressive less for what his widow learned – 'Tell them there is no death but everlasting life' – than for their remarkable technical detail. Two years later Price invited a journalist to hear the spirit of Flight-Lieutenant H. C. Irwin, pilot of the R-101 airship which two days earlier had crashed, killing forty-eight passengers and crew, including the Secretary of State for Air, Lord Thomson. Again, the analysis was highly specialized and astonished Major Oliver Villiers, a senior intelligence officer at the Ministry of Aviation who then arranged seven sittings of his own. Seeking further proof, Villiers also attended Mrs Duncan's materialization seance on 9 December, as the LSA register reveals.

Price had done well. Apart from the publicity he attracted through the journalist's magazine, he sold the story to the *Morning Post* (as an 'exclusive') and received ninety guineas for the American rights. Buoyant, especially because SPR members were defecting to his National Laboratory, he moved to more spacious premises in Roland Gardens, ten minutes' walk from the LSA, and invested in new equipment. All he lacked was a medium to make his own. Mrs Duncan he coveted, having first heard about her from James Souter's notice in *Light*. During her stay in London, although the LSA refused him admission to their sittings, Price did manage to meet the Duncans in private, and found them pleasant and intelligent. Early in 1931 the sculptor Stevenson gave him not only his pictures of Helen's seance but the ectoplasm sample, made into microscope slides. Price courted Henry Duncan who told him they had accepted the LSA's offer, but might put themselves at his disposal in the future. Meanwhile Price's suspicions about the ectoplasm were confirmed by chemical and microscopic analysis. In Eva C.'s sample, Schrenck-Notzing had found 'numerous skin discs; some sputum-like bodies; numerous granulates of the mucous membrane; numerous minute particles of flesh; traces of sulphozyansaurem potash'. Mrs Duncan's was similar but also contained coagulated egg-white. For the moment Price kept this to himself, but the knowledge was spreading from other directions. The following month Mr Montagu Scott contacted the LSA to say that the Charing Cross Medical School had found his sample to be little more than paper and cloth bound together with albumen.

Helen spent February 1931 regaining her strength after a bout of bronchitis and mustering the courage to return to London. Henry was keener to get back, bewitched by the offer of £9 per week – three times what an average family lived on. Surrendering to his wishes, Helen placed an advertisement with the Dundee Labour Exchange for a maid to join her on a long engagement and hired a feckless young woman named Mary McGinlay. In the second week of March the Duncan household decamped to 8 Beulah Crescent, Thornton Heath, Surrey, a comfortable house

126

arranged for them by the LSA at an annual rent of £85. On 9 March Helen and Henry agreed a six-month contract with an option for the London Psychical Laboratory, the newly formed research branch of the LSA, to re-engage them for a further year; Helen signed 'Victoria Duncan', fluffing the first letters as if nervous or unused to styling herself thus. Excitement among the research community was intense, unaffected by the analysis of the ectoplasm, details of which the LSA chose not to publicize. The ink was scarcely dry on the contract before the SPR was making overtures to Helen in a letter she dutifully showed to her new employers; the LSA Secretary, Miss Phillimore, in turn invited an SPR observer, promising of Mrs Duncan: 'I could vouch for her honesty as I could for my own' – which, given what she now knew about the composition of the ectoplasm, was not really saying very much.

The twice-weekly seances resumed on 13 March bringing more ectoplasm, at first the size of a cherry on Helen's tongue, then masses of drapery and a figure substantial enough to shake hands. On the following Tuesday at a sitting attended by, among others, a general practitioner from Bournemouth, a military staff officer, a theatrical producer and a continental baron, Peggy appeared, sang 'Baa, baa, black sheep', expressed a preference for water over lemonade (because of the gas), then handed over to the medium who stole the show by escaping from her seance suit and appearing quite naked except for a 'bridal veil' of ectoplasm. Dr Margaret Vivian, the GP, was deeply impressed, an opinion she communicated to her friend Maurice Barbanell and other figures influential in the Spiritualist press. New controls were adopted – stitching up the seance suit using a secret pattern, padlocking the suit shut, enclosing the medium's hands in buckram mittens and so on – but still the phenomena amazed guests between March and May, the names of whom today read like the society pages of the *Tatler*: Madame Destrees, Major and Mrs J. S. Swayne, Lady Harris and daughter, Lady Culme Seymour, the Hon. Mrs Wild, Susan Countess of Malmesbury, the Countess Ahlefeldt Lauring, Mr and Mrs Staveley Bulford, Major Stewart, the Countess de Lavradio, Lady Doreen Knatchbull, Dr E. S. Reid, the Hon. Mrs Cooper and Mrs Dickin OBE to name but a few. On 20 March, at an LSA research sitting to which Baron von Pohl was invited, Albert was asked to leave his mark on an ebony hand mirror. Helen's fingerprints were taken and compared with a magnified photograph of the mirror by an ex-police chief inspector, but without significant outcome.

The LSA was not the Duncans' sole source of income. Henry was still drawing his army pension and on her days off Helen held seances at home in Thornton Heath. They could now afford to live as a lower-middle-class family, eating well, travelling by taxi and keeping a maid. But inevitably young Mary McGinlay had begun to notice strange things. Mary's Irish grandmother (whom she occasionally mentioned to her mistress) materialized at a seance, although her grandfather – who, unknown to Helen, was a Scot – seemed to have acquired his wife's accent in the spirit world. Further suspicion was aroused by a spirit baby, allegedly one of Helen's own, which bore a striking resemblance to a doll Mary sometimes helped the Duncan girls to dress. Mary wondered why the children were employed to cut faces from periodicals such as *True Story Magazine*, and why she was sent to buy butter muslin and instructed not to tell Henry. Rubber gloves, for which they had no need, she found in a cupboard and again was told not to say anything; on another occasion she saw Bella burying a pair in the garden. In a drawer, Mary also came across the luminous star worn by a little spirit girl whenever she returned to see her mother.

Elsewhere, Helen's work was receiving even closer scrutiny. In the spring of 1931 the LSA published two broadly favourable reports on the Duncans, concluding that 'physical forces by some supernormal agency have been observed'. The weight of negative evidence, however, was by this stage overwhelming. A strip of ectoplasm was discovered to be surgical gauze soaked in Canada balsam or pine resin, and later in the month proved a match for a sanitary towel Mrs Duncan left in her dressing room. Ectoplasm was 'extruded by obvious movements of the mouth and throat muscles'. In Harry Price's opinion the only place a medium could not be searched without anaesthetic was the stomach, and when the LSA made Helen swallow a staining tablet of methylene blue no ectoplasm appeared. Their dilemma was that what was good for science was not good for business. The seances for members and guests, paying 21s or 25s respectively, over the full term of the contract could have been worth as much as £500, twice what the Duncans were being paid in the same period. Business triumphed.

Even though these doubts were not shared with the Duncans, they still sensed that all was not well and, like the alert, troublesome Golighers and the sensitive and peculiar Crandons, 'watched the researchers with the eyes of super-researchers', as Mercy Phillimore recalled. When the code-stitching of the seance suit was found to have been tampered with no one said anything, yet the trick was not repeated. Henry tried to rekindle the LSA's interest with Helen's clairvoyant profiling of a man wanted for murder; but even if this had not been so feeble – the culprit, she said, was sturdily built, married and wore boots – reconciliation was a forlorn hope. Only commercial gain, and perhaps fear of public ridicule, kept the Executive Committee of the London Psychical Laboratory from tearing up their contract. In the meantime, antennae twitching, Harry Price wrote to Miss Phillimore asking to borrow Mrs Duncan, knowing this would be denied and, without waiting for a response – indeed, the same day – offered Henry £100 as a retainer, £10 for a weekly seance and £100 at the end. This proved irresistible. After a meeting where the Duncans sampled the environment of Price's laboratory at 13d Roland Gardens (which they found congenial), Price sent out invitations to the first secret seance, in which, like a Victorian impresario, he billed his monster as 'the most brilliant materialising medium ever seen in this country'. Price's colleague Mollie Goldney, at that time training at the fashionable Queen Charlotte's Midwifery Hospital, was to conduct the physical examination, recalling the days when midwives led juries of matrons to strip suspected witches to search for the devil's mark.

The seance room which unkind souls had likened to a hunting lodge decked out in trophies of exposed mediums, Price preferred to think of as 'nothing so much as a gentleman's library, comfortably furnished with a home-like atmosphere'. Others said it resembled an operating theatre crossed with a torture chamber, although this description better fits the adjoining workshop with its tool racks, bell jars, microscopes and box cameras on high tripods. Certainly, Houdini's portrait on the mantelpiece was a warning to phonies. Arriving for the first seance at 7.30 p.m. on Monday, 4 May, Helen seemed nervous as she was introduced to the sitters, including Professor McDougall from Harvard who had examined Margery. After she had been searched and helped into her suit, the performance began – the standard offering with Albert hosting, the medium snoring and ectoplasm forming first a veil, then an apron, its odour a curious mustiness tinged with latex. Another four sessions were spread over as many weeks, at two of which the rectum and vagina were examined, revealing nothing untoward. Suspicion lay elsewhere. A piece of ectoplasm fell down, leaving a safety pin attached to the cabinet curtain. Another pin was visible in one of Price's flash photographs, as was a face cut from a magazine and a dangling hand, which seemed very like a glove attached to a length of muslin. 'I must say that I was deeply impressed,' Price declared. 'I was impressed with the brazen affrontery that prompted the Duncans to come to my Laboratory . . . I was impressed with the amazing credulity of the Spiritualists who had sat with the Duncans for six solid months.'

The day after the first session, 5 May, Helen returned to the LSA and was perturbed to see in the front row Mollie Goldney again who had been invited as an SPR observer. The seance began. Also present was Dr Nandor Fodor, a Hungarian barrister-turned-journalist on Lord Rothermere's staff whose surprise at being struck by a stump-like thing was eclipsed by Albert ceremoniously handing him the medium's shoes. But the dramatic climax came when the train of ectoplasm became caught, or, more likely, was trodden on by Mrs Goldney, and had to be yanked free. Helen began screaming, always a chilling effect in the still darkness. Afterwards, Mollie hurried into the cabinet and, although relieved to find Mrs Duncan fully clothed, was alarmed by blood on her face at which the good midwife dabbed with a handkerchief. Meanwhile the story about Helen's naked escape from the LSA's seance sack had spread. The same evening it was discussed in a debate at the Cambridge University Union Society, one speaker spoofing Wordsworth to describe how Mrs Duncan came forth:

> Not in entire forgetfulness,
> And not in utter nakedness,
> But trailing clouds of teleplasm . . .*

---

* The motion for debate – 'That this House has no faith in the Black Magic of Spiritualism and the Occult Sciences' – was carried, but by a margin of only eight votes (twenty-six to eighteen).

The glory and the dream were fading, and Helen spent the night vomiting – a reaction which, the maid Mary noticed, had become a regular occurrence. The next day Henry telephoned Harry Price to tell him about two small burns near her navel and a letter she had written for the coroner were she to commit suicide. Some days later Price met the Duncans and managed to calm Helen, although that evening at Queensberry Place, Albert disclosed, she was 'all shaking and trembling'. At the second NLPR sitting on 14 May, Price and a Harley Street doctor, William Brown, examined the livid and scaling burns and, as a precaution against shock from the flash of Price's camera, Mollie Goldney provided one of her black silk stockings to use as a blindfold. The performance was a disappointment. Albert bowed out early, Peggy could not be lured from paradise with chocolates, and Helen hurried on to tea and biscuits, smoking prodigiously throughout. For the next fortnight she complained of stage fright, bronchitis and money problems, at least once telephoning Price, who sent a cheque for £5. He for one was determined to press on and, having recorded Albert's voice, prepared to use X-rays – to detect a safety pin at least. His claim that she volunteered to undergo this, and to have her stomach pumped, seems improbable, given her anxious state. Five-year-old Gena noticed how anguished her mother seemed and one day overheard her say that a man called Harry Price would be the death of her.

At the fourth National Laboratory of Psychical Research sitting on 28 May, David Fraser-Harris, a retired Canadian physiology professor, was not impressed by the 'vague trivialities' Albert uttered in his affected drawl, nor by the obvious muslin hanging from the medium's nostrils. At the first flash of the camera Albert announced that all was not well and the curtains opened to reveal Helen's nose trickling blood, a sample of which Dr Brown took with his handkerchief. Confronted by chaos, Price had to act swiftly if he was to get his X-ray picture. With theatrical sympathy, he led his wobbling prize to the chesterfield where she sat sweating, reluctant to lie down as he suggested, and even refusing a cup of tea. Professor Fraser-Harris described what happened next: 'Several times she tried to rise and leave the room, which was not easy as the bulky X-ray apparatus barred the exit. Her agitation increased with every request that she should lie down for the X-ray photograph, until at last she sprang to her feet, struck her husband a violent blow on the face, and fled from the room.'

In a state of intense agitation she said she needed to use the lavatory, but on being followed changed her mind and simply plonked herself down in the entrance hall like a sulking child. As a glass of water was being fetched, she jumped up again, unfastened the front door and hurled herself into the street. According to Price, who was getting some brandy, the clock was just striking midnight. Outside, Helen collapsed and clung to the railings like a suffragette, screaming hysterically and tearing at her seance suit. Henry, first on the scene, tried in vain to calm her. A policeman arrived and was disconcerted by the sight of several men in dinner jackets gathered around a seventeen-stone woman clad in black satin combinations wailing on the pavement, but once she had stopped swearing at everyone Price was able to get rid of him. He then turned back to the Duncans, suspecting that something had been passed to Henry – a suspicion reinforced by the medium's sudden insistence that she be X-rayed after all. When Price asked Henry if he could search him he refused, giving the excuse that he was wearing dirty underwear; he also hinted that he had been carrying sanitary towels but, as Mollie Goldney pointed out, his wife was not having a period. In the cold light of day Professor Fraser-Harris arrived at three firm conclusions: Albert's voice was that of the medium 'altered by long practice so as to be unrecognizable'; some kind of material was concealed in her body, hence her reluctance to be X-rayed; and the bleeding was meant to influence them, but might have been the natural outcome of pushing material up her nose.

Contrary to what is sometimes said, the Duncans did return to the NLPR, despite Helen's growing fear of Mollie Goldney whom she accused of having set her up by planting a safety pin discovered in the tuck of her seance suit. Fear was compounded by infirmity: at the NLPR Helen complained of a badly swollen arm due to an abscess; at the SPR she arrived wearing a sling – now with a suspected *broken* arm. Perhaps as a consequence the phenomena were poor, although a woman who claimed to have seen Madame Blavatsky in the medium's transfigured features saved the day. Albert did not deny that the great theosophist was present.

At the next sitting Henry went to the cinema, as he had agreed he would, allowing enough time for a pair of doctors Price had drafted in secretly from a London hospital (he said St Thomas's*) to explore thoroughly the dark continent of Mrs Duncan's body: 'They brought a bag of tools with them, took off their coats to the job and really got down to it. But they found nothing. Every orifice and crack where an instrument or a hand would go was thoroughly explored; every nook and cranny was examined; but at each fresh place they drew a blank.' 'This all sounds very terrible,' Price remarked, 'but it is modern psychical research: a technique forced on us by the amazing tricks of the mediums.' The doctors could tell she was not in the best of shape: her eardrums had old perforations (probably from the mills) and

---

* Although the doctors were almost certainly men, to soften the impression given by the episode, in November of that year Price informed the SNU President, J. B. McIndoe, that they had been women.

there were signs of middle-ear disease, including a purulent discharge. The turbinate bones of her nose were also infected and seeping pus. Her uterus was described as 'small and ante-verted', her cervix 'small and scarred' and her rectum was empty 'except for some soft foecal matter'. It had been agreed that an ectoplasm sample would be taken and, to be sure of getting it, Price issued each sitter with a pair of surgical scissors, which glinted in the half-light. But Albert was shy and sluggish. 'The helplessness of thwarted purpose seemed to have settled like an incubus on that gentle spirit,' sniped Price, 'for although not exactly inarticulate he uttered only indistinct and uninforming platitudes.' Helen produced just a few inches of ectoplasm; but within a second of Albert giving his permission, one of the doctors pounced. Helen shrieked, jerked back her head and the ecto-plasm tore off like a slimy pancake; the remainder – of what turned out to be a flattened tube of paper folded zigzag – she swallowed. As Helen emerged from her trance her eyes rolled and arms flailed, until the doctors spoke loudly at her and panic subsided into a daze. Blood smeared around her face, they discov-ered, came from a small prick on the nasal septum and it was noted that an abscess on her arm was suppurating. 'I am in an awful mess,' she whimpered.

Price concluded that Mrs Duncan produced artificial matter 'by regurgitation, or reversed oesophageal peristalsis, with the help of the diaphragm and the muscles of the anterior abdom-inal wall'. He had the chemical analysis; he was ready. On Thursday, 11 June, seeking an explanation for the similarities between his wife's ectoplasm and cheesecloth, the NLPR Council interrogated Henry, pointing at the warp-and-weft in enlarged photographs and speculating about inflated surgical gloves. Henry was philosophical. Citing the famous examples of Margery, Eva C. and Rudi Schneider, he reaffirmed his belief that his wife's productions were supernormal, but admitted that he did sometimes suspect her of concealing things, albeit unconsciously. 'I have taken her into the bathroom and made her take all her clothes off,' he said, 'and I have on two occasions given her a vaginal examination.' He had also made Mary McGinlay search her clothes before a seance. Amazingly, Henry left the meeting with another seance booked for 2 July. The next day, after a disastrous seance at Queensberry Place – she tried to pass off her protruding tongue as ectoplasm – Henry met the LSA Committee and declared that his wife's materializations were the result of regurgitation. Although the contract was declared void, the seances for paying guests went on and the LSA continued to distribute handbills advertising Mrs Duncan's 'Experiments in Physical Phenomena'.

Helen was in no state to give any kind of seance. She fell into a violent despair when she learned what had happened, besides which her arm had become septic and she had to be admitted to St Thomas's Hospital, where they drained the abscess and detained her for observation. But as her body healed, her mind festered and on a reckless impulse she swallowed half a bottle of Eusol, an antiseptic solution of chlorinated lime and boric acid, and so ended up having her stomach pumped after all. The doctor, who believed it to be 'an hysterical histrionic performance' rather than a genuine attempt at suicide, nonetheless strongly recommended that she should terminate her seance-giving forthwith. The LSA, who were looking forward to the final curtain anyway, were informed of this in a letter from Henry received on 15 June in which he said Helen had *twice* attempted suicide. Dr Fielding-Ould immediately recognized hospitalization as an opportunity for Helen's urine to be analysed by a chemical pathologist, but nothing unusual came to light. In the meantime, feigning concern, Fielding-Ould organized a contingent from the LSA to visit Helen as she recuperated in bed, a gesture for which she thanked them by screaming obscenities until they left.

On Friday, 19 June, a convalescent Helen met Miss Phillimore at Queensberry Place to sign an agreement whereby the LSA undertook to pay the £7 1s 6d owed to her (after deductions of rent, rates and tax) and, on condition they were gone within a week, to foot the £40 bill for the repatriation of her family and furniture to Scotland. Meanwhile, for purposes of comparison with Mrs Duncan's ectoplasm, Price was busy taking photographs of his secretary Ethel posing with a length of Woolworths cheesecloth, one of which shows her with all 6 foot by 30 inches of it concealed in her mouth. So engrossed was he that he only discovered by chance on the Monday that Helen and Henry were going home without granting him the sitting booked for 2 July. That evening, Mollie Goldney tracked the Duncans down at a seance in Eaton Terrace, SW1, where Henry explained that they were leaving because Helen needed a holiday. Mrs Goldney, who was used to getting her own way, took him straight back to Roland Gardens where Price attempted to cut a new deal, offering Henry £100 for the opportunity to film Helen regurgitating cloth. So desperate was Henry to get out of London that he was forced to decline, but before he left, Price showed him the two sets of photographs: Helen in full flow and the mock-ups with Ethel. It perhaps indicates Henry's anxious and befuddled state of mind that he needed Price to point out that Ethel was half Helen's size before he was able to tell the pictures apart.

On 23 June the Duncan family boarded an overnight steamer and breathed the fresh air not only of the sea, but of liberty from the disgust and disgruntlement of the London research societies. The next day little Gena was nauseous from the pitching of the boat but mostly from overexcitement, her constitution not helped by the sight of her jubilant father downing a hearty breakfast of kippers as they sighted Leith in the distance. Over her tea and early-morning cigarette, Helen too contemplated with some satis-faction their homecoming and what had been achieved in the past three months. After all, the trip had not been a complete failure: they had been paid. Including expenses, the Duncans had cost the London societies over £500 within the space of a few months, enough to buy a suburban semi-detached house in the Home Counties. Helen left behind some semi-digested blotting paper and a few of her photographs, including the portrait of herself she had packed the previous autumn and on the back of which she had written 'Return to Mrs Duncan, Ferry Road, Dundee' before lending it to Price. But Price never did return it and even used it without permission for the frontispiece of his next book.

Having seen off the Duncans, Price prepared to trounce the LSA – 'the people down below,' as he used to call them at Queensberry Place – repayment for all their slurs and slights against him. Early in July 1931 he finished a draft of *The Duncan Mediumship: a Study in Regurgitation*, although on legal advice he made cuts and retitled it *Regurgitation and the Duncan Mediumship*. With insufficient time to publish before the LSA's own report appeared, Price gave an interview to the same *Morning Post* reporter who had covered the R-101 story and lent him an advance copy. At no point did Price mention the LSA, but hints about a well-known Spiritualist society did the trick. On 14 July the news broke with the headline: SPIRITUALISTS HOAXED. TELEPLASMS FROM CHEESE CLOTH 'MEDIUM' EXPOSED,

REMARKABLE FACULTY OF REGURGITATION, regaling readers with stories of wood-pulp ectoplasm and pronouncing the episode 'one of the cleverest frauds in the whole history of Spiritualism'. The story also appeared in the *Liverpool Post* and on Sunday in the Manchester *Empire News*. Just three days before the publication of *Light*, therefore, the LSA were humiliated – 'spitting blood' according to Mollie Goldney. A furious volley of letters was fired off from Queensberry Place towards Roland Gardens, Dr Fielding-Ould refusing to believe that Price had not written the article himself.

The 'adverse' report printed in *Light* on 17 July 1931 stated that 'on nearly all points the conclusions are disappointing to those interested in psychical research'. All the suppressed doubts now came flooding out. Mollie Goldney read it with indecent haste and wrote to her SPR colleague Eve Brackenbury straight away: 'They were a long time coming to this!!' To the SPR Executive Committee the most astonishing thing about the whole affair was the way the LSA had changed their minds about Mrs Duncan as a credible character. The LSA, in turn, decided that blame lay with Henry: he exerted a malign influence, they said; 'the lure of gold' was mentioned. Over the summer the Duncans put their side of the story to Ernest Oaten, editor of *Two Worlds*, who wrote a leader which occasioned some spiky debate between himself and Dr Fielding-Ould regarding the relevance of Jungian analysis to the Duncan case.

Reactions to Price's book were mixed. The SPR carped that the psychical research content was nil, Count Berovsky-Petrovo-Slovovo doubting that regurgitation had been proved. Price, of course, defended his work as a contribution to medical science; but to him profit and publicity were paramount, and to that end the book had a soft cover (so cost only 5s), but plenty of pictures including a set of stereograms – pairs of identical photographic images for which readers were advised to buy a cheap American 3-D viewer. Although *Regurgitation and the Duncan Mediumship* went on sale in the USA, and despite McDougall's opinion that Mrs Duncan was a fraud, the American SPR was even more divided than its English cousin and refused to publish Price's findings on the grounds that 'the principal facts are in controversy'. In Italy, the editor of *Luce e Ombra* was scathing, pointing out that ectoplasm *always* looked like cloth! The Spiritualists were more indignant still. J. Arthur Findlay, Vice-President of the Glasgow SPR, sent testimonies to Price who returned them with the stinging reply: 'When these people produce as good evidence for the abnormality of Mrs Duncan's alleged phenomena, as we have produced for the fraudulent side of her mediumship, I will listen to them. I have not seen or heard a shred of real evidence which would persuade me that Mrs Duncan had any psychic power whatsoever.'

Meanwhile, Helen had resumed her seances in Scotland. The Glasgow SNU was exercising great caution, J.B. McIndoe assured Price, but so far had detected no sound, smell or sight of regurgitation; in any case, the doctors who X-rayed her at Dundee had laughed at the idea. Ernest Oaten denied that what Price had seen and what others saw were the same thing at all, to which Price, ever more exasperated, replied: 'If you had felt, smelt, and photographed the stuff as I did, you would have not the slightest doubt that it was cheesecloth, swallowed and regurgitated: I would stake my life on this fact.' But he was wasting his time, for Helen was higher than ever in the estimation of her supporters. Montague Rust continued to rave about phenomena. At one seance, he said, the cabinet opened to reveal 'Mrs D. standing, one foot on the chair, and masses of white material streaming from nose, mouth, ears, breasts and from the region of the vagina'. In November 1931 he told Mollie Goldney that they had known all along that London would be a fiasco and that the sceptics there would never get good results from such 'a *very* sensitive human creature'. Sarcastically, he referred to all her miracles as regurgitations:

> In fact she regurgitated my brother-in-law, Charles Ross, and my driver, Andrew Barclay, and my dog Hector. We had long conversations with them in their own character-istic voice and varying memories, Hector being lifelike in all his actions and ran about the floor as he did in life. Forms came out and sat on some of the sitters' knees and spoke and ate apples and drank water, and also others who removed my boots forcibly and put them on and walked about with them.

Dr Rust had also seen Helen dematerialize, levitate, suck back a spirit in a split second and produce a football-sized lump of ecto-plasm, which crashed to the floor.

With all this support behind them, the Duncans hit back at an article in the *Empire News*, which carried the headline HYSTERICS OF CLEVER WOMAN MEDIUM and a touched-up picture of the medium, a knot of ectoplasm partly obscuring her face. A few days later the editor rang Price about a letter received from a firm of solicitors stating that their client 'has never been photographed in the position indicated and she is satisfied that the photo is really one of a person whom she knows as Ethel who is a typist with Mr Harry Price'. To cap it all, an expert certified that the picture was a fake. 'The Duncans fly from one folly to another,' Price complained to Oaten. 'What *are* you to make of such people?' But the SNU showed what it made of them by granting its prized diploma, allowing Helen to express gratitude to the LSA who 'definitely put me on the map as a medium'. The work flooded in. Price realized that his report had acted as an advertisement so that, as he recalled, 'Spiritualists on both sides of the Tweed began falling over themselves in order to obtain sittings with her.' In December she accepted Dr Margaret Vivian's invitation to Bournemouth Spiritualist church where sitters were delighted with an apported cucumber, the realistically rotten smell of the ecto-plasm, and the headaches and exhaustion they suffered as creative juices were sucked from their bodies. The resident minister, Rev. Frank Blake, declared Helen 'the most valuable medium for physical phenomena in the British Isles'. In the same month a correspondent to *Two Worlds* described how Albert had been asking sitters to consider Harry Price's inter-pretation and had suggested that if it were true, then Mrs Duncan must have the swallowing powers of a crocodile. Out of trance, Helen conducted herself at seances with an air of abused innocence, lifted by the heady martyrdom upon which in the future she would be borne aloft.

The Duncans moved back to Edinburgh where at first they found only a one-room tenement flat, Henry and Helen sleeping in a bed recess in the kitchen, but soon swapped this for a three-bedroomed house with a bathroom. However, with the excep-tion of sixteen-year-old Bella (and the maid Mary McGinlay) the family were rarely at home. To allow her to travel, Helen sent her children to a corporation-run home forty miles away at Kelso where, traumatized by the regime, Gena wet herself frequently and prayed hard to God and Albert, especially for her sickly sister Nan. But Helen had taught them the principles of the Fatherhood of God and Brotherhood of Man, and they understood that she had to spread the message further. In the spring of 1932 the President of the Southend Society of Spiritualists shuffled off his mortal coil, only to spring back at a house in Leigh-on-Sea thanks to Helen, who on this occasion also found time to reunite a man with his singing grandmother, to manifest a woman seeking praise for her ectoplasmic dress, and for Peggy to draw kisses with pad and pencil. After this, the Duncans were in London, where Will Goldston, founder of the Magicians' Club and the author of forty books on legerdemain, attended a seance where Helen consumed a double helping of coffee and teacakes before materializing eight spirits. At Easter they were in Bristol (Gena remembers them bringing chocolate eggs on their way back) whereafter they returned to London. At the invitation of Spiritualist hack Maurice Barbanell, Goldston attended another seance where he attempted in vain to incapacitate Mrs Duncan with sash cord and hand-cuffs, and wrote up the experience for Barbanell's newly founded *Psychic News*. As he had said of Rudi Schneider in 1929, Goldston swore to having seen things no trickery could achieve. It was also impressive when things went wrong. After a seance where a woman screamed, Helen said she felt as if she had been bashed over the head, a physical reaction which seemed to be corrobo-rated by the thin trickle of blood issuing from her nose as she spoke.

Adulation aside, Helen would never now be left alone by her enemies. One day early in 1932 a man, probably a journalist, stopped Bella and Mary in the street and for £10 – probably as much as the maid was paid in a month – was told that they kept masks and a dummy in the bathroom. At home the girls admitted this, causing Henry to remark that the price of Judas had risen, and adding to Gena's distrust of Mary who shortly afterwards was dismissed and went home to Dundee. Helen's belief that Harry Price was behind this incident may have contained some truth. In February 1932 Price received a letter from Mary McGinlay who had read a newspaper article of his and thought he might like to hear her stories of 'the Great Materialized [*sic*] Medium, Mrs Duncan'. She claimed that she had been made ill through overwork. Sensing his eagerness to meet her, Mary prevailed upon him to send a cheque to buy clothes and a railway ticket, and on the morning of the 15th caught a morning train at Dundee station, which ten and a half hours later pulled in to Euston. From there, she was escorted in a taxi to the Harrington Hall Hotel in South Kensington where she felt she was becoming someone at last.

The next day she described to the NLPR Council the things she had seen and heard: the rubber gloves, the doll, the luminous star, the vomiting and, of course, the ectoplasm: 'Mrs Duncan used to get me to wash out a length of this muslin. The muslin had a rotten smell. It put me in mind of the smell of urine . . . occasionally it would be stained a little as if it had been washed beforehand. At other times she would give it to me just as she had used it, and then it would be much stained and slimy.' Not only were the rips shown in Price's photographs the same as she remembered in Mrs Duncan's muslin, but she had been made to separate eggs, the whites of which her mistress said were a treatment for her abscess. Before every seance, Mary said, Mrs Duncan had a snack – usually a couple of biscuits and a cup of tea – then took a bath, and then disappeared into the potting shed for five minutes or so. Why she did not know. There was more. On the night of 28 May 1931, after the hysterics at Roland Gardens, the Duncans had arrived home and had proceeded to row until Henry stormed out and Mary was sent after him. He told her the game was up and gave her the cloth passed to him in the street. Her statement was incorporated in the form of a statutory declaration, read before a Commissioner for Oaths, published by the NLPR as a supplement to its report and found its way into the *Daily Mail*, which had covered the story the previous October. Two days after Mary left London Price refused her request for money so that she could get married, a brush-off which J. B. McIndoe believed explained why when he interviewed her she said she had no reason to think Mrs Duncan fraudulent. He sent a letter to the *Daily Mail* to announce the turbulent maid's change of heart, but they declined to print it.

In December 1932, like cat and mouse, Harry Price travelled to Edinburgh, Helen to London. At a Spiritualist society in Wigmore Street, sitters felt Helen's hands, then Albert's – the former calloused, the latter soft – and an old man was invited to compare his materialized mother's gums with the medium's teeth – although presumably not too closely because, as Miss Phillimore could have testified, they were not her own. On his visit to Auld Reekie, Price bought a ticket at the Theatre Royal, where the variety bill included Marie Lauton and her Harp; the Harum-Scarum girls and their 'Merry Madcaps'; and Michel & Nan: the Dancing Xylophonist and his Stepping Sister. Price, however, was interested in only one act, Kanichka the Human Ostrich, to whom a female contact in Edinburgh, identified only as 'E. M.', had alerted him. In her opinion Kanichka's proficiency as a regurgitator indicated that Helen Duncan was nothing of the kind. True, she vomited pieces of paper – which explained why many of her materializations were coughing old women – but the swathes of cheesecloth seen by Price had to originate elsewhere. After seeing Kanichka for himself, Price accepted the point and may even have reconsidered the public denial Helen had made so many times: 'I did not swallow the cheesecloth, they give me credit for far more than I can do.' What is certain is that he took an active interest in E.M.'s allusion to a forthcoming 'Government Enquiry' into fraudulent mediumship, for now he understood that impostors could not be defeated by rhetoric or experiments alone. Only the law had teeth and in the future that was where Price would watch for opportunities, assuming the law did not come to him first. Although Helen had been brought into the limelight, it seemed dark days lay ahead for her.

5
CHANGING FORTUNES
A Brush with the Law and the Coming of War

During an American lecture tour in 1922, Sir Arthur Conan Doyle attended one of Mr and Mrs Tomson's materialization seances in New York City. As the spirits drifted through, Conan Doyle – always more Watson than Holmes – gradually became suspicious, especially when his own mother appeared. In one of his thrillers, Holmes's advice to Watson, bereaved by the death of his wife, is that work is the best antidote to sorrow; but this was not a view shared entirely by the author who spent the last decade of his life preaching the comforts of spiritual

'Madame Victoria Duncan studying the crystal', 1933.

communication. Yet however passionate his beliefs, Conan Doyle did accept that fraud was rife. And the Tomsons did have a dubious reputation: Houdini and Sir Oliver Lodge had corresponded about them; and now the New York Police Department was taking an interest. Three nights later the Tomsons manifested 'Aunt Emma' for a Mrs Martin, whereupon she and her 'husband' – both undercover police officers – leapt to their feet, a whistle was blown and an NYPD squad came crashing in. Willie and Eva Tomson were fined $100 under the Fortune Telling Act, legislation based on that in force in Britain. 'All of us are eager to know, of course, what becomes of our loved ones after death,' observed Harry Price, retelling the story for a newspaper some years later. 'So deep-rooted and sacred are these longings to open communication with our departed that it is difficult to conceive anything more cruel and heartless than deception in such a matter.'

At the Tomsons' trial, a witness to their deceptions expressed the cautiousness shared by an increasing number of believers: 'If a spirit fades out of your grasp it is indeed a spirit. But if it screams and rolls over on the floor – it is just another fraud.' If only things had been that simple. The truth was that even cases of manifest imposture could be covered up by a dazed and emotional medium, falling this way and that, creating a smokescreen of chaos and protesting ignorance or diminished responsibility. Spooks stitched from bedsheets, furthermore, could be spirited away almost as quickly as the real thing. Most fraudulent mediumship, moreover, was not physical but mental and therefore almost impossible to prove – unless, of course, it were presupposed that the act of mediumship, irrespective of intent, style, circumstance or outcome, was *de facto* illegal.

This problem was an old one. In eighteenth-century England property was deified, and fleecing the credulous became another area in which the State sought to restrain the individual. By 1800 the authorities were committed to suppressing gypsies. The 1735 Witchcraft Act, which legislated for the prosecution of fortune tellers, was not commonly used because it required there to be a jury trial; more often offenders were tried as vagrants, summarily by magistrates – a policy given added definition by a new Vagrancy Act in 1824, Section 4 of which specifically outlawed fortune telling and palmistry as acts of deception. Arrests under the 1824 Act increased in the 1850s when county police forces were established, plain-clothes officers using marked coins to prove that money had changed hands. And by this time, because fortune tellers could be prosecuted not just for who they were (itinerants) but solely for what they did, it meant that the Act could be applied more generally to Spiritualist mediums sitting in their parlours.

The first high-profile trial was that of D. D. Home. He had been cut into the will of a wealthy but deluded widow who adopted him in his mid-thirties, but during a spell of lucidity, brought on by disappointment that her 'golden-haired boy' refused to have sex with her, she saw through communications from her husband and Home's promise that her artificial hand could be brought to life. In 1868 the great floating medium was made to return the deed of gift by a judge who condemned his 'mischievous nonsense'. In 1876 Henry Slade, an American medium whose speciality was automatic writing on sealed slates, was exposed by eminent zoologist Edwin Ray Lankester and Dr Horatio Donkin, his colleague for what would be a forty-year crusade against fraudulent mediums. Despite a ringing endorsement for Slade from no less a figure than Alfred Russel Wallace, a naturalist whose work on the theory of natural selection in the 1850s had anticipated and accelerated Darwin's, the magistrate at Bow Street Police Court reached a decision based on 'inferences to be drawn from the known course of nature' and Slade was given three months' hard labour under the Vagrancy Act, although the sentence was later quashed. This, and the prosecution of Francis Monck, a physical medium who did serve his sentence, drew public attention not just to the possibility of fraud but the ways it could be perpetrated using mechanical tricks: masks, veils, gloves, wires and double slates cunningly hinged to conceal a pre-prepared message until the climactic moment.

These cases, and others in their wake, also stirred debate about the legal prosecution of Spiritualists, the pro-lobby lamenting a return to medieval superstition, the opposers the folly of witch-hunting. Police action continued into the twentieth century, although in an age where class was still synonymous with authority, the gentility of many mediums – and their well-heeled clients – was a restraining factor. Questions were asked in Parliament, to which successive Home Secretaries – in 1911, Winston Churchill – replied by defining the 1824 Act and re-affirming that wherever prophecy led to imposition, there would the law intervene. In 1912 a surge in fortune telling in London's West End precipitated a Metropolitan Police clampdown: issuing cautions, banning advertisements and incurring the wrath of the likes of Madame Nita of the Edgware Road who cited the parliamentary questions in her defence. Others were prosecuted. An Egyptian who predicted tragedy at sea for an undercover police-woman – in the year when almost 1500 lives were lost on the *Titanic* – pleaded at Bow Street that he only told people things to make them happy. The boost war gave to occult services, on Bond Street and Margate promenade alike, elicited a commensurate response from the police and, in turn, sparked protests from those who sought to protect mediums from obsolete legislation and *agents provocateurs*. In 1915 the Home Office opened a file (later closed until 2024), which contains a letter from Sir

Oliver Lodge expressing his fear that 'there is an Anti-Occult League afoot, anxious to put in force an antique Act against necromancy of all kinds'. Lodge had intended to draw in A. J. Balfour, First Lord of the Admiralty and former SPR President, but received only a tight-lipped legal disquisition and some passing comment about impostors 'cruelly trading on the feelings of bereaved relatives'. But the rules were unclear. Another metropolitan purge in 1917 led the *Justice of the Peace* to observe that although this social evil needed to be curtailed, 'the law concerning alleged dealings with the supernatural has fallen into such a tangled condition that the public, even the educated public, has but a very confused idea of what it actually is'.*

A culture of persecution grew up around Spiritualism, reflected in a 1921 petition to the King – kept secret for eighty years – asking that mediums be protected from the law and signed by the usual suspects, Lodge, Barrett, *et al.* The complaining pen of Sir Arthur Conan Doyle, another signatory, was in almost constant motion in the 1920s, squaring up to the authorities with a self-righteous rhetoric much imitated in the Spiritualist press. In October 1925 Madame Estelle, a society *clairvoyante*, was convicted in a court teeming with her supporters and thereby earned the sympathy of the editor of the *Morning Post*, likewise the *Daily Express*, which printed the pungent reaction of Conan Doyle who condemned sting operations as 'foreign to the spirit of British law'. Enclosing both clippings, Conan Doyle sallied forth in a letter to the Home Secretary, censuring the police for inciting an offence which the law condemned.

---

* In 1920 the foundation of the British College of Psychic Science was inspired by the wartime prosecutions, especially the imprisonment on remand (in Holloway Prison) and subsequent trial under the 1824 Vagrancy Act of an American medium, Almira Brockway. She was deported as an undesirable alien.

By the 1930s, trials relating to such matters were common and never failed to attract attention from the press. In 1932 Mrs Louise Meurig Morris, a trance medium, sued the *Daily Mail* for libel and received accolades from, among others, Sir Oliver Lodge who testified that he had heard about fraudulent mediums, but had yet to come across one. Harry Price endured all eleven days of the action (which reached the House of Lords) and was predictably amazed by the cheek of the medium and the credulity of the witnesses. Justice was not left entirely to the courts. In 1936 the *Sunday Times* conducted an exposé of Holland Park psychic photographers the Falconer brothers, after they manufactured a 'spirit-extra' from a French painting seen in a Spiritualist newspaper. The police confounded suspicions current before 1914 that there was one law for the rich and one for the poor by seeking to protect not so much the middle-class medium as the poor client. In the mid-1930s the confidential policy of the Metropolitan Police was explicit, namely 'not to proceed except (a) where the activities of the fortune teller are such as are likely to become a public scandal – and (b) where the clientele are people of modest means – as distinct from the "idle rich"'. The key factor here was money; and even Spiritualists had little time for con-artists, nor for genuine mediums who abused their gifts through greed.

In the summer of 1932 Harry Price informed Dr Gerda Walther in Munich, a corresponding member of the NLPR International Research Council, that what he saw as the pernicious Jewish alliance of Maurice Barbanell and the conjuror Will Goldston was faltering. Not only had a rival conjuror disputed Helen Duncan's genuineness, but Barbanell had warned her in *Psychic News* about the perils of sitting every evening for a fiver. 'One of these days', Price predicted, 'someone will take some action and she will find herself the subject of a prosecution.'

Miss Esson Maule was a stout, mannish, no-nonsense forty-something who cut her hair short and dressed imposingly in blazer and tie. A spiritualist with a small 's' at least, she invited mediums to hold seances at her gloomy Victorian town house, 24 Stafford Street, a short distance from Edinburgh city centre. Naturally she took an interest in Helen Duncan, by now a celebrity on the materialization circuit, and, after attending a seance at the Edinburgh Psychic College and Library on Heriot Row, obtained some photographs taken by a Dundee press photographer, W. M. Scott. The most famous of these depicted the medium at home, entranced and blindfolded, with a Punch and Judy, papier-mâché coathanger-and-muslin mannekin at her side purporting to be a materialized spirit. Intrigued, Miss Maule had shown the pictures to J. B. McIndoe who then borrowed the negatives from Scott and subsequently lost them. They turned up again shortly after Scott threatened to sue.

Helen, meanwhile, had been working closer to home since taking the children out of boarding school due to Nan's deteriorating condition. The diploma under her belt, she had secured a weekly slot at the Edinburgh Psychic College, but relations with the SNU soured after a sitter said she was worth more than his 10s ticket, and the realization dawned on her that from every seance the college received as much as £20, of which she was paid only two guineas. In any case Helen resented the lack of freedom and decided to go it alone, unprotected but unfettered; and so, to Maurice Barbanell's consternation, she started sitting for a few pounds a time. Gena, too, was concerned that her mother always looked so tired, but Henry dismissively told her not to worry so much. In fact, Helen's workload had shrunk. Loss of income combined with Nan's infirmity earned them a council house on a new but impoverished estate in Craigmillar where, according to Gena, Helen became a philanthropist, paying the medical bills of sick neighbours. Helen herself suffered further gynaecological problems and needed a hysterectomy – an operation which she survived, it was said, due to Albert's advice in the operating theatre. A few months earlier *Light* had reported how the life of the R-101 medium, Mrs Eileen Garrett, had been saved by a spirit guide, 'Abduhl Latif', who in twelfth-century Parsee and Hindustani somehow advised surgeons performing a tonsillectomy how to staunch the bleeding.

Helen depended on her Glasgow seances until private work in Edinburgh picked up. As early as March 1932, Miss Maule had made bookings with Henry, but she had not been satisfied and, after taking expert advice from a contact in London, by the end of the year had decided to set a trap. On 5 January 1933, wearing her favourite tight brown dress, Helen had been performing at the Holland Street Spiritualist church in Glasgow where, *inter alia*, she filled the room with the scent of roses and materialized the wife of a man who returned the red rose he had placed on her coffin. Afterwards the organizer, Mrs Drysdale, informed Helen that while she had been in trance Albert had warned her to be careful that evening. Blowing away smoke, Helen promised she would, but did not give it a second thought as she packed a gift of home-made scones and jam into her seance case, and pulled on her big leather coat. Though tired, she had to rush back to Edinburgh to keep an eight-o'clock appointment confirmed the previous evening by Miss Maule's secretary, Hilda Sowden. Before leaving Glasgow Helen telephoned to say she was running late. Arriving at Waverley Station in Edinburgh shortly after nine, she hurried a taxi driver to Stafford Street where she was met by Mrs Sowden wearing a red jersey.

As Helen entered the fusty, dimly lit hallway, one of the first things she saw was a wall-mounted cutlass, which it was easy to imagine Miss Maule using in emergencies. She was led up the stairs without a word and into the cluttered morning room, which Miss Maule was fond of calling her 'den'. After greeting a handful of sitters, Helen was seated beside a desk, where she lit a cigarette and was handed £4 in a sheaf of ten-shilling notes. Leaving the money on the desk, she stubbed out her fag-end before being led upstairs to the top of the house and into the seance room where the other sitters (some of whom had responded to an advertisement in a local newspaper) were seated in a semicircle facing a cabinet of chintz curtains across one corner. The only lighting was a forty-watt red electric bulb covered with a Turkey red cotton bag, and a single candle burning on the mantelpiece; the temperature in the room was falling, the electric fire having fused minutes earlier. Still wheezing from climbing the two flights of stairs, Helen shuffled into the cabinet, the curtains were drawn and, quietly taking off her shoes, she began to breathe very heavily as the sitters commenced their singing in order to raise the vibrations.

A long whitish thing appeared and introduced itself as Albert but withdrew when Miss Maule asked for a better look. Just then, however, another figure appeared who Albert said was a gentleman for the lady in the red jersey. Mrs Sowden recognized the figure at once: it was Mrs Duncan with a length of cloth hanging from her head; but she managed to suspend her disbelief for long enough to express surprise that the spiritual gentleman, whose solid form she patted, was the proud owner of a large pair of female breasts. While this was going on Miss Maule reached into the cabinet and felt the unoccupied chair. For an hour a succession of spirits (all of whom smelt of stale tobacco) dropped by to say hello until finally Albert interjected to say how awful he thought Miss Maule's singing was, before handing over to the star turn. Peggy popped up behind a vase on the sideboard beside the cabinet before climbing down to dance. Miss Maule wished Peggy a happy New Year, then, bored with her chatter, approached the little scamp who everyone could see was Mrs Duncan on her knees manipulating something white and speaking childishly. Then the unthinkable happened. Miss Maule grabbed Peggy to find that she was made from soft, stretchy material through which her finger tore as the challenge turned into an ugly tug-of-war – a contest won by the defender. As arranged, one of the sitters, a solicitor named Elizabeth MacKay, switched on a powerful hand-lamp to reveal Mrs Duncan sitting in the cabinet, desperately trying to bundle the lifeless Peggy under her clothes. 'Mrs Duncan, you are taking money for producing fraudulent materializations purporting to be the deceased friends of sitters,' announced Miss Maule. 'It is disgraceful and I refuse to stand by it any longer.'

Laid bare in the glare of the lamp, the woman who taught her children that to be angry was to lose an argument felt the old, blind, passionate swell of rage rise within, and began to scream and curse at Miss Maule. Silenced momentarily by the sitters who were heckling to see the white material visible beneath her dress, she shouted back that she would not show men her knickers, but Miss Maule, injecting some steel into her voice, insisted she strip. Helen snapped. She raised a heavy wooden chair and swung it at Miss Maule, bawling: 'I'll brain you, you bloody bugger!' but missed, due to the intervention of one of the male sitters who then received a blow to the wrist from a shoe. With what a sitter described as 'one prolonged, savage yell', Helen swung her arm like a fast bowler and pitched the other shoe at Miss Maule who managed to duck. Calming slightly, Helen agreed to undress if the men left the room, which they did –

and, leaving the door ajar, peeped in from the landing. Under Miss MacKay's spotlight, she crouched down and pulled her dress and petticoat over her head in a single swoop, but just failed to make 'Peggy' travel with them. The white stockinette vest landed short of the other clothes and her female examiners simply stared. To distract attention Helen pulled off her knickers – which turned out to be bright blue bloomers elasticated at the knee – and displayed the inside to show there was nothing within. In a brief peaceful interlude, this exchange took place:

MISS MAULE (*pointing at the vest*): That is Peggy.

MRS DUNCAN: I'll no say it's no.

MISS MAULE: You cannot deny that is Peggy. Look, there is the tear.

MRS DUNCAN: It might have been . . . you dirty swine.

Another violent row ensued, Miss Maule insisting she take the vest, Helen first refusing, then offering all her clothes and proposing to go home in the nude. In the end she threw the vest at Miss Maule and again attacked her with a chair, which this time Miss Maule parried. She quietened when the men returned, but as Miss Maule explained to them what had happened, despite herself she flashed her big blue knickers by way of illustration. Finally, tiring of Helen's 'threatening attitudes and hooligan tactics, swearing and cursing', Miss Maule said she would call the police and left her guest screaming 'The Police!' while Miss MacKay and Mrs Sowden tried not to look too bothered. When the constables arrived, Helen swooned a little and asked for glass after glass of water, and on being accused of fraud replied politely: 'If God should stand between us just now I know nothing about it.' Even though one of the men was bleeding from the head where a flying chair had caught him, no one – neither Helen nor the sitters – wished to press charges so the constables left.

This tragi-comedy concluded in the hallway while they waited for Mrs Duncan's taxicab to arrive. First, it was noticed that she had somehow managed to reclaim the disputed vest (which she did return after some argument); then she denied there had been any arrangement for payment but, unable to bear seeing the ten-shilling notes refunded, snatched them from Miss Maule. Her hand shaking, Miss Maule drew up a receipt in pencil on the back of an envelope, which the medium signed with a confident flourish. Her last words before she blessed them all with her absence befitted a modern celebrity. Fixing them with the dark intensity of her stare – Miss Maule in particular – Helen said: 'I don't know how far this, tonight, will go, but I don't want anything in the papers, mind.' And with that, the cab engine ticking over outside, she scuttled off into the winter night.

The story did reach the papers, but by an indirect route. Eleven days after the incident Miss Maule and five of the other sitters appeared before a magistrate to testify that Helen Duncan had been detected by them in a criminal fraud. In support of this charge they produced their evidence: the grubby undervest, ripped and riddled with pinholes, to which now were attached a fringe of manila luggage labels each signed and dated by the witnesses and sealed with wax. A summary of facts was compiled and soon afterwards an indictment framed of which Miss Maule received a copy. In the days that followed, with clinical precision Miss Maule arranged for a photographer to capture the entire *mise-en-scène* from the various rooms, down to a pile of ten-shilling notes restored to the desk to show how things had been left prior to the seance, and next to the money, presumably for purely ironic purposes, her copy of the indictment. Two months

158

later Miss Maule was called to the office of the Procurator Fiscal, James Adair, to discuss the prosecution for which a date in May had been agreed. In the meantime, a summons to answer a charge of fraud was sent to the Duncans' home on the Craigmillar estate where, on receiving it, all was despair and disarray. A solicitor explained the situation to Helen and she waited.

Proceedings began on the morning of Wednesday, 3 May at the Sheriff Summary Court of the Lothians and Peebles, George IV Bridge, Edinburgh and for the first time Helen Duncan, trembling in her Sunday best, surveyed the physical machinery of the law, at once banal and malign, predictable and capricious. The court was crowded with reporters, thrill-seekers and supporters, the latter mostly female Spiritualists. Shortly before 11 a.m., the judge, Sheriff Macdonald KC, called the court to order and the charge was read. It was alleged that Helen Duncan had pretended to the complainants that she was:

a medium through whom the spirits of deceased persons were openly and regularly materialized in such a manner as to become visible to, and to speak to, and to converse with, those present in a room with you . . . and having each paid to you a sum of ten shillings of money, you did pretend to hold a seance there and to materialize the spirits of certain deceased persons including that of a deceased child named Peggy.

Struggling to be audible, Helen pleaded not guilty. In accordance with Scottish law, counsel – Mr Adair prosecuting, Mr Ian Dickson defending – made no speeches, and a succession of witnesses said their piece and were cross-examined. The taxi driver who had picked her up at the station became embroiled in a discussion about where Mrs Duncan had been told the seance would take place: at Miss Maule's house, or the 'Psychic

Research Centre' next door. The Defence also called a doctor, Marguerite Linck-Hutchinson, who had attended J. B. McIndoe's seances in Glasgow after her uncle – the theatrical producer present at the LSA in March 1931 – suggested she might find Mrs Duncan interesting. She said it was impossible that cloth could have been concealed and rejected the regurgitation theory, not least because she had seen the medium devour a meal of ham and eggs before the seance. On the second day, when the crowds were even bigger, McIndoe himself was called and recanted his initial opinion about events at Stafford Street, the cause now proving more important than the case. Ernest Oaten, too, did what he could, although he could not find it in himself to be as extravagant as Montague Rust who entertained the court with tales of Mrs Duncan dematerializing out of her clothes and issuing a vast snake of ectoplasm, which had lifted him off his feet. Expert witness Harry Price could hardly believe his ears, but he was at least impressed by the passion of the defence witnesses whereas the conduct of the Prosecution seemed half-hearted. Sheriff Macdonald decided to reserve judgement for a week – a week of anxiety and misery for the Duncans.

On 11 May well-wishers who had waited in the rain for over an hour, inside the courtroom bowed their heads in silent prayer. Ian Dickson, whose maiden case this was, pleaded clemency on various grounds: she was thirty-four (in fact, she was thirty-six that November); she had to support a family of eight (if one included herself and Henry) without a husband's income; and, with Browning's 'Mr Sludge' in mind, he said she had only this once 'stooped to manipulation'. Until this point Helen had spoken only to make her plea and to say she remembered nothing of the seance because she had been in trance. On hearing this slur however she shouted out 'But I never!' at which the court gasped in unison. Dickson, tiring of his first client, closed by expressing weakly the hope that the Sheriff would take into account the great faith many people had in Mrs Helen Duncan. It was a vain hope, dashed by Macdonald's terse judgement: 'Whatever psychic powers the accused may possess, I find that this charge against her has been proved.' Helen was fined the sum of £10 payable within one month, or one month's imprisonment, which she received stoically until the moment just before she left the court-room when she called out, 'God forgi'e ye!'

Predictably, the local newspapers had a field day. Excitement at the Dundee *Daily Record and Mail* can be gauged from its usual subject matter, of which the stories surrounding the account of the trial are representative: Dundee's highland singers, a contested will, a stray cuckoo and the annual audit of the Glasgow Local Savings Committee. PRAYERS IN COURT FOR MEDIUM FOUND GUILTY OF FRAUD, therefore, was a refreshing change. Harry Price returned to London vindicated but still needing to face off critics. In *Two Worlds*, Oaten painted him as a sinister presence in court, silently passing notes to the Bench, a description which had Price reaching for pen and paper once more. Not only should the Spiritualists thank the National Laboratory for purging the movement of frauds, he protested, but he had sent only *two* notes; and in any case the verdict was eminently reasonable: 'I think Mrs Duncan is very fortunate to get off with £10 and I suppose the poor, credulous fools who support her will find the money. And as regards the witnesses for the Defence, I have never heard such a display of the most utter credulity – or sheer lying – as I heard in court last week.'

Harder to deny was the suggestion from other quarters, not least from the Duncans, that Price had set the whole thing up.

The machinery of entrapment – advertising for sitters who would be credible witnesses, ensuring that Mrs Duncan took the money (and left a receipt), securing the signed evidence of the under-vest, the making of a photographic record – all bore his trade-mark. And the key revelation here was that the 'E. M.' who alerted Price to Kanichka the Human Ostrich was none other than Miss Esson Maule; and the contact in London from whom she sought advice was none other than Harry Price. Plenty of clues tie them to one another. Between appearing before the magistrate and meeting the Procurator Fiscal, Miss Maule visited the NLPR in Roland Gardens where, in contempt of court, she delivered an evening lantern lecture, 'My Experiences with Mrs Duncan'. The police citation calling her to give evidence is filed among Price's papers, although the strange absence of any correspondence makes it impossible to establish how far Price was implicated in events of 5 January. There is little doubt that he followed the investigation closely and probably suggested that Miss Maule take the photographs, a set of which he received, together with a print of the 'Mr Punch' spirit. On the back, Miss Maule wrote 'This photograph is for you' and, disregarding Mr Scott's copy-right now, gave Price permission to reproduce it.

The Duncans were depressed. It remained Gena's habit to retreat into a spiritual bubble, from which invariably she emerged refreshed and buoyant. After a difficult night she had been rewarded with the comforting vision of a lambent female form and in the morning was moved to song. 'Shut up,' said Lilian, to which her mystical sister replied: 'I know something you don't know' and ran off to tell her mother. Yet it would seem that the stark reality of the trial had immunized even Helen against Gena's viral optimism: 'She [Helen] was preparing breakfast, looking so tired, her eyes usually so full of life and joy were now so dull and she appeared absolutely listless. Going up to her and putting my hand in hers, I said: "Please don't worry, it's going to be alright, they promised." Squeezing my hand she nodded and told me to sit down and have my porridge.'

There were, though, some reasons to be cheerful. Price was right: £10 was not a lot for someone with her earning potential, and she may well have received that and more from private sources or from the SNU in whose favour she was held again. Maurice Barbanell thought the airing of amazing testimony had done Spiritualism much good: people listened now whereas until recently 'there would have been as little seriousness in such a trial as in one for witchcraft'. For the SNU, furthermore, a martyred fraud was a martyr first and a fraud second. Whatever harm the conviction caused, it did bolster the legacy of her victimization. That vest became her crown of thorns, and Gena would not be the last to draw parallels between Christ's introspection in Gethsemane and Helen mooching tearfully around the kitchen with a cigarette in one hand and a saucepan in the other. Like God at Calvary, ruminated Gena, porridge sticking in her throat, Albert had forsaken her mother. Her clients, however, had not. Harry Price's book, *Leaves from a Psychist's Casebook*, published in October, contained a chapter marvelling at the 'cheesecloth worshippers', a mania which had launched Mrs Duncan's 'meteroric flight across the firmament' – although on second thoughts he withdrew from the image of an airborne Helen. But the great pretender was resilient to insults and, resolving in the future always to have independent witnesses inspect her clothes (and never to wear white underwear), she got on with the job.

Many notable engagements were recorded for 1933. Helen was applauded at public meetings, including one where she established clairvoyantly that a man in the audience had brought along his wife's ashes in a tea caddy. Frank Smith reported how his Aunt Lizzie returned to him, as did his nephew killed in the war;

Mrs Smith, meanwhile, was pleased to see her sister Maggie because even though she was actually still alive, she did have a dead sister Nellie and thought this was near enough. Smith counted eleven manifestations, of which all were recognized except for one lost soul who, unknown and unloved, sank pitifully into the floor. In July a twilight seance was held in the garden of an old house in Liverpool where, despite the interruptions of a motorcycle and an express train, spirit forms were reported to have manifested between the branches of a rhododendron tree, and a flame like an old-fashioned gas burner was seen fluttering in the medium's cleavage. Helen was on top form, as well she might have been, given that three weeks earlier at the Annual General Meeting of the SNU at Doncaster a vote of confidence in her mediumship had been carried by fifty-seven votes to two and her diploma renewed. From here on the perceived quality of her seances ensured that she would be required to provide them in quantity. That summer, to meet all of her far-flung engagements, Helen made arrangements for the children to be looked after, packing Gena off on holiday with a family friend, Jean Beatson, who lived in a big country house in Fife. One day Gena was startled by a fairy dressed in green who doffed his hat, then vanished. Using words that might have come straight from Kirk's *Secret Commonwealth* or Frazer's *Golden Bough*, Jean explained that fairies were God's gardeners who also helped clairvoyant folk blessed with 'the sight'.

During these years of depression, the popular press thrived on a literate public's addiction to three things: for prosperity, job advertisements; for entertainment, football (which had grown as a mass spectator sport); and, bridging prosperity and entertainment, the horoscope. Furthermore, as Houdini and Harry Price had discovered, the new tabloid newspapers with their half-size format, copious photographs and accessible style were hungry for tales of mystery and magic and, conversely, provided a vehicle for self-promotion. And so, in September 1933, the Duncans were given a full-page column in Scots weekly the *People's Journal*. 'My Second Sight Secrets by Madame Victoria Duncan', which ran for fifteen weeks, was almost certainly ghost-written from Henry's scribblings, and achieved an arid tone stranded somewhere between moralization, sentimentality and titillation. 'My role is that of counsellor and friend,' she explained on 23 September. 'If I can let in a ray of sunshine where all is sad and dreary how happy I am to guide the brightening beam.' That particular instalment, in which Helen used clairvoyance to reunite a husband and wife, depicted her clutching a letter and pointing at an imaginary client. The specially commissioned photographs show her in various poses: staring intently into a crystal, stroking her chin over an open book; desk-bound, sucking a pencil; giving a psychometric reading; and smiling engagingly with a new hairdo. Another week, another problem solved, mostly concerning relationships, money and emigration to Australia, with headlines such as MENDING BROKEN HEARTS, LOVE KNOTS WHICH I UNRAVELLED, and GIRL WHO WANTED RICH HUSBAND. The final piece was tinged with irony. Having earned the gratitude of the police for helping to trap a burglar, she held a seance in a police station, materializing the son of a constable and two soldiers who spoke to their uncle about visiting their graves in France. 'I swear that I have given you the whole facts,' she said in another piece, 'and that I have told you nothing but the truth.'

Helen's rehabilitation enabled her to return to the Edinburgh Psychic College and Library, where in November 1934 a Mrs Wright of St Albans saw her deceased sister incarnated in a foam-like wave billowing from the medium's body. Local bookings were welcome, for illness restricted travel and often prevented work altogether. A neighbour, hearing she was laid up, brought a bottle of whisky at which she tippled until she fell into a coma. Gena told of how the spirit physician Dr Johansen sent her to the kitchen to prepare a reviving snack of tomato on toast, Albert thoughtfully apporting the principal ingredient and thereby saving Helen's life by a whisker. Albert was often around for the Duncan children while their mother was away. To demonstrate his presence, once, when Helen's youngest son Peter developed an earache and cried as Nan cuddled him in her bed, Albert was said to have levitated a full ashtray from the bedside table, setting it down on the floor without spillage. The pain subsided and the boy slept. Menial chores devolved to a new housekeeper, Sadie O'Hara, who had said at Helen's trial that *she* had torn the stockinette undervest while ironing it. After she moved away, the disaffected and disfigured Bella cared for her half-siblings until she married (and, after the war, fled to Australia), whereafter a new maid was hired who herself cleared off within weeks, taking the family linen as a souvenir. One maid allegedly laced the leek-and-potato soup with arsenic, hospitalizing Peter, so naturally she had to go. All of which left the sickly Nan in charge until Sadie returned – her husband having died of alcoholism – to see the remaining children through to adulthood.

Henry needed looking after, too. For ten months pleurisy confined him to the flat to which the family had moved, after which rheumatic fever and his heart condition prevented him from using the stairs. Helen, who found stairs a challenge at the best of times, was also struck down by pleurisy, Albert having interrupted a seance at Glasgow as its debilitating effects took hold. The solution to their restricted mobility lay in the purchase of a pleasant cottage in Kirkhill Drive, which Helen christened 'Albertine' in honour of her guides, Albert Stewart and Peggy Hazeldine, who after all had helped to pay for it. In more salubrious surroundings, Helen recovered sufficiently to work further afield and spent a good deal of her time in coastal resorts popular with the elderly – Bournemouth, for example, where in February 1936 Albert permitted a photographer to record her in trance, her face swathed in gauzy ectoplasm. Fame spread through the Spiritualist press. Early in 1937 – a year when the Archbishop of Canterbury, Cosmo Lang, conceded that the population of Britain was largely non-Christian – the *Psychic News* published an article by Rev. E.B. Fry who had attended one of Mrs Duncan's seances at a house in Monmouthshire and had been particularly impressed by the manifestation of an 'angel':

A form of a young woman appeared in the corner, as if a foot or so off the ground. We were directed to allow the moonlight to shine on it by removing the blind for a moment. The effect was radiant until, in a moment, the form disappeared from our physical sight. The resonant voice of Albert then spoke of a baby which had lived only a few moments. He commanded the medium to stand up and carry the baby out of the cabinet. Then was seen, in the red light, the tall form of Mrs Duncan, in black, and in her arms a snow-white bundle containing the baby.

In February 1937 Helen visited Treherbert, a Welsh mining community in the Rhondda Valley where the vicar, Rev. C.G.R. Lewis, was worried about the poor saving 3d a week in a club so that they could see her again when she returned in April. After reading Price's *Leaves from a Psychist's Casebook*, he spoke to his friend the Bishop of Monmouth who was interested in Spiritualism and encouraged him to write to Price. This Lewis did, saying that if she were the fraud Price described her to be, 'is there not some way of preventing her from robbing these people of money they cannot afford to waste?' Price sent a copy of the NLPR report and even offered to lecture in Treherbert, but sensed the magnitude of the barrier to be overcome when Lewis confessed that he remained half persuaded by the doctor seeing his father and a pit undermanager being kissed by his sister, witnesses he described as 'two fairly hard-headed men who would not easily be gulled'.

In the winter of 1937–8 Richard Howe, a young soldier stationed with the Black Watch at Perth, not far from Helen's birthplace, managed to get a ticket to a materialization seance through the President of the town's Spiritualist church, Mrs Macbeth. Although it cost him 10s (a third of his week's wages), to encounter the dead and sing 'Sweet Mystery of Life' with Peggy was, he said, 'an investment in experience'. Earlier, he had seen Helen perform clairvoyance in a large, crowded public hall and was captivated by her eyes, 'deep, mystical, inscrutable'. The conjuror Will Goldston once asked Albert whether he would consent to Mrs Duncan performing in theatres and had been told: 'I cannot stop her but she will be alone.' But when she did succumb to the roar of the greasepaint and started playing such venues, it seemed that he stuck by her. The performances brought praise and applause, and drew bigger audiences than Price's debunking lectures, even those he illustrated with lantern slides and recordings of Mrs Duncan putting on funny voices.

Price believed that explanations for ninety-nine per cent of paranormal phenomena were to be found in human nature. So what kept him going? Critics say an insatiable hunger for publicity: his account of a small girl, 'Rosalie', materializing at a south London house in 1937 and, most famous of all, the haunting of Borley Rectory, have been put down to invention. Others attribute his commitment to a sincere faith in the remaining one per cent of phenomena. These two views can be reconciled. What mattered most, and what Price understood better than anyone, was that the pluralistic, individualistic, consumerized population was profoundly interested in this one per cent and that it was an interest which could be exploited indefinitely. That, after all, was what orthodox churches had been doing for centuries. In 1936 the young Oxford philosopher A.J. Ayer published *Language, Truth and Logic*, which advanced 'logical positivism' – the idea that all meaningful questions must be answerable – and so rubbished all forms of the supernatural. Popular though this book was, however, the market would always be stronger for works suggesting the opposite. While Ayer was crystallizing his thoughts in Vienna in 1932, Harry Price was investigating the case of a talking mongoose on the Isle of Man which, it was claimed, sang hymns in six languages, had a smattering of Arabic, Russian and Welsh, and expressed distaste for Price as 'the man who puts the kybosh on the spirits'. In the same year Price took his philosopher friend Professor C.E.M. Joad, another sharp journalist reviled by purist colleagues, on an expedition to the Harz mountains in Germany to try an ancient spell to transmute a goat into a fair youth. Weird stories such as these offended the Spiritualists, alienated the psychical researchers, but sold newspapers and books by the van-load. Significantly, the goat experiment was performed at the invitation of the Goethe Centenary Committee, which hoped that witchcraft might do for the local tourist industry something of what the Romantic poets had done for the Trossachs.

According to Price, by the mid-1930s witchcraft was being practised in London 'with a freedom undreamt of in the Middle Ages' and, sensational though this was meant to sound, by the terms of the law he was right. Dipping into the SPR archives, one finds no shortage of mediums surrendering to experiment and becoming famous for being infamous – as Helen Duncan's entry in Nandor Fodor's 1934 *Encyclopaedia of Psychic Science* demonstrates. In that year Fodor, the Hungarian given Mrs Duncan's shoes by Albert, was appointed assistant editor of *Light* and Research Officer of the newly created International Institute for Psychical Research, which took a latitudinarian stance to the investigation of all phenomena, including ectoplasm and materialization. 'For doing the one hundredth part of what is done by men of science every day,' a promotional article suggested, 'our ancestors would have been burned alive.' Fodor saw some bizarre things. There was Mr Woodward who psyched himself up by drinking heavily and in trying to levitate a vase managed only to fall on it, whereupon he was made to stop and promptly fell asleep and began snoring. There was Mrs Hammerton, a squat woman from Chiswick who issued warnings about investments in the basso profondo of her male control, apported worthless trinkets coated in scouring powder and gave off a mouldy smell in the cabinet. Other women made slits of their eyes to claim they had transfigured into Chinamen, photographs of Mrs Everett and 'Woo Fang' being the most entertaining; others looked fierce and pretended they were Zulus – in the case of Mrs Bullock from Manchester, complete with bullet wound to the head. Brighton transfiguration medium Annie Scoggins did a sculptor called Chow, an ancient Persian called Hassef, but best of all, and most tellingly, she became her own sister who had died as a child.

Men, too, laid claim to such powers, although male mediumship was popularly associated with spinelessness or effeminacy. Welshman Jack Webber was an ex-miner who had literally seen the light when lost underground, but did not become a Spiritualist before he married one. A plain man who preferred children's comics to books, he came to accept his guides, 'Paddy' and 'Reuben', who, without a cabinet, enabled him to levitate and churn out ectoplasm at more than 200 seances a year, some of which were reported favourably by the press and the BBC.

The sound company Decca even cut records of Reuben singing hymns. Revered by followers, Webber was also extensively photographed, showing him paranormally removing his jacket while lashed to the chair, allegedly duplicating his own head, and extending an ectoplasmic tentacle from his mouth to which a claw-like gripper was attached – once used to play with toys hanging on a Christmas tree. Albert-like and Christ-like, he died suddenly at the age of thirty-three. In 1936 Dr Fodor offered another Welsh miner, Trefor Davies of Merthyr Tydfil, £5 for sitting at the IIPR, and another £20 (plus fifty per cent of the rights) if he could film him producing ectoplasm with an infra-red camera. Whether Fodor used infra-red on Davies is not recorded, but he did on Dundee engine driver Charles Stewart, 'a slightly built, nervous man, apparently suffering from an inferiority complex'. Intensely shy, he left the talking to his wife – 'a very big woman' – who ran the business side of things. In the early 1930s the Stewarts had met Helen Duncan who had shared her wisdom, showed them inside her cabinet and encouraged them to form a circle, which they did in their tiny flat in Rose Bank Street. 'Brazen frauds,' concluded Fodor whose photographs today show a scrawny man disporting himself wrapped in a sheet, butter muslin stretched over his face.

Meanwhile, Harry Price was investigating Kuda Bux, a fire-walking Indian with X-ray eyes, who had arrived in London in the spring of 1935 and for the next three years became a press sensation. Assisting Price was Mollie Goldney, at this time also active in the IIPR where she participated in the exposure of a medium from the LSA, Agnes Abbott. Breaching seance etiquette, Mollie took an illicit infra-red photograph in the darkness, which showed a 'floating' luminous trumpet stuck on the end of Mrs Abbott's thumb, and on a separate occasion spotted 'ectoplasm' poking out of her dress. Mrs Abbott, whose cod-Irish control 'Pat' would *pat* sitters, was induced to sign a confession, but soon cried that the photographs had been faked; her husband, a bullying drunkard, went on record saying: 'As God is my witness, I'm honest as the day.' Mollie Goldney also led a group of SPR members calling themselves 'The Probe', who set out to expose fraud after Hylda Lewis, a medium who apported flowers, reached the attention of the public. In April 1935, Harry Price sent Mollie a card on which he had drawn a red poppy labelled 'Apport!', adding: 'Of course you have heard all about the Flower Medium. Oh dear, oh dear!' Miss Lewis welcomed the press (except for Price, of course), and consented to an examination lasting several days at Oxford University where the Wykeham Professor of Logic and future SPR President H.H. Price (no relation) and his colleagues concluded that she was a fragile, volatile, self-deluded mental case who hid thornless roses on and in her body, burned herself on less sensitive regions with an electric iron and bought toy animals in Woolworths to pass off as apports; a lead sheep was discovered lurking in her handbag, awaiting its moment of psychic glory. Interestingly, her seances appeared to bring her almost narcotic relief from pent-up anxiety. The Probe investigators did their best on her, but scored a greater success in 1936 with Dorothy Henderson whose muslin ectoplasm was grabbed and photographed. Pulse racing, she had promised to mend her evil ways, while her hysterical daughter distanced herself both morally and physically from her mother.

No mere killjoys, Probe members protested that the activities of Hylda Lewis and others led to 'hundreds of pounds being drawn from the pockets of a gullible or bereaved public'. In February 1939 Countess Nora Wydenbruck and a medical friend attended a seance in West Kensington – 'an impertinent and ludicrous exhibition of fraud' – where the medium collected 10s 6d from each sitter, as she did in her two other weekly circles, which had been running for a decade. Assuming an average of twelve sitters and a steady work rate, she would have earned almost £10,000 in this time – equivalent to perhaps half a million pounds today. This was nothing new. In 1920 the *World's Pictorial News* exposed a medium who swindled clients out of £1000 a year. Yet this, some argued, was just capitalism and what was true of mediumship applied to all work. 'It is surely better for a medium to heal broken hearts and prevent suicides, as they often do,' reasoned one Spiritualist, 'rather than scrub floors, wash clothes, peddle matches, or even gamble on the stock exchange.'

The decade which had begun with the collapse of the New York stock exchange ended with a European war that most spirits had said would never happen. In the mid-1930s the novelist Somerset Maugham had visited a fortune teller on the Riviera before leaving for Paris and learned he would narrowly escape death, that he would be followed by two friends carrying a corpse and that Hitler would die or fall that year. He crashed his car into a tree, his friends picked up a sick man (who died) and, a gossip columnist reported, 'Mr Maugham and his friends are now anxiously awaiting grave news from Berlin.' The news never came and spiritual prognostications about the threat to peace abounded as the expansionism of the dictators became bolder. During Mussolini's war in Abyssinia in 1935, nine-year-old Gena Duncan went to the cinema to see a Tarzan film and was shocked to witness the Pope blessing Italian guns on a Pathé newsreel. Soon afterwards she was told by omniscient Albert at a seance that she was too small to take on the world's problems – that was her mother's job. But Albert was one of the few spirits to admit that a major war was inevitable and it was said that he further predicted the coming of a great British leader, the failure of German invasion, the Russian alliance and the survival of the Empire – although memories of this last prophecy were to fade.

As she watched her fiancé Ronald sail off to sea, Ena Bügg, the shy Gosport girl, contemplated ominous messages from a high spiritual order, the White Brotherhood, which had been received in the circle of a gypsy called Mrs MacHattie. So in August 1939, when Ena's spirit guide 'Chiefy' predicted a terrible tragedy for her, she guessed what it would be, despite the banner headline in *Two Worlds* that month which read NO WAR – the Spiritualist consensus after the Munich Crisis the previous autumn. Gloom hung over the Duncans, too. Nan, married now, had defied doctors by becoming pregnant and had given birth to a baby boy, Thomas, Helen's first grandchild and her pride and joy. But in 1938, at eighteen months, Thomas contracted meningitis and died, whereafter Gena was haunted by the child's disembodied voice. These days, Gena was often found to be in a 'devham' (a dialect word for 'trance'), and her siblings considered her to be 'not quite the full shilling'. In 1939, when her sister Lilian married Angus Douglas, an ICI employee, Gena earned a clip round the ear from the still grieving Nan for saying that the marriage would not last long; nor was her precognition of their father's death well received. But her black outlook would prove well-founded and, indeed, was shared by her mother. That summer, the whole Duncan family went on holiday to the coast, but as Helen sat on the beach – her favourite place in all the world – feeling the sea breeze blow away the cobwebs of the seance room, she sensed it was the last time they would all be together.

Once hostilities had begun, mediums spread confidence in victory but, as in the First World War, their most important role was as private counsellors. The scale of the killing was smaller than before, but the anxiety was, if anything, greater, especially due to bombing raids. The Britain of 1939 was also far more security-conscious and intelligence-obsessed than in 1914, and starved its people of information. Alternative sources were sought. Mass-Observation, studying social habits and opinions, revealed that a quarter of the population was gripped by paranormal beliefs, reflected in a craze for horoscopes, and encouraged by uncertainty and an enhanced sensitivity due to the blackout. Air-raid forecasting was a popular service offered by some mediums, and Spiritualist churches found that people of all creeds and classes started attending services, although it was not unknown for Catholics to disrupt them, crying 'spooks!' and other insults from the street. By 1944, Spiritualism was said to have a million believers worshipping at a thousand churches, as many affiliated mediums and over 50,000 home circles. These beliefs were not just confined to the home front. Lady Rhondda, who visited an army camp as part of a BBC *Brains Trust* entertainment, found the soldiers innocently open-minded about the paranormal. In 1942, when the army was at its greatest strength with 3 million men, even though only 521 soldiers were registered as Spiritualists (and were free to worship as such), many more of that persuasion had stated conventional denominations on joining and an even greater number were curious without deep devotion. In 1941 the Royal Navy finally recognized Spiritualism as a religion and sailors were allowed to hold services at sea, space permitting. Interest extended up the ranks. No fewer than 504 of the 521 Spiritualists registered by the army were officers. The home circle of Charles Glover Botham, a thick-set middle-aged medium who had first shown promise as a child, was said to include certain generals from the War Office staff and for three years was visited regularly by Air Chief Marshal Sir Trafford Leigh-Mallory who conversed with his brother lost on Mount Everest in 1924; after 1939 he attended occasionally until 1944 when he too was killed in an accident.

War changed life at Kirkhill Drive, most immediately with the requisitioning of 'Albertine' as a billet for army officers, Polish intelligentsia and the like. The extra income helped Helen to feed her family, although she was always short of decent cigarettes and was therefore thrilled to be given a tinful by a grateful sitter whose husband got them from the navy. Once the phoney war was over in 1940, the demands of battle started to take their toll. Bella's husband was reported missing at Dunkirk, but turned up at Folkestone on a fishing boat; and Nan's husband, a Scots Guardsman, suffered the worst of the Blitz in London. Lilian's husband Angus joined the RAF and went off on active service as a wireless operator and gunner, leaving her and their baby, Dawn, in Aberdeen. Harry Duncan, too, joined the RAF in the spring of 1941, soon after he had attended a seance in Kirkcaldy where he remembered Albert predicting that the war would last half as long again as the last one, and would end with two big bangs. By then the family was in mourning. In February Lilian, pregnant from his last leave, had heard that Angus had been killed over Norway and laid to rest in the same churchyard as British sailors drowned at Jutland in 1916. Helen did what she could, offering spiritual comfort and drawing morning sickness upon herself, but Lilian spent her days in a fugue drifting between picture houses with her little girl, movies washing over her like waves. When the baby was born she took little interest and was put in a sanatorium for ten months suffering from tuberculosis. Her mother, meanwhile, despite the onset of diabetes kept her engagements south of the border while Henry and the girls looked after Dawn and the new baby they had named Joan.

Because of traumatized women like Lilian, physical mediums were in demand as never before. None travelled further, or was more talked about, than Helen Duncan. Early in the war, Jean Baker remembers her coming to tea at their Gloucester home, after giving a seance at the local church where her aunt's baby had materialized down to its little jacket with the ribbons in the cuffs. Over in Somerset a widow was reunited with her husband, an RAF pilot recently killed in action. The stories are legion. In 1942 Arthur Oram had left the RAF to take a job in the Ministry of Aircraft Production when, staying with his parents in Wiltshire, the family attended one of Helen Duncan's seances. In what Oram thought was a ridiculously affected accent, Albert mocked his audience as a 'pretty hopeless crowd', but nonetheless ushered in a procession of spirits which glided around the room, stopping before each sitter and ultimately sinking into the floor as described so often. Elsewhere, a Suffolk couple were amazed by spirit forms produced by Helen, including that of a pet rabbit which returned to its tearful owner who greeted it with the words: 'To think I boiled you in a pot!' A German friend of their daughter conversed with her authentically perfumed mother in their native tongue. Such stories were widely dispersed, and not just by word of mouth. In October 1942 the SPR received a letter from a psychical researcher in Liverpool claiming that Helen Duncan's phenomena were 'at least as remarkable as those which Sir William Crookes is said to have witnessed in the personage of Katie King', to which the SPR replied that the evidence recorded at the LSA was still held to be 'unfavourable to the genuineness of the mediumship'. Refuting that evidence, in the same year B. Abdy Collins, a Council member of both the SPR and the International Institute of Psychical Investigation, published a laudatory evaluation of Mrs Duncan's powers in *Psychic Science*, of which he was editor, and a few months later J. B. McIndoe did the same.

Helen spent most time in places where the need for her services was greatest. Portsmouth was a secretive, sealed-off naval port, a place where every other family had a husband or son on a ship and to which the *Luftwaffe* were frequent visitors. Ernest Homer, who hailed from Staffordshire, and Elizabeth, the dumpy and voluble Welsh ex-entertainer who called herself his wife, ran a chemist's shop at 301 Copnor Road, above which they kept a room where seances were held. Grandly known as the 'Master Temple Psychic Centre', it was reasonably sized but drab and sparsely furnished. At the far end a cheap print of Leonardo's *Last Supper* hung from the chimney breast and upon a raised rostrum stood an altar with a wooden crucifix. In the opposite corner, near the large bay window overlooking the road, chocolate-brown cabinet curtains hung from a curtain pole supported by the picture rail, behind them a solidly constructed Jacobean chair with a leather seat and arm rests. Many of the mediums were as seedy as the premises, men such as Llewellyn Rosser and Reginald Scott-Horscroft, both known sex offenders. In November 1943 Dorothy Evans was told by Rosser that her husband, who had been killed on HMS *Illustrious* in 1941, was actually still alive and would be coming home soon – news which reached her children who became irrepressibly excited.

Helen had been visiting Portsmouth from the start of the war, if not even earlier, but by the end of 1943 she had become a regular at the Master Temple, boarding for days on end with a Mrs Bettison in Milton Road. Her reputation preceded her and grew among local people, a mixture of truth and myth ubiquitous in wartime and characteristic of the Spiritualist tradition. Mrs Homer, always drumming up trade, was fond of retelling the story where, holed up in an air-raid shelter, Helen had healed a soldier's baby afflicted with a disease of the legs by laying on her hands and frowning her way through an earnest prayer. Soon, many people in Portsmouth were clamouring to enter the darkness and witness Helen's miracles, and each fond farewell to the town only sharpened the desire for her return. At the end of

1943, Helen booked a fortnight in January at the Master Temple for which she was promised the sum of £8 per seance (sixteen times the *weekly* old age pension at that time) and with that booking under her belt left to spend Christmas with her family in Edinburgh. The seventeen-year-old Gena, in her special way, sensed that this holiday was the lull before the storm and on New Year's Day dreamt that two men were chasing her mother into a river where she thrashed about in the muddy water. The night before Helen left for Portsmouth, Gena lay awake mulling over this dream – and imagining Christ's final hours in Gethsemane – and in the morning, suitcases by the front door, pleaded in vain with her mother not to go. Watching from the window, Gena sobbed bitterly as the taxi disappeared at the end of their road, fatefully bound for the station.

6
A KIND OF CONJURATION
Trial and Denial at the Old Bailey, 1944

O n the afternoon of Tuesday, 25 November 1941, as Helen celebrated her forty-fourth birthday, several hundred miles away in the eastern Mediterranean HMS *Barham*, veteran battleship of the First World War, was cruising with HMS *Queen Elizabeth* and HMS *Valiant*, screened by destroyers on either side. At 4.26 p.m., a barely submerged German submarine, U-331, commanded by Kapitänleutnant Hans-Diedrich von Tiesenhausen, passed through the screen on the port side and fired four torpedoes, the force pushing up the hull and causing the conning tower to break the surface. Few on the *Barham* could

---

The Master Temple Psychic Centre, 301 Copnor Road, Portsmouth.

have missed the first thud, followed by two more, after which the ship began listing as the port battery flooded. Von Tiesenhausen's engineers put the U-331 into a dive a hundred yards from the fleet, just escaping the *Valiant* steaming straight at them, guns blazing. As the angle of the *Barham*'s list increased, sailors were starting to jump from the upper deck, when a colossal explosion from the 15-inch magazine threw most of those remaining into the water. Men sucked down as the ship sank were thrust up through the oil and flotsam on an enormous air bubble. Among them, Midshipman A. E. H. Sladen clung to a raft until he was picked up by HMS *Hotspur* where he found another 300 survivors, in shock deeper than they knew, laughing and singing over tea and rum. They were lucky: in all, 868 of their comrades had been incinerated, blown apart or borne down to the seabed.

The catastrophe only added to what Churchill called 'a sudden darkening of the landscape' after the fall of Greece and the air raid of 10 May, which wrecked the House of Commons and killed 1500 Londoners. On 24 May HMS *Hood* had been sunk and on 12 November, less than a fortnight before the *Barham*, the carrier HMS *Ark Royal* was lost off Gibraltar. Only two British battleships remained in the theatre and by the end of the year even they would be damaged. Von Tiesenhausen was not even aware of what he had done, guessing only that a cruiser had been sunk. Nor did his crew give it a thought as they lingered at a perilous depth waiting for danger to pass, oblivious to the 31,000 tons of the *Barham* falling silently past them. U-331 was hunted until 7 a.m., when von Tiesenhausen filed his report and was summoned to Berlin to make a propaganda broadcast. British Intelligence, who heard this on 16 December, already knew from decrypted Enigma messages that the Germans did not know they had sunk the *Barham*, confirmed by Italian ignorance of the same.

The precious time this bought for reorganizing the Mediterranean battle fleet made it impossible to announce the sinking in Britain; it was not even mentioned in the secret Weekly Intelligence Reports. The relatives of the deceased were not informed until late January 1942, whereupon von Tiesenhausen and his crew were decorated. The haunting film of the death of the *Barham*, taken from the *Valiant*, became a newsreel seen by people all over Britain who, three months after the event, reflected blackly upon the loss.

In Spiritualist circles, however, the news had been out much earlier. HMS *Barham* was a Portsmouth ship and it was almost inevitable that in the end a relative or friend of one of the crew would attend one of Helen Duncan's seances. The story has several versions, but all share the same essential features. At a seance soon after the sinking, the spirit of a dead sailor materialized for his mother, upon his cap-band the name HMS *Barham*. The next day the woman telephoned the Admiralty to ask for confirmation and was visited by two naval officers demanding to know the source of her news. She told them. Meanwhile word reached *Psychic News* editor, Maurice Barbanell, who called his friend Percy Wilson, a civil servant at the Ministry of Transport, to see if he knew anything. Wilson, a Spiritualist in Charles Glover Botham's home circle and future SNU President, first drew a blank, then learned confidentially that the *Barham* had been lost but that an announcement was not in the public interest. Among Spiritualists, this episode has for many years explained why Helen Duncan was pursued by the authorities; it has even been suggested that they feared she would disclose the secret that Britain had cracked the Enigma code. One might safely guess that a story which places humble Nell Duncan at the centre of wartime intrigue would not be entirely true; but then again, nor is it entirely false.

Recently declassified records have lifted the lid on wartime intelligence procedures. The two Admiralty investigators were probably MI5 officers from 'D' Division, which dealt with naval security. And this was not the first time Helen Duncan's name had entered MI5 files. In May 1941 Roy Firebrace, a Royal Artillery brigadier and head of Military Intelligence in Scotland, had attended one of Helen's seances in Edinburgh, possibly in the home circle of a Mrs Waymark, where Albert announced that a great British battleship had just been sunk. Firebrace, a Spiritualist who had seen Helen perform at the LSA in 1931 – he was the staff officer recorded on 17 March – was a regular member of Mrs Waymark's circle and had several spirit communicators, including Sir Arthur Conan Doyle, Lawrence of Arabia and a soldier called Mick he had known at Vimy Ridge in 1917. Later in the war, as well as serving as military attaché in Riga and Moscow, he sat on the Executive Council of the International Institute of Psychical Investigation, always dividing his time between these two sides of his life. Anyway, on returning to his office, Firebrace telephoned the Admiralty who said they had heard nothing, but received a call later that evening informing him that the flagship battlecruiser HMS *Hood* had been split in two by the mighty *Bismarck*, killing all but three of its 1418 crew in the icy waters off Greenland.

As a seance-goer, Firebrace admired Mrs Duncan, but as an intelligence officer he feared her. A year earlier the *Daily Sketch* had alleged sensationally that German agents were attending British seances to glean secrets from the dead and it seems that something of the rumour stuck. However fantastic it may seem that mediums could have been taken seriously in this way, it is important to remember that in wartime secrecy was mundane and habitual. The security problem was huge, especially 'leakage' of information at ports, matched by a paranoia that extended beyond fear of spies to the belief that a Fifth Column existed at the heart of the nation. Churchill, who liked to cast an eye over relevant files personally, saw to it that the *Daily Mirror* was investigated for criticizing the Government's conduct of the war, suspicions were raised that yellow pullovers were a badge of subversion and prior to D-Day, a *Daily Telegraph* crossword setter was arrested after code-named beaches appeared as answers. From 1940 security had been tightened through various committees, notably the Home Defence Executive, which coordinated the efforts of Home Office, MI5, MI6, police, Admiralty and other service departments, and pooled information between MI5 and the Special Branch of the Metropolitan Police. Mail, telephones and Irish radio broadcasts were monitored, and loose talk by anyone from Jehovah's Witnesses to Finnish officers on American ships – even to members of Churchill's Cabinet – was looked into and reports filed.

In fact, the addiction to secrecy – what Richard Crossman called 'the British disease' – dated back more than a decade when labour unrest and the fear of socialism had crystallized a relationship between Home Office, judiciary and police, which in practice worked to suspend civil liberties whenever national security was deemed to be at risk. Even before the First World War Churchill, as Home Secretary, had given the Secret Service powers of arrest without troubling Parliament for its opinion, and by 1931 MI5 had infiltrated Special Branch to exploit its expertise and use it as a cover. In 1940 the Home Office instructed all chief constables to report security news, however humdrum, twice a month to their MI5 regional security liaison officer and any 'matters of special security interest' at once. Soon, this became routine administration, likewise communications between police, the Director of Public Prosecutions and a legal section of MI5 known as SLB, which silenced indiscretions in the courts. In

1943 SLB split into two parts, one concentrating upon prosecutions, the other leakage of information; SLB2 had its origins in B19 formed in 1940 to investigate rumours, especially regarding shipping movements. By the time Helen Duncan hove in sight, chief constables were accustomed to referring even trivial offences against the defence regulations to the DPP who then liaised with SLB2.

Security notwithstanding, mediums remained a matter of public fraud and the courts continued to prosecute them whenever complaints were received. Dorothy Evans, whose children were told their dead father was coming home from sea, reported Llewellyn Rosser and thereby became one of the first people to alert the Portsmouth City Police (motto: 'Heaven's Light Our Guide') to the nefarious activities of the Master Temple. While all this was going on, Helen had been leaving dissatisfied customers in other coastal towns. After a seance at Torquay in March 1940, a group of friends decided that they had been the victims of a hoax and one of their number, Mrs Martin, wrote to the SPR requesting that they take action, but was disappointed by the reply. The SPR, she was told, existed not to identify frauds but to investigate genuine phenomena and in any case 'it must be remembered that a public exposure of any medium, however conclusive to sensible and impartial persons, usually produces a vigorous defence from the medium's less critical supporters'. The following summer Helen was sunning herself a short distance along the coast at Paignton in Devon. Mrs Marion Gray paid 15s to watch 'the doings' (5s more than at Torquay), but before things got under way she was asked to help examine the medium who was waiting in a bedroom. Mrs Duncan was an unpleasant surprise to her: 'A coarse and immensely fat woman, partly naked, was sitting on a chair smoking the fag end of a cigarette. The very sight of her revolted me and I'm afraid she noticed my expression. Anyhow she fixed me with a persistent stare, muttering all the time, "Oh what shall I do if Albert doesn't come tonight?"'

Albert did come, but was not the radiant ambassador for the afterlife Mrs Gray had anticipated; in fact, all the spirits looked like the medium, the seance was boring and she wanted to call the police. Instead, her son Peter, a doctor in Gosport, directed her to a sailor he knew called Jones who forwarded to Harry Price her letter, which requested advice about literature and asked: 'Don't you think something should be done to stop these harpies from battening on the misery and agony of others?' Price did and, agreeing with Jones that Mrs Duncan was 'a most repulsive and unpleasant woman as well as a fraud', dispatched a copy of the NLPR report to Paignton forthwith.

Gradually something was done. In May 1942 a medium named Stella Hughes, wife of a Hampstead borough councillor, was fined £10 plus costs under the Vagrancy Act, a prosecution which psychical investigator B. Abdy Collins condemned 'while the daily papers are allowed to feature astrological predictions, and fortune tellers openly advertise their trade in the London streets'. A year later the two policewomen who had arrested Hughes trapped another medium, Gladys Spearman, but themselves were gaoled for robbery before her case came to trial. Outrage was compounded the same month by Brighton magistrates fining a former soldier, Benjamin Misell, who had performed psychometry for another pair of undercover police officers. Barely a week later, in June 1943, a request for Stella Hughes to be pardoned was dismissed by the Home Office, intransigence which spurred on J. B. McIndoe to establish a Freedom Fund so that competent (and sympathetic) defence barristers could be appointed in every instance regardless of merit. As he had felt at the Edinburgh trial in 1933, the cause was more important than the case. The cases kept coming. One reason that newspaper horoscopes were tolerated and mediums were not was the perception at the Ministry of Information that astrology helped to keep people's spirits buoyant as it had during the depression, but by providing false information mediums had the opposite effect. Maurice Barbanell was warned about this by plain-clothes officers from Scotland Yard as early as 1940. By 1943, things had reached a head. In August a woman at Birkenhead was tried for telling the mother of a prisoner of war that he would be home soon and another client that her missing husband was still alive. The charge was fraud; but for this and at least three other prosecutions in 1943 – at Cardiff, Birmingham and Yarmouth – to the phrase 'pretending or professing to tell fortunes' from Section 4 of the 1824 Vagrancy Act was added a form of words closer to the 1735 Witchcraft Act: 'pretending to communicate with the spirits of dead persons'.

In subsequent months, similar cases were heard in magistrates courts around the country, with fines of up to £20 being imposed. This increased volume of prosecutions can be attributed in part to small groups of private citizens – operating in the spirit of The Probe – who refused to tolerate bogus mediums any longer, especially for the way they preyed upon a bereaved public, lowering morale essential to the war effort. Most prominent was the exclusive conjurors' club, the Magic Circle, which had maintained an Occult Committee as far back as the early 1920s. By late 1943 the committee (chaired by 'Ding' Dingwall who had seen both Rudi Schneider and Helen Duncan in action) was largely redundant, and was bypassed by the Honorary Secretary, Douglas Craggs, and other magicians who were organizing members nationwide into small teams to investigate mediums with the cognizance of the police. Craggs liaised with Scotland Yard, corresponded with Harry Price and was responsible for the prosecutions at Cardiff. Meanwhile, security was intensified further in the run-up to the invasion of Europe, and with greater zeal and urgency than ever before.

Official interest in Helen Duncan belongs to both campaigns: to flush out fraud and to strengthen security. By December 1943 she was being investigated by Detective Inspector Frederick Ford of the Portsmouth police, a ruddy-faced, down-to-earth detective of sixteen years' service, who had received several complaints about her and was happy to accept assistance from the Magic Circle. Despite a warning from a Charles Burrell, a dockyard worker and medium who had threatened to shop them unless they stopped their 'money racket', Mr and Mrs Homer continued to behave brazenly, even advertising in the *Portsmouth Evening News* – publicity which greatly assisted the police in their surveillance operations. One report of a Master Temple seance described the appearance of 'a white shrouded figure which purports to bring messages from the spirit world in the voices of dead people. Some of the things divulged are shocking.' One man who found these things shocking was Stanley Worth, a twenty-eight-year-old bespectacled RNVR lieutenant based at a Portsmouth shore establishment. Home on leave at Ashford in Middlesex, he had been intrigued by his mother's experiences at a local Spiritualist group where spirit guides spoke through trumpets, played the piano and performed healing through mediums. On his next leave, however, he was worried by how involved she had become and back in Portsmouth, hearing that people went to 'the spooks' above the chemist's shop in Copnor Road, decided to investigate for himself.

In the winter of 1943 Lieutenant Worth attended several services at the Master Temple where a gathering of mostly middle-aged women sang hymns, accompanied by a small organ, and clairvoyance was performed. Worth might have stopped going had Mrs Homer not told him that in the New Year an amazing materialization medium called Mrs Duncan would be visiting, but that tickets would be scarce. Back in the wardroom, when Worth told his fellow officers, the Commanding Officer was concerned he would become hooked and spoke to the Medical Officer and Worth's friend, Surgeon Lieutenant Elijah Fowler, who asked Worth if he could join him at the next seance. Worth consulted Mrs Homer, explaining that Fowler was not a believer. 'Bring him along to see Helen Duncan,' she said. 'I'll give him a seat in the front row and scare him stiff.' At a quarter to three on the afternoon of 14 January 1944 the two officers arrived at 301 Copnor Road and were led through the shop, past the advertisements for Vaseline and Virol, by a northern medium, Taylor Ineson, and into the room at the back where others were waiting. At last, with Worth leading the way, the twenty or so sitters, including a soldier and an RAF wing commander, were ushered towards the stairs where Mrs Homer ticked them from her list.

On entering the seance room, the first thing Worth saw was the weak glow from three lamps – red, green and white – all light from the street kept out by blackout curtains. Each of the seats bore a name slip, an arrangement Mrs Homer was eager to police, likewise a ban upon blackout torches which had to be deposited with Mrs Homer like guns left at the saloon door in a Western. After the usual preliminaries of searching the cabinet, examining the seance clothes and dressing the medium, Mrs Duncan entered and took up her position. Eyes shut, she slumped backwards – arms hanging, head lolling over – and began making groaning noises as the curtains were drawn. Mrs Homer led everyone in the Lord's Prayer, then called upon 'all friends to give their love and sympathy to Mrs Duncan and her guide' before initiating a rendition of Albert's favourite 'South of the Border', which petered out like a hymn at a wedding. The white and green light bulbs were unscrewed, leaving just the red one, situated behind the sitters, making it hard to see anything clearly even once their eyes had adjusted to the gloom. They were greeted by a voice, apparently that of a man but with a higher pitch, which expressed pleasure to see so many familiar faces, after which Albert appeared, looking like a length of cloth with a piece cut away where the face should be. Lieutenant Worth met the substantial physical form of his 'aunt' (dead from bowel trouble) even though all his aunts were still alive, and a similarly bulky spirit came through for Taylor Ineson, claiming to be his brother, who shook his hand and in Ineson's Yorkshire brogue confided that he didn't think much of the medium: *too fat*. The dead returned from the war: a woman whose son was missing in action received a soldier; the ghost of a man killed in an explosion in Singapore proffered a stump. On a lighter note, Peggy sang a chorus of 'Loch Lomond' before melting away with the words 'I'm gaun doon noo'; and then came Bronco the parrot who said 'Pretty Polly', followed by a cat and a rabbit, both nondescript white oblongs – the former miaowing, the latter realistically silent. The show closed with the medium lurching from the cabinet flailing her arms and crashing down next to Mrs Homer, nicotine levels dangerously low. At Mr Homer's request, Worth gave her a cigarette and the lights came up.

In the morning Worth visited Portsmouth police station, where he was interviewed by Detective Inspector Ford who asked him if he would attend a meeting the following afternoon; Worth already had a ticket. This was an ordinary service where, in broad daylight, a hymn was sung, prayers said, and Helen Duncan, dressed in white and eyes closed, delivered a sermon in the voice of Albert, exhorting the congregation to aspire to more spiritual things. Suddenly, to sustain interest, Helen announced that the spirit of a little girl called Audrey had taken her hand and pointed to Captain Barnes, a retired Indian Army officer, known to have lost a daughter – a daughter called Shirley. 'I'm sorry, I made a mistake,' she admitted upon correction. 'I should have said Shirley; I got the name wrong.' The leading lady sat down, rolling her eyes, and let her new travelling companion, Sunderland collier's wife Frances Brown, do a turn; she too saw invisible spirits and waved her arms. On the Monday Worth was issued with a policeman's torch and whistle, and that evening returned to Copnor Road where he booked two seats for the next seance on Wednesday the 19th. His sidekick was to be his good friend Rupert Cross, a bookseller and War Reserve Constable. They arrived shortly before seven and gave Mr Homer 25s in the kitchen before going upstairs and taking their places in the second row behind the chairs reserved for the Homers. Preliminaries over, one of the thirty sitters, Able Seaman Peter Pickett from Kent, who had lost his mother as a baby, received a burly woman shrouded in white, arms outstretched. Another spirit form took her place, then another, and it was from this third manifestation that Cross took his cue, Worth reaching for the illicit torch in his pocket as his partner raised himself from his seat.

Exactly what happened next is disputed, but it was something like this. Barging through the front row, Cross threw open the cabinet to reveal Mrs Duncan pushing away several yards of cloth, which he grabbed. Mr Homer then kicked Cross, someone knocked Worth's torch and the cloth was yanked away. 'It's gone into the audience,' said Cross agitatedly, to which a surprisingly composed Mrs Duncan replied: 'Of course it's gone; it had to go somewhere.' Pointing his torch, Worth saw her, still in her black satin seance dress, bending down hell-bent on putting on her shoes. Task completed, she screamed she was sick – indeed, that she was dying – and needed a doctor. Worth blew his whistle, signalling for Ford and three other detectives to enter, they having been let into the shop by another policeman attending a separate meeting on Ford's instructions. Frances Brown urged Mr Homer to make sure his daughter Christine, a geriatric nurse, kept her mouth shut. Ford switched on the light and, while a cursory search was made, asked if anyone had the cloth, but ignored the pleas of Christine Homer and others to be frisked; nor did he challenge a woman wearing a large sling on her arm. Instead, armed with a magistrate's warrant, he ordered the crestfallen medium to get changed (under the supervision of the policewoman), bundled up the seance clothes as evidence and arrested her on suspicion of contravening the Vagrancy Act by 'pretending to hold communication with the spirits of deceased persons'. After she had been led away, Ford heard Mrs Homer remind everyone that Jesus had suffered like this and made a mental note to add blasphemy to fraud.

Accompanied by a nurse, Jane Rust, a defence witness who was to impress Mollie Goldney, Helen was taken by car to Kingston Cross police station where she was cautioned. 'What can I say?' she replied limply, but remembered to warn them she was a diabetic with coronary problems, whereupon a police surgeon was called who certified that she was suffering from 'palpitation due to a fatty heart' but well enough to be put in the cells. In the morning she was photographed and fingerprinted, fed breakfast, tea and a cigarette, then hauled unrepresented before the magistrates who, at the request of Chief Constable Arthur West, remanded her in custody until 25 January. Once Ford had collected her insulin kit from Milton Road, the weeping prisoner was driven to Holloway Prison in north London where she languished in a cell, unaware of the intensity of activity elsewhere. Apart from the Portsmouth police, who at once set colleagues in Edinburgh to work, the newspapers, both national and provincial, seized the story – CONSTABLE GRABS 'SPIRIT' AT CITY SEANCE: SHOCKING THINGS DIVULGED, blared the *Portsmouth Evening News* – and even the BBC announced the arrest. The Spiritualist press was naturally quick to mount its soapbox, a typically hyperbolic headline from *Two Worlds* reading:

FREEDOM VERSUS THE HOME OFFICE

DEAD HAND GRIPS GOVERNMENT

THE GOVERNMENT IS STILL AFRAID OF GHOSTS!

Percy Wilson at the Ministry of Transport, at this time President of the SNU London District Council, had already heard of Helen's plight and was making arrangements to use the Freedom Fund to appoint learned counsel for the next hearing, even though representation by a solicitor would have been normal at this preliminary stage of proceedings. One man seemed ideal for the job, C.E. Loseby, a Spiritualist barrister who had defended mediums in the past and who had acted as chief spokesman for an SNU deputation to the Home Office six months earlier. Once he had agreed to accept the case, therefore, it was him that the SNU's solicitor Godfrey Elkin briefed.

Charles Loseby has been much criticised by Spiritualists, not for lack of commitment and effort, but because he was young and inexperienced. In fact, he was neither and it was precisely because the defending counsel in 1933 had been rather green, and not a Spiritualist, that he was chosen. Loseby was sixty-two years old. Called to the Bar in 1913, the following year he had pulled strings to get a commission, and during thirty months' service in France was gassed (which gave his voice a husky quality) and badly shot through the arm, both of which injuries left him wondering whether he would ever practise again. To say that the mental trauma was worse has become a cliché of modern warfare, but it was nonetheless true in the case of Captain Loseby. When in later life he sat down to write a memoir of those days, he thought of his working-class men, 'like sheep to the slaughter', their expressions indescribable; and he thought of the two square inches a sniper needed to take off a head, the corpses mortared with slime into the trench wall and the hum of the rotary fans as German sappers tunnelled beneath them. The war became part of him, as it became part of English culture and belief, and it was more natural than it may seem now for the first part of his honeymoon in 1921 to be spent on a tour of the battlefields of Flanders.

Proud of his service, especially his Military Cross and command of the 1st Lancashire Fusiliers, he did not relinquish his commission until 1920, by which time he was already a Conservative Member of Parliament. He campaigned on many social issues including female emancipation, establishing a Ministry of Health and, most energetically, pensions for disabled and 'nerve-shaken' servicemen, for whom he secured an extra £20 million. In 1921 he joined Lloyd George to fight godless socialism, but crossed the House again in 1929 and was returned as Tory MP for West Nottingham; in between he worked as a barrister on the Midland Circuit and in 1922 sent a labourer to the gallows for murdering his sweetheart. Emotionally reserved, he was passionate about the beliefs war had inspired and liked to play devil's advocate, believed he could detect impostors and relished challenges – on the golf course, at the dispatch box, or in court. As for so many, his Spiritualism (not shared by his family) was the product of agnosticism, empiricism and a hunger for a metaphysical truth able to make sense of the past and offer hope. So by the time that Ernest Oaten pointed him towards 'the irresistible conclusions to be drawn from the accurate observation of phenomena', his conversion was already virtually complete.

At the Home Office, where the first file on Helen Duncan was opened, officials privately expressed surprise that Loseby and the SNU should be defending 'such a patent charlatan . . . a barefaced and not particularly skilful fraud'. But even if Loseby had known their feelings he scarcely would have cared. Indeed, he had taken up the challenge of defending Mrs Duncan with alacrity. Quite indifferent to those who could not accept what he believed to be incontrovertible truths, he dug out his dog-eared copy of Ellis Powell's pamphlet *Psychic Science and Barbaric Legislation* (1917) and, against a passage about gifted mediums being at the mercy of ignorant policemen and prejudiced magistrates, he penned a note: 'True a quarter of a century later. Do not rest until an end is put to it.' This he had adopted as a crusade and he knew the Duncan brief could be his finest hour. For in this proletarian housewife could be seen the epitome of the persecuted minority described by Powell and for that reason Loseby, patrician paragon of the officer class, humbly subordinated himself to her. He had probably forgotten acting in a knockabout production entitled *An Eastern Episode* on the Western Front, where he took the part of Second Slave to Captain North's Plumi Jham – an Egyptian sorceress. But there was real irony in this, for farce was about to be repeated as tragedy and Loseby would be playing the role for real.

At Portsmouth Magistrates Court on 25 January, the police were surprised to see a barrister, still more by his arguments. Helen Duncan was a distinguished medium whose life had been endangered, Loseby told the court, and by arresting her, finger-printing her and denying bail, the police had made her into 'a furtive and dangerous criminal', out of line with the Home Secretary's wish that the pre-trial machinery of the 1824 Vagrancy Act be suspended. This raised cries of 'hear, hear', swiftly silenced by the magistrates. After five days in Holloway – where she alleged a wardress had thrown a bucket of cold water over her for complaining that her bath was too hot – Helen's head was swimming and she felt as if they were speaking about someone else. The first thing she had said on being arrested was 'I have nothing to worry about'; but she was worried now. Detective Inspector Ford relayed Chief Constable West's plea for another two weeks' grace while the Director of Public Prosecutions considered the case, but added that the police no longer objected to bail. Moreover, the Portsmouth police wanted representation by counsel if that was the way the SNU wished to proceed. Helen was released on sureties of £100 (put up by J. B. McIndoe) and another hearing timetabled for 8 February. It is safe to assume that as Chief Constable, West had consulted his MI5 officer regarding the pronouncements about HMS *Barham*, if not now, then fourteen months earlier.

From a small dusty office called 'C' Division (Criminal Matters) in the Home Office an assistant under-secretary, Francis Graham-Harrison, was tasked to maintain contact with Detective Inspector Ford and the Director of Public Prosections who had agreed to represent the Portsmouth police in court. On 2 February Ford submitted a report to the DPP, Sir Edward Tindal Atkinson, summarizing events surrounding Helen Duncan so far, adding: 'This may or may not be true, but I have reason to believe that she is a person who is addicted to drink.' Every possible type of personal information was gathered in support of the case and here police in Edinburgh were happy to help. Records showed that Henry Duncan owned the cottage at Kirkhill Drive, but paid no income tax – although this was not surprising, given that his wife's occupation was illegal. The police also paid him a visit, and learned that he settled all the bills and that Helen had no bank account of her own. The Edinburgh Criminal Investigation Department said that Mrs Duncan, well-known as a medium in the city, had been fined for fraud in 1933 and supplied details of this in an extract of her conviction – for which they charged their Portsmouth colleagues a fee of 2s.

Having read his report, the Assistant DPP, Arthur Sefton-Cohen, met Ford and concluded that given the limited evidence, a charge of conspiracy to defraud would be preferable to vagrancy. This way, there would have to be a jury trial and in the event of conviction a custodial sentence. Sefton-Cohen appointed a representative, J. E. Robey, instructing him to request summonses against the Homers and Frances Brown, and to challenge the claim that Helen Duncan 'was capable of holding communication with deceased persons and causing the spirits thereof to materialise'. The Home Office were notified of the modified strategy. At 10.50 a.m. the next morning, 8 February, Helen was charged in the presence of her solicitor, Mr Elkin, who advised her not to reply, and was driven to the magistrates court. A long queue stretched up the steps to the front door, people in hats and coats posing for photographers, all smiling faces and Victory-V signs. Proceedings were brisk. When Helen heard the charge again she fainted and had to be helped up by the policemen at her side. Fresh summonses were issued, the Homers' served upon them that afternoon at the Master Temple, Mrs Brown's dispatched to her home at Houghton-le-Spring, County Durham, to which she had fled. The court was adjourned, pending arrests, and a new date set for 29 February. Mrs Homer, too, had recently gone to ground, although W. A. E. Jones from the *Daily Herald* tracked her down to her bedsit in South Norwood where she described Helen as 'a comparative stranger', but a natural medium to whom she had paid £8 per seance, amounting to £112 over six days – the equivalent of three months' wages for a lorry driver. Ford, meanwhile, reported to the Home Office, interviewed navy widow Dorothy Evans and pressed Edinburgh for more details of the 1933 trial.

Protests poured in during February. Manchester MP Eleanor Rathbone received a letter from a constituent, enclosing the front page of *Psychic News*, complaining that the arrest of Mrs Duncan ran counter to the struggle for liberty in Europe. Rathbone's search for information ended with the Parliamentary Under-Secretary at the Home Office, Sir Osbert Peake, who, having met the 1943 SNU deputation, was in a good position to inform her that the police did not use the law as a means of oppression, 'but to protect the public against those who trade on the ignorant and credulous, and especially those who in wartime exploit the anxiety of people about the fate of relatives and friends serving with the Forces'. The Home Office itself was pestered. Herbert Morrison received a petition from Morecambe in Lancashire signed by, among others, several soldiers and a Glasgow policeman, but used Ford's latest report to stand his ground: the police had acted lawfully and Helen Duncan had not. On the evening of Monday, 28 February, J. E. Robey met Chief Constable West at the Queen's Hotel in Southsea to give the charge a final polish, then, like his comedian father before a big show, got a good night's sleep.

At the hearing the next morning there were distracting noises-off. Somewhere, someone was bashing out dance tunes on a piano, overlaid with the dull drone of RAF bombers, the raids over Germany intensifying as D-Day drew closer. Today, however, Charles Loseby was fighting his own war of liberation and squared up to the youthful Robey who was brimming with disparaging theatrical phrases. After the four accused had pleaded not guilty, Robey gave Mrs Duncan's act the thumbs-down, judging it inferior to the great Victorian conjuring shows; but his real point, and one stressed by the Prosecution throughout the trial, was that it was not the truth of Spiritualism that was at stake but whether the defendants had conspired to commit fraud. Rupert Cross denied that Mrs Duncan had looked either blue or distressed, nor had she fallen over. Ford admitted she might have looked blue but, glancing at her in the dock, added: 'No bluer than she is in court today.'

The involvement of counsel at a preliminary stage, the conspiracy charge and the securing of the DPP's support, all made the relocation of the trial to the Old Bailey – the Central Criminal Court in London – rather inevitable, however fantastic it seemed for a fraudulent medium to be so extravagantly handled. The DPP's office within the Bailey got weaving and the Clerk of the Court set about framing an indictment that could not be picked apart by a clever barrister. The Clerk's discoveries were significant. Mr Homer could not be indicted as a chemist, because under the 1933 Pharmacy and Poisons Act he was not one; he was merely a drugstore proprietor. Nor could Mrs Homer be indicted by that name because she was already Mrs Elizabeth Jones, a revelation which solved one problem for the Prosecution, namely that husband and wife could not legally conspire together. In the first week of March prosecuting counsel was appointed. Usually the Central Criminal Bar Mess, a permanent Bar attached to the court, dealt with cases on a rota system, leaving only the most serious trials for Treasury Counsel and the Law Officers of the Crown. Sir Edward Tindal Atkinson, however, considered this to be 'a case of some difficulty' and so, on the advice of the Attorney-General, nominated John Maude, whom he thought 'likely to handle this rather unusual case with ability'. Maude, the son of a well-known actor, product of Eton, Christ Church and the Middle Temple, had been Treasury Counsel in 1942 and became King's Counsel in 1943; had funds permitted, the SNU would have been well-advised to have appointed Treasury Counsel against a KC. Now the odds were stacked against them. Maude's junior would be the gawky, inexperienced but able Henry Elam for whom the case was just another brief until he saw its full implications.

On 15 March a private meeting took place between Maude, Elam and the DPP, which would be a turning point in the history of Spiritualism – albeit one, its details buried in secret archives for more than half a century, hitherto unacknowledged. To the DPP and to Chief Constable West, even a charge of conspiracy to defraud seemed shaky because they would have to prove beyond reasonable doubt that money had been paid to see materialized spirits, whereas seance organizers were usually careful to avoid promising anything. Clearly, something else would be needed to nail the case down. By the end of the meeting, which lasted one and a half hours, a solution had been found in a single clause of a largely obsolete statute: Section 4 of the 1735 Witchcraft Act. When James I's 1604 legislation had been expunged from the statute books, its terms were imported into an act of repeal in order to make explicit their nullification, and a new section interpolated for 'the more effectual preventing and punishing any pretences to such arts or powers . . . whereby ignorant persons are frequently deluded and defrauded'. Thus Helen Duncan's perception that she was being tried as a witch was about to become much more vivid, and her mother's prophecy that she would be burned at the stake as such borne out to a far greater extent than she ever could have foreseen as a second-sighted child in Callander.

Like Mollie Goldney, Harry Price declined to participate as an expert witness – he had been ill with angina – although he was present in the Old Bailey on at least one day. He did, however, contribute indirectly. Predictably, he sent Chief Constable West a copy of *Regurgitation and the Duncan Mediumship* who, in turn, passed it on to the DPP with remarks about the maid, Mary McGinlay. Maude thought she should be present so that she could be 'called in rebuttal' should the Defence attempt to demonstrate Helen Duncan's good character and most especially if Helen went into the witness box. The stereograms in Price's book were also invaluable ammunition for cross-examination and would corroborate Cross's assertion that the ectoplasm was really old cheesecloth. The 1933 prosecution was also held in reserve, likewise the discovery that Frances Brown had served two gaol terms in 1929 for the theft of goods, a list of which was typed on ten foolscap sheets. In mid-March the DPP requested more photographs from Price who arranged for the Librarian of the University of London – his books having found a home there in 1938 – to hand them over to the police. By 22 March the brief for the Prosecution was complete, predicting that Loseby's proposed strategy of calling up to fifty witnesses would not succeed because they were bound to describe events from before January 1944, which were irrelevant to the case. Anyway, as far as Maude and Elam were concerned,

It would seem that the Prosecution should succeed in establishing that Duncan was not acting as a genuine medium at Portsmouth by the cumulative effect of the witnesses for the Prosecution stating what they saw and heard, which any person with an ounce of common sense would liken to a Punch and Judy show, which had as its climax the seizure of the medium and the disappearance of the white cloth.

The Prosecution's evidence did not amount to much; but then what Maude understood at once, and Elam came to understand, was that the Witchcraft Act rendered this unimportant. What they needed to establish was not so much that Helen Duncan was an impostor, but that she had *pretended* – falsely claimed – to conjure up the spirits of the dead; and the Defence, in its endeavour to demonstrate that the dead could be brought back to life, would do that for them. Loseby's only hope was, first, to focus on the Prosecution's failure to produce the sheet under which Mrs Duncan masqueraded as a ghost, and, second, to field a witness able to undermine Worth's credibility. But even if it had mattered that much, Loseby, the righteous crusader, was far too head-strong to listen to advice.

The trial began on the morning of Thursday, 23 March 1944 in Court No. 4 of the Blitz-damaged Old Bailey. The public gallery remained out of bounds, and eager spectators squeezed past each other in the precincts and corridors, hopeful of a downstairs seat or at least a place outside the door. It is possible to recover the court's experience a little too authentically, conveying the list-lessness and ennui felt by all but a few as Loseby's twenty-fifth, thirty-fifth and, finally, his forty-fifth defence witness took the oath. More revealing are the emotions of that strange week in March, not least those of the quixotic, ill-starred Charles Loseby, the tragic figure fated to do right by no one.

Long before he was unnerved by stifled yawns and judicial obstruction, Loseby was troubled. After breakfast at his Kensington home he had paced the hallway in the manner which suggested to his wife and daughter that a great burden was weighing down on him. In court, once again he noted the impres-sive effect of John Maude's good looks and stature, his strong voice contrasting with Loseby's own softer, smoother drawl.

Loseby was supported by Mr Simpson Pedler, a fellow member of Gray's Inn with two decades' experience at the Bar; but even as the junior he did not look up to Loseby the way Elam did to Maude, a figure whose self-assurance no amount of swotting, zeal, or casuistic ingenuity could assail. 'He spoke', Loseby admitted, 'with such adroitness, skill and economy of words that any ill-informed person might well imagine that there could be no effective answer to the case as he set it out.' The judge, Recorder of London Sir Gerald Dodson, a practising Christian, was even-handed with his contempt, measuring out professional irritability to all and sundry without breaching the Old Bailey custom of humane treatment of prisoners in the dock. By the end, however, even Dodson could not conceal his desire to be elsewhere, perhaps back at the opening night of *The Rebel Maid*, the humorous musical he had part-authored, which may have caused him some wry amusement when he heard about the Duncans' rebellious servant, Mary McGinlay.

The witnesses were nervous, the exception being Stanley Worth whose testimony had become the vanguard of the Prosecution as the charge evolved from vagrancy to conspiracy to witchcraft. At the Portsmouth hearing, moreover, Cross had appeared uncomfortable whereas Worth, dapper in his lieutenant's uniform, Loseby noted, 'gave his evidence with skill and a good eye to effect, being assisted in the latter by a flickering smile which seemed to be under command'. And he could do all the voices, including Albert's. More worrying was Loseby's dilemma, one faced by all defending barristers: whether to let his clients testify and have them incriminate themselves under cross-examination; or deny them the privilege and make it seem they had something to hide. Daunted as they were, in the case of all but Mr Homer, Loseby chose the latter which, Elam remembered, looked very bad indeed. As for others present, the spectating public were boss-eyed and garrulous, the psychical researchers serious and studious, the Spiritualist women pious and lachrymose. W.A.E. Jones of the *Daily Herald*, who attended on all seven days, did not warm to Helen the martyr and her disciples, many of whom had come up from Portsmouth. 'As she waddled her way to face the judge and jury, women threw their arms around her, kissed her, sobbed over her and blessed her in whispering voices.'

The first, electrifying day was taken up by the opening speech for the Prosecution and Worth's account of the seances of 14, 17 and 19 January. Maude's gentle but cruel mockery, deftly poised ironies, learned perspectives and calm appeals to common sense lowered the Defence into a slippery-sided pit from which it would struggle to emerge. As Loseby cross-examined Worth, the formal protocols of the exchange – begged pardons and craved indulgences – gave way to raised voices, the Recorder interjecting that the court could hear them both perfectly well. They squabbled over whether Worth thought himself to be a spy and, indeed, which of them had first used the word, Worth protesting that Loseby had put it in his mouth so he had used it. To Loseby's sarcastic parody of Mrs Duncan 'playing bogey-bogey with a sheet over her head', he needed to add nothing, acceding effortlessly to this interpretation. Worth was unshaken and Loseby knew it. More than that, he was utterly persuasive, a seductive quality which smoothed over the inconsistencies so hotly scorned by the psychical researchers. The Recorder wound up proceedings for the day by asking for a sketch plan of the seance room, and releasing Mrs Duncan and her co-defendants on bail. Outside, Frances Brown was not her usual talkative self and shielded her face from the cameras.

The second day began with Worth, examined by Elam, defending his eyesight – he had a lazy eye – until the Recorder cut him off before he started on his optician's opinion. Next

Elijah Fowler, in his diffident Scots voice, confirmed Worth's account of the first seance; a police photographer amused the jury with his imitations of spirit photographs seized from Frances Brown; Mr and Mrs William Lock said their piece, which included the story of the return of Pinky, an RAF pilot shot through the head; and Mr Burrell likened Peggy to a fairy in a Christmas pantomime. Kitty Jennings, an Air Raid Precautions supervisor, related how at an afternoon seance on 19 January 'this wretched Scotch child' (Maude's words), jigging up and down, had confessed to using Christine Homer's perfume and lipstick. When she hesitated before describing Peggy, Maude raised a laugh by asking whether she looked more like Helen of Troy or a pillowcase. A seasoned actress before the war, Mrs Jennings agreed with Loseby that the regional accents would be hard to mimic – unless, of course, one were used to doing such a thing. Finally, after Rupert Cross had corroborated the second part of Worth's testimony, Detective Inspector Ford was brow-beaten by Loseby for failing to search the sitters and his defence that it would have been pointless without the presence of a doctor was received sceptically. Again and again, Loseby asked for the significance of this until the Recorder stopped him, as much from boredom as a desire to save Ford's blushes, whereupon Maude stepped in: 'It is obvious there are certain places where things can be concealed?' 'Yes, sir,' replied Ford briskly. And with that, Maude rested the case for the Crown.

That evening Loseby paced some more, while he rehearsed the Defence's opening speech. In the morning he steeled himself and, before another crowded court, did his level best to discredit the Prosecution's witnesses, while steering towards the assertion that Helen Duncan was a genuine materialization medium. The Recorder, for the time being, kept his feelings to himself, but they resembled those expressed by the Lord Chief Justice in the mid-1930s, namely that the validity of Spiritualism as a religion was a topic 'better discussed in the bracing air at a conference in Blackpool'. Loseby carried on obliviously, digging his hole deeper, making the sides ever more slippery. His attempt to call the prisoners out of order was blocked, as was his proposal to present Mrs Duncan for a test seance later on. He spoke of Mrs Duncan having 'gone down like a shot rabbit' when Worth shone his torch, and referred to the burn on her cheek where ectoplasm had re-entered her body; all eyes turned to the dock but no mark was visible. The whey-faced, unassuming Mr Homer who followed, did little to incriminate himself – describing a materialization of Mrs Homer's grandmother joining her to sing a Welsh hymn – but neither did he say anything to exculpate Mrs Duncan, still less to substantiate Loseby's thesis that the bodies of gifted mediums were portals through which the spirits of the dead revisited earth. Pathos turned to bathos when, once more, Loseby sought approval for Mrs Duncan to perform a private seance for the jury and this time the Recorder explained his refusal. Like a medieval ordeal, he argued, such a demonstration 'might operate unfairly against this woman because, supposing the spirit, if such a thing there be, was not mindful to come to her assistance on this occasion, then the verdict would have to be against her'. If Loseby quailed inside, he did his best not to show it as he called the first of his witnesses.

The twinkle in the eye of George Mackie, the RAF wing commander present on 19 January, did not alter the court's impression that, like Loseby's other 'skilled investigators', he took himself too seriously. Of the fact that he had been reunited with his mother who had died in Australia in 1927 he was quite sure. 'A man knows his mother,' he observed. 'I have the advantage also of knowing my father', to which the Recorder, eyebrows raised, responded politely: 'Well, that's something', causing some spectators to rub their smiling faces. Harold Gill of Southsea followed, Maude talking him through his recollection of the ectoplasm by dangling a piece of butter muslin, much to the consternation of the Spiritualists. Mrs Gill knew about the belief that ectoplasm could rush back into the medium's body from a lantern lecture given by a Mr Lilley of the Portsmouth City Police fingerprinting section in November 1943 – a curious detail not mentioned again.

The fourth day of the trial, Tuesday, 28 March, marked a watershed, the repetitiveness of the stories, however marvellous and poignant, eating away at the roots of the Recorder's tolerance. Proceedings resumed with some mild distraction in the form of documentary evidence: some receipts and letters of thanks for seance profits donated to the Wireless for the Blind Fund, the Two Worlds Publishing Company and the SNU Freedom Fund. The Homers claimed that all 'surplus money' went to charities, receipts for £450 of which the police managed to trace, although less than £30 of that came from the Duncan seances. The first witness was a Mrs Cole who, speaking of the manifestation of her friend, complained that some people present in court were laughing at her trying to remember how long Albert's beard was and, from that point, for the Recorder all was sorrow tinged with desperation and anger, a darkening mood which Loseby at least pretended not to notice. Towards the end of the afternoon, having heard a Royal Marine speak fondly of the return of his grandparents and unable to bear another second, Dodson interrupted Elam cross-examining a witness about the kind of fairy light she had seen in Mrs Duncan's hand:

THE RECORDER: We will go into that tomorrow. Mr Loseby, can you give us any help at all with regard to the witnesses?

MR LOSEBY: My Lord, I shall call no more Portsmouth witnesses.

THE RECORDER: Any other sort of witnesses?

MR LOSEBY: Yes, my Lord.

THE RECORDER: How many more? I want to know, roughly.

MR LOSEBY: It is hard for me to estimate. I had in mind forty to fifty.

By way of reply, and yearning for his tea, the Recorder said nothing but merely scraped back his chair and made good his escape through the door behind the Bench.

Day five brought no relief to Sir Gerald Dodson. On top of his feelings of malaise, he became squeamish when Loseby, encouraged by the presence of Harry Price, speculated too long on the appearance of regurgitated cheesecloth. Basil Kirkby, a retired businessman, said he had spent twenty years researching 'the stuff known as ectoplasm', behind which lay a power almost as amazing as radium had been to Marie Curie, and which he had observed alongside Sir Oliver Lodge and Sir Arthur Conan Doyle. Mention of a spirit budgerigar which, according to Kirkby, said 'Pretty boy, pretty boy' (words a budgerigar of his acquaintance had used) led the Recorder to take over the questioning whereupon he learned that everyone has a spirit guide. 'Have we?' Dodson asked incredulously. 'Yes, every one of us,' replied Kirkby, who had Chang, a Chinaman with an eighteen-inch moustache and a swinging pigtail. 'Well, I don't seem to have one with regard to this evidence,' said the Recorder. Next came an RAF officer who had seen Mrs Duncan at the Edinburgh Psychic College and Library in 1937 and again, since the outbreak of war, at Preston;

Lilian Bailey, a medium employed by the IIPR; and Hannen Swaffer, the journalist who had trumpeted the British visit of American medium 'Margery' in 1929, and the first defence witness to give Elam a run for his money.

After the wife of a Glasgow forgemaster had told of meeting her dead father in 1931, – complete, if that is the right word, with missing eye – it was the turn of B. Abdy Collins who earned the Recorder's respect by his having been a magistrate and sessions judge in India. Mrs Duncan's manifestations radiated an unearthly phosphorescence, he said, providing evidence of survival almost as compelling as that offered by the ex-miner Jack Webber and quite unlike a deception he himself had exposed at Reading. Testimony for this, the fifth day, ended with a Battersea medium describing the spirit of her husband Alf, and a man convinced by his wrinkly old granny's Suffolk accent. The Recorder shaved off ten minutes' free time and the court adjourned. Next morning the Recorder's spirits were lifted a little by Loseby's announcement that this would be the last day on which he would call witnesses. First up was Alfred Dodd, the Shakespeare hobbyist (he believed that Bacon wrote the sonnets) who had seen his first sweetheart Helen. The Recorder's patience being fresh, Dodd was permitted to speak at length, for instance, claiming that Mary, Queen of Scots, a seance favourite, had struggled in vain to materialize at a seance in 1940 but had managed to pass on the message that she was a lady attired in 'an old-world dress' who spoke Scots tinged with French and had lost her head on the block – the sort of historical sketch one can imagine Mr Cumming having once made at Callander Parish School.

Thus far Helen's 1933 conviction had been kept quiet, because by the terms of the law of evidence it was no indication of guilt, and but for Loseby's strategy it would not even have been mentioned. Now, Dodd's allusion to 1933 prompted Elam to ask for the fact to be disclosed in rebuttal of the Defence's continued claim that Helen Duncan was a genuine medium. The jury retired, the story was revealed through Dodd's cross-examination and the question of whether the evidence would now be admissible was discussed. Elam hesitated and asked that Maude be brought back (remember he was simultaneously defending an accused murderer in Court No. 1), whereupon the Recorder ruled that Loseby had chosen to draw upon events pre-dating January 1944 and now the Prosecution should be allowed to do the same. Loseby's hopes were fading and the failure of his case was etched into the faces of the newly returned jurors, who remained unmoved even when Dodd, retelling the story of the Edinburgh trial, reduced a murmuring Mrs Duncan to tears with his affirmation of her qualities. 'She is a genuine materialization medium,' Dodd stated firmly, 'and anything I can do to help that lady in her distress, I come here to do it, because I owe her a debt.'

Throughout the trial, Helen was surrounded by people who felt similarly obliged, if not always for what she had done for them personally, then at least for what she symbolized to the Spiritualist movement. Released on bail, she stayed at SNU official Percy Wilson's house in Wimbledon, where she conducted six test seances, others having already been held before the start of proceedings, both there and at the Marylebone Spiritualist Association. At least one of these sessions was attended by Charles Loseby. As Percy Wilson recalled in the 1950s:

> After a day's hearing, we took her straight to Wimbledon, gave her some tea with good red jam – we were thinking, of course, of the regurgitation suggestion – and then upstairs to the seance room . . . I have never seen such a mass of ectoplasm. It bundled up on her bosom, dropped to the

floor and then jumped up to her hand. It was as a result of this experience that we offered the court a sitting.

Wilson's son, Laurence, was almost knocked over by a tube of rubbery ectoplasm upon which a mischievous Albert had invited him to tread. Another son, Geoffrey, an undergraduate on vacation (later a scientific officer for the Admiralty), was appointed as a messenger for the Defence and was present throughout the trial, which bored him as much as it did anyone else. The seances at his home, however, were something quite different, with ribbons of wriggling grey ectoplasm and an abundance of apported flowers, Hylda Lewis-style. Loseby, too, was convinced and once he had agreed to suggest a test seance to judge and jury, Wilson and his wife hastily built a portable cabinet from copper gas piping, black cloth, curtain rings and an adapted standard lamp fitted with a rheostat.

Loseby made the most of his last day by calling another fourteen witnesses. Dr John Winning, Assistant Medical Officer for Glasgow and a committed psychical investigator, claimed to have seen over 400 of Mrs Duncan's manifestations, speaking not just in different accents, but in Gaelic, German and Hebrew. Relatives he had met in spirit were quite unlike the medium: his mother was slim, his brother quick in his movements, his grandmother eighty-four. Indeed, stretched over forty seances, Winning had attended the family reunion if not from hell, then from somewhere lighter and brighter. Aunt Elaine called by, as did several uncles including one whose features were entirely different from Mrs Duncan's, not least his beard and moustache. Winning was followed by a psychic healer from Baker Street, dewy-eyed veteran of 150 Duncan seances, who saw a child with withered arms; a Frenchwoman whose one-legged daughter sang *Au clair de la lune* and displayed dancing skills denied her in life; and a

212

retired sanitary inspector from Kendal, slightly deaf, who received a message from his drowned daughter tapped out in Morse code. Vincent Woodcock, an electrical draftsman from Blackpool, identified first his wife from the spirit's palpitating heart, then his stepmother from a fatal wound sustained during the Manchester Blitz. The only witness who brought anything new to proceedings was Sir James Herries, an Edinburgh journalist and magistrate whose class and credibility were invaluable to Loseby. His friend Sir Arthur Conan Doyle had returned to him at a Duncan seance, if only to answer 'yes' to a question before fading back, his legendary stamina for public engagements now sadly diminished. Herries had disagreed with the verdict in 1933 and, prompted by Loseby, pronounced Price's cheesecloth theory 'perfectly absurd'. For poor Sir Gerald Dodson the afternoon ended in an evidential blur – more glowing dogs and birds, another one-legged relative, boasts about spiritual healing, a doctor talking to his mother (in Swedish), the return of a French youth killed on the Maginot Line in 1940 and a South African called Gilbert who had perished in a plane crash. At last, Loseby said that he had called enough witnesses and the Recorder, in full agreement, asked that the case be concluded the next day. 'One would like to reciprocate the patience the jury have shown', he remarked with an economical smile, 'by not inflicting more upon them than we can help.'

That evening, a dinner was held in Helen's honour at the Bonnington Hotel in Southampton Row. After they had finished eating, Loseby suggested she try to procure a spiritual message on a pad which he placed under the tablecloth, and which she held while she continued chatting and smoking. After a while, they were rewarded, but with scrawled words which made the dinner seem even more of a valedictory last supper: 'Two will be convicted and two will go free.' In the morning, judgement day found the court jaded, the defendants more alert now, fearing the worst. For simplicity's sake all the charges were dropped – including 'effecting a public mischief' by exploiting the war bereaved – except that of conspiracy to contravene the Witchcraft Act. In Loseby's closing speech, the two hours and 11,000 words of which persuaded the Recorder that his optimism had been premature, the jury were asked whether they felt that the Prosecution had proved beyond reasonable doubt that Helen Duncan had exercised or pretended to exercise a kind of conjuration, and whether the 1735 Act was an appropriate statute upon which to try her and her co-defendants. Perhaps this was the point when someone passed Henry Elam a note reading: 'The only evil spirit is now known as Hooch; in 1735 all spirits were evil.' If so, Loseby was too busy with his own mockery to notice Elam smirk, so engrossed was he in heaping derision upon the tribunal which had convicted Helen in 1933 and, indeed, upon the whole of Scotland, a country, he said, which had objected to the introduction of the potato as an act of impiety.

John Maude's cool-headed response was every bit as withering as Loseby had feared, a rhetorical *coup de grâce*. The world beyond the veil, he put it to the jury, was a dull and ridiculous world, not awesome, merely awful:

> Let me ask you to imagine an afternoon in the Other World. They are sitting round Mary, Queen of Scots. Her head is on. St Sebastian, the pin-cushion saint, is there, perfectly normal. There are various persons who have been mutilated, looking perfectly all right. No arm or leg cut off, no eyes out. Then suddenly someone says something that is sad. Off comes the Queen's head – under her arm, I suppose – St Sebastian begins to bleed, and unmutilated persons become mutilated.

The entire scenario was too fantastic. 'If this is the sort of thing we are coming to,' advised Maude, 'it is time we began to pull ourselves together and exercise a little common sense.' And why did famous people so rarely return? Never did they see Napoleon, Socrates, Shakespeare, Keats or Shelley, the last of whom Maude quoted to address Bronco the parrot: 'Hail to thee, blithe Spirit! Bird thou never wert', adding: 'For it was not a bird, but a fraud.' Like defending counsel in 1933, he also referred to Browning's 'Mr Sludge, the Medium', pointing out that dealing with the occult had attracted charlatans for centuries.

After lunch, the Recorder delivered his summing-up, at two and a quarter hours a masterpiece of compression, shaming Loseby whose case, he suggested dispassionately, may well have defeated itself 'by being so prolix and multiplied'. At 4.32 p.m. the jury – the wartime variety of six men and one woman, all from the surburb of Barnes – retired, returning twenty-four minutes later with four guilty verdicts. Chief Constable West was then invited to give an account of their records, calmly demolishing the ruins of Mrs Brown's and Mrs Duncan's credit, referring to the former helping herself in Selfridges (which had her shouting in denial) and adding the following censure of the latter, who by now was murmuring protests of her own. Paying little notice, West continued:

This is a case where not only has she attempted and succeeded in deluding confirmed believers in Spiritualism, but she has tricked, defrauded and preyed upon the minds of a certain credulous section of the public who have gone to these meetings in search of comfort of mind in their sorrow and grief, many of whom left with the firm conviction that the memory of the dead had been besmirched. She thought fit to come to Portsmouth, the first naval port of the world, where she would find many bereaved families, and there she practised her trickery.

Interrupted by the Recorder, West expressed a wish to finish what he had to say, which was granted. And then came the rub. West made an unexplained fleeting reference to the darker danger Helen Duncan had presented to public and nation in 1941, when a report was filed about her 'having transgressed the security laws, again in a naval connection, when she foretold the loss of one of His Majesty's ships long before the fact was made public'.

The Recorder postponed sentencing until 10.30 a.m. on Monday, 3 April, Loseby having requested a non-custodial sentence in view of Helen's poor health; he was not optimistic, but at least this way he had time to prepare his appeal application. While he paced and scribbled, Helen and her dishevelled gang spent the weekend in the cells, Albert having at last deserted her. When the Recorder gaoled her for nine months, she shouted back: 'I didn't do anything!' W. A. E. Jones described how 'she sobbed. She moaned. She groaned. And then she collapsed on the floor, hat off her head, her fur coat flapping round her as prison matrons and the three other defendants helped to raise her to her feet.' Another reporter affected surprise at her keening cry as to whether there was a God: 'For one professedly in touch with the world beyond this one, it was a strange query.' Frances Brown received four months for aggravating Helen's offence, whereas the Homers were saved by their guilelessness, clean records and charity receipts, and were bound over. With the last of his strength, Loseby arranged for notice of appeal to be given on behalf of all four defendants and vainly attempted to have the case declared *sub judice*, again to restrain the press who were champing at the bit to get back down Ludgate Hill to Fleet Street in order to bash out their witch-trial stories. But the Recorder was in no mood to indulge Loseby and ended the trial with a sardonic remark indicating his view that it was rather rich for him to be resisting the press now when in the course of the previous week he had presented 'rather a temptation to them'.

'My Lord, I respectfully agree,' said Loseby with a modest bow.

Later that same day, Victoria Helen Duncan, aged forty-six, suffering from angina, began her sentence in Holloway Prison. Decommissioned, deactivated, she lay idle and inert like a defused bomb and without even having had her say or demonstrating her gifts. Loseby she resented for having failed to sell the test seance to the court; even when the Recorder let the jurors decide whether they wanted it or not, they had declined. Now, her hopes were pinned on the appeal; her fears were for her family. They too were sick with worry, sure, now, that she would die a martyr; Albert was afraid that she was not long for this world. One gloomy night after the arrest, Henry had sat speculating to Gena and Lilian as to what might happen, when Gena heard a sudden noise like a released window blind wrapping itself around the roller, followed by a voice which came from nowhere saying 'nine months'. 'No, no, no!' cried Henry when Gena told him, tears rolling down his cheeks. Lilian, now an invalid, told Gena to shut up; but Henry reprimanded her, supposing that his youngest daughter, so like her mother, would be proved correct. In the last week of March Nan, more pallid and frail than ever before, accompanied Henry to London for the trial and broke down when the verdict was announced, certain of the consequences of a gaol sentence. Outside the courtroom she told a reporter from the *News of the World* – who described her as 'a slender blue-eyed girl' – that the Duncans were ordinary working-class folk, adding: 'If Mother were a fraud as a medium, she wasted her time in Spiritualism. She could have made a fortune on the stage.' Over the weekend of 1–2 April Nan's condition deteriorated to such an extent that Henry had to take her back to Edinburgh, leaving Helen in her cell to await her fate, prompting the sneering remark from one Spiritualist supporter that only rats leave sinking ships.

Reunited with his other daughters (the spirits had already told Gena about Nan's state; Lilian had silenced her), Henry carried Nan to bed and called for the doctor, who diagnosed jaundice and rheumatic fever. Gena, who had had to stay behind to care for Lilian and her children, probably took the trial hardest, having trusted in God and Albert. Escaping for a couple of hours, she went to the theatre but even there a comedian made a joke about 'the witch' and she stormed out. Newspapers were hard to stomach as well, with most of the popular dailies out to milk the kind of sensationalism usually only derived from murders: the *Daily Express* printed a cartoon of a pair of ARP fire watchers spotting a witch flying a broomstick and to the *Daily Worker* it was simply the 'witchcraft trial', irrespective of legal semantics. Other headlines read: GHOST INVITED TO GIVE EVIDENCE and SPIRIT CALLED PEGGY LIKED LIPSTICK. The London *Evening News* and the *Daily Mail* both went for what Fleet Street was now used to calling 'the woman's angle', commenting on every detail of what Helen was wearing, although they disagreed as to whether she was well-dressed or not.

Reporters bothered the Duncans constantly and Henry, under pressure from Helen's estranged sister Florence, agreed to an interview with a Sunday broadsheet to set the record straight. The resulting exclusive was headed: SEVENTH DAUGHTER OF

SEVENTH DAUGHTER CHARGED WITH WITCHCRAFT, which would have been unsatisfactory to the family even if Helen hadn't been the fourth child of an only child.* Bereft that truth had not won the day, Gena remembered what her mother had taught her – you can bind the hands of a thief but not the tongue of a liar – and, disillusioned, vowed never to develop as a medium. When word reached Helen's sons – Harry with the RAF in Egypt and Peter who was serving as a signalman on HMS *Formidable* – both fired off anxious letters to their father asking for something to be done. Peter, believing his mother to be a finished woman and not expected to live, was granted compassionate leave. Broken-hearted, Henry received a letter from the Edinburgh City Police requesting that he collect a parcel sent up from London containing his wife's clothes – presumably the seance outfit confiscated as evidence.

And so this sad, strange episode drew towards a close. The records were all made straight: old files closed and archived, new ones opened with a letter here, a cutting there, and the indictments, depositions and exhibits delivered to the Registrar at the Criminal Appeal Office. The receipt for Helen's things, signed by Henry, was posted back to London; her fingerprints were dispatched to the relevant branch of 'C' Department (Crime) at Scotland Yard; and Detective Inspector Ford compiled a final report of which copies were sent to the DPP and the Chief Constables of Sheffield, Sunderland and Edinburgh, all of whom had assisted with the Portsmouth investigation. Officers at Scotland Yard, who also received a copy, were especially thanked for the advice and support they had provided.

---

* In her newspaper column, Helen (or Henry) falsely claimed that her mother was the seventh daughter of the seventh daughter of a seventh daughter: *People's Journal* (9 September 1933).

Finally, Ford sent a note to Harry Price enclosing correspondence Price had lent him, plus confirmation that his photographs were safely back at the University of London Library. But that was not all. Arriving home at Pulborough, West Sussex, for the weekend of 8–9 April, Price found a parcel containing his loaned copy of *Regurgitation and the Duncan Mediumship*, three more of his pictures of the convicted medium in mid-flow and a personal letter from the Chief Constable of Portsmouth, Arthur West, expressing his 'very real thanks and warm appreciation for all the kindly help and assistance you so readily rendered me in connection with this presentation'. And with it West offered an apology: 'The book has been in many hands and it is a matter of some regret to me to find the covers have been somewhat soiled but having regard to all the good it did perhaps you would forgive me for this.' Albeit by remote means, Price felt he had had his day in court as an expert witness after all and now, finally, he could sleep the sleep of the just. The practice he had once branded as 'cheesecloth worship', a decade later the law had successfully formalized as 'a kind of conjuration' and as a consequence the vilification of hellish Nell Duncan was complete.

PART III
HELEN VINDICATED

7

SQUARING THE CIRCLE
Phenomena and Fraud at the Seances

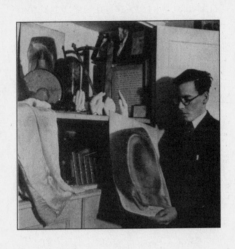

I n November 1925 Harry Houdini bought a copy of the *Atlantic Monthly* and, fountain pen in hand, turned to page 666 for details of the latest Harvard investigation into the mediumship of Mina Crandon, alias 'Margery'. A year earlier, sitting on the *Scientific American* committee with Professor William McDougall and others, he had been utterly sceptical about her, references to which he now underlined, likewise a key passage about the luminous levitating doughnuts (actually cardboard rings). 'What I saw holding the doughnut', wrote Dr Hudson Hoagland,

Donald West in the SPR museum, *c.* 1950. Note the cloth to the left of the picture.

'appeared to be a human right foot, the toes clamped over the periphery of the disc, creasing it in a way verified by examining the doughnut after the sitting.' 'Aha!' annotated Houdini, relishing the exposure. This was more than just a casual interest. Houdini was waging an obsessive war against Spiritualism, demonstrating to packed theatres on Broadway how to fake every kind of phenomenon – an ironic reversal for an entertainer whose career began in dime museums performing feats of escapology copied from Spiritualist stage shows – he even used a cabinet. A passion for debunking was fuelled by failure to contact his beloved mother, disappointment which peaked in Atlantic City in June 1922 when the entranced wife of his friend Sir Arthur Conan Doyle acted as amanuensis for a letter from a spirit which used the correct idiom but the wrong language: English rather than an inimitable mishmash of Hungarian, German and Yiddish. Four years later, the spirits were to warn Conan Doyle: 'Houdini is doomed, doomed, doomed!' and sure enough, on Hallowe'en that year he died after a student ruptured his appendix with a muscle-testing punch. However much Helen Duncan feared and loathed her nemesis Harry Price, she should have been grateful for this intervention before she rose to prominence. For Houdini eschewed Conan Doyle's genteel respect for the sensitivity of mediums which, to his mind, only preserved them in mischief; by comparison, even Price was inhibited in his dealings with the people the great magician called 'human vultures'.

It may seem perverse to begin the vindication of Helen Duncan with a discussion of fraud; but as much as deception and false-hood, this chapter deals with perception and truth – a kind of truth which sees the phenomenal in the mundane, and inspires meaning and purpose in the beholder. In 1944 the prosecution witnesses may well have demonstrated that Helen was guilty of fraud; but that does not invalidate defence testimonies describing

224

vividly intimate engagement with the spirits of relatives and friends. The intention is to conjure up an alternative reality – a reality hardly less substantial than the knowledge of the tangible world trusted by secular minds. A similar problem underlies historical writing: how to be certain about anything when all we have are faulty data, fallible senses and a secret or subconscious desire that things should be one way rather than another. This tendency to make 'truth' in the image of this desire applies equally to storytelling as to our scientific understanding of the universe and of our place within it as human beings.

Houdini's example illustrates blurred divisions in opinion. His attitudes, superficially those of an arch scoffer, were actually those of a hopeful agnostic angry that his search for real spirits was frustrated by impostors. And there were many like him, broadly believing but specifically sceptical. Dr 'Ding' Dingwall was a man who wavered about Margery's mediumship, but did not hesitate to condemn Houdini as a prestidigitator hostile to science, and told Schrenck-Notzing so when Houdini doubted the mediumship of Eva Carrière. In truth, like his SPR and Magic Circle colleague Harry Price, Dingwall expressed profound scepticism about physical mediumship, but even here consensus was elusive. Extraordinary though it seems, Price was too *credulous* for Ding and therefore unsuited to investigating with the SPR where, in any case, Mrs Sidgwick refused to have him on the Council because he was 'not a gentleman'. One thing upon which Price, Dingwall and Houdini all agreed was that conjurors were best placed to detect fraud because of their skill in what Price called 'the art of mystification' – or, as Houdini put it, 'It takes a flim-flammer to catch a flimflammer.' Charles Dickens's satires against mediums – for example, *Worse Witches than Macbeth's* – had been rooted in the contempt which he, as an accomplished amateur conjuror, felt for the likes of D.D. Home. Moreover, another

Victorian conjuror, J. N. Maskelyne, who had not been convinced by Eusapia Palladino's Cambridge seances (but did believe in apparitions and table turning), maintained that scientists were the easiest to dupe because they were too rarified in their thoughts, too idealistic, to detect simple legerdemain.

There were many books about the fraudulent methods of the seance room, one of the earliest, *Modern Spiritualism*, written by Maskelyne himself in 1876. Not all were by magicians – *Confessions of a Medium* (1882) speaks for itself – and similar anonymous works came from the USA. Thanks to publicity generated by Spiritualists trying to buy the entire print run, *Revelations of a Spirit Medium* (1891) had a huge impact, not least on the adolescent Erich Weiss who was struggling to escape from Wisconsin to become Harry Houdini. At once an indictment of Spiritualism and a veritable textbook of seance tricks, it asserted that 'No individual can become a spiritual medium and retain all his moral qualities', implying that even the genuine article exploited others. The following year, Julia E. Garrett's *Mediums Unmasked*, published in Los Angeles, told the story of a medium whose foot, draped in a handkerchief, was kissed by a sitter who said it smelt like the corpse of a deceased relative. From London in 1902 came *A Séance with the Lights Up* by Philip Astor (author of *Conjuring at Home* the following year) and a classic work from SPR stalwart Frank Podmore who borrowed Maskelyne's title, *Modern Spiritualism*. Demand for such books, which spread to France and Germany, was boosted by the First World War. By 1916 David Phelps Abbott's *Behind the Scenes with the Mediums* (Chicago, 1907) had reached its fifth edition and several new books were appearing each year. In the 1920s Maskelyne's descendants kept up not only his conjuring but his anti-Spiritualism with exposés such as *Spiritualism Exploited*, *Bogus Séance Secrets Exposed*, *Rogues of the Seance Room* and

Exposing Ghost Frauds – their inventiveness for titles seemingly endless. Periodicals carried articles and serializations, which spread awareness over an even wider area of the public. In 1921 the popular magazine *John Bull*, which had done so much to demonize the Germans during the war, turned on mediums in a piece entitled: 'Indian rubber spooks: kings and clowns on tap for the credulous'. A year later Price and Dingwall published a facsimile edition of *Revelations of a Spirit Medium*, the Victorian original of which by this time had become the impostor's bible.

Most fraudulent mediums restricted themselves to clairvoyance, psychometry and so on, where the only hazard was being wrong and for which excuses were legion: spiritual interference, inability to raise the vibrations, the weakness of the communicating spirit, or sceptical feelings harboured by the sitter. Good results, by contrast, were produced by 'pony books': card indexes containing the personal details of local Spiritualists which could be lent to visiting mediums. Travelling companions and booking agents could also make surreptitious enquiries. Harry Price advised giving nothing away when visiting a medium to the extent of not speaking and removing rings several days before a sitting to let the marks fade. But once information had been aired, a good memory could produce impressive readings. In 1938 Mollie Goldney revisited a medium who mentioned 'Bessie and Alec White', names that Mollie had invented at a seance with her two years earlier; in the interval 30,000 names may have passed the medium's lips, but these she was able to recall. According to psychic investigator Arthur Wilkinson, forgetting 'when things got sticky' was also important, as were an innocent face and a quick wit. The medium's best asset, however, were the high expectations of their clients, which were raised still further by high fees. Clairvoyants usually had their vague insinuations confirmed because most sitters wanted to help them make contact, not to test them. In any case, seances tended to be social engagements where politeness and chivalry were likely to preclude open challenges to the medium's genuineness, even if scepticism was consensual among the sitters.

Frauds were thus emboldened. 'If you have the flair for stunts and some showmanship,' advised Wilkinson, 'well, the field is wide open for you.' Materialization mediums, he added, require only 'muslin, masks, trumpets and a colossal cheek'. Again, in private sittings especially, expectation and etiquette allowed physical mediums to get away with the clumsiest of manipulations. 'With the paid performer you pounce upon him and expose him the minute you have seen through his trick,' reasoned Conan Doyle. 'But what are you to do with the friend of your host's wife?' Darkness also helped: the dim light required to protect ectoplasm happens to be the condition most conjurors would choose to put on a good show. Even red light was often dimmed as a seance progressed. Props were daubed with luminous paint – from Margery's doughnuts to the ubiquitous trumpets and crucifixes – so that they could be seen. And that which aided perception also assisted in deception. A luminous business card allowed a medium to read in the dark, and luminous plates either side of the face framed many a ghostly mask. Harry Price once saw a medium use a flask of phosphorized oil to project a pale spectral light, and silver of ferrocerium – lighter flints – had its uses. Books on chemical conjuring had been around for years: John Scoffern's enticing *Explosive Spiders and How to Make Them* and *Firework Pie for a Picnic* dated from the 1880s. Light shows, from lantern lectures to the movies, inspired ambitious frauds, a point illustrated, tangentially, by the German accusation in 1930 that the Angels of Mons had been motion pictures projected on to clouds from aeroplanes to suggest that God favoured the British. Overall, arbitrary restrictions imposed by mediums said more about them than about the spirits they claimed to invoke: as one sceptic observed, the remote movement of objects by the extension of ectoplasmic rods never actually exceeded the muscular powers of the medium. Against this, it was sometimes argued that spirits rejected extravagant demonstrations as distastefully vulgar – a sensibility which would explain why no medium ever gave cause for the laws of physics to be revised.

Most of the conditions described here will already be familiar from Helen Duncan's seances. 'There is a lady here beside me who entered the spirit world quite recently,' confided Albert. 'On the earth plane she suffered from a serious and painful ailment situated in the lower part of the abdomen; eventually her heart was affected and she passed away.' A description made hundreds of times, it is trite, yet the quotation comes from a sitter who identified the spirit as his wife in Blackpool in 1942. Perhaps awe and joy helped palliate the manner in which, as a clairvoyant, Helen sometimes bullied sitters into accepting her messages, becoming red in the face when they did not. An appreciation of what could be achieved with educated guesses and deftly solicited information downgrades these miracles – and helps to explain the predictions about sinking warships. There were many stories about how news of HMS *Barham* entered circulation: it came from survivors sent home from Alexandria; a German propaganda broadcast had been picked up; Mrs Duncan was an enemy spy. To these speculations might be added a simpler solution: that the prediction was never made – or, at least, not in the way described in the canonical version. The same applies to HMS *Hood*.

Mediums were full of hope but also foreboding and in 1941 anyone wishing to make doom-laden pronouncements could have done worse than to focus on battleships, of which there were but a handful and all in peril. Italy's entry into the war in June 1940 left the Royal Navy isolated in the Mediterranean, and it was common knowledge that the *Barham* had already been torpedoed off the coast of Scotland in December 1939 and bombed during the withdrawal from Crete in May 1941. The *Hood*, sunk the same month, was famous as the largest warship in the world in 1939 and would have been an obvious choice if one aspired to foretell the greatest naval catastrophe. At the seance attended by Brigadier Firebrace, the prediction concerned only a 'great British battleship' and was made during the protracted Battle of the Atlantic, costly from early on in the war when HMS *Courageous* and the battleship *Royal Oak* had been sunk. With the *Barham*, the loss of the *Ark Royal* in the Mediterranean days earlier concentrated minds and in Portsmouth, the port where the families of many of the *Barham*'s 1200 sailors lived, it was as much a target for a medium as for a U-boat. Knowing that a sitter had connections would have clinched it. Percy Wilson considered the sailor's materialization to be 'rather straight evidence of the survival of the boy who came back to speak to his mother'; but one can also see how a generic cheesecloth shape could have been claimed and embellished into a boy with 'HMS *Barham*' on his hat, either through a fault of perception or, more likely, fond retelling of the tale. In fact, the classic story was wrong: not only was the anxious woman the wife of the sailor not his mother, but he was a petty officer and as such would have worn not a round hat but an anonymous peaked cap. Even if he had been recently promoted and was therefore still 'square-rigged', in wartime all cap-bands read just 'HMS' for security reasons. Finally, witnesses reported later that although the *Barham* was mentioned, the name was extracted from the sitter by Mrs Duncan speaking as 'Albert'.

The defence testimonies at the Old Bailey suggest that it really would have been possible for the widow to have recognized her husband. Of course, it should also be remembered that the seance conditions at the Master Temple were optimal for creating illusion. It was never possible to adjust one's eyes completely to the darkness, as Stanley Worth testified, and the forty-watt red bulb which Mr and Mrs Homer described to the police turned out to be more like a five-watt. The cabinet concealed all, the music muffled all, and Mrs Brown's and Mrs Homer's commentary helped to keep things moving, identifying shapes and calling on sitters to claim the spirits announced by Albert. The Homers were helped further by the seating plan which, ostensibly, allowed visitors to be settled in the room quickly and without fuss, but actually extended a measure of control when paying strangers were admitted. And good mediums always knew who was sitting where. 'Here is another case', concluded Professor McDougall after visiting the NLPR in 1931,

> which justifies the general principle that when the general procedure and circumstances demanded by the medium are such as suggest fraud and favour fraud, the observer is justified in regarding the phenomena as fraudulent, even if he is not able to suggest any plausible explanation of the phenomena; and, still less, to demonstrate the truth of any hypothesis he may entertain as to the manner of that fraudulent production.

This stringent position has much to commend it; but it does draw a veil over the phenomena, which, after all, need not have been genuine ectoplasmic manifestations to be phenomenal. They remain phenomenal for as long as they cannot be fully explained. And in any case, it would be an incurious enquirer indeed who, having written off ectoplasm as cheesecloth, stockinette, paper, wood pulp, egg-white and so on, had no interest in how such household sundries were artfully arranged to create the illusion of the returning dead.

Traditionally, materialization mediums had relied on props. In the 1870s Madame Blavatsky was forced to leave Cairo after a ghostly arm was discovered to be a long glove stuffed with cotton wool and suspended by threads, and Maskelyne detected Eusapia's dummy hands at Cambridge in 1895. But props were difficult to use wherever pre-seance cabinet searches were conducted – the Homers even obliged a man who asked that the cabinet chair's upholstery be ripped open – and by 1930 fraudulent mediums on tour could safely use only what they could hide on their own bodies. Usually, this meant white cloth, but discreetly inflated balloons and rubber gloves also made an appearance. As we saw earlier, the Crandons were more inventive: the knobbly, clammy matter Dingwall felt on Margery's thigh may have been a lung from a freshly killed animal, pumped up from between her legs. Keeping it simple became essential. Dr W. J. Crawford had said of Kathleen Goligher: 'The experimental results are so impossible by fraud . . . that it would have been quite unnecessary to take any means to prevent fraud.' And yet when she came out of retirement in 1936, a carefully positioned camera revealed a thread running down one leg attached to ectoplasm creeping across the floor. The SPR Research Officer, the aristocratic C. V. C. Herbert, experimented by dragging a handkerchief attached to a length of cotton, slowly winding it towards him round the stub of a pencil. In weak light, observers found the trick almost impossible to detect.

But how were full-figure materializations achieved? Lighting from beneath a piece of silk treated with phosphorus, olive oil and alum water produces a fine luminous vapour, and may have been a method used by David Devant, associate of the Maskelynes, who once made a 'ghost in silken gauze' glide across a hall, then evaporate before twenty puzzled people. For Helen Duncan the conventional explanation is that she did what Charles Loseby sarcastically suggested: she played bogey-bogey with a sheet over her head. But still the question was asked repeatedly: how could the waddling five-foot-six-inches Helen transform herself into lithe young people, little girls and especially the six-foot Albert? Easily, is the answer. A bogus ghost can gain as much as eighteen inches by draping an arm extended vertically and it was not uncommon for tall spirit forms to have use of only one arm. The most important evidence here is provided by a set of photographs for which the Edinburgh ghost-buster Miss Esson Maule posed, mocking up Helen's tricks, all the more remarkable because their porcine bodies and bovine faces made them look rather similar. One shows her with a hand-kerchief over her face and an undervest over her head, face poking through the armhole; in another she pulls the cabinet curtains around her to determine how much of her white-swathed body was visible. Add to this thick black stockings, quiet on wooden floors and invisible in semi-darkness, and the effect was of a slim floating figure. An odd noise heard prior to Peggy's arrival was traced to a squeaking floorboard: Helen had been lowering herself to her knees in order to manipulate the vest. Disappearing through the floor, it turns out, was an old trick: working downwards, one simply gathers in white material behind something dark; one can also fake the reabsorption of ectoplasm by these means. At the LSA sessions in 1931, Eve Brackenbury had reached similar conclusions, suggesting that Helen's face could be reduced in size using a dark surround, and that 'the appearance of shortening might easily be produced if the lower end was gradually covered by the black buckram gloves'. A decade later things were the same. Elijah Fowler told how plump spirits appeared when the curtains were open, slimmer ones when they were drawn. Stanley Worth remembered heavy thumping as the spirit retreated into the cabinet and also heard the rustling of cloth – something Mrs Homer attributed to 'psychic winds'.

After the war, Donald West was appointed SPR Research Officer and through Mollie Goldney obtained Harry Price's photograph of the Punch and Judy mannekin – the one Price dubbed 'the old witch concoction'. West thought this would make a fine illustration for the article he was preparing because, unlike Price's stereograms, the raddled papier-mâché gargoyle of a face would persuade even an agnostic that what had been recorded was not the dawning of a new scientific age but some daft puppetry in the back room of a terraced house in Dundee. As West and others observed, even the nail which attached the angular rag person to the door was – and is – plainly visible. Photography and searching investigation imposed limits upon other mediums, too. Fru Lára Agustsdóttir was Iceland's Helen Duncan. Well-built with dark wavy hair, obstreperous, nervous and prone to hysteria, she was plagued by poor health and bleeding piles, but produced remarkable materializations, such as a girl, 'Minerva', and a Spanish woman who spoke the language like a native. Arriving in England in the summer of 1937, she received national press attention, but seance reports were damning. An old photograph plainly depicts a young girl dressed as a nun attached to the comotose medium by a cloth umbilicus. Furthermore, in the archives of the International Institute for Psychical Research are envelopes containing flakes of pink paint found in the cabinet and thought to have come from a papier-mâché mask. Cloth, too, was mysteriously produced and manipulated between areas of greater and lesser illumination before she drew it up under her skirt. Ironically, Dr Margaret Vivian, the Bournemouth doctor impressed by Helen's LSA seances, believed Agustsdóttir to be genuine because 'nobody could fake that dreadful smell which clung to me till the next day . . . We used to get the same smell with Mrs Duncan when her results were genuine.' The stench was so foul that she joked that others in her hotel would think she was a body-snatcher.

At the Old Bailey, Rose Cole described the odour emanating from the materialized form of her friend Mrs Allen: 'It was just like death and made me feel terrible. I had to stand back because I could not stand the smell. I was told it was ectoplasm smell.' She was followed in the witness box by Bertha Alabaster who, asked whether the ectoplasm smelt of vomit, agreed with Mrs Cole that it was more like death. Perceptions varied. In 1931 Harry Price described the odour as 'reminiscent of a bit of ripe gorgonzola'; meanwhile, at the LSA, the perfume Henry Duncan likened to old cloth – and Albert said was nicer – at least one sitter called 'strong and objectionable'. Some said Helen's ecto-plasm had an earthy smell, others that it reeked of urine and one, more courageously, that it smelt like semen. For those who disputed that ectoplasm was what Spiritualists said it was, there was only one explanation: lightweight cloth, tightly packed, was concealed in the body; and so in 1944 the regurgitation contro-versy was revived. Price's friend and colleague, C.E.M. Joad, caused outrage by suggesting in the *Sunday Dispatch* that physical mediums might have second stomachs like cows. Maurice Barbanell retaliated, reminding Joad, 'We have not yet discovered *everything* about nature', while others referred to the X-ray photo-graphs taken in 1930 and the report certifying that Helen's stomach and oesophagus were normal. Hannen Swaffer had copies of both at the trial, but was not allowed to produce them and had to vent his frustration in a ditty which he passed to Barbanell with his regards:

> *I'd swallow until I were drunken,*
> *But not the bunk on Helen Duncan.*
> *(If I were swallowing, more and more,*
> *Things spiritous or beery,*
> *I'd swallow anything before*
> *The Price regurgitation theory.)*

Doctors in Dundee were said to have laughed at the idea that Mrs Duncan was a regurgitator, especially because on one occasion it took them half an hour to fit the tube of a pump into her stomach, although what poison she had swallowed they did not disclose. Helen was also sick of people asking if she was a regurgitator – literally on one occasion in Belfast when she stuck her fingers down her throat at the request of a sceptical sitter and vomited spectacularly upon the floor.

Price had heard it all before and for years had an interest in stage swallowing, as he had in every type of trick and legerdemain. The nucleus of his library was his childhood copy of Angelo Lewis's *Modern Magic*, from which he graduated to such desirable volumes as his copy of Scot's *Discoverie of Witchcraft*, prized not just for its Shakespearean connections but because it was the first English book to contain an illustrated chapter on conjuring. Another early English work of his was Peedle and Cozbie's *The Fallacie of the Great Water-Drinker Discovered* (1650), which told the story of a Frenchman brought to England for tests (paid for by private subscription) to determine how he regurgitated two different colours of water. Across early modern Europe, showmen ate and vomited stones; one who set up a sideshow in the Strand in 1788 charged 2s 6d per person and invited his audience to bring their own stones. Others swallowed live frogs, snakes, glass and nails; in Prague, Price himself witnessed the swallowing of a watch (which could be heard ticking); and Houdini saw the glow of an electric light through a man's chest. Most modern performers, however, were unable to regurgitate, an assertion of Price's proved in May 1944 by Arthur Haylock, a swallower who hit the headlines after a crowd blocked the London traffic to watch him eat razor blades. The SPR thought it important to document such acts, in Mollie Goldney's words, 'for occasions of the Duncan variety' and so hired Haylock and watched him feast on a light bulb, a gramophone record and a bunch of flowers, all of which he kept down. But there was a better example. In 1935 Professor Fraser-Harris, the Canadian physiologist who had reported on Helen Duncan at the NLPR, performed an experiment where Victor Dane regurgitated seven feet of butter muslin which came up 'very wet, thick and cord-like'. Elsewhere Fraser-Harris argued that the existence of an *oesophageal diverticulum* – a secondary stomach or pouch – might allow separation of, say, cloth and food, and would be hard to detect using X-rays. Not that this was necessary for regurgitation if, like Dane, one were well-practised, patient and able to exercise control over the gag reflex.

Other parallels present themselves. An observer from the American SPR likened Margery's ectoplasm to 'lace made of heavy white cord', cool, clammy and malodorous. On one occasion she could also be heard struggling to swallow this vile matter, causing her cruel-hearted spirit guide 'Walter' to joke: 'Put some salt on it, it will go down better.' Comparison between Helen Duncan and Margery offers another explanation for how they were able to produce ectoplasm: both frequently had nosebleeds during seances, suggesting another hiding place – the conclusion of William Brown, the Harley Street doctor who attributed the phenomena at the NLPR to 'clever prestidigitation'. After his sittings William McDougall told Harry Price: 'On the first occasion, I suspected an oesophageal diverticulum, in the second Dr William Brown's observations led me to suppose the material might have been packed in the nostrils and nasal cavities.' This was possible. In 1895, Freud allowed Wilhelm Fliess (a proponent of universal bisexuality) to perform nasal surgery on a patient, Emma Eckstein, after cocaine failed to quell the neurosis Freud attributed to masturbation. The case is of interest not just because a great length of gauze was accidently left up her nose, but because Freud explained her subsequent haemorrhaging as hysterical attention seeking, a trait which he likened to diabolically inspired witches of earlier times and which earned his sympathy for 'the harsh therapy' of witch-hunting judges.

Dr Crandon never consented to an examination of his wife's digestive tract on the grounds that it 'would be a painful inconvenience to the medium'; but because the Harvard investigators had searched the outside of Margery's body so thoroughly, they concluded that her ectoplasmic articles, in Hudson Hoagland's words, 'must have been stored away internally'. Houdini underlined this five times in the *Atlantic Monthly*, adding: 'Yes sir, H.' But, of course, Hoagland's words were discreetly ambiguous for, as Houdini knew well, swallowing was not the only means of bodily concealment (he had hidden tools on his naked body to escape from dozens of prison cells). Dr Dingwall's suspicions were confirmed by eminent gynaecologist Dr Florence Willey, wife of SPR founder Sir William Barrett, who informed him in May 1925 that 'of course it would be quite possible to pack a considerable portion of such substance into the vagina . . . By muscular contraction (which however I should think would be obvious) the substance might be wholly or partially expelled.' Quite what this substance was is another matter: the possibility that it was a lung has been mentioned, but Margery's other ectoplasmic extrusions were likened to cold raw liver, half a human brain and the back of an armadillo. At a test seance in London in 1929, Dr Willey found her vagina and cervix to be abnormally soft for a woman who had not just given birth; she was also haemorrhaging. Later, Margery explained that she had begun to menstruate, but Dr Willey had her doubts due to the diamond-shaped bloodstain in the medium's underwear which to her suggested 'something laterally distending the vagina'.

When Detective Inspector Ford hinted that Helen Duncan's missing sheet may have been secreted thus, he was using information already received by the Portsmouth police. Early in March 1944 Chief Constable Arthur West received a letter from Varina Taylor of Southport, a coastal resort in Lancashire. She had helped Helen Duncan to undress before a seance in the summer of 1943 and thought that 'under the tremendous folds of flesh, or in the vagina, Mrs Duncan could easily conceal the amount of diaphanous drapery used for her various ghostly visitors'. And just as the smell of the ectoplasm kept all but the emotionally automatized at a distance, Helen was afforded immunity from detection at this stage too. 'Most women asked to witness her undress to the skin', Mrs Taylor explained, 'out of decency do not look, touch, or examine her too closely; but if a lady doctor were to examine her in these parts (lower abdomen) I am sure they would find room for concealments of this nature.' Esson Maule had known this back in 1932. After a performance by Kanichka the Human Ostrich (which persuaded her that Helen Duncan was not a true regurgitator), she had been out to supper with a party of female doctors, one of whom told how she had treated Helen for chronic cystitis and had noticed that 'the urethra was so stretched with the introduction of abnormal and unnatural foreign bodies, that its natural elasticity was gone, causing frequency of micturition, which her age does not justify'. Contrary to what some said, Helen often ate a large meal before a seance, which pressed on her bladder, causing incontinence – hence the splashing sometimes heard. This also proved that she and Albert were one and the same. A puddle discovered where he had been standing during a seance might have been blamed on the spirit guide himself, caught short on his lengthy astral excursion, were it not for the uterine blood mixed with the urine, identified as 'catamenial discharge in its primary degree'. Delicately, Miss Maule informed Price that Helen possessed 'enormous depth of pelvis', adding that 'pelvic concealment of articles is one of the commonest acts of insane females, especially if there is any taint of immorality in them. One, two and three large bath towels, secreted in the pelvis, is of common occurrence in any Female Lunatic Asylum.' The mind wanders to the apported objects of modern mediumship: Helen's cucumber; Hylda Lewis's thornless roses; Eusapia's dead rat; Elizabeth Hope's rubber plant; Jack Webber's brass flamingo . . .

Unsurprisingly, Helen Duncan's ectoplasm does not exist in the same quantities as, say, the books, letters and papers that constitute the bulk of the historical sources used here. There is a small quantity, framed by Harry Price, hanging on the wall in the University of London Library; and a square of gauze in an envelope labelled 'Ectoplasm' was stored at the old LSA (today the College of Psychic Studies) until it was stolen in 1999. The slides made by Mr Montagu Scott in 1931 are still there somewhere in a cupboard jammed with boxes of notebooks, portraits of luminaries, and luminous trumpets long silent. But what about a bigger piece, a piece so large that it could be wrapped around the body and fluttered through the air to recapture what that trick might have meant half a century ago? The absence of such a sheet, of course, was a bone of contention at the Old Bailey in 1944. The point was this: had all the sitters at the Master Temple been searched and the cloth still not been found it would have been embarrassing for the police, and, in the end, the Witchcraft Act ensured that such evidence was superfluous anyway; for what it matters, Ford, Worth and Cross suspected the woman with the sling. After the war, however, a rumour from the time of the trial developed into an intriguing story. In 1946 Denys Parsons (ejected from the Old Bailey for donating his seat to Mollie Goldney), was put in touch with James Robinson, a naval instructor at Portsmouth in 1944. Two of his fellow instructors, who shared an interest in the paranormal, had sat next to each other at the fateful seance on 19 January: one was called Jacobs, the other was Peter Pickett, the Spiritualist sailor from Kent whose burly mother had supposedly manifested for him. This is what Robinson was told:

> Jacobs and his friend were sitting at the front of the audi-ence, and were becoming more and more convinced that the show was a lot of tripe, when, suddenly, there was a disturbance, and Jacobs made a grab at the 'ghost', and contacted with a fistful of cheesecloth, which he immedi-ately stuffed into his greatcoat . . . They both made a hasty exit after this and returned to barracks.

It was said that the piece of cheesecloth, eight feet square, was commandeered as a hammock! Parsons passed the story to Donald West, who traced Jacobs via Henry Elam who had obtained his address from the police. At an interview in March 1948, Jacobs laughed at Robinson's account and suggested that Pickett might have concocted it because he 'was always being teased about his interest in spooks'. And where was Peter Pickett?

241

'Discharged dead' in 1945 and lying in Naples War Cemetery. The SPR closed the case.

Before the war, however, a sheet had been snatched successfully and bundled away. On 2 April 1939 a seance was held by Helen Duncan at Cefn Coed on the outskirts of Merthyr Tydfil in the Welsh valleys, where she was stripped and searched beforehand, but without an internal examination. Several sitters noticed that the medium was out of her chair when she was supposed to be in trance and a Mr A. J. Miles was unconvinced by a manifestation of his brother, which lacked an identifying deformity. Deciding enough was enough, Miles and another sitter grappled with the burly Helen who punched Miles in the eye to retain ownership of the cloth, but in vain. Five sitters signed a statement to say what had happened. A few days later Harry Price received a letter from Miles, and by May both cloth and statement were in his possession. Price began his inquiry at once and pressed Miles for more details, especially about the washed-out bloodstains, which he hoped to have analysed. Three days after the outbreak of war, Miles obliged with a full account:

The material was draped over her. That was the reason for my pulling it from her. I could see quite plainly that it was cloth when I was examining the supposed spirit form . . . the cloth was damp but I am not sure whether the stains were fresh. I did not examine it owing to the terrible odour that was issuing from it and from the smell of it quickly suggested where it had been concealed. I suggest that it was concealed within the lower portion of her body. Although it seems incredatable [sic] the fact remains that it is possible and the odour says that it is definitely so.

Miles hoped this would help Price with his investigations and trusted that his writing to *John Bull* would not interfere with them. Price was certainly pleased with the discovery, as were the Portsmouth police in 1944 for it was Miles's correspondence that Price lent to Detective Inspector Ford, returned with thanks at the end of the trial. Whether there was any talk of using the cloth as supporting evidence is not recorded. A clue to what happened to it next comes from a photograph from the early 1950s, showing Donald West standing by the SPR cabinet of curiosities, examining a huge photographic enlargement of one of Margery's spirit thumbprints.* Among other strange objects, including imitation plaster casts of alleged spirit hands, is a length of cloth described as 'a piece of white drapery, supposed to be ectoplasm, captured from a fraudulent materialising medium'. The old archive handlist confirms its provenance as 'Duncan Mrs Helen Cloth (alleged Ectoplasm)'. Today, staff in the Manuscripts Room of the Cambridge University Library are curiously reluctant to produce the cardboard box with its hinged lid containing a fat brown envelope addressed to Mollie Goldney at the SPR. Inside is a large piece of white satin, or perhaps cotton-silk, measuring eighty by a hundred centimetres, faintly stained at regular intervals. These marks, a typed note by Mrs Goldney suggests, were caused by the cloth being folded and secreted in the vagina where blood seeped in. A single stitch of fine twine can be seen about a quarter of the way in from each side, suggesting a means by which the cloth could have been invisibly retrieved, and perhaps that it was suspended to create a ghost effect. Released from this point at head height, it traps the air, billowing out as it floats to the ground with a tantalizing shimmer.

---

* In 1932 she was caught out after it was discovered that a thumbprint left in a piece of dental wax after a seance belonged not to her spirit guide 'Walter', but to her dentist – who else?

Tricks have the power to awe because a relationship exists between conjuror and spectator of which only the conjuror is fully aware. A willing suspension of disbelief allows a magician's audience to pretend they are witnessing miracles (just as theatre-goers are moved by drama) and the spell is broken only if the trick is explained – which is why the Magic Circle is so secretive. The magic resides not on the stage but in the space between performer and percipient. However, if that were an end to squaring the circle, we could rejoin Helen staring at the ceiling of her cell forthwith. But mediumship is unlike magic because however similar suspended disbelief and real belief seem, the emotional factor shaping interpretation and motivation is absent in the former and essential to the latter. Spiritualism is religion, and magic is recreation, otherwise nothing makes sense: the psychical researcher's determined agnosticism; the Spiritualist's refusal to accept as fraudulent even exposed mediums; the defence witnesses at the Old Bailey – a solicitor, a doctor, a businessman, an air force officer, a midwife, a journalist, a peer of the realm.

Against such believers the debunkers were doomed, for Spiritualists had little to fear from demystification. Harry Price was dumbfounded when Mrs Duncan received her SNU diploma after the Edinburgh conviction, feelings shared by Houdini when, as part of his war on mediumship, he demonstrated how to fake spirit hand casts, only to have a woman in the audience recognize the finger of a girl who had been lost on the *Titanic*. Famously, big, bluff Sir Arthur Conan Doyle was unshaken in his conviction that Houdini was guided by spiritual forces which allowed him to turn his bones to ectoplasm, and, in a perfect illustration of how finely balanced such beliefs could be, was able to pronounce confidently that his small, supple friend was not only the greatest medium baiter of all time, but also the greatest physical medium.

Today, many of Helen Duncan's sitters acknowledge that fraud may have been resorted to *sometimes*, but insist that that was not what *they* experienced: that could only have been genuine. Their position is reinforced by certain paranormalists who, without hiding their contempt for teacup-rattling proletarians emoting in the darkness, nonetheless feel that well-documented exposures like those by Esson Maule, A. J. Miles and Stanley Worth do not necessarily condemn every phenomenal occurrence; such sweeping judgements would betray the guiding spirit of the SPR, namely Joseph Glanvill's dictum that phenomena should not be dismissed simply because they cannot be explained. Whether one subscribes to this prescription or not, the fact remains that it is difficult to explain fully the testimonies recorded in Helen's favour and why what seem to have been obvious conjuring tricks remained so convincing to so many for so long.

Let's start with the assumption that some materializations were real. Anyone who feels insulated against this realm of hyperreality may easily meet Spiritualists, including some who attended Helen Duncan's seances. By the 1950s, perhaps 20,000 people had seen her perform, many of whom are still alive and are invariably friendly. More, they seem sane and relaxed as they describe Spiritualism as a world of reality shored up by demonstration not faith. For they too are materialists, just as our cave-painting ancestors were: one need not understand gravity to experience its earth-hugging certainty, nor to appreciate the orchestration of the planets to expect to wake up with the sun. Enlightenment empiricist David Hume detached reason from the ideology which sustained God's ascendancy. When a man tells you he has seen a corpse restored to life, Hume argued, one should treat both the fact and his belief as phenomena, and then decide which is most likely to be true. As a guide, Hume advised that 'no testimony is sufficient to establish a miracle unless the testimony be of such a kind that its falsity would be more miraculous than the fact which it endeavours to establish'. The laws of nature, applied with dreary repetition in daily life, were too precious to suspend just because a trick was taken seriously by a mere mortal.

Surely, though, the omnipresence of mechanistic science and rationality in western society only makes the Spiritualists' position more understandable. The difference between the believer and the non-believer – as between deists and atheists – is not one of innate nature but unconscious choice: a choice of competing realities. Confronted by the stories of the Spiritualists, even a hard-boiled secularist might suspect that to allow our love of technology to dismiss metaphysical feelings as neuroses is to abdicate responsibility for explaining the human nuances that make us who we are. When the last physiological, chemical and genetic puzzle in the body is solved, the emotions will still mystify; and because of that much of the world's population will continue to seek refuge in religion and will choose mystery over pragmatism – what Hume called 'the usual propensity of mankind towards the marvellous'. After all, mysteries and marvels do at least offer guidance in shadowy regions of consciousness where empiricists can but shrug their shoulders.

Our taste for the marvellous may be a product of the emotions, but it can only be satisfied because our senses distort things. That the same event could appear different between observers had been noted with regard to materialization a decade before Helen Duncan was even born. For his article about the Duncan mediumship, Donald West's mentor, Mollie Goldney, directed him to a statement made in 1887 by Professor Horace Furness who had been required to spend $60,000 bequeathed to the University of Pennsylvania to allow a commission to investigate Spiritualism and prove its ineluctable truth. Risking wrath from beyond the grave, Furness was unable to oblige:

> A woman, a visitor, led from the Cabinet to me a Materialized Spirit, whom she introduced to me as 'her daughter, her dear darling daughter', while nothing could be clearer to me than the features of the medium in every line and lineament. Again and again, men have led round the circle the Materialized Spirits of their wives, and introduced them to each visitor in turn; fathers have taken round their daughters, and I have seen widows sob in the arms of their dead husbands. Testimony such as this staggers me.

And, as we have seen, this amounted to more than just a contest between the men of reason and the rest. Bewitched by the spirit 'Katie King', poor Sir William Crookes complained of 'an antagonism in my mind between *reason*, which pronounces it to be scientifically impossible, and the consciousness that my senses . . . are not lying witnesses when they testify against my preconceptions'. Fellow Nobel prizewinner Charles Richet was scathing: 'How could I suppose that the savant who has discovered thallium and the radiometer, and foreshadowed the Roentgen rays, could commit himself to be duped for years by tricks which a child could have exposed?' But, of course, Richet himself was duped in the end.

Experiments demonstrated that testimony was a compound of vision, environment, predisposition and memory; with alarming helplessness witnesses saw things which never happened and missed things that did. And in the dark, how much greater the error. At the time of Helen's seances in 1931, at the SPR Theodore Besterman, inspired by tests from the 1880s, was mocking up seances using red light at which sitters saw stationary objects move, badly misjudged time and failed to describe correctly a scene exposed by flash. Commenting on a draft of Donald West's article in 1946, Cambridge psychologist Robert Thouless explained how people adapt differently to semi-darkness and, with reference to materialization, 'the relative insensibility of the fovea in semi-darkness makes testimony as to recognition peculiarly uncertain' (West appropriated the remark almost verbatim).

Weariness played a part. Professor Joad told of seances where the same record was played repeatedly – 'the taste of the spirits is deplorable' – and painted a picture similar to that of an investigator in 1941 who said: 'At the end of a long sitting in semi-darkness, when you are tired, if something appears suddenly, nothing is harder than to say exactly what happened.' Donald West also took advice from Denys Parsons who in June 1944 had published in the arts magazine *Horizon* an article entitled 'Testimony and truth' in which he did not doubt that seeing was believing, only that belief was different from proof. C.E. Bechhofer Roberts, a barrister and editor of the Old Bailey Trial Series (which included a volume on the Duncan case) also offered advice to the young researcher. Himself the author of a sceptical work on Spiritualism in 1932, Bechhofer Roberts shared his opinion with West that the defence witnesses 'were trying to tell the truth but were incapable of doing so'.

In a *Sunday Times* review of Bechhofer Roberts's edited transcript of the trial, Desmond MacCarthy recalled a seance where a spirit 'was so obviously a fake that I was amazed that others present did not notice it, but, on the contrary, declared afterwards that the séance had been most unusually impressive'.

To him, this suggested that the hopes and sorrows of such people rendered them physically unable to detect fraud. Besterman had not been shy of the word 'hallucination', but his work pre-dated an understanding of how this could be caused simply by bereavement. Today, manifestations of a deceased partner are well-documented. In 1998, a sample of Swedish and Japanese widows and widowers revealed that hallucinations were experienced by eighty-two per cent and ninety per cent respectively, although the experience tends to be under-reported in cultures where percipients fear stigmatization; among the Hopi Indians it is a normal part of death. Grief is an engine of desires which, Joad explained, 'make us extremely receptive to so-called evidence which, if our attitude was purely dispassionate, we should not consider for a moment'. Many preferred at least to suspend judgement after a materialization seance rather than go home disappointed. Everything hinged on expectation that the medium was genuine and that the dead would behave as they had in life. Humans were thus well-placed to impersonate spirits, the hallmarks of flesh and blood confirming more than they confounded. When the spirit-guide Bien Boa turned Richet's barium oxide solution cloudy in 1905 (proving that he exhaled carbon dioxide), everyone applauded this vital sign. Mrs Hannah Ross, a Bostonian medium of the 1880s, had only to paint a face on one of her breasts and poke it through the cabinet for bereaved mothers to rhapsodize about the warm soft skin of their materialized babies.

Mrs Ross narrowly escaped lynching when a newspaper exposed her, but the history of Spiritualism suggests that, more commonly, internalized experience of spiritual reunion was sufficiently intense that neither vigorous debunking nor psychological explanations had much impact. The story is an old one and is evidenced in a pocket-sized calf-bound volume in the Cambridge University Library containing Dr John Ferriar's *Essay*

Towards a Theory of Apparitions. Published in 1813, it is a short disquisition which criticizes John Beaumont's well-known *Treatise of Spirits, Apparitions, Witchcrafts and Other Magical Practices* from 1705, a work which followed the old conservative tradition of Joseph Glanvill, ever fearful that the end of ghosts and witches would spell the end of the kingdom of heaven. But Beaumont was more of a waverer than Ferriar made out, as indicated by his comment that: 'If you ask me whether I think these Apparitions to be Spirits, or only an effect of Melancholy, I can only say what St Paul said of the Nature of his Rapture, God knows, I know not, but they appear'd to me Real.' And Ferriar, the modern physician who described the Salem trials as a 'memorable fit of national insanity', was careful to preserve the doctrine of divine providence, even the idea that ghosts might be sent in its service. But Ferriar did enter the nineteenth century with his ideas about the effects of brain irritation, delirium and hallucination, the symptoms of which could be seen in the sort of romantic temperaments 'which dispose men to cultivate the higher and graver species of poetry' and the highland tradition of second sight whereby apparitions warned of deaths. But it is a pencil annotation at the end of this particular copy of Ferriar's *Essay* which is most telling about the popular thinking that connects contrasting eras over the last four hundred years. Here an irate reader, probably in the inter-war period, took the debate back to Glanvill: 'This is all very well, but when one has seen and conversed with a spirit it doesn't exactly satisfy one that it was all bosh! All [that is] proved here is that one may see spectral illusions, which was never doubted.'

The annotator had a story, perhaps about Helen Duncan. But stories can be piled on and on, and still the question of genuine versus fraud would be unresolved. Trickery is part of the problem of belief, not its solution. Evidence of Helen's shenanigans was plain, yet belief endured. Not all Spiritualists considered her to be on the level and most who did knew she cheated occasionally, allowing Laurence Wilson, son of Percy, to say she was one of only two genuine materialization mediums he had seen and even she used fraud. Many Spiritualists expected genuineness, so regarded poor evidence as an aberration and advanced the idea of 'mixed phenomena'. A Spiritualist who saw Mrs Duncan in London in 1942 wrote to the DPP, saying: 'To my mind the features of every "spirit" that appeared were precisely the same, viz. the thick lips and rather coarse features of Mrs Duncan enshrouded in a muslin veil', concluding: 'I do not contend that Mrs Duncan has not got the power which she professes to possess, but I *do* say that occasionally she appears to lose that power (possibly thro' overwork) and then stoops to fraud rather than return the entrance money which has been charged.'

Another piece of chicanery had the *spirits* providing bogus evidence. Trial witness Dr Winning was unfazed by the idea that props were used, believing 'the controls might be obliged to make use of "earthly" materials'; and Abdy Collins wondered 'whether Albert does not apport rubber gloves and cheesecloth and masks on some occasions as a leg-pull for the audience'. Finally, as Margaret Vivian argued, 'If the sitters are strongly persuaded in favour of the fraud theory they will get manifestations that have every appearance of trickery.' Montague Rust agreed and explained the LSA fiasco thus: 'One sitter with a hostile critical mind is quite enough to put everything wrong, and this is the element which the London people forget.'

Even if mediumship is ultimately in the mind's eye of the beholder, we might also consider the mind of the medium. Although many historians would think this territory out of bounds, it is impossible not to wonder just what was going on in Helen Duncan's head. Was she a cool, calculating impostor? Or does this only explain the problem away? Was her psychological make-up in fact incompatible with such deceitfulness? In 1938 Dr Nandor Fodor, sacked by the IIPR for his avant-garde theories, was fighting a war on two fronts: against Spiritualists for their miracle mongering and psychical researchers for their narrow-mindedness. In the autumn of that year, however, as hopes for peace in Europe ebbed away, the embattled Fodor was relieved by none other than Sigmund Freud, a corresponding SPR member who, having read the manuscript of his book, reassured him: 'Your turning away from interest in whether the observed phenomena were genuine or fraudulent, your turning towards the psychological study of the medium and the uncovering of her previous history, seem to be the important steps which will lead to the elucidation of the phenomena under investigation.' Perhaps there is more to Helen Duncan than meets the historical eye. Having explained everything in 1931, Harry Price was still perplexed by the fact that she had come to London to commit such a bare-faced fraud, and asked: 'Why did the medium dare to pirouette among us, in a bright light, with a teleplasmic tail trailing round our feet?' Who the hell did the Duncans think they were?

Henry Duncan's role is yet another grey area. Many mediums were thought to use accomplices, sometimes in elaborate scams: in 1930 Lady Terrington discovered a trapdoor and remotely operated lights and bells in premises vacated by the British College of Psychic Science. But for a travelling medium like Helen, a companion was the key asset and in the 1930s, at least, this was Henry, variously described as booking agent, minder, business manager – even pimp. Almost certainly, he pressurized his wife to perform and when the going got tough he dematerialized faster than Albert in a police raid. Here we need to return to Henry's confessions from 1931. According to one pundit, Henry's acceptance of the regurgitation theory was a way of admitting that the game was up without implicating himself; but, as a secular judgement upon people inhabiting a very non-secular world, this cannot stand alone as an explanation. Ten years of experience had taught Henry that mediums tended to have childlike dispositions, simple and shy, but wilfully obsessed with meeting the expectations of others. To this end, he protested jesuitically to the NLPR Council, fraud might be motivated subconsciously: he believed Helen was genuine, but also believed in an 'automatism of the will', which enabled her to swallow cheesecloth. The theory was more than the NLPR could swallow, but may still have held some truth. The following day Henry informed the LSA that 'Mrs Duncan was in the habit of losing her will (entering an altered state of consciousness) for a time about three hours before the sitting and said he believed that in a state of unconsciousness resembling hypnosis, Mrs Duncan secreted things in or about her person and that she could retain these things in her stomach and eat and digest food.'

In this, Henry may have had a hand, for he was adept at hypnotism – a skill he later used to ease his daughter Gena's birth-pangs. SPR pioneer Frederick Myers had been one of the first to notice how hypnotism could effect automatism in suggestible subjects (today witnessed at many a seaside theatre or college ball) and the idea was popularized by George du Maurier's novel *Trilby* (1894) where the eponymous girl is manipulated by the hypnotist Svengali to sing, to the extent that, the author ventured to suggest, she was not just asleep but had actually ceased to exist. It may be just a coincidence that the story was released as an Oscar-winning film in 1931, and 'Svengali' entered the English language.

No one who has witnessed stage hypnosis will doubt that the effect could be interpreted as spiritual control. Reading about Margery in the *Atlantic Monthly* in 1925, Houdini was interested in Dr Hoagland's views about mediumship and hypnotic trance: 'A narrowing of consciousness is obtained by darkness or by concentrating on some simple sensory stimulus . . . the subject is urged to render his mind passive. He is then lulled to sleep by the operator . . . with the parting suggestion to do what he is told. In a trance, the subject is apparently bereft of a will of his own.'

Acting as a guide, the accomplice – Dr Crandon, say, or Henry Duncan – could not only manipulate the medium, but could call upon sitters to focus their energies and attentions on helping to produce evidence of the truths which, after all, they had paid to see. And here's the clincher: it was possible that even he, as protagonist, was subsumed within the alternative reality of his own drama. Theoretical psychologist Nicholas Humphrey, who has no truck with any form of the supernatural, has suggested that Jesus may have been a conjuror who sincerely came to believe in his own powers because of the way others responded to his tricks – what Humphrey calls a 'virtuous circle' whereby faith and action became self-confirming and even initial self-doubt could provoke a yearning to inspire wonder in others without pretence. Today, psychoanalysts recognize similar behaviour in many relationships, describing 'congruent fantasies' and 'complementary fantasies' where one or more people cooperate to act out their innermost desires. That the LSA were sympathetic to the possibility of this in 1931 is suggested by a letter from the Secretary, Mercy Phillimore, to the SPR Research Officer, which referred to 'proof to us that conscious deception had been practised by the Duncans'. Reading over her typing before she sent it, Miss Phillimore decided to be more circumspect, inserting 'or subconscious' in ink.

Mediumship could weave a spell of fascination between husband and wife who otherwise had little in common. Some mediums could no more renounce their gift (or confess to being frauds) than they could admit that their marriages were farcical. The entranced wife of W. B. Yeats scribbled automatic messages to distract her spiritualistic husband from his poetic musings about the revolutionary Maud Gonne, and thereby became, in his words, 'a perfect wife, kind wise and unselfish'; her revelations helped to inspire *A Vision*, published in 1925. In a more intimately sexual way, mediumship formed a bond of interest between Kathleen Goligher and her husband in the 1930s. In 1938, Mollie Goldney's exposure of Agnes Abbott at the IIPR also revealed some home truths: she said she cheated because her beery, unemployed husband forced her to perform mediumship – although she had once been a true medium, a role he genuinely believed in and admired. How could she disappoint him? What had Mina Stinson, a poor divorcee from Toronto, to offer doughty Harvard physician Dr Crandon except her incarnation as world-famous medium 'Margery'? In William McDougall's opinion, nothing, and once he appeared to tire of her she invented the mediumship 'with the hope of regaining his confidence and affection'. Privately, Dr Hoagland expressed the view that:

Dr Crandon is a man who has never learned to play. He takes everything very seriously. Dr Crandon took up Spiritualism as a violent hobby and Mrs Crandon played it for all it was worth. I think that there may have been elements of hysteria that made her believe her own phenomena at those early stages but this is relatively unimportant. It was all good fun for her anyway and she found that her husband was quite fascinated. They both found themselves at the center of attention.

Harvard colleagues agreed that Dr Crandon could be both accomplice in deception *and* sincere ambassador for her mediumship, and that the phenomena were 'the product of an autonomism built up by direct and auto suggestion in a way of which Dr and Mrs Crandon were unconscious'. At least this explanation indicted the mediumship while limiting the ignominy heaped upon the estimable Boston socialites themselves.

For a medium like Helen Duncan the best compliments were back-handed ones. To her more cultivated supporters in 1944 she was 'a simple, quaintly gifted, but honest unlettered woman'; 'not a woman of any great intellectual attainments, but she is a medium'. Charles Loseby remembered her as 'a humble and ignorant woman with certain physical attributes in respect of which she suggested no special virtue in herself'. Her childhood may hold the key to her character, at least insofar as she resembled what Frank Podmore termed 'a child of larger growth', displaying the same dissociative, regressive tendencies as he had noticed in entranced Victorian mediums. She was Madame Victoria Duncan, the aggressive hysteric, swearing and blaspheming, swinging chairs and punches at those who challenged her; and then she was Nellie MacFarlane, the passive child whose utter compliance during an intimate examination astonished the doctors Harry Price hired in June 1931. At the time, the doctors also noted an infantile dreaminess, and a tendency to slip easily into trances from which they roused her by speaking loudly and directly into her face.

Many direct-voice mediums supposedly received messages from children, or were controlled by them. Mrs Osborne Leonard's juvenile control 'Feda', it was argued, was a classic Jungian complementary character, a dramatic projection of the medium's subconscious self in trance. Freud's parental archetypes and childhood sexual conflicts are plausible motors of trance mediumship: within the SPR the austere Eleanor Sidgwick, with her fondness for pure mathematics and the colour grey, always found favour with the childish secondary personalities of mediums who saw in her a strict mother who could be gentle and kind, even though she never had a child of her own. Nicholas Humphrey offers an even more tantalizing proposition: young children witness daily the miraculous way in which their needs are met and have to grow out of thinking they are magicians; even sulky adolescents are prone to the fantasy that they are specially gifted and misunderstood by the world. These fixations, at once introverted *and* extroverted, selfish *and* magnanimous, do not just describe Helen Duncan: they come close to defining her inasmuch as a person can be defined by psychology. By the time she was old enough to perform real magic – her petty prophecies and scholastic triumphs – her self-awareness was shaped by the reactions of her peers, and even when these were adverse the sense of being special was the same, an effect visible in her mystical daughter Gena every time Lilian told her to shut up. To inspire awe or fear (perhaps both) is to stir the emotions of others and it can be addictive.

Afraid of dark enclosed spaces, Helen could become hysterical if the cabinet curtain was drawn before she was ready; she would always leave a room if someone was present she disliked; in the dressing room before a seance she muttered her fears that Albert would let her down, afterwards that the faces of the sitters betrayed suspicion and disappointment when she had given them everything she could; her histrionic displays at the Old Bailey persuaded a *News of the World* reporter that 'she is unbalanced, and seems always to be under the compulsion of extreme reactions'. Sometimes, Helen – the young innocent banished from her family home with her unborn child – would take on the personality of a lost orphan, the cloyingly sentimental refrain, 'I don't know where my mammy is' betraying the darker, deeper and sadder causes of her mediumship.

Attitudes to women are also relevant. However much the old world was shattered by the Great War, inter-war Britain remained a highly stratified society where the more progressive alternative to landed indifference among the ruling class was the condescending *noblesse oblige* of liberal élitists. But at least most men, however poor, got to be kings in their own households, backed by the law. Women may have been allowed to vote, smoke and display their knees in public, but they had not slipped the leash: it had just been lengthened. Most women were not like the suffragettes whose ghosts haunted the cells of Holloway; they accepted the petty inequalities and indignities because they knew no other way. Yet still they suffered, their frustration internalized, and sometimes exteriorized in mental illness, religious fanaticism, or other eccentricities. The legal label of 'witch' attached to Helen Duncan seems superficial as a parallel between the seventeenth and twentieth centuries compared to the way witchcraft and mediumship were both sustained by institutionalized fantasies of female power in a man's world. In the medium's parlour, men paid women to hear what they – or the spirits – had to say. Entranced women swore obscenely in polite company and were congratulated for it: the chief control of the prim Mrs Piper was a foul-mouthed French doctor. Profanity, blasphemy, exhibitionism – symbolic rebellions against every form of social restriction – had once been features of the diabolic possession of female adolescents, from the pornographic poses of the Ursuline nuns of Loudun in absolutist France to the weepy bible-hurling tantrums of girls in colonial America. In England, even minor possession cases once had doctors and clerics from Oxford and London rushing to the scene, sometimes borrowing the afflicted young women for special study. Away from home, they were often exposed as frauds, but not before the virtuous circle of pretence, amazement, expectation, phenomenon and their own sincere belief in their powers had been closed.

These were rarely conscious bids for attention and respect, rather the symptoms of complex psychological episodes which, in extreme cases, were manifested not just verbally or gesturally, but physically. 'When a child has grown up to be a woman,' Freud suggested, 'she may find all the demands she used to make in her childhood countered owing to her marriage with an inconsiderate husband.' Illness, real or imagined, allowed her to withdraw her obedience and make demands of her own. And many mediums were sickly. Helen Duncan's frequent cuts, sores and burns (almost invariably caused by cigarettes) may have been the product of low self-esteem, even self-loathing, likewise her apparent propensity for swallowing rubbish: matchsticks, cigarettes ends and carpet tacks were found inside her during an abdominal operation, rendering less wholesome the 'vacuum cleaner' effect of which Mrs Homer had boasted to Stanley Worth. But these effects nonetheless elicited sympathetic responses. Likewise, the fact that she really was a sick woman gave her supporters something with which to magnify the scale of her sacrifice.

Childbirth was also treated as a form of illness and offered a stage to the rebellious female hysteric in that it was one vital thing women could do which men could not. Traumatic though this was at the best of times, evidence exists of a kind of freakish maternity, a ripple sent by a subordinate woman across the still pond of nature. In sixteenth-century Germany the medical spotlight fell on a young woman in Esslingen whose belly had swollen monstrously – until she was exposed and executed; mere ridicule awaited Mary Toft of Godalming who, in the 1720s, simulated delivery of a litter of rabbits by storing them in her uterus, but not before medical men had lent credence to the phenomenon. That said, after 1600, doctors in Germany and England were beginning to associate the symptoms of possession with gynaecological disorders, hence the term 'hysteria' (wandering womb) and here parallels to physical mediumship three centuries later need not be laboured. Just think back to Montague Rust seeing ectoplasm streaming from Helen Duncan's every orifice, an event related by J.B. McIndoe to Harry Price in 1931. By 1942 McIndoe had made the story his own, embellishing it into a *tableau vivant* of luxuriant fecundity:

> She stood there, in trance, white material of some sort streaming apparently from her eyes, her ears, her nose and her mouth. It seemed a white jelly-like substance right up to the orifices from which it seemed to be flowing. But even more weird and fascinating was the spectacle of a liquid spurting from the nipples of her breasts, apparently transparent as it left them, then becoming white as it fell, condensing into threads which somehow seemed to merge into some sort of fabric which draped the lower part of her body and hung like a kilt down to her knees.

Not content with being a prolific natural mother, within Helen's body grew the stuff of life by which the dead would be reborn and many people, she discovered, thanked her for it.

When the ectoplasm took shape as the dear departed, the possibility arose that 'multiple personality disorder' played a part. In modern psychiatry the existence of this condition is contentious and when it is accepted it is more likely to be termed 'dissociative identity disorder'; but after the First World War it became popular as a means of characterizing various forms of abnormal behaviour from the suspended consciousness of shell-shocked soldiers, to dysfunctional phobias and obsessions, to the voluble *dramatis personae* of the seance room. The way had been paved by a study of an American student who, shy and submissive in herself, under hypnosis became someone far more demonstrative and spiteful.

In July 1931, Chairman of the London Psychical Laboratory Committee Dr Fielding-Ould concluded that this sort of explanation was the only way they could acquit Mrs Duncan, asserting that 'her total personality was accustomed to be disintegrated under her husband's hypnotic influence and the fraudulent practices that have been witnessed are due in some measure to her secondary and less responsible personality'. In his presidential address to the SPR in 1939, Professor H. H. Price commented on the widespread acceptance of the idea and the way it had 'thrown great light on some of the most obscure phenomena of the human mind'. By 1944 it was a concept even mass circulation newspapers were using to explain Helen Duncan's mediumship, although in his analysis of the case Donald West was more trenchant: 'A more likely explanation would seem to be that her personality is subject to some degree of dissociation at all times, but that at her séances it is so extreme that her whole character may change from that of an ordinary, dull, rather clumsy woman, to a very deft and resourceful cheat.'

Albert, the cultured but irascible gentleman with the accent universally described as 'Oxford' – the BBC's voice of authority – made for a perfectly comprehensible alter ego, especially set against a manipulative and overbearing Henry. Helen Duncan's sitters were mocked and mimicked by Albert, and in 1931 he never missed a chance to ridicule and chastise Henry, addressing him sternly as 'Duncan', meeting him eye to eye as an equal in debate, and occasionally slipping into the vernacular when he told him to go and lose himself. But, like 'Walter', Albert could be strict with the medium as well, occasionally making asides to her in the darkness, even though she was supposed to be in trance. One thing he could not stand (apart from Henry) was coughing, from Helen or anyone else. At a seance in Glasgow in the 1940s, hearing a cough from within the cabinet, Albert said loudly and sharply, 'Stop that!' and then a few moments later, so quietly that hardly anybody heard it, he whispered: '*Stop smoking.*'

In the mid-1980s, Manfred Cassirer, an SPR Council member with a special interest in Helen Duncan's mediumship, concluded that the balance of fraud and genuineness was 'a problem of such complexity that as yet no conclusive solution can even be imagined'. Perhaps this outcome will never avail itself. The quest for conclusive solutions and squared circles presupposes a consensually agreed definition of reality, which is wholly inappropriate to the worlds of fantasy, belief and spirit communication. It is possible for us to rise above the debate in line with the psychologist Carl Jung whose interest in Christ's virgin birth had nothing to do with whether the famous miracle was true or false, only the fact that such an idea existed. Fictions can be as revealing as more verifiably true stories. So when, in 1946, Donald West declared that 'the truth is that Mrs Duncan is an unsolved riddle', he chose not to consider that broadening his workaday concept of truth to embrace alternative interpretations of the universe would simply have left no riddle to be solved. And the men and women whose lives compassed these alternative interpretations – those able, at least in some measure, to take Helen Duncan at face value – were not just simple-minded fools, Freudian basket-cases, or even eccentric scientists and aristocratic dabblers, but some of the most publicly influential and politically powerful people in the British Isles.

8

MANY MANSIONS

Public Life and Prominent Men

hrough books such as Estelle Roberts's *Red Cloud Speaks*, Ena Bügg had converted her friend Bob Brake to Spiritualism, so that when he was posted to an RAF radar station in Preston, Lancashire, it was natural for him to join his local SNU church. One evening in 1941 he was invited to the President's house where he met a coarse, corpulent woman, introduced to him as Mrs Duncan. The guests were chatting by the fireside, when Helen, until then merrily slurping tea and smoking, suddenly slumped and began speaking as 'Albert'. The light was switched off and, flickering flames illuminating their faces, the

Mr John Maude KC, counsel for the Prosecution, 1944.

company leant forward to hear the first message, which went to Bob from a gentleman who had passed with kidney trouble. When the light was switched back on, Helen thought she had been asleep. Bob was to meet Helen again, this time at a trumpet seance, which she attended as a sitter and so herself received messages. The guide, 'Joe', a rough-and-ready soldier from the trenches, put her in touch with Estelle Roberts's father who sang an aria from Gounod's *Faust* and was followed by a wireless operator tapping out a message in Morse code, which he decoded as a mayday. Not just any distress call, this belonged to the stricken liner *Titanic* aboard which the operatic communicator – veteran journalist, W. T. Stead – had perished with 1489 others on the night of 14–15 April 1912.

With his straggly beard and mustard suits, in life Stead had cut a distinctive figure on Fleet Street where, as editor of the *Pall Mall Gazette*, he perfected the blend of piety and prurience characteristic of the modern tabloid press. But by the 1890s his crusade against vice was surpassed by a passion for Spiritualism. Though sceptical about materialization – he once sent Estelle on a tour of drapers' shops to match up a piece of 'ectoplasm' – he abhorred the SPR and believed in the authenticity of spirit photography. He was not long silent after death. Mrs Etta Wriedt, a medium he had arranged to meet in New York in 1912, was urged to go to England where she was to hold hundreds of seances, which encouraged Estelle Stead to develop her own powers. Other mediums brought messages from Stead. One which began 'I am one of the passengers on the steamer Titanic. A more awful disaster than the wreck may not be conceived', initiated a dispute about Stead's will – one of several similar cases. The poet Yeats was contacted by a friend's nephew, Sir Hugh Lane, who had been drowned when the *Lusitania* was sunk in 1915. The spiritual Lane, however, was less concerned with the codicil to his will than with rumours that he had committed suicide. Yeats tended to accept such communications as real and, like Oscar Wilde and George Bernard Shaw, was influenced by theosophy. On a mission to Paris Yeats saw something like 'a fragment of the Milky Way' in Eva Carrière's lap and in 1917 attended a seance with Sir William Barrett, from which he concluded that Lane and other spirits were angst-ridden entities who 'should be treated as a doctor would treat a nervous patient'. This, he argued, would be appropriate even if they turned out to be no more than the secondary personalities of the mediums.

Spiritualism had been a part of professional life in Britain from the 1870s when its founder, Kate Fox, married well-connected London barrister H.D. Jencken (the wedding table was said to have reared up on two legs). Middle-class concerns and beliefs were indulged in different ways, but by 1914 academic interest in materialization had abated, the Sidgwicks' attention now focused upon the 'cross-correspondences' – dovetailed messages received by the likes of Margaret Verrall (a classics lecturer at Cambridge), Leonora Piper in Boston, and Rudyard Kipling's sister, Alice Fleming, in India. Crucially, this research was fuelled not just by religious longing, but the desire for knowledge otherwise unobtainable on earth. Traditionally, this had been a classic motive associated with becoming a witch, of which Faust was the best-known literary example. In pursuit of superior intelligence, Renaissance princes had employed magicians and astrologers (famously Elizabeth I's Dr Dee) and conversely sought to protect themselves against sorcery deployed by their enemies: in 1607 James I's Witchcraft Act was amended to make it a more effective weapon against treason. It was perhaps inevitable, therefore, that the next time spirits were taken seriously in British society, men prominent in public life would show an interest in the enlightenment to be derived from them. Where they did not, the infectiousness and purposeful creativity of Spiritualist lore could be relied upon to make up the difference. The story which emerges reaches beyond the quest for religious and scientific truth about the afterlife described in earlier chapters, and centres on power and those who exercised it in government, politics and the public sphere.

A prominent figure is Abraham Lincoln who in 1831, it is said, visited an elderly negress in New Orleans who informed him that he would become President and abolish slavery. During the Civil War, when Spiritualism flourished in America, Lincoln was devastated by the death of his son and entertained a medium, Nettie Colburn, in the White House. In 1891 she wrote a book which asked *Was Abraham Lincoln a Spiritualist?* to which the answer is: no, but for a while at least he did take mediumship seriously. (For an American hero who *was* a Spiritualist, look no further than gunslinger Wild Bill Hickok.) Across the Atlantic, the crowned heads of Europe patronized mediums. D. D. Home attended courts as far east as St Petersburg and in England Queen Victoria's legendary grieving for Prince Albert was such that even if she had never flirted with Spiritualism, rumours would have been inevitable. A watch supposedly presented to medium 'Georgiana Eagle' by the Queen, and later given to Etta Wriedt by W. T Stead, was a fake (there was a misspelling in the engraving), but it is more plausible that conversations with royal ghillie John Brown had Spiritualist content, given his highland primitivism. Rumours that he acted as her medium, accounts of which allegedly were burned, are unfounded. Evidence for the dabbling of Victoria's longest-serving Prime Minister, William Gladstone, is more compelling. Besides his well-known approval of the SPR's work, in 1877 he told a newspaper that he knew of no rule which forbade Christians exploring Spiritualism, adding the following year: 'I do not share or approve the temper of simple contempt with which so many view the phenomena.' Work alone prevented his greater involvement, but it seems he did visit at least one medium, the materializer and Fleet Street editor William Eglinton who, like Home, toured widely and was received in Russia by the Tsar.

Not every great man was impressed. Darwin walked out of his only seance in 1874, and was bewildered that his colleague Alfred Russel Wallace viewed Spiritualism as a 'science of vast extent' and an everlasting basis for religion and philosophy. More outspoken was Darwin's ally T. H. Huxley who famously declared: 'The only good that I can see in a demonstration of the truth of "Spiritualism" is to furnish an additional argument against suicide. Better live a crossing-sweeper than die and be made to talk twaddle by a "medium" hired at a guinea a seance.' Like many conjurors, Dickens was said to be a medium, but this seems unlikely, given the derision he too poured upon mediumship. The fact that such men went to seances at all tells us something. In the era of the cross-correspondences, distinct from the crepus-cular melodramas of materialization seances, a forum was taking shape where dignified mediums at ease in the groves of academe and on the London circuit were employed by the well-to-do. In the 1920s Geraldine Cummins, shattered by her brother's death at Gallipoli, began a fifty-year career as a medium, dividing her time between west London and her family's farm in Cork. Her most famous works were *The Scripts of Cleophas*, a supplement to the New Testament, and later *A Swan on a Black Sea*, commu-nications received from Mrs Winifred Coombe Tennant, the first British female delegate to the League of Nations. Miss Cummins had many well-heeled clients. In 1939 she visited the Surrey mansion of Lord Gerald Balfour where she was silently received in the drawing room and, entering a trance, produced a sheaf of messages of which Lord and Lady Balfour took custody. Then everyone sat down to lunch during which matters psychic were not mentioned once.

Prominence in life increased the chances of returning after death. In 1947 Irish Spiritualist writer Shaw Desmond addressed a meeting in Newcastle-upon-Tyne at which he broadcast that American President Franklin D. Roosevelt, who had died two years earlier, had visited mediums to seek political guidance. Before the end of the year, Geraldine Cummins had reported that FDR's spirit had spoken through her, predicting US economic imperialism, labour unrest for the British and the rise of a strong leader in France. In nineteenth-century America the most common communicators were Edgar Allan Poe, Thomas Jefferson and Benjamin Franklin, although these and other communicators bear out SPR investigator Alan Gauld's impression that 'if the great minds of this world degenerate so much in the next the prospect for lesser fry is bleak indeed'. Anyone familiar with the mathematical beauty of Christopher Wren's buildings will recoil from the monstrous Victorian Arnewood Tower in Hampshire; that the architect was possessed by something is certain but it was not, as he claimed, Wren. In the 1920s Margery knocked off the odd Wren sketch and came up with passable Wildean witticisms; in 1923 the *Occult Review* reported good examples of the latter coming through, although utterances from Shelley 'would have shamed that genius on earth and certainly outraged his memory in the world beyond'. Harry Price once met a midwife allegedly controlled by epic poet Homer, but whose verses 'might have originated in a box of Christmas crackers'.

The silliness was abundant. A spiritual Sir Walter Scott told Mrs Piper that there were monkeys in the sun and Gladstone, in life faultlessly patrician, confirmed his identity with the words: 'Yis, I'm 'im.' After the war, Alan Crossley, a medium who had no doubts about Helen Duncan, saw a woman who claimed to be von Ribbentrop looking for his army; when Crossley informed her that von Ribbentrop had been the Foreign Minister and therefore had no army, she became abusive. He also told of a sitter controlled by the spirit of her pet dog who, to cries of 'God bless you friend!', crawled around the floor – barking. Transfiguration circles witnessed more than just bellicose Zulus and inscrutable Mandarins. In 1935 a medium, straining to produce Abraham Lincoln, got as far as the mouth, whereas Edith Balmer could do the whole face, plus Byron, Tennyson, Joseph Chamberlain and Cardinal Newman. One sitter saw a materialization of Lord Northcliffe in Mrs Balmer's ear and in 1948 Denys Parsons, though sceptical of Mrs Duncan, was impressed by an SPR test at which elastic Edith assumed the appearance of Queen Victoria, Gladstone and Sir Philip Sidney. Houdini often returned in spirit, but after three years of messages his widow wondered if she would ever hear their private code word. In 1936, on the tenth anniversary of his death, once more Bess Houdini's precious Erich failed to come through at a special seance, whereupon she resolved to turn out the light at his shrine.

The personalities destined to toil hardest after death were those who advanced Spiritualism in life. Despite his intellect and credentials, for many in the scientific establishment Sir Oliver Lodge went too far with his Spiritualism, which he had taken up twenty years before the death of his son Raymond. The confidant of radical thinkers from Joseph Chamberlain to George Bernard Shaw, he was lambasted by Sir James Dewar, inventor of the vacuum flask, and Charles Mercier, a psychiatrist of the behaviourist school, although the analyst Freud did accept that telepathy might be 'a kind of psychic parallel to wireless telegraphy' and possibly a form of atavistic communication. For a physicist whose life spanned the Battle of Balaclava and the Battle of Britain, it was understandable that Lodge's specialization in electricity and telegraphy would be accompanied by an interest in animal magnetism, mesmerism, hypnosis and telepathy, all invisible media by which physical effects were achieved remotely. The metaphor for brain function, which during the Renaissance had been hydraulic and in our own time is digital, was in Lodge's lifetime telegraphic. The idea extended across society. In 1886 Marie Corelli's novel, *The Romance of Two Worlds*, made electricity the connecting matter between God and creation; French peasants resisted the installation of 'evil' telephone lines; and by the 1920s mediums were likened to radio transmitters (Helen Duncan to a *huge* radio transmitter). In 1931, J. Arthur Findlay's *On the Edge of the Etheric* taught that the universe consisted of orders of vibrations of which the highest – the mind – merged into the ether at death, an idea which appealed to Lodge who *knew* conventional physics could accommodate mediumship. In the 1920s he took this message on a lecture tour of the USA and there joined the debate over the 'Margery' mediumship. Initially determined to resist Houdini's prejudices, his hopes that Mina Crandon would produce Raymond's fingerprints gradually dissipated and by July 1925 he had rejected even the idea of her 'mixed mediumship'. The need to protect genuine mediums, however, remained close to his heart. In 1928 he protested to Prime Minister Stanley Baldwin who politely suggested that for him to ask for legal immunity for mediums might be interpreted 'as a request to the Government to connive at the fraudulent exploitation of the public'. The same year, the Home Office filed news cuttings reporting two suicides of youths who had dabbled in Spiritualism.

Lodge's attitude to physical mediums was a reluctance to allow the probability of fraud to obscure their possible significance should they be genuine. Whatever disappointment he felt in Margery, therefore, an invitation to the LSA to see one of Helen Duncan's first major performances he accepted with hope in his heart. On the afternoon of 30 October 1930 Harry Price – conspicuously absent from the guest list – heard noise from 'the people down below' and came out from his laboratory: 'Looking over the banisters as they trooped up the stairs, I could not help wondering what the afternoon would bring forth. I was soon to be informed, however, as very shortly the floor of my office reverberated to the "Hurrahs!" and "Bravos!" of those beneath, and I knew that Mrs Duncan had received the *cachet* of the Spiritualists.'

Lodge had watched while Helen, sitting like an outlandish rag doll, had been examined and dressed, and had escorted her into the seance room where the other sitters were waiting. Seven minutes after she was tied into her sack and the lights switched off, a strip of white ectoplasm a foot long appeared at the cabinet curtains and Lodge, whom Albert complimented on his nice name, was asked to step forward and feel it. It wriggled over his hand and he returned to his seat, swapping with another sitter so that he could hear better. As they waited 'for some person to come and get her out of here and take the atoms to pieces', as Albert put it, what self-respecting physicist could have resisted a peek? Peering into the cabinet, Lodge saw Mrs Duncan sweaty and snoring, and then the ectoplasm again: 'It was heavy, cold and clammy, its texture was like a number of parallel threads forming a bundle two inches thick. It might have been separated into strands. It was not like woven material but was stringy. A curiously unpleasant slight odour remained either on my hand or in my nostrils as an occasional whiff for 12 hours afterwards.' Lodge watched as the ectoplasm coalesced into a blob. 'It looks like a baby's head!' enthused Henry, to which Albert's predictably curt reply was: 'It isn't a baby's head, do you think I have no brain!' Lodge, who had a very good brain, was not overly impressed with these vaudevillian inanities; but then neither did he criticize them. Instead, he continued to act as a public ambassador for Spiritualism in all its forms.

The following year Lodge lectured to over two thousand men at the Portsmouth Brotherhood, to whom his example was a shining and inspiring one. They would have known him best as the author of the best-selling account of his son's spiritual survival after his death at the Battle of Ypres in 1915. This filial reunion had little to do with the physical mediumship offered by Helen Duncan and others. Lodge had been impressed by Eusapia Palladino on the Ile Roubard in 1894, but the likes of Mrs Piper and Mrs Osborne Leonard were more his cup of tea, and it was through these more sophisticated women that he enjoyed his regular chats with Raymond's spirit. Etta Wriedt he liked so much he gave her a cello and was not deterred by accusations that other-worldly noises in her seance trumpet were achieved with a pharmaceutical powder used to coat pills. Doubts about her mediumship were surpassed by the ability of her guide, an eighteenth-century Glaswegian émigré to Indiana, to connect her to spirits speaking in most west European languages, plus Arabic, Norwegian and Croatian. Her communications were not just evidential, but emotional in that they built the bridge of love to his adored son, a subject about which Lodge received many letters. In 1933 a Miss Wainwright, a retired schoolteacher from St Leonards-on-Sea, was impelled to write after reading his books and receiving messages on a Ouija board from an ex-pupil also killed at Ypres. 'Dear Sir Oliver,' she marvelled, 'what you are to us who grope so blindly cannot be told in words.'

Her fawning admiration was shared by the Rt. Hon. W.L. Mackenzie King, Canada's liberal and idealistic Prime Minister, who sought guidance in the spirit world after being thrust into the political wilderness in the early 1930s, attending the first of many seances in 1932. In the following year he wrote, thanking Lodge for a signed copy of his autobiography, and expressing sadness at the passing of Lord and Lady Grey but also his certainty that they had survived death. He said he now knew Etta Wriedt well, and that she spoke fondly of Lodge and her cello. Mackenzie King had first met Lodge at the home of the Greys in 1926, at which time he was still Premier and in Britain for the Imperial Conference at which equal status for the dominions was established. Lady Pamela Grey was a devout Spiritualist who would send her driver to fetch Mrs Osborne Leonard from her cottage in East Barnet and sometimes went there herself. She also provided a rousing foreword for Rev. Charles Drayton Thomas's *Life Beyond Death with Evidence* in 1927: 'There have been some in all ages who have held they spoke with the dead, and who have given us their message. It may be the message is being recorded, fruitfully, at last.' Back in office in 1936, Mackenzie King's express wish to abandon public life and devote himself to Lodge's writings may have been just flattery, but is still significant. Mackenzie King, who that year opposed sanctions against Italy for invading Ethiopia, enclosed a copy of a Remembrance Day broadcast in which he called upon nations to 'preserve the blessings of peace' and trusted that the prayers of children would bring down 'legions of angels each with its power to save'. When prayers failed in 1939, and after consulting the spirits, he wrote to the dictators urging peace but feared the worst. Nor was this the last war he would see coming. In 1947–8, while still in office, he sat several times with Geraldine Cummins and at one seance at the Dorchester Hotel in London was advised to pay attention to serious developments in Asia. He died in 1950, just before outbreak of the Korean War.

The history of Spiritualism illustrates how memories of one war fed into foreboding about the next, but also that spirits offered a way of coping with Freud's 'accumulation of death'. The spirit of Raymond Lodge seems to have helped many a diffident serviceman (in both world wars) to return to the other side, an idea which acquired an eerie solidity in photographs taken at the Cenotaph, London's principal war memorial. In January 1924 Sir Oliver Lodge received a letter from Sir Arthur Conan Doyle enclosing a picture taken by Mrs Ada Deane during the two-minute silence on the previous Armistice Day showing a white miasma dotted with dozens of men's faces. 'It is worth examining with a lens,' Conan Doyle recommended. 'My son is certainly there and, I think, my nephew.' Later that year Mrs Deane commenced sittings with W. T. Stead's daughter Estelle, which led to the publication of a booklet in 1925, *Faces of the Living Dead*, which shrugged off accusations made by the Magic Circle's Occult Committee that the photographs were faked. In the Westminster of the 1920s the Cenotaph symbolized the *public acceptance* of death, unlike Conan Doyle's 'Psychic Book Shop and Library' around the corner (telegraph: 'Ectoplasm, Sowest'), which represented a *private denial* of death. As a Spiritualist campaigner, Conan Doyle lacked Lodge's academic status but made up for it with wealth and energy, and from 1918 tirelessly toured Europe, the USA, Australia, New Zealand and South Africa. He is said to have spent £250,000 of his own money educating the public and badgering politicians, the equivalent today of about £5 million.

In the spring of 1929, Baldwin's government was facing an evenly three-way general election in which competition for votes (including those of all women for the first time) was intense.

Conan Doyle had a questionnaire sent to candidates, promising electoral support (50,000 votes) to any party named by the SNU Parliamentary Committee, which undertook to reform the law. The Liberals and Labour both offered written pledges, and after a meeting of the Cabinet's emergency business committee the Home Secretary invited the Spiritualists to draft a bill, which would receive sympathetic consideration if the Conservatives were re-elected. In the end, support went to the Liberals – not that it did them much good: Labour won and Ramsay MacDonald became Prime Minister.

The more established the SNU became in political life the more their patience with the SPR ran out. In 1930 Conan Doyle led a wave of resignations, realizing that the future lay in practical political action not in addle-headed academic speculation. On 1 July 1930 Conan Doyle led an SNU deputation to the Home Office, which included Hannen Swaffer, Charles Drayton Thomas and Mrs Philip Champion de Crespigny, Principal of the British College of Psychic Science and daughter of the Rt. Hon. Sir Astley Cooper-Key. Home Secretary J.R. Clynes listened to claims that Spiritualism had 'a great contribution to make towards the moral and spiritual uplift of society', and that freedoms granted in the USA and the dominions should be extended. Clynes sympathized, but the bottom line was the law, which, he said, existed to protect the public against fraud and 'mental terrorization'. Non-Spiritualist MP William Kelly, who had introduced the deputation, departed with a joke, hoping that liberty would *materialize* before too long. Six days later Conan Doyle was dead, though not out of touch. On 8 July the Marylebone Spiritualist Association held a seance in the Albert Hall for over 6000 mourners, at which Estelle Stead – now Mrs Estelle Roberts – clairvoyantly saw Conan Doyle in his empty chair and whispered a message to his softly smiling widow. From that point on, Conan Doyle stepped up his campaign, sending messages to an all-night seance in Paris, to Harry Price via R-101 medium Eileen Garrett and to another medium, Grace Cooke, who was inspired by his attentions to found the internationally successful Spiritualist society, the White Eagle Lodge. The face of Manchester transfiguration medium Mrs Bullock was hijacked by Conan Doyle's and a Canadian medium was photographed vomiting ectoplasm containing not only his image but that of Raymond Lodge. As we have seen, Brigadier Roy Firebrace received a message and Helen Duncan even managed a fleeting full-form materialization.

Viewing developments from the sphere of contemplation, the spiritual Conan Doyle must have been disappointed. Clynes had stymied the SNU's ambitions and even though he consented to the drafting of a bill this project was doomed. The Spiritualism and Psychical Research (Exemption) Bill, calling for the licensing of mediums by officially approved churches, was first read in the House of Commons in November 1930, and was mocked in Parliament and by the press. Sir Oliver Lodge, who had advised that it was too ambitious to push for recognition under civil law when the battle against the criminal law had not yet been won, was proved right. The Home Office, which kept a careful eye on public opinion, privately branded the bill 'ridiculous' and after its second reading wrote to the party whips to have it blocked. And so the Tory MP who amused the House with his remark that it was a shame to spoil traditional associations between mediums and witches on broomsticks had his way.

Further behind the political scenes lay a stranger story. In October 1930, Ramsay MacDonald sat down to dinner at Chequers feeling uneasy about the R-101, which his friend Lord Thomson had joined for its maiden flight. The bad news – predicted that day in a newspaper horoscope – did not surprise him. MacDonald's life had been shrouded in grief since the death of his wife Margaret whose presence he felt often. Shortly before the formation of the National Government in August 1931 a friend, Effie Johnson, informed him that during an automatic writing session Margaret had said: 'Tell R. M. I *need* him now; I *need* him now.' In the weeks which followed Grace Cooke (by now in regular contact with Conan Doyle) received similar messages from Margaret who said her husband's work was building the Brotherhood of Man upon which the future of the Labour Party depended and advised that Britain should ally itself with the USA to guard against coming global disturbances. Mrs Cooke's claim that she enjoyed a long correspondence with the Prime Minister rings true with MacDonald's biographer.

Of course, he would not have been the first premier to be so involved. Arthur Balfour (Prime Minister 1902–6) had been SPR President in 1893, a position held in 1906 by his brother Gerald (former Chief Secretary for Ireland and President of the Board of Trade), and their involvement with mediums was common knowledge. Less well known is that in 1924, between his resignation as Prime Minister and election as Liberal leader, David Lloyd George wrote to Sir Oliver Lodge to enquire about a sitting with Mrs Osborne Leonard, to which Lodge replied that he thought it best for him to send a car to collect her as Lady Grey often did. Like Gladstone, MacDonald admitted he should have been more interested in Spiritualism than he had time to be, but did attend at least one seance. In April 1925 he was connected with the recently deceased Foreign Secretary Lord Curzon who charged the Labour leader to promote spirituality in order to avert another war. This he was unable to do and, a decade later, his pacifist dreams crumbling, MacDonald retired to become Lord President of the Council. In October 1936 he made a speech at the opening of a college library in Edinburgh and, having noticed a 300-volume section entitled 'Demonology and Spiritualism', referred to 'a wave of extraordinary credulity among young and up-to-date people'. No longer young and up-to-date himself, a year later he passed away on an ocean liner, and his ashes were united with those of his wife in the same Scottish kirkyard.

For Helen Duncan, the price of fame was not just vilification and imprisonment, but the forced acquisition of a persona shaped by a wider context of public life. The Spiritualist interests of the great and the good, which framed Helen's life, help us to understand her obliquely within her time, but of course also had a more direct bearing on the vicissitudes of her fortunes. The men (and to a lesser extent women) who populated politics, entertainment, science, the press, the law and so on also lavished attention upon her; and they did so not because they loved her, but because they recognized in her a resource to be exploited. This was even true of many of her supporters who barely tolerated the woman they revered as a medium; the vanity and ambition in this story belongs to them as much as it does to her. In this way poor Nellie came to star in her own end-of-season pantomime, one where she played all the parts – the princess and the pauper, the heroine and the fool – and found herself stranded on stage, blinded by the footlights and deafened by the jeering of the audience.

After Helen's Duncan's trial, Spiritualism intruded upon political life far more than the other way round. Sir Ernest Bennett, who had worked in Admiralty Intelligence during the First World War, became a Labour MP in 1929 and joined the British delegation to the League of Nations in 1934. He did not hide his other side: he listed his recreations in *Who's Who* as shooting, fishing and investigating haunted houses – about which he published a book in 1939. In 1930-1, at the time Helen was being tested, he was Vice-President of the LSA and attended no fewer than eleven of her seances, including the one where Sir Oliver Lodge was present, and her first performance where he saw a small face. On 5 December his watch was taken and, feeling a touch, he looked down to see tiny fingers; in March of the next year a larger spirit hand took his and shook it. By then, Bennett's feelings had become cool towards 'that awful female Mrs Duncan'. On 15 May 1944, at the Reform Club in Pall Mall he bumped into Harry Price, with whom he idled away an hour or so swapping Duncan memories, and Price was gratified to learn that even in 1931 Bennett had thought that her spirit faces were achieved by draping a hand in cheesecloth. And yet by this time the agenda had moved on and it mattered less what Bennett or any other politician thought about the genuineness or fraudulence of Helen Duncan's mediumship, only what her conviction under the Witchcraft Act represented for Spiritualist and, by extension, British liberties – a question which, from the spring of 1944, fell to the Home Secretary, Herbert Morrison.

Early in 1945, Morrison met his old socialist ally Hannen Swaffer for lunch at The Ivy off Shaftesbury Avenue and had a friendly argument about the legal plight of British mediums. Before they parted, Morrison grinned and said, 'Well, I'll see you on the Other Side', to which 'Swaff' replied acidly, 'Herbert. You *are* on the other side.' To the tabloid-reading nation Swaffer – said to be sceptical about everything except Spiritualism – was a folk hero and, as the king of gossip and lost causes on Fleet Street, reigned even longer than W. T. Stead. Cadaverous, dishevelled and nicotine-stained, his biographer likened him to an out-of-work ham actor, his trademarks a black cape, floppy bow-tie and a cigarette butt screwed into his drawn face. One cartoonist in 1935 portrayed him as Don Quixote tilting at windmills with an oversized quill, another saw him as a minister in a fantasy Cabinet, with Bernard Shaw as Prime Minister and Sir Oliver Lodge as Foreign Secretary ('This World and the Next'). A member of Maurice Barbanell's home circle, he kept in touch with his old boss Lord Northcliffe and was a friend of artist Austin Spare, taught to paint by a witch boasting ancestry back to Salem. Like Lodge and Conan Doyle, Swaffer was as keen a campaigner as he was a seance-goer and had been a member of the 1930 SNU deputation to the Home Office. In playful but determined correspondence with Morrison about convicted medium Stella Hughes in 1943, he suggested that, to be consistent, the Home Secretary should also enforce ancient laws against making mince pies, selling short lobsters and walking with a lighted cigar – 'I tremble to think what you will do to Winston about this.' In 1945 Swaffer reproduced the letters in a book, which preached the importance of socialism and Spiritualism to deliver the world from future wars, an objective close to the hearts of the entire nation.

It was in defiant spirit that Swaffer had entered the witness box at the Old Bailey on 29 March 1944 and irreverently rattled off the oath like grace said by a hungry schoolboy. 'Now take the oath properly,' ordered the Recorder, Sir Gerald Dodson, tetchily. Swaffer had taken the precaution of looking up Dodson in *Who's Who* and, being a merciless scourge of thespians, was delighted to find that he had co-authored a play, which Swaffer knew from experience would have been atrocious. Although similar to that of the other defence witnesses, Swaffer's testimony was delivered with considerably more aplomb and he alone, with reference to the spirit guide Albert, dismissed his Oxford accent as an invention of the BBC. Swaffer's first seance with Helen

Duncan had been in 1932, the same one where she had escaped magician Will Goldston's handcuffs and knotted sash cord, and at which, he recalled, the flame of a cigarette lighter had caused her nose to bleed. More recently, Swaffer had attended the London test seances, including the one at Percy Wilson's house in Wimbledon, and had seen ectoplasm like living snow form a thick rope which poured from her nostrils, adding that anyone who mistook it for butter muslin would have to be a child. Nor was there any chance that she was acting, a point which gave rise to some droll banter between judge and witness, momentarily author and critic:

LOSEBY: Have you been a dramatic critic?

SWAFFER: Unfortunately, yes.

THE RECORDER: For whom?

SWAFFER: What for, my Lord?

THE RECORDER: You said 'unfortunately'. For whom?

SWAFFER: Unfortunately for the poor critic who has to sit through it, my Lord.

The Recorder, however, got his own back by denying Swaffer the opportunity to share with the court his evidence of Helen Duncan's normal oesophagus, nor would he permit him to try swallowing the cheesecloth which the Prosecution had brought along. Although Swaffer put Henry Elam through his paces, his subsequent boast that he ran rings round Treasury Counsel and then stormed out was too rich and the jury had looked unimpressed when he announced that he himself retained the services of a guide, 'Darak Ahmed'. On this occasion the reporter became the reported, his colourful performance giving his jaded fellow journalists plenty to write about. In the *Daily Mail* the next morning the headline bleated: SWALLOWING TEST BARRED BY JUDGE IN 'SÉANCE' TRIAL.

It was proper that 'the Pope of Fleet Street' should canonize Helen Duncan as the 'St Joan of Spiritualism' in the popular press. Her trial, comparable to that of Socrates said Swaffer, was a sign that 'orthodoxy was back to broomsticks' within an Establishment which cared little for the aspirations towards tolerance laid down in the Atlantic Charter in 1941. After Helen's conviction the style and substance of Swaffer's arguments influenced many an outraged citizen chewing on the end of a pen, from whom the Home Secretary received sacks of correspondence alluding to the machinations of a British Gestapo and the persecution of witches – 'one of the great amusements of the Dark Ages', said Swaffer. In November 1944 a Mrs Vernon-Smith of Folkestone accused Morrison of betraying his roots and forgetting that socialists had once been 'on the people's side, the side of the under-dog, the side abused by the world, taken advantage of by party politics and repressed by legal jugglery'. Like others of its kind, the badly typed letter was repetitious and festooned with exclamation marks, underlining, and ink corrections; but it expressed sincere and emotive truths, all diligently picked out in blue pencil by a civil servant at the Home Office where, in an age of universal adult suffrage, sound administration increasingly meant listening to the general public rather than just telling it what to do.

Slightly more eloquent in his protests was Air Chief Marshal Sir Hugh Dowding, a household name since the Battle of Britain during which he had used radar to deploy fighters surgically, in opposition to the more aggressive tactics of his fellow Spiritualist, Leigh-Mallory. Soon afterwards 'Stuffy' Dowding was ousted and in 1942 retired to concentrate on informing the common man about life in the Great Beyond. In 1943 he caused controversy by publishing in the *Sunday Pictorial* letters from dead servicemen received in automatic writing – many his own pilots from 1940 – and the same year wrote *Many Mansions*, a Spiritualist manifesto which he rushed into print 'while all these lads are having their souls violently torn from their bodies, and leaving inconsolable dear ones behind'. Inspired by *Raymond*, Dowding also drew upon another collection of messages from the spirit of an ordinary soldier published in 1917 by W. T. P., a serving officer. Here, the eponymous Private Dowding (no relation) describes how he had tried to help his comrades carry his body to the dressing station but fell behind when he realized he was a spirit. Sir Hugh Dowding's messages from the Second World War were similar: a drowned sailor waking up in a strange place; a Norwegian shopkeeper told by God to forgive the Nazis who executed him; a fugitive Polish pilot who wondered why he was not tired or hungry; a burned tank officer whose colonel, seemingly oblivious to the bullets flying all around, took him by the shoulder and said: 'Don't you see, Kit, we are dead.'

Dowding's contribution was welcomed by the Spiritualist movement. In July 1943 he led the SNU deputation of which Charles Loseby was spokesman and was received at the Home Office by Under-Secretary Osbert Peake, Morrison having refused to see them. Dowding called the recent prosecutions of mediums 'most lamentable' and was praised by a Spiritualist MP present, Thomas Brooks, for raising public awareness of survival. Subsequent correspondence between Morrison and the SNU, some of it acrimonious, was widely publicized. Morrison did make enquiries among the chief constables and in November 1943 issued a circular recommending concentration on preventing the 'exploitation by impostors of credulous members of the public for private gain'. The private response of the Metropolitan Police was that this had been their policy for years, 'the rock bottom point every time'. Nevertheless, the SNU now suspected that a widespread campaign against mediums was imminent and warned a select number believed to be in greatest danger to exercise extra caution in their work. These few included Helen Duncan.

Dowding sat with various mediums, including Estelle Roberts, and before the end of the war was attending materialization seances. Whether he sat with Helen Duncan is unknown, although Mrs Homer said he had expressed an interest. Previously having thought of ectoplasm only as an 'extremely mysterious but apparently well-authenticated phenomenon' and spirit forms as 'toys of the kindergarten', he was now astounded by what he saw. Like Conan Doyle and Lodge, Dowding took to the stump, preaching about fallen servicemen clamouring to reach loved ones, and describing the universe as a set of concentric spheres each representing a state of spiritual development. On 3 November 1943 he addressed a large crowd at Portsmouth, which included Harold Gill, an Approved Society official, who had thought Spiritualism 'a lot of hooey' but was impressed by Dowding, and was soon attending meetings at the Master Temple where he and his wife were in the front row on the night Helen Duncan was arrested.

After Helen's trial, Dowding wrote to the Lord Chancellor citing the Home Secretary's previous recommendations, only to be reminded early in 1945 that the Witchcraft Act related to imposture just like the Vagrancy Act. Another Home Office memo was sent to chief constables reminding them of this fact, accompanied by an extract of the Lord Chancellor's reply to Dowding. To open laughter in the House of Commons, Thomas Brooks challenged the Home Secretary on 3 May, and Morrison only just wriggled out of a tight situation by blaming the capriciousness of legal interpretation. This, however, only exposed the position of the Government further, leading future health service architect Aneurin Bevan to ask trenchantly and prophetically: 'Is not ambiguous law the worst kind of law; and if there is any dubiety about this matter ought it not to be put right by fresh legislation, so that citizens may know what their rights are under the law?' Five days later the war ended and the democratic spirit of Bevan's question fast pervaded every area of British public life.

Helen Duncan's supporters muttered darkly about conspiracy. The State, they said, had dusted off an archaic statute to prevent her revealing secrets likely to prejudice the success of the Normandy landings – the greatest seaborne invasion of all time. Early in 1944 Maurice Barbanell was writing a propaganda pamphlet: 'It is the Vagrancy Act which we are determined to have amended. We do not fear the operations of the Witchcraft Act of 1735, for it is very rarely invoked. Apparently, the minions of the law realise that to accuse anybody of witchcraft in the 20th century might sound just a little ridiculous.' Even before publication, this was already out of date and a correction slip had to be added, stating: 'No one could have foreseen that in the year 1944 the might and majesty of the law would be invoked to initiate a prosecution under the Witchcraft Act of 1735, as was done in the Helen Duncan case.' No clairvoyant powers would have been needed, however. Not only was the language of witchcraft already creeping into charges under the Vagrancy Act, but the statute had been used more often than the Spiritualists claimed.

In June 1805, at Kirkcudbright in Scotland, where a century earlier Elspeth McEwen had been executed for bewitching her neighbours' livestock, Jean Maxwell was sentenced to a year in prison under the Witchcraft Act for telling fortunes from tealeaves, rubbing an intoxicating liquid on a girl's head and frightening people with Satan's scratches on her arm. The trial of the 'Galloway Sorceress' aroused great excitement in legal circles, as it did among local people for whom a best-selling pamphlet was printed, its title page bearing the same passage from *Macbeth* quoted in chapter one (p. 21). The sensational response suggests that the 1735 Act was not used often, especially after the introduction of the Vagrancy Act in 1824, which allowed for fortune tellers and the like to be tried summarily. It was the appeal judgement in the case of convicted slate-writer Francis Monck in 1877 which brought to public attention the fact that such offenders could be tried under the more serious Witchcraft Act and, therefore, that there was no incentive for the court to misuse or twist the 1824 Act.

From then onwards, mediums who objected to being branded as vagrants were made to feel fortunate that they had not been tried as witches. A Cornish cunning man was indicted under the Witchcraft Act in 1894, although the judge was uncomfortable with a charge framed according to 'an almost obsolete statute', feelings shared by a London magistrate ten years later when fortune tellers Charles and Martha Stephenson were committed for trial. In this case the Act was out of print at the King's printers and the Stephensons were acquitted. Despite distaste about the word 'witchcraft' being used in court, Section 4 of the Witchcraft Act did cover the offences committed by mediums and fortune tellers, and so police continued to use it. In the 1920s at least two gypsies were tried under it: one in Northamptonshire received a month's hard labour for selling charms; the other in Cornwall was sentenced to six months' imprisonment for taking £500 from a sick man in return for counteracting the effects of the evil eye. In 1935 Bournemouth magistrates issued warrants against several mediums, including Welsh clairvoyant Nesta Lewis who had been fined £7 the previous year, an issue raised in the House of Commons at that time by her MP, E.A. Radford, later a member of the SNU deputation. This time, Mrs Lewis – alias 'Nesta of the Forest' (her husband was a Druid) – was fined £25 under the Witchcraft Act after a drunken undercover policeman had visited her business premises situated between Marks & Spencer and the Electric Theatre. The Home Office received a letter of protest about the trial from Lady Knollys and opened a file. In 1936 Nesta Lewis sued *John Bull* magazine for libel at the Court of King's Bench where she was represented by Quintin Hogg, the future Lord Hailsham. He lost; but the judge, Lord Hewart LCJ, could not resist asking the plaintiff about the fate of Spain then being torn apart by political strife, to which she replied: 'The King and Queen will return there.'

Nesta Lewis was able to fight her own battles and later admitted that the publicity generated by the action brought her many new clients. But for lesser mortals the higher echelons of the Spiritualist movement were ready to help. In 1937, *Psychic News* took up the cause of A.H. Clive-Holmes, a materialization medium gaoled in Wormwood Scrubbs – in effect for conjuration – after a man grabbed a spirit form; a piece of crêpe bandage seized survives in the IIPR archives. Maurice Barbanell pestered Sir Samuel Hoare at the Home Office, spread word of how burial alive in the trenches had made Clive-Holmes terrified of his cell and set up a fund to support his family. The trial of Helen Duncan, therefore, could not have been quite the shock Barbanell and others pretended it to be, nor were they ill-prepared. In 1942, following a sting operation by two policemen dressed as convalescent soldiers, mediums Austin Hatcher and Emily Little were imprisoned at Cardiff for 'pretending to hold communication with departed spirits to deceive persons'; and when Hatcher was denied Spiritualist ministration, the SNU swiftly used his case as a lever against injustice. By this time, then, battle had been joined in different parts of the country. But this degree of activity suggests that Helen Duncan was prosecuted not so much as a threat to national security, but simply as another nuisance lowering morale in Portsmouth – a key point of departure for D-Day – at the most crucial moment of the war. To cap it all, it turns out that the Witchcraft Act had been used once before by Portsmouth magistrates: in 1939 a gypsy called Bessy Birch was bound over for receiving money for advising a woman that her ring was bewitched and that she should bury a pound of steak with a human hair, then burn a glove with a needle and pin in it. This was to prove an important legal precedent in 1944.

After all, the authorities wouldn't really have been afraid of Helen Duncan's prognostical powers . . . would they? The Nazis, of course, took the occult seriously enough. Obsessed with astrology, mesmerism and spiritism, Himmler set up an 'Occult Bureau' and a special team to study the witch-craze – although here the aim was to understand the mechanics of persecution more than witchcraft itself. Hitler believed his fate was determined by divine providence, an idea he elaborated with Hans Goldzier's 'earth electricity' creation theory and von Reichenbach's 'odic force', seen by some people in luminous emanations from crystals. Dowsing maps with a pendulum to find warships was another of Hitler's eccentricities. Little about British attitudes can be inferred from all this; and yet a basic principle of modern intelligence gathering is: think the unthinkable or your enemy might. Dr Walter Stein, a Viennese occultist, escaped being pressed into the Nazi Occult Bureau and fled to Britain, where he became an adviser on Hitler's beliefs, which included, he said, an obsession with the power of a relic alleged to be the lance used to pierce Christ's side. The War Office employed an astrologer in Grosvenor House, Louis de Wohl, who cast Hitler's horoscope in order to predict his moves and after the war a shadowy figure by the name of Ernesto Montgomery claimed to have been part of an MI5 psychic unit from which he travelled behind enemy lines in astral form – presumably like Henry Duncan visiting his sister in Arbroath but more dangerous.

One might expect the story of the occult in wartime to be flooded with fantasies; but we should be careful about dismissing everything. In 1940–4, Geraldine Cummins performed psychic work 'of an investigative nature undertaken for patriotic motives', one account of which is said still to be in the custody of a government department; another, made in 1949, remains under lock and key in the SPR archives. In 1938 Colonel Maltby from MI6 asked witchcraft expert Cecil Williamson to compile a list of high-ranking Germans who dabbled in the occult, work which led Williamson to establish a 'Witchcraft Research Centre'. At the outbreak of war he served in the Royal Signals and, as well as monitoring the work of Nazi astrologers, also broadcast propaganda and 'degenerate' jazz to U-boat crews. Maltby thought the occult was nonsense; but that was not the point. The intelligence services existed to collect information; sources were a secondary consideration. Williamson, a believer, also claimed to have witnessed 'Operation Mistletoe', a ritual performed in a Sussex forest in 1941 by occultist Aleister Crowley at the behest of MI5, where a dummy in Nazi uniform was burned, surrounded by white-robed soldiers. After the Fall of France, 'Operation Cone of Power' was launched by a convention of witches in the New Forest, a ceremony intended to prevent Hitler invading, and groups such as the Society of the Inner Light performed many similar acts in what has been called the 'Magical Battle of Britain'. Sir Hugh Dowding was a supporter of the 'Cross of Light' campaign in which Grace Cooke's White Eagle Lodge distributed posters across London with the intention of concentrating positive thought and invoking spiritual power against the forces of darkness. Whether he shared their view that it was this surge that won the Battle of Britain is less certain.

Perhaps the security services did not have to believe that Helen Duncan was a genuine medium in order to be concerned. Information flowed from her at a time when victory depended on secrecy, and MI5 were unlikely to have ignored such a woman, however strong the hunch that she was harmless. There was certainly something unusual about the way she was treated. One should be wary of the Home Office's explanation that the responsibility for sending a case to the Old Bailey belonged to the committing magistrates; that it was convenient to hold the trial in London because many of the witnesses lived there (few did); and that the case would otherwise have had to wait for a long time until the next assizes. It could have been heard summarily by the Portsmouth magistrates under the Vagrancy Act, or it could have gone to the local quarter sessions. But that did not happen; nor is it entirely true to say that the decision rested with the magistrates: the Clerk at the Old Bailey sent a note (which survives in the Public Record Office) to inform them that the case would be removed to London 'for the special reason that there are special circumstances which make the case an unusually grave and difficult one and that delay and inconvenience would be occasioned by committal to quarter sessions'. Why was delay so undesirable in what appeared to be a simple case of vexatious imposture?

Although the Metropolitan Police deny having any records relating to Helen Duncan, Brigadier Firebrace claimed that after the sinking of HMS *Hood*, Scotland Yard asked for his advice about how to silence her and that because, 'from the point of view of the authorities Mrs Duncan was a dangerous person', she was targeted. But by whom? Since 1944, Stanley Worth has been called a mole, a spy, a stooge and so on, and although little was said in court about his association with the police, his father had been a senior sergeant in the Metropolitan Police transferred to Portsmouth; his uncle, Percy Worth, was the Chief Constable at Scotland Yard; and before the war he himself had been a special constable in the Met at Harlington in Middlesex. He had also become friends with Chief Constable Arthur West and his family after they attended a function at his naval base. There was more. After the war, Percy Wilson's son Richard claimed that 'the whole affair was a conspiracy by the Portsmouth police, which proved more difficult than they expected'.

And from the Wilsons came an astonishing claim. At Christmas 1943 John Lock, a storeman at the Cowley motor works, visited his parents in Portsmouth – William and Bessie, the licensed pedlar and his wife present at the Master Temple on 19 January 1944. William Lock told his son that a naval officer called Worth had joined their Spiritualist church a few weeks earlier and that, as an ex-policeman himself, he sensed that Worth was working for the police to expose Mrs Duncan. (Of this the Locks denied all knowledge at the trial, although they were friends with Charles Burrell, the dockyard medium who had warned the Homers against fraud. Nor did Worth admit to knowing the Locks at all before criminal proceedings began.) Furthermore, the Wilsons alleged that on 3 January 1944 John Lock was discussing materialization seances with William Spencer, a foreman welder, who had been to Duncan seances and was convinced she was genuine. Lock bet him 5s that she would be arrested within a few weeks and so it proved. Percy Wilson arranged for Spencer to appear as a witness at the Old Bailey, but he was never called. The story informed the thinking of both Prosecution and Defence, but just how true it was is impossible to establish. In 1958 Percy Wilson repeated his account at the College of Psychic Science annual conference in Brighton, but here added not only that it was actually *Spencer* who was privy to the secret information but that he was Worth's nephew!

Stanley Worth denied being a police stooge and that he was involved with anyone except Detective Inspector Ford regarding Helen Duncan; his uncle was never involved, nor did he have any nephews. Clearly, however, he held back a little: SPR man Donald West claims to have buttonholed him and found him 'much more frank and revealing than when put on the defensive by badgering in the witness box'. Although he may not have dealt directly with Worth, Chief Constable Arthur West did oversee the investigation personally and in a BBC interview in 1975 admitted that the Admiralty had wanted Mrs Duncan out of the picture without too much concern for how she had obtained knowledge about the sinking of warships. By the start of 1944 there was a sense that something had to be done and, following his report to the DPP, a prosecution under the Vagrancy Act was discussed. 'But none of this seemed to cover what we were getting at in these circumstances,' he recalled, 'and therefore the Director said, look here, we'll use the old Witchcraft Act. Old it is, he said, but it'll cover what we want. And that's the one we took.' Word of approval soon came from the Admiralty.

West did not mention the assistance of Douglas Craggs and the Magic Circle. In a letter to Harry Price dated 29 January 1944, Mollie Goldney shared her suspicions that the Magic Circle had been involved in Mrs Duncan's downfall; but then Price already knew this. The next day Craggs wrote to him to say that the Magic Circle's investigation at Portsmouth had now become a police matter and that: 'We are asked to help and wish to if in any way possible. We have recently been in *constant* touch with Scotland Yard and I am hopeful that we may eventually get results.' Price's response is not known; but it is certain that he lent his expertise, books, photographs and correspondence to Chief Constable West, and that the trial went pretty much as he had predicted. On 9 February 1944, West sent Price's *Regurgitation and the Duncan Mediumship* to the DPP's representative, J. E. Robey, saying that having reviewed the facts of the case in relation to the charge, 'I feel satisfied that these four people will have some difficulty in proving their innocence.' Another clue: among Harry Price's papers is a compliments slip from the small Portsmouth bookshop run by War Reserve Constable Rupert Cross. This must be more than coincidence.

However satisfied the police, DPP and Admiralty were, after the trial the Home Office became concerned. Assistant Under-Secretary Francis Graham-Harrison contacted his senior, Sir Frank Newsam (both present when the Home Office received the SNU in 1943), after he had been told by J.E. Robey in conversation that the Prosecution had added the witchcraft charge without consulting the DPP. Newsam asked Under-Secretary Theo Mathew to find out whether this was true, and on 6 April 1944 Mathew wrote to the DPP, Sir Edward Tindal Atkinson, to ask why the Witchcraft Act had been used, indicating that the Duncan episode was becoming a public relations headache for the Home Office. Instead of trying the defendants for fraud, Mathew said, the authorities had played into the hands of the Spiritualists who 'will exploit to the utmost the fact that Helen Duncan was convicted under an Act which they can with some reason represent to be an anachronism and quite out of harmony with contemporary feeling'. In reply, Tindal Atkinson asserted that personally he would have preferred the main charge to have been common law conspiracy to defraud, but that it was his usual practice to allow counsel to settle their own indictments. On this occasion, he explained, the Attorney-General had nominated John Maude KC who thought the case would best be proved according to the Witchcraft Act.

One final point seems to have gone unnoticed by posterity: the presence of a Secret Service officer at Helen Duncan's trial. If MI5 were to prosecute persons who contravened security laws, it made sense that they should themselves see the case through to the end – as at the trial of traitor William Joyce (alias Lord Haw-Haw) in 1945, for example. However, some officers were reluctant to appear – wearing uniform as they were required to do – because testifying revealed their identities. No such uniformed officer was in the Old Bailey in March 1944, although MI5 involvement is beyond doubt. A Major Nicholson present at a meeting of chief constables on 17 May 1945 was, given his military rank, almost certainly an MI5 officer and in discussion about fraudulent mediums argued that greater coordination was needed due to the 'difficulties he had experienced in the recent prosecution in this area', presumably the Duncan case. In 1943–4 the work of the Inter-Services Security Board – which united the Admiralty, Air Ministry, War Office and MI5 – was dominated by preparations for D-Day and at every meeting the latest public rumours were discussed. To gather stories, 'B' Division of MI5 (Counter-Espionage), led by a former Scotland Yard subversion expert, relied on its network of a dozen regional security liaison officers to whom chief constables reported 'matters of special security interest'. During the war, MI5 recruited what were called 'men of discretion': Britain's natural rulers hailing from the public schools who followed class instincts rather than the dictates of a corrupt bureaucracy – the European model. Many were drawn from the legal profession and were given the honorary rank of major in the Intelligence Corps.

One of these was John Maude. In 1939 he had joined MI5 and, as usual, was described simply as 'Temporary Civil Assistant to the General Staff at the War Office'. At the outbreak of war he received his Intelligence Corps commission and in December 1939 was put in charge of a section dealing with leakage of information. In the spring of the following year this work was done by section B19 of which Maude was also head until B19 lapsed, was renamed B1K and, by May 1943, had been absorbed by SLB2, the subdivision of MI5's legal unit responsible for leaks. Maude himself would travel undercover to investigate the source of rumours (on at least one occasion to Scotland) and was responsible for implementing a scheme to plant agents posing as domestic servants in foreign embassies. From 1942 he worked specifically for the Offices of the War Cabinet. Surely, then, the Attorney-General's choice of Maude for the grave and difficult case of Helen Duncan was made with this experience in mind. Mollie Goldney, who kept her ear very close to the ground, suspected not only the involvement of the Magic Circle but the Admiralty, which to her mind explained the presence of a naval officer as the leading prosecution witness. Spiritualist B. Abdy Collins told her not only that he believed the Duncan trial stemmed from the *Barham* incident, but that prosecuting counsel had offered to scale down the prosecution on condition that the Defence consented to Mrs Duncan being locked up for six months 'over the coming offensive'. Loseby refused. Could it be that the 'witch-finding activities' Churchill once criticized in MI5 had literally come true?

Spiritualists have long held that Churchill was outraged about Helen Duncan's conviction because he was one of their number. Escaping from a prison camp during the Boer War, it is said, he plotted his orientation with a planchette, a pencil mounted on a wheeled cradle used by mediums for automatic writing. As a politician, he attracted various letters from Spiritualists. In 1922 a Canadian woman sent him poems from the spiritual Shelley including 7350 words of 'A Song of Italy', which told of Christ approaching the darkened earth through the etheric spheres of light. Conan Doyle also corresponded. 'I wish you would yourself look into this psychic question,' he pleaded in 1923. 'It is far the most important thing upon the earth and we want leaders of energy.' That Churchill would one day be Prime Minister had been predicted by the spirits in an unsolicited message sent to him in 1915 when he was one of Asquith's ministers. After the Dardanelles disaster, Churchill served in the trenches with the Royal Scots Fusiliers for a few months and, although there is no evidence for the Spiritualist notion that he and Charles Loseby were comrades in arms, they may well have met as battalion commanders at Ploegsteert in 1916. After the war they certainly knew each other well. In 1919, as Secretary for War, Churchill received a deputation from Loseby concerning the promotion of other ranks to commissions and also dealt with him in connection with war bonuses. In fact, covering the period 1918–22, Loseby's curriculum vitae reads: 'Worked closely with Winston Churchill for whom I did several missions – never lost touch' – a relationship borne out in correspondence from the 1920s and by Loseby's daughter who remembers Churchill visiting their house. All this may explain cryptic Spiritualist references to Loseby having been one of Churchill's spies, but in no way proves that Churchill shared Loseby's Spiritualist sympathies, even though he must have been aware of them.

From the letters he received in 1944, Churchill may also have been conscious of public feeling about Helen Duncan. After her arrest a housewife from Bath drew the Prime Minister's attention to police interference in the work of mediums who had 'brought knowledge and spiritual comfort in these dark days', and said that her son, missing since the Battle of Crete, was 'just one [of] many who fought, and still fights, for the preservation of an idealistic way of life for these islands'. News of Helen's conviction moved her good friend Mr Latimer in Alloa, twenty miles from Glasgow, to inform Churchill of all the wonderful things he had seen – the spirits dressed in shimmering robes, the light divided prismatically – but said he was sure Churchill knew all about spiritual power already, 'for no mere man could have carried your burden without help'. Like many others, his letter ended with a plea: 'You are a great man but be a just man and see that this woman get[s] justice or your Charter is in vain and the Gestapo of religion still lives.' Typically, such letters were forwarded to the Home Office, and may not even have reached the Prime Minister's desk, but Churchill nonetheless heard about Helen Duncan and was impelled to comment. On Monday, 3 April 1944 he sent a personal minute to Herbert Morrison which read:

Let me have a report on why the Witchcraft Act, 1735, was used in a modern Court of Justice. What was the cost of this trial to the State, observing that witnesses were brought from Portsmouth and maintained here in this crowded London, for a fortnight, and the Recorder kept busy with all this obsolete tomfoolery, to the detriment of necessary work in the Courts?

On the same day Morrison forwarded the letter to Theo Mathew who composed a reply stating that it was not the Home Secretary's job to interfere in a criminal prosecution; that the police were right to act against fraud, especially 'in wartime when relatives of men killed or missing are easy victims'; and again that magistrates, not the police, allocated cases to particular courts. The question of the Witchcraft Act was left open, proposing further consideration when a full report had been made, a point Mathew explained thus: 'I put in this sentence in case we have to do something to placate the prevalent opinion that a law is unsatisfactory because it is old. My own view is that the Act of 1735 is a very sensible and natural measure which compares favourably with the superstition and irrationality rampant in 1944.' Finally, Mathew advanced the view that expense and inconvenience were 'part of the price to be paid for maintaining the right to be tried by a jury'. Morrison excised a passage admitting that ninety per cent of indictable trials were tried summarily – this would only have emphasized that Helen Duncan's case *was* peculiar – and the answer was retyped, signed and sent on 6 April. Churchill was doubtless satisfied and that was an end to it.

Churchill's minute had not been quite 'the call for an inquiry and a reprimand' some Spiritualists still make it out to be, nor did he stand up in the House of Commons to 'let the world know where he stood about the trial of Helen Duncan'. If anything, he felt irritated that resources were being wasted at a time when national efficiency was crucial and in any case his emotions were dominated by the death of Orde Wingate, the impetuous leader of the Chindits in Burma in whom Churchill saw himself as a young man. Morrison's was just one of several personal minutes sent on 3 April – other business preoccupying Churchill included the political situation in Italy and the Russo–Japanese agreement about North Sakhalin. Churchill and Morrison met the same day in the War Cabinet where they focused on such weighty matters as bombing policy in occupied territories, fears of industrial unrest and reports of a successful attack on the last German battleship, the *Tirpitz*; nor was *l'affaire* Duncan mentioned during the rest of the week's business, whereas inland transport, national water policy and civil aviation were.

At times in the past when Churchill had been required to deal with Spiritualism, he had shown all the constructive pragmatism one would expect from a man who counted bricklaying among his recreations. As Home Secretary in 1910–11, he had done nothing to restrain the Metropolitan Police in their periodic swoops on fortune tellers and mediums, and may even have deliberately sanctioned their policy. When challenged on the issue in the House of Commons in 1911, he blithely referred his interrogator to the terms of the 1824 Vagrancy Act. As Chancellor of the Exchequer in 1928, Churchill was called upon to suppress a lecture by the widow of Captain Walter Hinchcliffe whose aeroplane had been lost over the Atlantic that year. Mrs Hinchcliffe told of his return through mediums such as Estelle Stead and Eileen Garrett, whom she had been encouraged to meet by Sir Arthur Conan Doyle, and how the spirit of W. T. Stead had helped her husband to get in touch. Churchill was all for remonstration, but the Public Trustee advised against antagonizing 'the Stead–Conan Doyle gang' and instead the lecture was mildly censored.

The story that Churchill was a regular seance-goer who visited Helen Duncan in Holloway, had a private sitting in her cell and promised to make it up to her, was an inevitable fantasy. Needless to say, suggestions that other sitters included Mackenzie King, General de Gaulle, the Queen Mother and Chief Sitting Bull should be treated with caution, although ironically the fact that Sitting Bull died in 1890 made him the most likely candidate if any one of these ever did pay her a visit. From the autumn of 1945 onwards, Mackenzie King's friend Mercy Phillimore did arrange seances for him at the LSA and in 1947 promised 'some of the best mediums', although whether these included Helen Duncan (as Spiritualists assert) is not recorded. He did sit with

Lilian Bailey whose own development as a trance medium was inspired by Helen's materialization of an officer from the First World War, but that was probably as close as Helen ever got to a head of state. The suggestion that, as Sagittarians, Helen and Winston would have understood one another may well be true, but says nothing about the great man's beliefs. He did not use a planchette pencil to escape the Boers, yet that was the metaphor he chose to describe the instinctiveness of his trek. Remembering his South African adventure, Churchill spoke of 'the assistance of that High Power which interferes in the eternal sequences of causes and effects more often than we are always prone to admit'.

Churchill was a man of extraordinary personal qualities, and as well as a ruthless pragmatist he was a romantic freethinker, spiritual without being a Spiritualist and, like his grand adversary Hitler, believed himself to be a man of destiny.* He was also capricious in his attitudes, and can no more be summed up by an anti-religious phase he went through after reading W. E. H. Lecky's *History of the Rise and Influence of the Spirit of Rationalism*, than he can by the metaphysical turn of mind which inspired him, in the late 1940s, to write a story where he dreamt that the spirit of his father returned to quiz him about the twentieth century. For Churchill, like the questing virtuosi of the seventeenth century, was interested in everything. He owned at least one book about spirits – possibly Joseph Glanvill's *The Vanity of Dogmatizing* (1661) – which in 1904 he lent to Pamela Tennant, who in 1922 became the second wife of Sir Edward Grey after the death of her husband. Her letter of thanks which accompanied the returned volume said that the Grey family, with whom

---

* Churchill's cousin on his mother's side, Clare Sheridan, did become a passionate Spiritualist after her husband, Wilfred, was killed in the trenches in 1915. She found him as overbearing in death as he had been in life.

she was already acquainted, had 'a copy of Glanvils book on Witchcraft' – *Sadducismus Triumphatus* (1668) – and expressed horror at the manifest injustice of the burning times. 'These poor innocent witches', she lamented, 'were no doubt people with psychical gifts. How much more advanced we might have been in that direction if so rigorous a treatment of this subject had never been.' The Spiritualism she flaunted after she became Lady Grey was therefore already in evidence long before she met Etta Wriedt or Mackenzie King.

The colossus of twentieth-century Britain, like so many of his contemporaries, ruled spirits neither in nor out. On 25 November 1947, three days after a sitting with Geraldine Cummins, Mackenzie King met Churchill and informed him that Roosevelt's spirit had sent him a message. Churchill asked to borrow a transcript. What he thought of it is impossible to ascertain, but Mackenzie King believed he took it seriously, recording in his diary that the account of the seance had been returned to him accompanied by 'a most significant little note'. The openness of Churchill's mind to such ideas can be further demonstrated by his earlier correspondence with an astrologer from Norwich called R.G. Hickling, whose rambling predictions and recommendations he took seriously to the extent of sharing them with Cabinet colleagues including the Prime Minister, H. H. Asquith, and Foreign Secretary Sir Edward Grey. Churchill's first letter, warning of some of the worst planetary conjunctions for forty years, was received in August 1911, less than a week before the Admiralty and War Office began their strategic planning for war with Germany. Messages over the next three years concerned strike action and the instability of the Balkans, and after Hickling correctly predicted a sudden end to the miners' conference in 1912, Grey wrote to Churchill to ask: 'Have you any indication of the nature of events of a far graver character that are to supervene?' In the months before the outbreak of war, Hickling spoke of the danger of conflagration but was confident that the planets would ensure British victory, as they had in the Boer War. During 1915, as First Lord of the Admiralty, Churchill continued to study Hickling's forecasts concerning the most propitious moment to initiate sea battles, although it is perhaps significant that the final letter in the archives, dated 28 April 1915, predicted that the Dardanelles campaign would be Churchill's greatest personal victory.

In 1964 Wellesley Tudor Pole – the anonymous W. T. P. who edited the spiritual communications of 'Private Dowding' in 1917 – wrote to the novelist Rosamond Lehmann with whom he maintained a long correspondence. Like John Maude, in the Second World War he had served as an MI5 officer at the War Office, where he warned the Prime Minister about bugs in the House of Commons and formed the opinion, confided to Lehmann in his letter, that 'Churchill has always feared the supernatural not because he thought of it as bunk but because he believed in it'. As Churchill lay dying a few months later, who knows what he thought would become of his soul? One authority maintains that there is no proof of his belief in an afterlife, and it is safe to assume he was joking when he said once that brandy and cigars kept ghosts at bay. And yet the evidence that he allowed for the possibility of a superior existence is compelling. In 1942 Churchill told the House of Commons that the recently deceased Duke of York had 'gone to join a happy family', leading the Spiritualist MP Thomas Brooks to ask him privately whether he really believed that. 'I do,' came the reply. 'Is it true then?' pressed Brooks, to which Churchill answered: 'No doubt about it in my mind.' It is possible, then, to interpret his letter to Morrison about the Duncan trial in a slightly different light, and however unlikely Hannen Swaffer's assertion (made to a journalist in 1944) that three members of the War Cabinet had attended seances and had therefore contravened the Witchcraft Act, it is by no means impossible. Perhaps, after all, Churchill watched Helen Duncan's appeal against conviction with more sympathy than his primary concern with economic efficiency and public accountability might lead us to believe. That he ever visited her in Holloway Prison is beyond credibility, but he might just have spared a thought for her plight as she marked off the days of her sentence.

9
NELLIE, KEEP YOUR CHIN UP!
The Path to Liberty

Holloway Prison in north London was a century-old Gothic fortress complete with loopholes and battlements, where hunger-striking suffragettes had once been force-fed and Oscar Wilde had pondered the iniquities of English justice. For forty years it had been a women's prison, the largest in Britain, and although the walls had been repainted a softer cream now, a pall of timeless, nameless wrong hung over the cell blocks which radiated from an open well like the spokes of a wheel. Individual cells were reached from galleries around the perimeter, a network of mesh-covered walkways and spiral staircases connecting them

---

Helen Duncan in the 1950s.

---

to one another and the main concourse. It was, in short, a panopticon where surveillance and servility, inspection and introspection, were intended to bring the fallen closer to God and the ideals of the State. On arrival, Helen Duncan and Frances Brown repeated the routine they had been through before: separated into gloomy reception cells, and from there to cubicles where a nurse weighed them, examined their hair and asked about varicose veins, fits and periods. Finally, a doctor came round with her stethoscope and indifferent manner, and decided that in Helen's case, once she had been bathed and dressed, she should receive attention for her diabetes and angina. Like most of her fellow prisoners – thieves, cheats, prostitutes, derelicts and abortionists – her senses were at once flattened by despondency and heightened by fear. She felt faint and expected to die.

In wartime Holloway everything was in short supply, including hot water, soap and clothing; and the contents of the bundle each new prisoner received were invariably soiled including the calico chemise, voluminous drawers and knitted black stockings which, without garters, drooped ceaselessly. The shapeless blue frock was no longer patterned with what Mrs Pankhurst had called 'the broad arrow of disgrace', but was nonetheless degrading attire. Shoes were mismatched, handkerchiefs scarce and against the cold (fuel economies were obsessive) each cell came with a grimy serge cloak, which prisoners wore to chapel and during their one hour of outdoor exercise each day. Cells measured thirteen feet by seven with a barred window, an armoured door, and contained basic necessities: an iron bed, table, chair, jug, bowl, mug and covered pail. Baths and the issue of clean underwear were supposed to occur weekly, but a wait of a month was not unusual. Toilet paper was highly prized and women often used pages from the bibles provided for their moral reformation. The food was monotonous – coarse bread, oily meat stew, dirty greens – and tended to cause either diarrhoea or constipation, depending on how the digestive system reacted to the shock; the only 'treat' was the cloying ship's cocoa from which prisoners would skim the grease to use on hands chapped from long toil.

Arranging to see the Medical Officer ('booking for the MO' as it was known), meant being locked up while one awaited a visit, missing companionship and exercise, and was therefore not a soft option for malingerers. Even so, women reporting sick were regarded with suspicion, although in Helen's case her abnormal pulse and bluish pallor were convincing enough. The prison hospital in which she found herself was not the light antiseptic haven one might imagine, but just another cell where in isolation she was confined to bed, incarcerated around the clock. As in all cells, there was an emergency bell but it often went unheeded as ringing annoyed the wardresses. To start with, Helen was probed and medicated, treatment which she received in her usual passive manner. Her diabetes was tamed with regular and precise doses of insulin, and a strict diet which she would have minded more had her voracious appetite not deserted her. She craved cigarettes, but there were none. Nor was there any privacy, yet little comfort was to be derived from the officious staff who monitored her. Whether she saw much of Frances Brown is not recorded. There were insipid novels from the library, but Helen was no bookworm and had always preferred Henry to read to her. Sleep came in irregular waves and waking offered no relief from the dark menace of her dreams. Reality was worse.

Prisoners were starved of information and newspapers were scarce, although from the furore of the past two months, Helen may have guessed what was happening in the world outside. In wartime, a shortage of notable criminal cases meant that those which did emerge generated extravagant interest among the bored populace. Parallels were drawn with a *cause célèbre* from the end of the First World War, a libel trial about the existence of a Black Book containing the names of thousands of perverts in high places, including Asquith, the Prime Minister. Now, as then, the popular press had a field day and became frenzied to uncover new angles. On the day she walked free from court, Mrs Homer told journalists that she would carry on at the Master Temple 'in the ordinary way', but in fact she kept a very low profile. The London *Evening News*, eager to know what happened to the takings from Helen's seances immediately prior to her arrest, sent a reporter to Portsmouth who found 301 Copnor Road closed, a notice about cancelled services chalked on a board and the sole occupant apparently a chow dog. The *Daily Mirror* became so excited, after tracing the carpenter who made the crucifix for the seance room, that they managed to refer to Helen as *Hilda* Duncan. Charles Loseby blamed all the printed travesties on the Prosecution who had, he said, spun a story at the Old Bailey which was 'clear, simple, blatant and vulgar and lent itself to headlines which were freely given'. To Mollie Goldney, however, the Spiritualist propagandists and the tabloid newspapers were quite as bad as each other, and she delighted in dubbing the lot of them the 'FFFs' because they were fifty–fifty in frightfulness. *The Times*, by contrast, followed the trial with utter dispassion and every day used the same sober headline: ALLEGED SEANCE DECEPTIONS.

Alone among the tabloids, the *News of the World* was sympathetic, having sensed that beyond the Spiritualists, broader currents of feeling held that the legal prosecution of witches and the war to liberate Europe were incompatible. Subtly and briefly, the historical image of the witch-hunts came to symbolize a class-ridden, patriarchal past at a time when British people were demanding a new world in reward for their sacrifice. And so, in the *News of the World*, Helen was painted as an infirm philan-thropist whose annual income had never exceeded £200 – less than half the national average for a man. Not that the articula-tion of public support in April 1944 was based only on sentiment. The *New Statesman*, serious and radical (with a small 'r'), argued that a conviction for 'pretence to exercise a kind of conjuration' had potentially serious consequences for ordinary Spiritualists and implied that Mrs Duncan's conviction was arbitrarily unjust if it did not. Another piece in *Truth* regretted that the 'mediaeval savour' of the 1735 Act allowed Spiritualists to cry persecution when it was not thereby elevating Mrs Duncan to sainthood. Likewise, the *Glasgow Herald* called for a new legal style, suggesting that 'in the coming epoch of reconstruction Parliament may take the view that a rewording would be worthwhile'. The Marquis of Donegall, who had been at the Old Bailey, wrote in the *Sunday Dispatch* that he saw no difference 'between a person who obtains money under false pretences by pretending to be a witch and one who does the same thing by selling shares in a non-existent goldmine. Why should the former be accused under a special archaic Act? To my mind, the so-called witchcraft part of it is purely incidental.'

At the Home Office these clippings were pasted on to paper sheets – as an economy, scraps of old propaganda posters – and filed with the letters of protest. Both Robey at the Director of Public Prosecutions' office and Chief Constable West in Portsmouth were asked for reports to help them to reply, and in his letter of 6 April to DPP Sir Edward Tindal Atkinson, Theo Mathew referred to the Marquis of Donegall. Under-Secretary Francis Graham-Harrison, who had also seen the *Sunday Dispatch* article, noted that 'On the face of it, it is a pity that Duncan was convicted under the Witchcraft Act and not simply of conspiring to obtain money by false pretences. It is already clear that the Spiritualists will make the most of the fact that she was convicted under an Act 200 years old, which they can represent with some show of reason to be archaic and out of harmony with modern feeling.' Mathew used almost identical words.

Confronted with this idealism, the DPP was unmoved: proving conjuration had obviated the need for proof of intent to defraud and the Witchcraft Act had therefore been appropriate. What the Home Office objected to was the implied notion that a citizen – innocent until proven guilty – simply *had* to be convicted and that the mere existence of a statute was sufficient justification for its use. Parliamentary representation and popular literacy meant that people were less passive in the face of despotism than they had been in the previous century. Added to rants about the British Gestapo were calmer criticisms from melioristic non-Spiritualists defending liberty for the post-war world. A man from York said there were more harmful things on which to spend money than seances, and another (writing from a mental hospital in Kent) asserted that the country had returned to the mentality of the reign of James I and that, like witch-hunters of that time, the Chief Constable of Portsmouth had lost his head. As he had anticipated, Arthur West himself received letters from Land's End to John o' Groats voicing opinions which, he claimed, were broadly fifty–fifty for and against his actions. He was quiet about an article in the *Police Review*, which took an almost identical line to that of the *New Statesman*, adding the point that the conviction of a medium whose fraud was unproved seemed to undermine the Home Secretary's assurance of November 1943 that only imposture would be pursued by the police. Few denied the validity of the observation and an embarrassed Home Office were forced to take refuge in their inability to comment while an appeal was pending.

Among the psychical researchers, Donald West felt that if Helen

Duncan had disclosed war secrets she should have been tried for that, but among his colleagues justice was not an issue of great interest – nor even the ontological status of her alleged spiritual manifestations – compared with the extraordinary testimonies presented by Charles Loseby. Waiting for the train to Putney after the trial, Mollie Goldney, who believed that the sentence had been just, spotted champion witness for the Defence, the Glaswegian Dr John Winning, and asked him whether he now thought Helen Duncan was a fraud. Smiling, he replied quietly that he did not and said he had in his possession photographs of the spirits of his relatives, but refused to show them to Mrs Goldney because he did not know her. She remonstrated politely with him until his train arrived. 'I wish the police had left Mrs D. to stew in her own ectoplasm!' railed SPR President W.H. Salter a few days later. 'She isn't worth all this fuss.' However, even he thought someone should write a proper report about her mediumship, but with typical bumptiousness forbade Mrs Goldney or any other member to contact or visit Helen in prison without the express consent of the SPR Council.

Not that Helen was short of visitors. It was difficult for Henry to travel because of his poor health and responsibilities, but the girls came when they could. Her friend Jean Beatson, who had taught Gena about the fairies, regularly travelled down from Fife with cigarettes hidden in bunches of violets. B. Abdy Collins visited too and was pleased to report that she was being well treated, attributing this to the guilty conscience of the authorities. Helen was also one of the first prisoners allowed to receive Spiritualist ministration. In 1936, Spiritualism had been disqualified as a religion in prison, but the SNU campaign on behalf of Austin Hatcher, the incarcerated Cardiff medium, forced the Prison Commission to reconsider in October 1943. Despite reservations that allowing ministration would aid and abet the crime for which prisoners had been convicted, it was recognized that Spiritualism was probably no greater deviation from orthodoxy than Christian Science or Buddhism, and the rules were amended. There is no reason to suppose, either, that Helen, now famous, did not give psychic readings in return for cigarettes, pennies or favours. Jacobean wizard to the Duke of Buckingham, Dr John Lambe, had extended his client base during a spell in the King's Bench gaol and Helen may have behaved similarly. But here mythology intervenes. She is said to have held full seances to which a blind eye was turned by sympathetic wardresses who, in any case, refused to lock her cell door. Another version asserts that Albert came to her as she slept and, like the Angel of the Lord dissolving St Peter's chains when he was gaoled by King Herod Agrippa, dematerialized the lock.

These and other rumours reported in the Spiritualist press fed back into the community in which they originated and further fuelled the campaign against Helen Duncan's conviction. Some condemned public ignorance of miracles. As editor of *Psychic Science*, Abdy Collins published an article by defence witness Alfred Dodd who shared his wondrous experiences with tub-thumping righteousness. 'With the advancement of knowledge,' Dodd declared, 'we shall cease persecuting the prophets and the smelling out of witches.' The activists received hundreds of letters from high and low. Lady Eleanor Smith, the novelist daughter of Lord Birkenhead, waxed lyrical to Hannen Swaffer:

Although I'm no Spiritualist, I regard Mrs Duncan's conviction as a disgrace to English justice, and another detestable attempt to interfere with our personal liberty. I don't want to go to one of her seances – that's all right – but why the devil shouldn't other people go, if they want to? Anyway, if she was tried under a Witchcraft Act of 1735, I'm only astounded that she wasn't sentenced to be burned at the stake. Wishing you every success in your campaign.

Maurice Barbanell had a diverse mailbag. Superintendent L. R. Russell of the Indian Police thought it scandalous that his country had no legal provision against witches, whereas England held up its democracy as a model to the world. According to Gunner T. A. Mead, a Spiritualist soldier serving in Italy, the case mocked the cause for which he was fighting. Many arguments were daft and ingenious. Technically illegal donkey rides on Sundays went unpunished, and it was hypocritical, some believed, to pay the Archbishop of Canterbury £15,000 a year for interceding between God and man when a poor medium could be imprisoned for a few shillings. On 8 April 1944, in *Psychic News*, Barbanell observed the absurdity of the situation when resurrection was central to Christianity, speculating that 'if every medium and Spiritualist who is wiping away the tears of mourners is to be imprisoned, then the building of jails will have to become a new war-time priority'. Finally, he assured readers – who, for this piece at least, included Theo Mathew at the Home Office – that they had only lost the first round and the fight would continue. A fortnight later the *Daily Mail* reported the SNU's intention to raise £5000 to meet the costs of an appeal and their determination to take the case to the House of Lords if necessary.

Meanwhile, as Helen grew stronger, she became bored in her hospital bed and the doctor allowed her to spend time each day in the workroom, engaged in handicrafts. Whether she attended the classes in making soft toys and home economics, we cannot say; nor whether she took the opportunity to earn pocket money, which women spent on cosmetics so that they no longer had to make rouge from exercise book covers. We do know that the deprivation of human company which resulted from being locked in a cell from 4.30 p.m. to 7 a.m. was what most affected every prisoner and made them grateful to escape solitude even in menial labour. Helen soon acclimatized to the routine of slopping out, work and worship, also the sounds and smells – jangling keys and slamming doors, undisinfected lavatories and institutional dankness. Alone at night, her bed surrounded by well-wishers' cards and notes, her thoughts turned to her family, and she did her best to put her trust in God and Albert. And she must have thought about the only man who could save her, Charles Loseby, perhaps unaware that five miles away in Kensington, Loseby was thinking of her as well. Holed up in his study preparing his case, again he sought inspiration in Ellis Powell's pamphlet, which described the 1542 Witchcraft Act as 'the first anti-psychic statute' and argued that 'the demon of Law, not the goddess of Justice' was the principal arbiter of truth. That much Loseby now knew. After the trial the Recorder, Sir Gerald Dodson, had refused to grant a certificate of appeal, but within two hours Loseby and the solicitor, Godfrey Elkin, gave notice that they would be appealing anyway. The grounds were essentially three-fold: the Witchcraft Act had been an inappropriate statute to use; the verdict had been 'unreasonable and perverse', given the Prosecution's dearth of evidence and its abundance with the Defence; and the Recorder's dismissal of the possibility that the accused was a genuine medium had been unjust.

Even though many saw the appeal as futile – Harry Price dismissed it as 'mere propaganda' – there was serious interest among lawyers. The editor of Archbold's *Criminal Pleading, Evidence and Practice* obtained a copy of the indictment for inclusion in his journal, the leading textual authority on criminal law. The *Law Quarterly Review* devoted a paragraph to the appeal, noting that 'an otherwise sordid case was given a dramatic quality' by the use of the Witchcraft Act. Contrary to W. H. Salter's opinion that Stanley Worth was a 'rotten bad observer and a rotten bad witness', C. E. Bechhofer Roberts, editor of the Old Bailey Trial Series, commented to Salter's minion Donald West that Worth was 'clearly a witness of trust in all essential matters', whereas his rhapsodic opponents – Loseby most of all – had been barking up the wrong tree by trying to prove the truth of post-mortem survival. Initially, the subtlety of this point had been lost even on junior prosecuting counsel Henry Elam who in court seemed to Mollie Goldney 'very much at sea, afraid of bungling it in consequence'. Notes pencilled by someone on the Prosecution side (possibly Elam) include this nervous observation: 'Issue is: Have Crown proved that Mrs D = Fraud?' when this was not the issue at all. Another note made here to the effect that the jury's refusal to attend a test seance was highly significant also missed the point. The jury was right to refuse, not because the test was unlikely to yield results, nor even because it would have constituted an ordeal as the judge argued, but because it was irrelevant to the question of whether or not Helen Duncan had conspired to pretend to exercise a kind of conjuration in January 1944. None of this, however, was lost on the wily Maurice Barbanell who recognized that 'under the Witchcraft Act there was no possible defence because it all turned on the word *pretending* to conjure up spirits, and legally it was maintained that *pretending* meant if you said you could produce materializations . . . it was witchcraft'.

By the time the appeal was heard, on 8 June 1944, D-Day had passed and the British had established a beachhead at Arromanches. The big secret no longer had to be defended, the pretence that the landings would take place at the Pas de Calais was over. The official reason why the appeal had taken ten weeks was that George Walpole & Co. of Chancery Lane had to prepare a full transcript of the eight days of proceedings. As news reached home that the Allies were fighting their way into France, British spirits soared, and for a while so did those of Mrs Duncan and Mrs Brown as the police van carried them from Holloway to the Royal Courts of Justice in the Strand where they met the Homers again. Far from being the wan and wasted figure many had expected, her friends and supporters were forced to admit that Helen had lost a bit of weight and looked rather well – certainly better than she had in April. Three judges presided over the Court of Criminal Appeal that day: Viscount Caldecote, the Lord Chief Justice and pillar of the Church of England; Mr Justice Birkett, son of a Cumbrian draper and an adviser on defence regulations; and Mr Justice Oliver who in 1932 had represented the Bishop of Norwich in the prosecution of the debauched Rector of Stiffkey, Harold Davidson. It was a sign of the times that after his defrocking Davidson had grown more famous than the Archbishop of Canterbury in his new career as a fairground attraction. His act was to stand in a barrel 'starving to death', a feat for which he was arrested for attempted suicide. Davidson's fate, however, lay not in the courts, but in a cage in Skegness where in 1937 a lion, also starving, ate him.

Between them, therefore, the three learned gentlemen brought experience of religion, security and tiresome impostors; perhaps Helen never stood a chance. The courtroom was packed with tearful Spiritualists, idle servicemen (including an American flying officer), curious lawyers and overeager journalists. One of the first things everyone noticed were the piles of books around the counsel benches – calf-bound, time-encrusted tomes of irregular sizes hunted down in the legal libraries – counsel on both sides having sought the wisdom of the past to make sense of the present. Loseby's speech was prevented from becoming a filibuster by persistent judicial interruptions, and although he displayed skill and grace in his replies, hope was stirred in Spiritualist hearts alone. On the question of the Recorder's bias at the Old Bailey, Loseby was forced to retract his allegation of impropriety, but when asked by Birkett whether he would have objected had the bias been in favour of the Defence, he laughed sardonically and replied that he should not have been in court today had that been the case. A debate about the disallowed test seance followed, Birkett asking whether the jury would have been able to handle animal materializations, then John Maude rose to speak. An argument ensued about the precise meaning of 'conjuration' and on the press bench Maurice Barbanell wondered what the spirits would be thinking. It was argued that the word did not appear in the Bible and against this that invoking spirits (and not merely evil ones) was as close to a legal definition of conjuration as could be imagined. A longer argument about the meaning of 'pretend' grew from this, the judges upholding Maude's definition of 'to claim untruly' – the inference being that Helen Duncan was an impostor as well as an idolator. Sitting far back from the lawyers, Helen listened to their mealy-mouthed pedantry, looking flushed and anxious, and was silent except for occasional sobs muffled by her handkerchief. Her confederates were more impassive, although Mrs Brown did squeeze out a few tears.

For two days the discussion wore on, touching upon such recondite matters as the translation of the Old and New Testament, the true nature of the Witch of Endor story, variations in the Witchcraft Acts from the reigns of Henry VIII, Elizabeth I, James I and George II, and the sententious opinions of Dr Samuel Johnson. Witchcraft, sorcery, conjuration, invocation, magic and enchantment were all dissected in meaning and nuance in a way that had not happened in an English court for over two centuries, and intellectual matters long assumed by triumphant rationalists to have died with the Enlightenment now seemed to have been merely dormant. Loseby read from a 1727 edition of the seventeenth-century magistrate's vade-mecum, Dalton's *Countrey Justice*, to argue that the spirits once associated with witches were diabolical familiars, and that this belief had been consigned to the dustbin of redundant superstitions. Nathaniel Bailey's dictionary published in 1735, a copy of which they had in court, must have served the Prosecution best, given that the definition of the verb 'to conjure' embraced not only 'to raise or lay spirits' but conspiracy as well. Volume after marked-up volume was passed to the Bench, ushers were sent to the library to fetch more and the court officials began to doze off. 'Look,' whispered Barbanell to his neighbour, 'here is another going into trance.' Snoring could be heard above the seamless etymological exchanges, the riffling of pages, and the sound of fidgeting backsides. At the end of the second day the judges muttered in consultation and announced that judgement would be given at the next sitting in ten days' time.

The following Tuesday, as Churchill stepped off a landing craft at the Normandy bridgehead, Hitler took his war to the heart of Britain. The first V–1 flying bomb – known colloquially as a 'doodlebug' – landed in east London killing six. Optimism in the capital was now leavened by panic and uncertainty; even the Government did not know quite what to expect and set up defensive belts of barrage balloons, anti-aircraft guns and fighter patrols, fearing that 10,000 a day might be killed. Prisoners in Holloway, starved of news and unable to join the million Londoners who fled before the end of July, felt especially anxious, and none more than Helen Duncan who was made frantic by the droning engines, followed by the eerie silence as the bomb exhausted its fuel and began its providential descent. Her reaction was not unusual: many prisoners showed signs of depression and hysteria, symptoms which the Holloway medical authorities did little to acknowledge or alleviate. Ironically, one V–1 may have given Helen some quiet pleasure: the one which landed on the Royal Courts of Justice, wrecking the chamber in which she had attended the learned symposium on witchcraft just days earlier. Had this really been a witchcraft trial, such a timely misfortune would probably have added to her guilt.

On 19 June, with the business-as-usual sang-froid at which wartime London excelled, an air-raid shelter was furnished with plain wooden tables and benches, and there the spectators queued just as they had at the start of the hearing. Fewer than fifty people managed to cram themselves inside and sat huddled together, Spiritualists cheek by jowl with pressmen and lawyers – and even Helen and her fellow applicants. At least the proceedings were brief, not that the Spiritualists gave much thought to mercy once Viscount Caldecote began to read the judgement, which he did so quickly that the journalists went into a flat spin. 'You'll never get this down,' whispered Maude to the reporter squashed next to him. It took the Lord Chief Justice twenty minutes to get through 4000 words – three a second. Even the expert short-hand writers knitted their brows. But the gist was clear. The grounds of appeal, eleven in all, were dismissed and Sir Gerald Dodson's conduct upheld. Regarding the legal interpretation of historical terms:

It appears plain that with the abolition of the felonies of witchcraft, sorcery, enchantment or conjuration the minds of men were making an advance. These things were no longer believed in, but the statute of George II did not go the length of allowing anyone to make the pretence of engaging in converse with spirits, not being evil spirits. Such a distinction would raise an issue of fact incapable of determination and based on no intelligible principle of law or religion.

Any kind of spirit – evil or benign – came beneath the terms of the Act, which was therefore applicable to the conspiracy alleged. In conclusion, Viscount Caldecote explained that the Prosecution had not sought to prove that spirits could not be materialized, only that Helen Duncan had pretended – that is, falsely claimed – to do so on the occasion in question, and that a demonstration of her powers in court would not have acquitted her on this count. Such a display might even have been misleading: today the ruling *R v Duncan* is best known in relation to a judge's power to exclude evidence likely to cloud the issue before a jury. Frances Brown, it was decreed, had served her sentence less remission for good behaviour and should be freed at once. The second round lost, Loseby applied to the Attorney-General for the case to be heard in the House of Lords – the highest court in the land. But that would not prevent Helen returning to her cell that same gloomy day. She looked utterly forlorn, her face purple from crying, and just before she was led out of the frowzy shelter, Maurice Barbanell snatched a few minutes with her. Smiling stoically, he told her to keep her chin up, and reassured her that the fight would continue as before and that she would be vindicated. Saying nothing, she simply groaned as she turned away.

More Spiritualist ink was spilled in correspondence and in the press, but serious hopes were fading. The Lord Chief Justice was criticized for his faulty reading of the Bible and attention drawn to the irony that he rejected Spiritualism but elsewhere had declared the Resurrection 'a fact beyond dispute'. But hot air quickly dissipated and did nothing to make the four walls of Helen Duncan's cell less real. At the Home Office, a civil servant stuck the last clipping about the appeal (from the *Yorkshire Post*) to a scrap of an old ATS recruiting poster and that particular file was closed. Loseby probably did not expect the Attorney-General to admit the case to the House of Lords and was already planning to draw a line under things by writing a book, *The Vindication of Helen Duncan*, where 'the evidence will be made to speak for itself'. It would seem that the eight days of the trial, and the three days of the appeal, had done nothing to alter Loseby's understanding of the relevant legal realities. Yet when he noted incredulously that the implication of the DPP's case was that Mrs Duncan was *defenceless*, he was closer to the truth than he knew – therein lay the ancient legal magic of the Witchcraft Act. This time, Abdy Collins set down his criticisms of Loseby in a Psychic Press pamphlet, never published because of libel, and Percy Wilson pointed the finger too. J. B. McIndoe was also writing a book, for which Loseby provided an introduction and here Loseby revealed that the only person he was really concerned to vindicate was himself. He may even have lost interest in Helen the felon, and only held a torch for her as a figurehead for the Spiritualist cause. The fact that he had begun carelessly to misspell her name 'Hellen' may not have been significant; but his allusion to her ectoplasmic manifestations as 'parlour games' certainly was.

Only at home did attitudes to Helen remain constant. Her children had pinned their hopes on the appeal, as had Henry who was being cared for by his daughter Lilian, while Gena, now a nurse, was at work. Henry also had his own immiseration as a householder to worry about, especially since he had ceased to accept a dole of £3 per week from the Edinburgh Psychic College and Library in protest against them quizzing Gena as to whether he had a job yet. 'Do you not think your mother has kept him for long enough?' they asked. Desperate now, he decided to petition the Home Secretary, the Prime Minister and the King. On 24 June 1944 he wrote three letters, each a variation on a theme: his wife was a good woman who had helped thousands, but now was broken in body and spirit. Buckingham Palace forwarded theirs to the Scottish Office who passed it to the Home Office; Churchill's Private Secretary did likewise; and Morrison's landed on Francis Graham-Harrison's desk where it was reunited with its siblings and logged into a huge ledger worthy of Mr Micawber. The Home Office had the perfect excuse to do nothing, having heard from the Governor of Holloway that Helen Duncan had made application to the Attorney-General, so that the case remained *sub judice*. The first step towards the House of Lords was for Sir Donald Somervell to grant a fiat – a certificate – indicating that the appeal ruling involved a matter of exceptional public significance and, until he made a decision, Graham-Harrison explained to Henry Duncan, his hands were tied. But Henry was not beaten yet. He had their family doctor summarize Helen's medical history in a letter, which he sent to the Home Office, pointing out that the earliest Lords hearing would not be until October and begging compassion. The Home Office reiterated that they were unable to help while the case was under review; but were careful not to promise future action either.

This was a prudent policy, for in August Somervell refused the application and with that the fight to overturn Helen Duncan's conviction ended. Meanwhile, the Home Office had sought the opinion of the Medical Officer at Holloway, wary of her martyrdom. Given everything they had heard, officials were surprised by the MO's report, which began by saying that her diabetes had been brought safely under control: 'Her present condition is entirely satisfactory as there is no evidence of any sugar in the urine with this treatment. As regards her heart there is some myocardial regeneration due to fatty infiltration of the heart muscle but this has been benefited to some extent by a loss in weight. On Reception she weighed 236 lbs, and now weighs 212 lbs.' It went on to say that there were no problems with her gall bladder, nor her abdomen. The only deterioration in her condition was mental. The flying bombs had caused anxiety and 'mild depression', and in general 'she has become very emotionally hysterical', although the MO thought twice about this and put 'emotionally *unstable*' instead. The bad news about the appeal did not help Helen's anguish. More downcast than ever, she arranged an interview with the Deputy Governor to inform the prison authorities that her present course of action was over and they, in turn, informed the Home Office. The very next day an official at the Home Office wrote to Henry Duncan to inform him that his wife was in good physical health.

Confusion in the Spiritualist camp as to what had been achieved by campaigning on Helen Duncan's behalf was made depressingly clearer by the continued activity of the police and courts. Within weeks of the Old Bailey trial, a magistrate at Hull offered to dismiss the case against a fortune teller charged under the Vagrancy Act if she could predict how much he had decided to fine her. When she declined – the answer was a tricky £3 – he called her a fake. More ominous still for Spiritualists, on 10 July 1944 Jane Yorke, a seventy-two-year-old medium, was arrested at her home in Forest Gate, east London. 'Why, after twenty-three years?' she asked the police. Mrs Yorke held seances in her basement where the spirits spoke through her Zulu guide who impressed sitters with his war-cry 'Umba, Umba, Umba!' Queen Victoria was a frequent communicator (Yorke scrunched up her face) and Sir Arthur Conan Doyle had been known to spare her a few moments, too. Her messages were not just vague but wrong, for which she blamed the bombing. Acting undercover, a police inspector was told that he had lost his father in the First World War, a policewoman that her dead baby was beside her holding a bunch of roses and a sergeant that his brother had been burned alive on a bombing mission. These messages were relatively harmless; but whenever Yorke came close to the truth the effect could be devastating. A woman, crying bitterly after Yorke attempted to impersonate her son who *had* been killed in the RAF, was warned that 'a loved one is going to meet with a serious accident but I fear it will be fatal'. She was not told who, but was advised to take care of her husband.

The case was referred to the DPP who paused while the Court of Criminal Appeal reached its judgement in the Duncan case and then, confident that he had escaped criticism, pressed ahead. He appointed Henry Elam as prosecuting counsel who, more sure of himself this time, framed an indictment under the Witchcraft Act using a near-identical formula to that used against Helen Duncan, the only change – albeit significant – a greater emphasis on the fraudulent acceptance of money. On 12 September Jane Yorke was convicted at the Old Bailey but, presumably due to her age and disability, Sir Gerald Dodson mercifully agreed to bind her over for three years.

Jane Yorke was not like Helen Duncan; she had divulged no state secrets, unless one counts Queen Victoria guaranteeing the success of D-Day ('Get your red-white-and-blues ready!'), or Conan Doyle predicting that the war would be over by October 1944. The reason that the authorities used the Witchcraft Act against her is simple: after Helen Duncan, they knew that they could. This confidence is further reflected in events at Altrincham, near Manchester, where two weeks after Jane Yorke's conviction police banned a Spiritualist meeting – an address by a spirit guide, 'Dr Letari' – on the grounds that it would constitute an act of conjuration. The London and North-Eastern Railway had already stripped advertisements from their stations, the

Altrincham Corporation withdrew permission to use the municipal hall and printers refused to print the propaganda about the case which the SNU was to have sent to MPs. Hannen Swaffer charged off to the scene but was not allowed to speak in Altrincham and had to decamp to nearby Sale. Such was the fear of the Witchcraft Act, cried the Spiritualists. In the House of Commons, Herbert Morrison laughed the whole thing off, but his officials were less complacent. When, in December, the President of Redhill Spiritualist church was instructed that clairvoyance and psychometry constituted conjuration indictable under the Witchcraft Act, and was required to supply a written undertaking that these practices would cease, public protests followed. That winter the Home Office started looking at ways to weed 'crazy old nuisance laws' from the statute books.

By the time the news about Jane Yorke reached Helen she had less than a fortnight of her sentence left to serve. To the end, she remained tormented by the bombing and, unlike many London mediums, found little relief in trusting her spirit guide. By then, many of the V–1 launch sites had been overrun by the Allies and eighty per cent of the doodlebugs which did make it over the Channel were intercepted; however, the announcement that the Battle of London was over proved premature once the first supersonic V–2 rocket landed on 8 September. The circle of anxiety and depression became still more vicious. In later years Helen remembered a wardress who came to her cell, seeking comfort after a rocket had exploded nearby; but it was as likely that it was the wardress who comforted Helen, the 'child of larger growth', shaking and weeping, alone and afraid. On the morning of Friday, 22 September, fear of the war became fear of the world as Helen was bathed, examined (usually no more than the touch of a stethoscope), and her clothes and possessions returned. Less the usual remission, she had served 172 days of her sentence and, free to go, she was met at the prison gates by several members of her family, and together they caught a train from King's Cross. The girls were overjoyed and back in Edinburgh saw their father crying as he watched his treasured Nell snoring in a chair, napping away an afternoon. For a while she was extremely tired and seemed somehow diminished. She was bitter about the conduct of the SNU and within a week had formally withdrawn her services as a medium. The SNU Freedom Fund committee issued a press release lamenting this 'grave blow to investigation, advance and progress', and reaffirming their position thus: 'We are satisfied that Helen Duncan . . . was completely innocent of the charge of pretending brought against her, that her trial violated elementary principles of justice, and that she was wrongly convicted.' When word reached Harry Price that Helen had retired from mediumship – the declaration was published in *Psychic News* – he was deeply sceptical. Back when she was just beginning her sentence, he had ended a letter to Mollie Goldney with a wry prediction: 'One last certainty: when Mrs D comes out, she will be at the old game again!'

Price was right. Henry, who blamed himself for having developed Helen's mediumship, felt uneasy when she started to give private sittings, but had to be content with her promise that there would be no more materialization seances. Helen regretted that by touring constantly, and then going to prison, she had missed so much of her children's teenage development, and so started spending more time with Lilian, Gena and Nan, and her grandchildren, telling them stories from her childhood and reflecting on the second shock-wave of war she had experienced in her lifetime. In due course her sons came home, Harry to hospital suffering from amoebic dysentery (he married his nurse), Peter traumatized by a Japanese kamikaze plane which had struck HMS *Formidable* and killed his best friend. Victory over Japan in September 1945 brought peace, but with it new dangers. The bombing of Hiroshima and Nagasaki (predicted by Albert), combined with the penetration of Britain's island security by the V–weapons, suggested that the next war would mean obliteration, perhaps on a global scale. In August 1942 a spirit had spoken through Gladys Osborne Leonard, warning of storms, earthquakes and tidal waves which would follow the war, and although she subtracted somewhat from the terrible drama of this by immediately hooking up with a lovely white cat and a dark-brown dog in spirit, the message was clear and was repeated at seances nationwide in the post-war era. Spiritualist aspirations for a new order of peace, light and the Brotherhood of Man seemed more relevant in the nuclear age than they had even in 1918.

More immediately, Helen was pleased to help a fresh cohort of war bereaved, the only irritation being a persistent woman seeking tips for the greyhound track. Before long, Lily Greig, a medium and friend of Helen's, had established a development circle at the Duncans' home, although this was disbanded soon after Albert came through to say that no one there would ever develop as a physical medium – including Helen's daughter Gena – and advised them to stop trying. A spirit once told Mrs Osborne Leonard that unreleased ectoplasm builds up in the muscles and can cause cancer, but it is unlikely that it was fear of the only major illness she had yet to contract which brought Helen Duncan back to physical mediumship: it was simply that materialization was what she did best. Her promise to Henry notwithstanding, she began to arrange sittings in Edinburgh where she amazed sitters with manifestations including a small African boy who had a conversation in Swahili with a colonial farmer present. Before long, she was accepting invitations to her old haunt, the Spiritualist church in Glasgow where she had been performing prior to attending Miss Maule's doomed seance back in 1933. Now bad luck struck again.

It was on one of these jaunts that she agreed to take her granddaughter Dawn but changed her mind at Waverley Station after she experienced a premonition and asked Henry to take the child home. Ever the martyr, Helen set off regardless of the risk; she refused a vendor's offer of cigarettes on tick when she discovered she had no change because she was not sure if she would be coming back. Just before the train arrived in Glasgow it crashed. Seconds earlier, Helen had clairaudiently heard Albert's warning and had hurled herself into a vacant lavatory cubicle, which afforded her some protection from the impact. She remembered being upside down among the splintered woodwork and arms reaching in towards her; but the next thing of which she was fully aware was that she was back in hospital where she was observed for a few days, then discharged. Even as she recuperated at home, clients were knocking at the front door, and she looked to Albert and the occasional stiff drink for assistance. One evening Gena brought home George Brealey, a soldier she had met at a football match. The house was quiet and dark, except for the fire in the dining room, so the pair left the light off before settling themselves. Suddenly Albert's voice boomed out a greeting and Gena realized that her mother was actually sitting in the room. Perhaps the strangest part of the story was George's reaction. It soon transpired that he was an aspiring medium himself, so when his future mother-in-law left her trance and introduced herself more cordially than her guide, he was quite unperturbed. But then Helen already knew this.

It was not long before the famous medium was back in commission, sitting more frequently and travelling further. June Moore was in her twenties when she attended a seance in a downstairs room of a semi-detached house in Warrington. Mrs Duncan was not long out of prison, and the organizers were secretive and protective, and would not allow the handful of sitters to meet her. The medium sat at one end of the darkened room looking fat and fishwifey, while a fog began to drift over, within it a spectral old lady. June recognized her as a woman from her village who had been knocked down by a bus, and here she was, just as in life, speaking in a wavering voice. Her niece, who was present, kissed her and said, 'It's lovely to see you, Auntie' and after that the spirit began to fade. Lancashire and north Wales seem to have been popular destinations for Helen, perhaps due to the golden beaches she loved so much (and to which post-war holidaymakers had by now been allowed to return) and the high density of elderly Spiritualists in retirement. At Blackpool, the kiss-me-quick jewel of the north-west coast, it was said that sandwich-board men advertised her seances, though this may have been just a malicious rumour among those who felt her standards had fallen. Reports to this effect filtered back to the SNU until they could bear no more. In a letter to active SPR member Lady Ruth Balfour, written early in 1946, Mollie Goldney shared the latest gossip: 'The Spiritualists are now so furious with Mrs D. that they have disowned her and withdrawn their so-called "diploma" from her. I understand she is giving sittings right and left and drinking hard.' Some said it was the drink which did most to turn the SNU against her; the new SPR Research Officer, Donald West, was convinced of it.

It was Mollie Goldney who suggested to Donald that he should write an article about Helen Duncan, Harry Price having declined to do a joint study with her. Mollie asked Lady Balfour to provide details of a meeting she had arranged with Dr John Winning in 1944, at which time she happened to be on war service in

Winning's native Glasgow. Ever since Mollie had first accosted him at the station, the SPR had been trying to see his photographs but he remained reticent. Lady Balfour, however, had seen all eight, the most striking of which showed a black-bearded Arabian physician called Abdul who knew the names of all the nurses at the local hospital. When Lady Balfour asked Winning about Price's regurgitation theory he had struggled to contain his anger and she made a hasty exit. Mollie liaised with several others on behalf of her protégé Donald, including Price who rather resented the newcomer, and Eric Dingwall who offered to read his draft, saying: 'I want this to be *the* paper on fat Helen.' Donald West also benefited from long conversations with Mollie who felt he needed educating in metropolitan ways and steering through the minefield of SPR protocols. She teased him for his 'leftish mind', played him Bach and was gratified to hear his Mersey accent disappear. When the time came to publish his study in the SPR *Proceedings*, President W. H. Salter was afraid of libelling Mrs Duncan, especially about her drinking. Donald protested that he had 'piles of witnesses' to support him, including Abdy Collins who had said, 'Mrs D. is a dreadful woman and has always drunk something like a bottle of whisky a day.' In the end, Donald did tone things down and in April 1946 submitted his draft, declaring his involvement with Helen Duncan at an end. In October he received a belated reply from a Mrs E. Homer of Portsmouth, 'Certified Masseuse, Diploma Holder, Healer, Speaker and Demonstrator'. Mrs Duncan, she assured him, was an honest medium, but she regretted to inform him that she had heard nothing from her since the trial.

Unlike Helen Duncan, Mollie Goldney was neither a drinker nor a smoker – she preferred to waste money on gramophone records, she confided smugly to Donald West. However, apart from the odd attention-seeking burn, the redolence of the saloon lingering around her more somnolent spirits and Albert's languorous slurring, Helen's vices never caused her permanent harm – she was far too ill for that. Her reputation did perhaps suffer in an age when female smoking had its place and drinking, which might have shamed a man, was positively scandalous in a woman; but this mattered little to her. Moreover, for every lack-lustre performance there was one which harked back to former glories, when the ectoplasm billowed like a quicksilver cloud and Peggy sang 'You are my Sunshine' like a mischievous angel. At her Liverpool home, the dead cousin of a medium named Susie Hughes – a casualty of war – materialized, as did her father who embraced his wife and lifted her over his head: half tearful reunion, half strongman act. Susie Hughes also attended one of Helen's public meetings at the Daulby Hall, where she reported seeing a Dublin colleen with long dark curls take shape from tendrils of mist that rose up before the girl's father sitting in the front row. In the later 1940s Helen frequently crossed the Firth of Forth to Dunfermline, where she performed in the Cooperative Hall, the basement of an orthodox church, and Mr and Mrs Lingwood's attic. The Lingwood children remember the seances well. Eileen, a friend of Lilian's (who had remarried), saw the usual glowing parade, plus Peggy cavorting and a small glowing fairy, which twirled around on Mrs Duncan's palm – a new member of the spiritual cast and uncannily like the miniature girl Madame Bisson said she saw Eva C. manifest in 1921. Eileen's brother Harvey, who had to tidy away his toys to make room for the sitters, was in the same Cub Scout troop as Lilian's son and was once invited to tea, where Helen, bespectacled these days, her hair tied back in a severe bun, forced cake upon him and told him he possessed healing powers. Demand for her seances seems not to have diminished, nor did her loss of the diploma condemn her in the eyes of those who admired her as a medium rather than just an emblem of mediumship. With them, her martyrdom was safe, and over post-seance tea and cigarettes she often told stories of her degrading searches at the hands of Harry Price and Mollie Goldney, like an ancient Quaker speaking of past sufferings.

Despite the family's vow to have nothing more to do with the Edinburgh Psychic College and Library, Helen continued to work there. Proper test conditions were applied, with vaginal and rectal searches by a 'committee of lady sitters', although there had been cutbacks since the war. Verbatim records of seances were discontinued – the excuse given to Donald West when he made enquiries about documentary sources for his article. In 1949 a young woman named Denise Hankey flew from London to Edinburgh to visit her mother Muriel, who was Deputy Principal for a term, and was lucky enough to be offered a place at a seance after a cancellation. Milky ectoplasm spilled from Mrs Duncan's nostrils like egg white solidifying in boiling water, she recalls, which sank to the floor and ebbed and flowed in a swirling carpet smelling of body fluids. Albert informed Denise that a girl who had 'passed with a condition of the lower part of the body' was there and before she could think who this might be the ectoplasm around her ankles sprang up to form the well-defined face of a schoolfellow who had died from cancer of the uterus. The spirit asked Denise to pass on a message to their headmistress which, in due course, she did. Everyone got someone except for two guests from Oxford. Today, Denise tells the story with all the awestruck ardour of half a century ago; Mrs Duncan she remembers as a coarse-mannered, gross heap of flesh who drank like a fish – a perfect vehicle for materialization.

It remained common for sitters to find some parts of a performance deeply suspicious, others utterly convincing. Mr S. M. Gardiner, a non-Spiritualist SPR member, attended at least eleven of Helen Duncan's seances in Dunfermline and, although he sometimes gave her a lift to the station on his way back to Glasgow, he was no fan of her as a person, nor, it would seem, as a medium. He was disappointed that the spirit of his father had only pointed at his moustache, thought that Albert was probably Mrs Duncan's secondary personality and hoped to borrow an infra-red telescope from the Admiralty (for whom he worked) to find out what was going on. And yet the materialization of his young daughter gave him pause for thought. Peering at him, her face no more than eighteen inches from his, she said 'I'm going to touch my daddy' and patted him on the head. His wife had a conversation with the luminous form of the child and was convinced. The Gardiners were aware of Mrs Duncan's past history, but they also knew what they had seen and believed that if some phenomena were fraudulent, there must be genuine content as well. A similar conclusion was reached by Leah Longman. One evening in 1949 she arrived at a private flat in Edinburgh and heard what she described as the 'powerful masculine voice' of Mrs Duncan who was chatting and smoking at ease with her sitters, each of whom had paid 10s 6d for the privilege of watching her perform. A tiny alcove had been made into a cabinet from where the first spirit form appeared. 'It bore no resemblance whatever to any communicator,' Mrs Longman said, 'but a marked resemblance to Mrs Duncan.' Despite her initial revulsion, she found the spirits which followed more convincing – differentiated, voluble and emotionally alive – and several women were reduced to tears. 'My view at the moment', she informed the SPR, 'is that it is as difficult to explain the phenomena of Mrs Duncan on normal lines, as it would be to accept the forms at the face value.'

Similar reports, which arrived from time to time at SPR headquarters in Tavistock Square, always raised interest, albeit sometimes more nostalgic than academic. Donald West still hankered after a proper test seance of the sort Helen Duncan had granted Harry Price in 1931, but had always denied the SPR. In 1947 the SPR increased its prize for proof of physical mediumship from £250 to £1000 and in the autumn of that year Donald asked Mr Gardiner in Glasgow to approach Mrs Duncan on his behalf. This Gardiner did – in vain. Helen was indignant, asking whether by 'the SPR' he meant Price and Goldney, and then launching into the full story: the choking seance bag, the sanitary towel, the double-stomach and the maid, Mary McGinlay (whom, according to Helen, no one would employ now). Emotional from her woeful recollections, Helen set her face against Gardiner and declared that she would not do it for a million pounds – although one suspects that if that had been the offer she would have been hailing a cab to Waverley Station post haste. Donald's response to Gardiner was that by refusing she only harmed her reputation – a bit much, considering that her traducement had gone as far as it could. Perhaps, like Harry Price poking fun at cheesecloth worship, West found it hard to accept that her popularity had survived, and would thrive, for as long as the martyrizing law remained unchanged.

It was also hard to accept that the Duncans were again reversing their material fortunes. They had moved a mile away to 36 Rankeillor Street on the edge of Holyrood Park, where Helen and Henry spared themselves the stairs by sleeping on the ground floor and let the upstairs rooms to respectable lodgers. The Duncan household was a favourite with the tramps who called by for food, marking the doorsteps with chalk to guide others. Helen must have seen herself as a young woman in a pregnant Welsh girl she took in and likewise in Maggie, an eighteen-year-old she met while shopping whose hair was falling out. Helen invited her to tea, bought her a couple of wigs and she stayed for four years. But even with guests in residence there was always plenty of space. Henry kept his books in a back room he called 'the library' and another room was empty except for a pianola. The busy, homely kitchen had a scrubbed pine table, a washing machine and a walk-in pantry stacked up with pickle jars. Gena came every day to help out, accompanied by her children, the infant Sandra (born on Helen's birthday) and a baby, Sheila – both destined to be psychic. When they were a little older they were afraid of the rumbling from the water tank, which Helen told them was the sound of some bogeyman she called 'Alligator Bill'. The environment in which Gena's children grew up was as suffused with spiritual power as that in which she herself had been raised, especially for Sandra who chose to live with Helen (who missed her own children) and who was most fiercely protective of her. Helen had known that Gena was pregnant with Ann even before Gena, and had got her spiritual physician, Dr Johansen (the one who saved her from a whisky-induced coma in the 1930s), to give her a once-over. Perched on Helen's lap, the girls would write questions on pieces of paper which she burned, rubbing the soot on her arm, thrillingly, to reveal the answer.

In the world beyond Rankeillor Street, Spiritualism was declining in vitality as a religion. Many who were disappointed that the spirits had predicted peace in 1938 had let their beliefs lapse and new converts were few. The efflorescence of Spiritualism after 1918 was not repeated in 1945: the loss of life was smaller, its public impact lessened by experience. Of course, the private grief of individual households – a third of a million of them – was just as devastating as during the First World War and for them mediums were on hand. There were too few, according to some dead soldiers, one of whom said he had met servicemen from the First World War in the spirit world who had lent him Lodge's *Raymond*. Physical mediums such as Minnie

Harrison (the sister of the exposed Agnes Abbott) helped many people between 1946 and the mid-1950s, during which time there were hundreds of ectoplasmic extrusions, materializations and trumpet levitations. At a special Armistice Day seance in 1947 a poppy and a Royal Artillery tunic button were apported. But the end of an era was nigh. In 1952, *Psychic News* reported a general decline in psychic phenomena, a decline mediums themselves had noticed. Belief in the supernatural was not the problem. A Mass-Observation study of post-war London indicated that two-thirds of men and four-fifths of women believed in God, a majority of whom believed in an afterlife; one vicar said his flock still imagined the world of troublefree leisure inhabited by Raymond Lodge. More than a third believed in contactable spirits, half in clairvoyance. The difference now was that the inclination to act upon such beliefs had faded. In 1944 Maurice Barbanell had claimed there were a million Spiritualists in Britain, but by the 1950s the SNU laid claim to a fraction of that figure. Originally a weekly, the LSA's newspaper *Light* had become a monthly in 1944, then in 1955 a quarterly no longer devoted solely to Spiritualism; in the same year the LSA was renamed the College of Psychic Science to reflect changing interests and to sustain the drift of members away from the SPR. In 1932 C. E. Bechhofer Roberts had predicted that Spiritualism would be 'doomed to perish by the hand of its own child, psychical research'. He was right; but for the wrong reason, for public interest in psychical research was weaker than it had been before the war. In 1948 W. H. Salter wrote a self-congratulatory history of the SPR, suggesting that the ambitions of its founders were as relevant as ever. The reality was otherwise. Britain was a long way, now, from the intellectual *noblesse oblige* of Sidgwick, Myers and Gurney seeking salvation from godless ruin. Nandor Fodor, who had escaped to New York where it was easier to indulge in theorization, now understood that 'psychical research has tried to be too scientific for years and has gone bankrupt as a result'.

The shift can be detected in the media revolution. Radio waves, which had hinted at an understanding of psychic communication, were by this time firmly established as a means of communication in their own right. As an aspiring national unifier, Spiritualism had given way to the BBC, and even secular interest in radar and radio waves from space were of little cultural consequence compared with the transformation of popular entertainment. Now, the new realms of experience into which people ventured more often existed in this world. On the eve of war, forty per cent of the population went to the cinema once a week and with victory even this was under threat, not so much from wireless – for which there were 34 million subscribers in 1939 – but from television. Ownership of TV sets grew exponentially once transmissions, suspended for the duration, resumed in 1946, especially after coverage was extended beyond the south-east. Whereas only a few thousand saw the 1946 Victory Parade, 2½ million households switched on to watch the Coronation in 1953. In television lay a paradox which would prove a bitter blow to Spiritualism: people went out less, but they knew more. Inter-war Britain had accepted what it was told (especially if said in an Oxford or BBC accent), and contained many who got seance phenomena if they expected them. Spiritualism was also a religion for gregarious activists; television was personal and passive. By the end of the century this generation of Spiritualists was lamenting a lack of discipline in the ranks of the movement and knew well that a generation brought up to expect instant gratification would never spend the hours apprentice mediums had once put into their development circles. An age awash with information cannot sustain this, nor can its people understand well those seance-goers whose innocence is easily mistaken for ignorance, and who used their senses differently. With all that expectation and all that effort, who knew what might happen in the darkness when the gramophone needle found its groove and the cabinet curtains began to part? And light was let in on magic in a more practical way after the war with the increased availability of infra-red cameras and optical equipment. In 1936 Harry Price was on the verge of being able to record a seance cinematographically and eagerly anticipated the day that it would happen. 'When we reach it,' he predicted, 'the day of the fraudulent medium will be over.'

Pre-war fraudulence was still in evidence. Without too much effort, a photograph of Minnie Harrison supporting a trumpet on an ectoplasmic pseudopod can be interpreted as cloth stretched from her teeth to a bandaged rod between her legs on which the trumpet has been fitted. There may be no photographs of Helen at work in these years but, on bad days at least, this was just the sort of thing she was up to. And she herself admitted that prison had made her deceitful. One of her friends, Ivy Northage, formed the opinion that although she possessed remarkable powers, Helen was nonetheless 'a very foolish woman' who was 'battened on' at home to make money, the implication being that she needed to resort to fraud to eke out her rapidly depleting energies. Stage fright affected her worse than ever before and a nip of Dutch courage went a long way. At a seance at the home of Mr Latimer in Alloa (he who had appealed to Churchill), the sound of breaking glass had her pack up pronto – or, if you prefer, a torch handed to a materialized spirit caused ectoplasm to rush back into her body. (As usual, even the mundane explanation is bizarre: upstairs, the Latimers' four-year-old son, unable to turn the handle of the lavatory door, had broken the glass with a hammer.) Helen was taken back to Edinburgh with a burned stomach. Confronted by such dangers,

Albert was more often wise after the fact than before it. Helen needed a more practical assistant, especially as six months after the Alloa seance she collapsed into a diabetic coma, her kidneys were shown to be in a poor state and she was rapidly becoming infirm. Spouting homespun philosophy about having to die some time of something, she forced herself back to work, but could no longer operate alone. Henry stayed at home and Helen could hardly ask Frances Brown if she felt like getting the old team back together again. It was fortuitous, then, that one of her first engagements was with Gert Hamilton who kept a seance room above her grocer's shop in Stoke-on-Trent.

Gert enjoyed what Spiritualists call a very 'evidential' seance, seeing a materialized airman, a printer who had lost his fingers on a cutting machine and the spirit of a woman who shone a torch on her face to show everyone her harelip; this time the white light did the medium no harm. On the strength of this, Gert became Helen's minder and travelling companion, making sure she took her insulin and keeping suspicious sitters away from the front row. Albert did his bit too, waking Helen in the night to warn her about a man with red hair who would come to the next seance. Gert watched out for him and directed him straight to the back row, her suspicions increased by the fact that he was wearing a wig. By the early 1950s Helen's health was deteriorating, and she was in and out of hospital. Eileen Lingwood, then training to be a nurse, saw her for the last time leaning out of the toilet window of the Edinburgh Royal Infirmary Eye Department having a crafty cigarette, but she did not stop to chat because it was raining and her starched cap was getting wet. The catalogue of medical disasters grew in length. Helen's sight was not what it was; Gert took her to Paris, but had to bring her back after her blood-sugar level escalated; she suffered a minor heart attack; a huge abscess in her groin was drained, at which point she was diagnosed with shingles; and one Christmas she was admitted to a Welsh hospital with her diabetes. Most devastating of all was the news she received on her way back from Wales: Gert had received a telegram from Henry to say that their daughter Nan had died.

Emotionally and physically, Helen Duncan was falling apart, a tragic symbol of the once flourishing religion and science she represented. Like Eusapia Palladino, who died in 1918 after a disastrous tour of the USA, she sensed the ratio of good to bad phenomena sliding away to her disfavour. There were poor reports from seances in London. Muriel Hankey and her daughter Denise attended a seance in a large hall where some ectoplasm covered Helen's face and, even though a friend of Denise's recognized her mother, the performance was unimpressive. An SPR investigator, Tony Cornell, was present at a similar gathering somewhere off the Seven Sisters Road, where despite the raptures of women around him, all he could see was cheesecloth and a coathanger glinting in the dim light. Elsewhere, Albert's sentences trailed away distractedly and the formalities of the old days were dispensed with. Instead of mannered introductions, a hand would poke through cabinet curtains, click its fingers and point at the lucky sitter; the other hand usually held a cigarette, the smell of which wafted out unmistakably. Gert Hamilton tried to keep things together. Chris Newberry had not long finished his National Service when he spent £1 on a ticket to see a Duncan seance in a nonconformist hall at Plymouth Hoe. Various spirit forms approached the audience, one of which Chris recognized as his grandfather, a lay preacher who showed his astonishment that he had not had to wait for the Last Trump to return. Gert, who sat at a table next to the cabinet, opened the curtains to reveal the medium still in trance, and the audience were tickled pink to see the hunched spirit of an old lady who asked whether

Helen was all right and should she take her a glass of water. At the end, Gert helped an apparently oblivious Helen to her feet, stretched out her hand for her, and the glowing fairy manifested there and did a turn. Everyone gasped.

The year 1954 was mixed. Alan Crossley, a medium shaken by his war experience (his spirit guide was a soldier killed at Dunkirk), met Helen for the first time in Liverpool and became devoted, although he recalls sitters muttering that she was not as good as she used to be. Alan saw dozens of materializations including his friend's father who encouraged his wife to get on with her life, twin babies in Helen's arms screaming their heads off and the mayor of Tewkesbury resplendent in his chains of office. Alan also saw Helen do a double act at Southend-on-Sea with Maud Gunning, another huge materialization medium who turned water into wine and apported fruit and flowers, which they donated to the local hospital. On another occasion he saw Helen dematerialize a cup of tea, which a sitter had spilt down her dress.

In London an investigator who had quit the SPR for the LSA found the medium dull and monosyllabic, but could not argue with the fact that his mother had returned to him from a cloud of white mist. In the same year, however, Mollie Goldney received a complaint from 'a sensible sort of girl' about a seance she had attended with her flatmate. Blackout curtains formed a cabinet, above which muslin was suspended from a hole where pipes came down. Albert was faceless and had Mrs Duncan's left arm for a backbone, and an Arab sheik – presumably Abdul – turned up still sticking on his beard. A manifestation which one lady swore was her teenaged daughter 'looked exactly like Mrs D. and more 70 than 17'. The same month a Lancashire Spiritualist wondered if Helen should be told what was happening, fearing she had been taken over by 'Powers of Darkness'. In May, a Mrs Quinlan from Manchester was grief-stricken but grateful when

Helen materialized her brother who, she was informed for the first time, had been killed in New Zealand. On receiving a letter from him in August, she was overjoyed and angry.

Helen continued to travel widely in 1955. At Gloucester, Jean Frost struggled to see a friend in the form of a young woman who built up from ectoplasm, but reached no firm conclusion before the spirit melted away; nor did the sad spirit utter a word. In West Kensington, Richard Sheargold, an SPR member, saw Albert – 'a long white streak with barely discernable features' – appear between Helen and Gert Hamilton. Albert showed the sitters his 'voice-box', described by Sheargold as 'a peculiar object rather like a large white potato', and by others in previous years as a large pair of pendulous lips, a square box on a rod of ectoplasm, and Mrs Duncan's draped fist held vertically. On this occasion about a dozen spirits came through – an Irishman here, a black baby there – all but one of which were recognized. One spirit, an old lady, resembled Helen Duncan wearing a grey hooded dressing gown. 'Another purported to be Latvian,' recorded Sheargold, 'but in response to floods of eloquence in that tongue from a lady sitter it made an unrecognizable sound which might have been anything and disappeared'. The following year saw Helen attending to the poignant desires of more refugees, this time from the Hungarian uprising, many of whom had found jobs in the coalmines around Dunfermline. Harvey Lingwood saw the spirit of a woman speak to her son at the Cooperative Hall and, although no one knew if these words really were Hungarian, the man's tears spoke for themselves.

Whatever scathing words Helen had to face, she was at least safer from the law than she and her fellow mediums had ever been

before. During the war, although the SNU deputation to the
Home Office had lost the battle to change the law, many smaller
skirmishes had been fought: ministration for prisoners; recognition for Spiritualists in the services; attacks on the BBC's embargo
on Spiritualist broadcasts; the status of churches and their endowments; permission to hold Spiritualist burial services. Nor had
the bigger ambition been shelved. Labour leader Clement Attlee
had pledged to repeal obsolete legislation and when he became
Prime Minister in 1945 appointed a Home Secretary who was
nonconformist in religion and libertarian in politics: James Chuter
Ede. Attlee's choice was propitious for the SNU, which redoubled
its lobbying efforts, sending a deputation to the Home Office
soon after the general election, and in general building upon the
righteous indignation of 'An Amazed Citizen of Gateshead' and
others who had written to Herbert Morrison. The Labour
Government of 1945 were self-conscious modernizers, and there
was no escaping the fact that the Witchcraft Act – indeed the
very word *witchcraft* – smacked of the Middle Ages, made the
police into witch-hunters and the courts into the Inquisition. In
key areas of national life – laws, institutions, schools, healthcare
– Britain seemed out of step with some other countries in an age
of US-dominated internationalism, and changing the law was a
small price to pay to prevent official attitudes to Spiritualism
being used as a symbol of this backwardness. From the time that
the Attorney-General denied that Helen Duncan's case was a
matter of public importance, Maurice Barbanell for one was
determined to make him eat his words. And the fact that some
legal experts were sympathetic meant he had a chance. 'The
present situation, in which both Spiritualists and quacks are prosecuted under two obsolete Acts', argued *The Solicitor* in 1944,
'is highly unsatisfactory, and calls for investigation.'

So far as the police were concerned, it had been agreed in

1945 that discretion over whether to prosecute mediums lay with chief constables who, due to the publicity generated by the Duncan trial, were now expected to refer all cases to the DPP. The Home Office, too, advised caution and took seriously an argument in Desmond MacCarthy's review of Bechhofer Roberts's book that 'the effect on a medium of public exposure is not what one might suppose: it brings a larger following and an increase in faith'. By degrees, the SNU was getting its way and in 1948 Chuter Ede's Criminal Justice Act finally stopped the police arresting suspected mediums unless there was good reason to believe they would abscond. Prosecutions became rarer, although each time a fortune teller was tried under the 1824 Vagrancy Act – thirty-nine of them in 1949 – it served as a reminder that a judicial sword of Damocles still hung over Spiritualists. This sense became more vivid in June 1950 with the Old Bailey trial of Leigh-Mallory's medium, Charles Glover Botham, who had assured Lady Wilson, widow of a banker and former Tory MP, that £1500 left behind a cushion would be dematerialized by her husband's spirit and given to charity. The banknotes did indeed dematerialize: into the medium's pocket and he was soon exposed – thanks to Mollie Goldney – and tried for false pretences. However, the charge was supported by an indictment under the 1735 Witchcraft Act in case it transpired that the dupe had believed her husband would actually appear – an offence now well-established as pretence to conjuration. The words of the judge – none other than Sir Gerald Dodson – were a significant departure from 1944 and thus straws in the wind. Upon conviction, Glover Botham was reprimanded for having 'done a great disservice to Spiritualism, which is held in great reverence by many devout people'. As it happened, the fraud was so blatant that Dodson discharged the jury from returning a verdict on the subsidiary charges, but the SNU were still able to capitalize on the fact that the Witchcraft Act had been mentioned at all.

In the same year, Charles Loseby who, despairing of England, had emigrated to Hong Kong, received a letter from Percy Wilson with the latest gossip. The editor of *Two Worlds* was a communist; Ernest Oaten was ageing fast; the secular Spiritualists were at war with the Christians; Hannen Swaffer had been experiencing blackouts; Maurice Barbanell had 'fallen on evil days', embezzling the proceeds of propaganda meetings to pay for a lost libel action; and 'Mrs Duncan is misbehaving again!'. The biggest news was that, as a Unitarian, the Home Secretary supported their fight for liberty and although their draft Bill had been rejected, an acceptable alternative had been drawn up by the Home Office and Parliamentary Counsel. On Monday, 16 July 1951, the Spiritualists' Parliamentary Committee gave a high-spirited dinner at the House of Commons in honour of Spiritualist MP Thomas Brooks and Sir Hugh – now Lord – Dowding, to celebrate the Bill receiving Royal Assent three weeks earlier. It had been read for the first time in November 1950 by Walter Monslow MP, not a Spiritualist but a Methodist who understood the importance of freedom of worship – as did Chuter Ede and his fellow Unitarians, and the Congregationalists, Catholics and Jews behind him in the Commons. Indeed, before the general election in February some 200 MPs had pledged support for the SNU's objectives. Brooks seconded the motion, calling the 1735 and 1824 Acts 'terrible measures to apply to decent folk', and alluding to the Glover Botham trial. After some concern about the exploitation of the war bereaved had been expressed, Chuter Ede stood up to say his piece.

Prior to the day's proceedings, he had paid a visit to the Home Office library where he had found a 1616 edition of James I's *Daemonologie* and had paused to reflect upon what witchcraft had meant to a previous government. His speech was the epitome of sound reason. Next, an under-secretary from the Home Office apologized for joking about the obsolescence of broomsticks during the 1945 election campaign, his reply to a question about the Witchcraft Act while he was speaking in public about the mass production of vacuum cleaners. Everyone in the House laughed. One backbencher remarked upon the peculiarity of the English that only last night they had been discussing the possibility of a Korean war and today not only were the front pages absorbed by the Australian Test Match, but here they were chewing the fat about witches. Chuter Ede, however, felt certain now that this was an end to it, and in the future fraud should be tried as fraud and witchcraft would be consigned to history.

After the second reading, minor amendments were recommended by a standing committee and in May 1951 the Bill passed to the House of Lords, where it was read by Lord Dowding. The former Lord Chancellor, Viscount Simon, agreed that they should be ashamed to use antique legislation against Spiritualists. The following month the Fraudulent Mediums Act of 1951 repealed the Witchcraft Act and substituted certain provisions of the 1824 Vagrancy Act, the central point being that intent to deceive or defraud would now need to be proved. There was a clause providing a special defence for 'anything done solely for the purposes of entertainment' and all prosecutions would require the consent of the DPP. After a century the Spiritualists were at last free to worship, and free from the stigma of a magical, maleficent past with which the Witchcraft Act allowed them to be branded. Indeed, for the first time since 1547 witchcraft, by whatever casuistical definition, had ceased to be a crime in England. Feeling was strong within the Spiritualist movement that, whatever her merits or demerits, Helen Duncan had accelerated this change – indeed, her example had been cited early in the first reading of the Bill. The trial had refreshed old arguments and had generated publicity, which extended and intensified the debate into the fresh pastures of liberty. The police were brought up to speed by the Home Office and Theo Mathew – now DPP – asked to see only the most serious cases and 'not those merely relating to a gipsy fortune teller on Epsom Downs' – a phrase he borrowed from an old file. On the ground, the police who had been foxed by the Criminal Justice Act, were now unsure how to adapt to the new definitions and confusion reached a point where one senior officer made the following bracing recommendation: 'I think the time has come to scrap all the existing instructions and make a fresh start.'

And what of Spiritualism now that it could bask in its hour of triumph, blessed with its new lease of life, its fresh start? Perhaps here lay one of the greatest ironies of the whole story. A movement which for so long had thrived on being maligned and misunderstood, and had built its objectives upon persecution by government, courts and police, now found itself accommodated and protected. It was no longer possible to struggle against authority and bigotry in the name of justice and truth. Helen Duncan had helped to bring the history of Spiritualism in Britain to its climax; but, equally, her career as a medium had been nurtured by its coincidence with the movement's finest hour. Now was a good time to be bowing out, for there was no one to lobby, nothing to rail against, and the people stayed at home listening to the wireless, watching television and speaking to each other on the telephone. In 1961 the editor of *Psychic News*, Bill Neech, summarized the decline neatly: 'Doyle died, the Second World War came and went. Swaffer stepped more and more out of public life, Spiritualism was recognized in an Act of Parliament. It was the kiss of death.'

EPILOGUE
BEYOND THE VEIL

In the darkest hour of the night, Henry Duncan awoke to see Helen fully dressed standing at the foot of the bed. She had gone away to give seances in Nottingham and he had not expected her back so soon. His first thought that something must be wrong was confirmed when, switching on the lamp, he saw her face was deathly pale and fat tears were rolling down her cheeks. When he asked what was wrong she replied only that she had been going to leave him – after forty years of marriage – but could not bring herself to. Perplexed, Henry reached for her hand, upon which her wraithlike form

Ena Bügg and Ronald Hill on their wedding day, 15 January 1940.

shimmered back into the shadows and was gone.

Unable to sleep, Henry got up, dressed and made a pot of tea as the sun rose over the hill of Arthur's Seat. The postman would not call for another two hours and Gena not till nine. Restlessly, he set off into the chill of the autumn morning to buy a newspaper and, returning home, let his eyes swim over the latest on the Suez Crisis: it looked like Britain would soon be at war again; what more was there to say? When at last Gena's face came round the door, he explained his fears and she did her best to reassure him; but she, too, was afraid and when a telegram arrived they could hardly bear to open the envelope. It was from Gert Hamilton and stated only the barest details: the police had raided a seance, Helen was seriously ill and Gert was bringing her home that same day.

It was Tuesday, 30 October 1956. Rushing out to meet the taxi, Gena led her wincing mother into the house, where she found that even a light embrace pained her. While Gert explained to Henry what had happened, Gena took Helen into the bedroom, started to undress her and, on removing her corsets, discovered the cause of her discomfort. Even as a nurse she was appalled and let out a scream which brought Henry and Gert rushing in. On Helen's right breast there was a livid burn the size of a tea plate and on her stomach another the size of a saucer – injuries, it was said, caused by the violent reabsorption of ectoplasm. Henry took over, easing his trembling wife into her nightdress. When the doctor arrived they were told that the burns were electrical, which led Henry to ask whether they could have been self-inflicted. The doctor doubted it, adding that she would have to go to hospital anyway for her diabetes to be treated. Henry swore that this time he would sue the police and, after Helen had been made comfortable in the Western General, he sat Gert down and made her go over again what had happened in Nottingham two nights earlier.

They had been invited to stay with a Mr Timmins, a chiropodist and healer, in West Bridgford, a suburb to the south-east of the city. In an upstairs room, Mr Timmins had arranged his sitters that evening, most of whom he knew well, although one man – introduced by a new patient as her husband – he had met only once before and two of their friends never. As Helen took her place, two women attested that they had watched her change into her black outfit, then the white light was switched to red. During a rendition of the twenty-third Psalm, Albert wished everyone good evening before introducing the first apparition. Twenty minutes later, two had been claimed – a local doctor and a foreign pianist – but the seance was brought to a sudden halt by urgent banging and ringing at the front door. Seconds later a swarm of police officers were upon them, cameras flashing, hands fixing Helen to the spot where she had fallen. Her face a ghastly grey, in the voice of Albert she reassured Gert that she was not dead. After the police had cautioned her, all hands were needed to carry her to a bed where she was guarded by a policewoman while Gert, protesting that a doctor should be called, was led back into the seance room.

The sitters were kept for over an hour while statements were taken, the police eager to find the beards, masks and 'shroud'. Fruitlessly, they ransacked Gert's and Helen's suitcases, ignoring Mr Timmins's pleas that everyone be searched, which he kept up until an inspector threatened to arrest him. It is said that a doctor, called by Gert, was asked by the inspector to search the suspect's anus and vagina but he refused, and simply examined her (finding no burns), gave her an insulin injection and left. Still sprawled on the bed in deep shock, Helen was questioned at length and told that if she 'came clean', the police could make it easy for her. Prison was unthinkable; yet how could she come clean? The next day the police told Gert they were free to leave Nottingham, but they stayed another night until Albert felt confident that Helen was strong enough to travel. Not wanting to worry Henry while he was powerless to help, it was only then that Gert had sent her telegram.

Henry Duncan at once secured the backing of the Spiritualist press. His wife was not the woman she had been, he told them, and it seemed as if she had come home to die. On 10 November, in an open letter to the Chief Constable of Nottingham, *Psychic News* accused his officers of behaving like the Gestapo and quoted the Fraudulent Mediums Act of 1951, namely that mediumship was only an offence if intent to deceive could be proved. In the meantime it is likely that either the Director of Public Prosecutions or the Chief Constable contacted the Home Office, because on 15 November Helen Duncan's files from 1944 were called up from the archive. One imagines that the police would have been advised to drop the case even if her health had not been poor. Given the inevitable publicity and possible martyrdom, she was best left unmolested. Besides, the charge – that a materialization had pretended to be a man who was alive – was insubstantial, the photographs inconclusive and there was no other evidence. And without the Witchcraft Act they would need it.

Helen's fifty-ninth birthday passed joylessly in hospital. A few days later she was home in Rankeillor Street, but that weekend, as November turned into December, the family could think of nothing to lift her spirits. A pain in her back worsened, she was unable to stomach food, nor could she sleep without tablets. Early on Monday, Gena made her daily pilgrimage down the Dalkeith Road and found her mother in anguish, her father morose, over a letter received that morning from the Chief Constable of Nottingham informing her in one sentence that her case had been passed to the DPP. Describing it as 'a calculated piece of cruelty', Henry sent the letter straight to the editor of *Two Worlds*, and sought sympathy and advice from anyone he could think of. Gena, meanwhile, stayed with Helen whose pain grew so intense she wished she had the courage to end her life. Breathless from angina and panic, she took to her bed and waited for the doctor who could do little except inject her with morphine. That evening when he returned to repeat the dose, her condition had deteriorated and he advised Henry to prepare himself for the worst. The next day the doctor administered more morphine and Helen withdrew further from the world of sorrows. On the Wednesday she gave out the few Christmas presents she had bought already, and spoke tearfully of her mother with whom she would soon be reunited in love and forgiveness. Nan, Etta and Alex, her children in spirit, were waiting for her too. Harry – 'her Henry' – paid a visit and, choking back his tears, sniffed the strange floral perfume in the room where his mother was ebbing in and out of consciousness. It seemed her prophecy that she would never live to see another trial was about to be fulfilled.

That evening an exhausted Gena kissed her mother's head, and went home to see her own family and to sleep. At about eleven o'clock the doctor came to give Helen her injection and left Henry reading to her at the bedside. Before long, he fell into a doze and did not wake up for several hours. At some point between three and four in the morning, with Albert and the legions of the beloved dead beckoning in her morphined dreams, Helen pushed softly through the veil, not so much raging against the dying of the light as drawn to the light which had guided her life. Gena, who knew her mother had passed from a solemn knocking at the front door, was ready when she was summoned at dawn. It was 6 December. The family issued no formal statement, declaring no interest in Spiritualist pledges to petition the Home Secretary and have questions asked in Parliament. 'We want to be alone with our grief,' was all they said. Henry did, however, meet Maurice Barbanell who came to Edinburgh at the first opportunity to reassure Henry of the financial support of the movement, and found the family composed and calmly determined to seek legal redress. Even without a statement the local and national press still covered the story: MEDIUM'S DEATH BLAMED ON RAID was the *Daily Express* headline on 8 December. From overseas, Charles Loseby issued a rare public statement: 'Helen Duncan was murdered!' Her death certificate recorded diabetes and cardiac failure.

Helen's body was returned from the Cooperative funeral parlour and laid out in Henry's library at Rankeillor Street, surrounded by the books which had shaped his vision of her and the papers which recorded how she had measured up. Accompanied by Gert Hamilton – Auntie Gert to the grand-children – ten-year-old Sheila peered nervously into the coffin, and remembers seeing a woman serene but bloated 'like a beached whale', even though her weight had fallen, some said to as little as twelve stone. 'That's not my grandmother,' Sheila told Gert with tearful defiance. Beneath a louring sky the funeral was held on Monday, 10 December at the private Warriston Crematorium and was well attended by family, friends, clients, ex-lodgers and the presidents of Spiritualist churches nation-wide. A representative came from the Edinburgh Psychic College and Library where a minute's silence had been observed at their last meeting. Maurice Barbanell returned to pay his last respects. Rev. Thomas Jeffrey, a Spiritualist Church of Scotland minister who had attended many of Helen's seances, conducted the short service in which he described her as Scotland's Joan of Arc. Beforehand, Gena had gone alone to the chapel of rest and standing over the open coffin had whispered that she loved Helen as she laid a red rose on her chest – a rose, she was assured by a medium, that one day would be returned to her. Gena gave the ashes to her sister Lilian who took them to America where she treasured them in her bedroom beneath the framed photograph of Albert's bust. Later, Helen's remains were brought home to Callander and scattered among the graves of the MacFarlanes in the ancient cemetery at Kilmahog.

Albert's portrait was one of Helen's few relics. The gold watch given to her by the man who won on 'Double Chance' was inherited by Gena who guessed that no one else was supposed to own it when it vanished. Today there remains little by which to remember Helen. The fine furniture and books at Rankeillor Street were sold off, and her clothes destroyed or given away, as Henry retreated into his shrunken world. A few photographs are scattered in archives, libraries and among her family. It is said that her trumpet was still in use in a home circle in Wiltshire in the 1980s; others she may have used lie in the cupboard at the College of Psychic Studies. Her ebony mirror tested for spiritual fingerprints is certainly there, broken and dulled. The ectoplasmic sheet seized in 1939 is safe in the basement of the Cambridge University Library. The fragile wax cylinders on which Harry Price recorded Albert's voice have not survived, although around 1955 Alan Crossley did make a tape on his Grundig reel-to-reel. The accents of the female sitters suggest that the seance took place in Lancashire or Cheshire, but the quality is poor and it is difficult to understand what is being said. Albert we can hear: he slurs and sounds breathless, wavering between a parody of clipped middle-class English and

coarse Australian, much of which is muffled gibberish and may
have been so at the time: 'I wahnt someone – jus' like thees, but
furthair beck, towards the cor-nah thay-are – to ask a yang laydee
aaht that passed . . . Now, I hev a feeling that she's hed an operation of sam koynd.' And so on.

The drive to remember Helen Duncan, and to see justice done,
started from the moment she died. Within a week, *Two Worlds* was
inviting contributions to a memorial fund and the Home Secretary,
Gwilym Lloyd George, was pestered until he replied that the
matter had to be taken up with the Chief Constable of
Nottingham. In the end the fund money was not spent in the
intended manner. Henry, a man crumbling inside, was being cared
for by Gena and was in no state to organize his own affairs, let
alone a lawsuit. In any case his solicitor, who at first had been
optimistic about their chances, now advised him to drop the case
due to insufficient medical evidence to suggest that the police had
caused Helen's death. In addition, Percy Wilson was concerned
that if the case was made *sub judice*, it might hold up action and
comment in other quarters. Mr Timmins dropped his action too,
announcing piously that turning the other cheek was behaviour
more befitting a Spiritualist. Why Helen Duncan had been raided
again after all these years therefore remains a mystery. There were
no rumours of conspiracy, as in 1944, and probably local police
simply heard about the seances, perhaps after receiving a
complaint, and intervened to protect the public. That said, prosecutions under the Fraudulent Mediums Act were very rare. And
there is one final intriguing piece of evidence: the Anglo-French
landings to reclaim the Suez Canal, which involved the Secret
Service, were the largest British seaborne military operation since
D-Day. The coincidence – and it is surely no more than that – is
stranger because the police raid occurred less than thirty-six hours
before the assault against Egypt began.

EPILOGUE

The legend of Helen's life continued to develop, but commanded less public interest than would have been the case before the war. Maurice Barbanell printed a selection of his memories, including the story of an impromptu performance for Estelle Roberts at which Helen wore nothing but a red table-cloth, and the time she materialized racing driver Sir Henry Segrave who had been killed on Lake Windermere in 1930 while breaking the world motorboat speed record. Segrave appeared to his widow as he had in life and even left his autograph on a notepad. Barbanell also recalled how Helen could make spirit messages appear on a slate – the trick she had been performing since the days of history tests at Callander Parish School. By mid-1957, tributes and reminiscences were still appearing in *Two Worlds* and *Psychic News*, although what before 1951 would have become a crusade to emancipate Spiritualists was little more than a trickle of nostalgia. These days, the movement seemed more preoccupied with spiritual warnings about the hydrogen bomb. Helen found her most fitting and enduring memorial in the private recollections of people she had helped. A housewife from Stockport described a seance she attended thus: 'It was as though the gates of heaven had opened and let me in for a short time. I cannot put into words the joy I felt.' An ex-miner from Yorkshire, who was reunited with his mother and saw Peggy guzzling chocolates, ended a letter to Alan Crossley with these words: 'At the age of eighty-eight, one is getting to the end of life's road, but it does not worry me as I shall only pass through a veil to a better life where I shall meet all my loved ones again.'

Helen Duncan transformed lives and none more than that of Ena Bügg, the girl from Gosport whose fiancé Ronald went to sea and whose friend Bob Brake was stationed in Preston with the RAF. Ena and Ronald were married in January 1940, but a month later he was killed when his ship was sunk by a U-boat. Although the spirits had prepared her for the tragedy, she was devastated and did not even have a grave upon which to focus her grief. All she had were his pyjamas. Ena sought solace in Bob and by the end of the year had agreed to marry him, provided Ronald gave his blessing from the spirit world. In the spring of 1941 they attended one of Helen Duncan's seances and Ena saw for herself the 'oceans of white' which poured from her mouth. First, Ena's grandmother appeared, then Albert called upon her to summon a young man whose body lay at the bottom of the sea. With Bob's arm round her shoulders she pleaded, 'Come on, Ron darling, come and speak to me', whereupon the cabinet opened and out stepped Ronald wearing a uniform of glowing ectoplasm. 'Hello, darling,' he said, 'I've come to give you my blessing. I want you to know that your happiness is my happiness always. Take care of her, Bob, until she can join me.' Their experience was not unique. Vincent Woodcock, a witness at the Old Bailey trial, received a similar blessing from his deceased wife when he decided to remarry; and then there was the widowed mother of Alan Crossley's friend, told to get on with her life. But what makes Ena and Bob special is that, now in their eighties with children and grandchildren, they are still happily married and living in Yorkshire, and they continue to speak of their small miracle – and of Helen Duncan – with the same reverence and gratitude they felt sixty years ago.

Although it is not hard to trace people who attended Helen Duncan's seances, most of the leading actors of 1944 are dead . . . Dodson, Robey, Morrison, Arthur West. Charles Loseby lived out his days as a tax exile on Guernsey; Maude and Elam became respectable judges. Hannen Swaffer died in 1961 and sent a message to Maurice Barbanell: 'Dear Barbie, it is quite untrue that I am dead, Swaff.' The man Swaffer ridiculed and reviled, Harry

Price, died of heart failure in 1948, smoking his pipe after lunch; he was rounded upon at once by colleagues in the Magic Circle, and Spiritualists and psychical researchers have been bashing his memory ever since. His sidekick – and some said lover – Mollie Goldney was awarded the MBE (for her work with the blood bank) and for years remained a stalwart of the SPR, crossing swords with more credulous members, before her sad descent into senility. Donald West became a psychiatrist, later Professor of Clinical Criminology at Cambridge, and recently stepped down as President of the SPR. He still feels that although Helen Duncan was a fraud, the case against her was never proven. Percy Wilson retired from the Civil Service in 1949, suffering from 'nervous overstrain', and as President of the SNU watched its prestige and finances go into steep decline – just as the spirits had predicted a decade earlier. His son, Geoffrey, messenger for the Defence at Helen's trial, lives in America and still remembers mostly how boring the whole thing was. Stanley Worth stayed in the Royal Navy until 1953 when he emigrated to New Zealand where he worked in real estate until retirement; he still denies that he spied for anyone except himself. In 1949 he married the sister-in-law of War Reserve Constable Rupert Cross who himself later left England for New Zealand. Number 301 Copnor Road, Portsmouth, to which they brought such chaos in January 1944, is currently empty and seeking a tenant. Demolition work on the old Holloway Prison began in January 1971. The Labour Party never did embrace 'the fundamental law of Spiritual Brotherhood', which the spirit of Ramsay MacDonald's wife predicted was the only hope for them and the world. The threat of nuclear war receded. The ghosts of the two world wars are fewer now that there are fewer survivors to haunt.

And what of the Duncans? Henry died in Edinburgh in 1967, his second wife having failed to penetrate the cocoon of sentimentality he had spun around himself. Helen's grand-daughters, Sheila and Ann, both nurses living in Staffordshire, share their mother Gena's conviction that the legacy of perse-cution led certain family members to neglect their psychic gifts and that the burden of blessed memory caused the break-up of her marriage. Cousins, nieces, nephews and grandchildren are spread across Scotland, England, Australia and America, and vary in their curiosity about their famous forebear. There are still MacFarlanes living in Callander where in the shops and pubs Helen is remembered with both forthrightness and furtiveness as 'Hellish Nell', although the origin of the nickname – her tomboyishness – has long been surpassed by the memory of her conviction at the Old Bailey and all the publicity which followed. In 1997–8, controversy flared up when a Spiritualist group, the White Rose Fellowship, presented a specially commissioned bust of Helen Duncan to the Callander Community Council who so far have been unable to find anywhere to put it on show. Stirling District Tourism Limited did not consider that the Rob Roy Visitor Centre was an appropriate home for the bulky bronze and because of Helen Duncan's associations some local people prefer that it not be displayed at all.

Of course, Helen's immortality does not depend solely on her post-mortem legacy. On the day she died, a Glasgow medium, Margaret Lyon, was conscious of the odour of ectoplasm and within a few hours had received a message from Helen, sending her love to Henry, and saying she had been greeted by Albert and reunited with Nan, and that the spirit world was more wonderful than even she could have imagined. Maurice Barb-anell passed the news to Henry who before long also experi-enced his wife's return. Lying in bed one night, the temperature dropped and a dark cloud billowed out the bedclothes as it floated towards him. A hand which gently grasped his he knew to be Helen's, and at once he felt reassured and encouraged. Much later, Helen's presence was detected at Gena's home circle and once a trumpet did levitate, but without her voice coming through it. Elsewhere, Helen communicated many times and acted as a spirit guide to several mediums; and yet, except for the reproachful arm in 1958, she had never actually materialized. Physical mediums capable of such feats were a dying breed and in any case, it was suggested, Helen had been so disillusioned with life on earth that she never wanted to return. But in the early 1980s rumours spread that a medium in Leicester, Rita Goold, was holding seances where Helen Duncan was the chief communicator (Raymond Lodge was another) appearing in full materialized form in the darkness. In 1983 Alan Crossley not only witnessed this, but spoke to Helen for three-quarters of an hour, felt the see-saw effect as she joined him on a sofa and nearly had the life squeezed out of him. Some of this he taped, including Helen's advice that he should take care, 'because you know what happened to me'. Helen protected Rita: once a man had tried to shine a torch but failed because Helen dematerialized the batteries, dropping them into his hand before he was banished. A year earlier, a reporter from *Psychic News* took Gena Brealey along, where for over an hour a shadowy spirit of her mother's carriage engaged her in private, esoteric conversation. Several objects were apported as well, including a single red rose on a long stem, sprinkled with dew as spiritually apported flowers tend to be. Gena wept bitterly – although whether she was fully convinced is open to question.

Today, Helen frequently sends messages and, free of her ailments and diseases, is happy in God's palace, enjoying the Communion of Spirits and the Ministry of Angels. The best-known recent communication occurred in September 1994 – the fiftieth anniversary of the trial – when a pristine copy of the *Daily*

Mail dated 1 April 1944 was apported to a home circle at Scole in Norfolk. The circle had grown out of the Noah's Ark Society, founded in 1990 to revive physical mediumship, and disagreement over the genuineness of their spectacular effects (apports from Churchill, extraterrestrial voices, coloured lights and images on unexposed film including St Paul's during the Blitz) has divided the Council of the SPR, an organization which limps on, seemingly unaware that the scientific establishment and the British public mostly neither know nor care about its preoccupations. Modern parapsychology is not much concerned with spookiness, preferring a diet of telepathy in twins, extra-sensory powers in pets, predictive dreams and previous-life experiences. To date, the outcome of this research has been, according to Nicholas Humphrey, 'a museum full of well-I-never curiosities and disputed laboratory data'; for him the natural world and its people are sufficiently complex and wonderful for there to be no need for the supernatural. But like modern Spiritualists, who still meet in small congregations in most British towns, parapsychologists continue to tell themselves comforting stories which help them to believe they are winning, and follow the dictum attributed to Sir James Dewar (the Lodge-bashing inventor of the Thermos) that minds are like parachutes: they only work when they are open. Others, however, prefer the cautionary advice of philosopher Jacob Needleman who recommends that we should always remain open-minded, but not to the extent that our brains fall out.

In modern Britain, belief in the supernatural is endemic, but has so many different shades and outlets that we fail to notice. Christianity, Hinduism, Islam, Judaism, Buddhism and so on are all established codes by which mortals put their faith in beings and realms for which no tangible evidence exists. Wicca – New Age paganism – is said to be the fastest-growing religion. Many more people engage with imaginary forces in subtle ways: reading horoscopes, walking round ladders, avoiding travelling on Friday the 13th. Like Helen, we are afraid of the dark, but cannot always say why. In 1993 four members of a jury at Hove in Sussex used a Ouija board to contact a murder victim's spirit to help them in their deliberations; the suspect named was convicted. And we should remember that the western world is the *most secularized* corner of the globe, a place where for over two centuries generations have learned to worship technology, industry and consumerism, and to forget about going to church. Elsewhere, the belief in witchcraft as a harmful and a healing force is indistinguishable from beliefs current in Britain a mere fifteen generations ago. In 1997 the Syrian state condemned and beheaded a man for the crime of witchcraft. A jumble of newspaper clippings collected over the past couple of years report witch lynchings in Assam, Fiji, north Sumatra, Kenya, South Africa, eastern Uganda and in Tanzania where as many as 5000 suspects are now thought to have died between 1994 and 1998. As I write, thirty people have been detained by police in the Indian state of Andhra Pradesh on suspicion of having been members of a frenzied village mob which beat up four women and a man believed to be witches, tied them to a tree, dowsed them in kerosene and burned them alive. Just three hundred years ago, at Kirkcudbright, Dumfriesshire, this was how both governors and governed saw fit to deal with the luckless Elspeth McEwen.

All of which leaves Helen as a more mainstream representative of human beliefs than she may at first appear. Animism – the belief in spirits – is probably the oldest religious belief, anxiety for survival our oldest emotion, and both stretch back tens of thousands of years to a time when hominids first became conscious of the fact that they would die but were unable to contemplate their own personal extinction. Imagining death remains a sublime paradox. Because of this, and because we continue to crave control over our destinies, it may be that our innate mentality as a species is not secular but magical. Perhaps our ancestors – like the people of India, Africa and South-East Asia – believed in witches not for want of better knowledge, but because intuitively and intellectually it made sense to explain the world that way. Even today, half-hearted superstitions aside, many more of us in the developed world than we care to admit spend our lives resisting the notion that fortune and misfortune might be determined by intangible forces and that there may well be a place to which we return at the hour of our death. We forget that we spent childhoods steeped in monsters and make-believe, and are surprised to find ourselves wishing and praying at moments of personal crisis. It will never be proven that God and the devil are scholastic fictions, that the heavens are empty and that Raymond Lodge is not up there in a spherical order of existence sipping a whisky and soda as his father believed. Even if the proof were there, the sheer *desire* to imagine an enchanted universe would inevitably be indulged in, and the idea would catch on. Thus spake the Fox sisters in 1848.

Perhaps an innate need to commune with the dead, and the real sense of purpose and comfort it can bring, makes Helen Duncan's conviction in 1944 seem unjust after all. Perhaps hers *was* an unselfish love for humanity, a tap you couldn't turn off. There are those, of course, who believe that the injustice resides simply in the fact of her genuineness as a medium. In 1997, the centenary of her birth, a campaign to have Helen's conviction quashed was revived by a group of Spiritualists advised by a retired Quaker barrister. When the Criminal Cases Review

Commission refused to refer the case to the Court of Appeal (because the conviction pre-dated the Fraudulent Mediums Act and had been made according to standards of fairness acceptable at the time), campaigners moved to secure a Free Pardon by exercise of the Royal Prerogative of Mercy – granted only once before in 1966 in the case of Timothy Evans hanged for murder in 1950. The press showed an interest, the headline in the *Guardian* for 31 January 1998 – PARDON HOPE FOR LAST WITCH BRANDED A WARTIME TRAITOR – being broadly typical. *The Times* showed a cartoon of Home Secretary Jack Straw recommending clemency to the Queen after his transformation into a toad. There is no agreement regarding what Helen wants to happen, and even in death she has been pulled this way and that. Leading activist Michael Colmer claims to have been told by her spirit to 'steer clear of the family, laddie'; but then, on the whole, her relatives believe she wants only to rest in peace. A rival pardon campaign claims to have been entrusted with her exoneration; but the President of the SNU maintains that Helen's spirit confided to her: 'It seems to matter a great deal more down there than it does up here.' Colmer appealed to his MP, Michael Ancram, to put pressure on the Home Office to act, leading the Italian parapsychology journal *Luce e Ombra* to revisit the Helen Duncan story in an article entitled 'Tony Blair and the last English witch'. Yet what was true of the Home Office in 1944 is true today: the Secretary of State cannot countermand decisions made constitutionally by the courts. By the summer of 1999 the case was no longer under active consideration and Michael Ancram returned the papers sent to him by Michael Colmer. The campaigners remain optimistic, however, and insist that their work has entered a 'discreet phase'.

'One day the truth will come out,' Alan Crossley assures us. 'It's all there in the archives, and when it does she'll be hailed as a martyr.' It will never happen, nor are the campaigners likely to get their way (unless a recent judicial ruling about standards of fairness can be exploited successfully). The elusive truth about Helen Duncan is that there is no truth to uncover, at least no single version that will banish speculation and controversy for ever. Getting to the bottom of historical mysteries can become harder the deeper one delves – the muddy water rises, the sides of the hole fall in – and in matters of wartime secrecy, in particular, one can appreciate what Churchill meant when he said of the preparations for D-Day: 'Truth is so precious that she should always be attended by a bodyguard of lies.' Some may feel that the raw material for this book is more inclined towards fiction than is acceptable in a historical biography and for this reason I have deliberately limited the extent to which I have stepped outside the world this material describes. As far as possible the seance-goers and psychical researchers have told their own stories, using categories which discerning readers will not need me to qualify for them.

Besides, the purpose of this book is not merely to valorize, vilify or vindicate Helen Duncan, but to do all those things – and with an ulterior motive. At one level her life, seen in the round, is fascinating and carries the same force to entertain as any adventure. There is no denying the truth of Alan Crossley's remark that her story is 'one of tragedy and absurdity, yet at the same time one of triumph over adversity' and, as such, that it deserves to be told. But there is something else. Helen Duncan tells us subtle things about the way we were by opening a window through which we glimpse the twentieth century – the age of extremes – not merely as a sequence of events but as a cultural drama where unspoken assumptions and ambivalent attitudes were as influential as conscious expressions and concrete actions. In a recent children's history book her trial is illustrated by a cartoon of a woman in 1940s clothing tied to a stake and about to be burned, at which point a member of the crowd turns to another and says: 'You don't think we might be overreacting just a bit?' The irresistible appeal of the joke suggests that the story of Hellish Nell is important, not just because it is her due, nor even because it teaches us about a broader historical terrain, but because it provides a commentary on the human condition, alighting upon, and illuminating, universal and eternal themes of love, truth, power and death – all things children understand as completely as they understand the allure of witchcraft.

NOTES

GENERAL

The most informative guide to Helen Duncan's life was her husband Henry's journal, but this seems not to have survived. Echoes of it are found in their daughter Gena Brealey's indispensable biography, *The Two Worlds of Helen Duncan* (1985) upon which I have drawn extensively, but which nonetheless contains factual errors. A lengthy ghost-written section describing the Old Bailey trial paraphrases Maurice Barbanell's splenetic but readable *The Case of Helen Duncan* (1945), which itself was based on his reports in *Psychic News*. Fans

'Mrs Victoria Helen Duncan, aged 32½ years' – the portrait Price never returned.

of courtroom drama may prefer C. E. Bechhofer Roberts's edited transcript, *The Trial of Mrs Duncan* (1945), which has a reliable introduction. Alan Crossley, who knew Helen Duncan well in her last years, writes touchingly of her in *The Story of Helen Duncan: Materialization Medium* (1975), though much of the information comes from Gena Brealey and Maurice Barbanell. The most recent book is Manfred Cassirer's *Medium on Trial: the Story of Helen Duncan and the Witchcraft Act* (1996), which trawls through a good deal of the archival material to assess the value of the mediumship for psychical research; he is cautiously optimistic. This seems to be the only work on Helen Duncan which, at the time of writing, is still in print, although I picked up the others from antiquarian book websites. Conversations with Sheila Downie and Ann Pooey were as valuable to me as the writings of their mother, Gena Brealey. Thanks to them I also learned much from Gena's unpublished autobiography and from an important letter written by her brother Harry in 1981.

What follows is a rough guide to the way these and other sources were used to write this book. It is also intended to give credit to the authors upon whose works I have depended, and may serve, too, as a bibliography for further reading on the history of Spiritualism and psychical research. Of necessity, these notes are simplified and highly selective. Page and chapter numbers have only been given where failure to do so would cause confusion.

Prologue: UNDER FIRE

Between them, Bechhofer Roberts and Barbanell provide a satisfactory account of the trial. Additional detail I gained from contemporary newspapers, local and national, found in the British Library's newspaper library at Colindale in north London –

although conveniently the Home Office were assiduous in amassing clippings in 1944. The files in which these clippings are found make essential reading for the serious student in any case, and can be consulted in the Public Record Office at Kew (PRO), classmark HO 144/22172. A restricted file from the office of the Director of Public Prosecutions – PRO, DPP 2/1204 – was made available to me at the Crown Prosecution Service's offices in Ludgate Hill; since then this has been opened to the general public at the PRO. Over on the Defence side, Charles Loseby's private papers are preserved by the Islands Archive Service on Guernsey. His notes relating to Helen Duncan's trial are also revealing; these are to be found in the archive of the Society for Psychical Research (classmark: SPR, Loseby) which is housed in Cambridge University Library (CUL). Among its many 'Mediums Files', the SPR archive has a scuffed cardboard wallet – strangely, unlisted in the catalogue – which is crammed with newspaper articles, notes, letters and other documents relating to Helen Duncan's mediumship. Fortunate enough to be allowed into the CUL's dingy basement, I spotted it lurking on the shelf and thereafter used it extensively.

1. YOU'LL BE BURNED AS A WITCH!: The Child-Prophet of Perthshire

The historical literature on witchcraft prosecutions is extensive. A sensible place to begin is Robin Briggs, *Witches and Neighbours* (1995), and Christina Larner's *Enemies of God: the Witch-Hunt in Scotland* (1981) is especially relevant. On witchcraft and the law, see the essay by C. R. Unsworth in T. G. Watkin (ed.), *Legal Record and Historical Reality* (1989). Keith Thomas, *Religion and the Decline of Magic* (1971) is the best introduction to beliefs about witches, ghosts, fairies, omens and so on; and for Scotland, Robert Kirk,

The Secret Commonwealth (c. 1691) – available in modern editions – is essential. The execution of Elspeth McEwen is described in Sheila Livingstone, *Confess and Be Damned* (2000) and Brian P. Levack (ed.), *Witchcraft in Scotland* (1992). The haunting of the Mackies is described in Alexander Telfair, *A True Relation of an Apparition . . . of a Spirit* (1696). Social historical insights I owe to T. M. Devine, *The Scottish Nation, 1700–2000* (1999) and John Stevenson, *British Society, 1914–45* (1984). Alastair Thompson, *Callander through the Ages* (1985) is exhaustive on Helen Duncan's home town; Sarah Murray, *The Beauties of Scotland* (1799) and John Thomas, *The Callander and Oban Railway* (1990) were also helpful. Other local colour was extracted from crumbling copies of the *Callander Advertiser* at Colindale. For a taste of the belief in prophecy, see Norman McCrae (ed.), *Highland Second-Sight* (1908). Genealogical details were obtained from the General Register Office for Scotland. Other details of Helen's early life are inconsistent and impossible to corroborate, but the outline of a story emerges nonetheless. Gena Brealey was the principal source; but closer in time to the events described are articles from 1933 published in the *People's Journal*, a Scottish Saturday newspaper, under the heading 'My Second-Sight Secrets by Madame Victoria Duncan'. The quotation from Mrs Foster Turner's seance comes from p. 298 of Nandor Fodor's *Encyclopaedia of Psychic Science* (1934). For other predictions about the First World War, see F. C. S. Schiller writing in the *Journal of the SPR*, 37 (1916) and Frederick Bligh Bond, *The Hill of Vision* (1919).

2. DEVELOPING GOD'S GIFT: Labour, Love and the Arrival of Henry

Most of the family details at the start of this chapter were provided by Sheila Downie. The birth certificate of the illegitimate Isabella helped to make sense of Gena Brealey's sanitized account. For a discussion of 'moral truths' in history, see Natalie Z. Davis, *Fiction in the Archives* (1987); other relevant works include: Gillian Bennett, *Traditions of Belief: Women and the Supernatural* (1987); W. Lance Bennett, *Reconstructing Reality in the Courtroom* (1981) and Ethel S. Person, *The Force of Fantasy* (1996). On the ambivalence of belief in spirits and witches in the eighteenth century, see R. C. Finucane, *Appearances of the Dead* (1984) and Malcolm Gaskill, *Crime and Mentalities in Early Modern England* (2000), chapter 3. The history of Spiritualism is well documented. Ruth Brandon, *The Spiritualists* (1983) ranges widely, and Simeon Edmunds, *Spiritualism: a Critical Survey* (1966) and G. K. Nelson, *Spiritualism and Society* (1969) are also useful. Specialized analysis can be found in Logie Barrow, *Independent Spirits: Spiritualism and English Plebeians, 1850–1910* (1986) and Alex Owen, *The Darkened Room: Women, Power and Spiritualism in Late Victorian England* (1989). Janet Oppenheim's *The Other World: Spiritualism and Psychical Research in England, 1850–1914* (1985) adds the dimension indicated in the title and here Brian Inglis, *Natural and Supernatural* (1977), a history of the paranormal to 1914, is worthy of mention. Other works which helped me to understand the shifting relationship between religion, science and philosophy were Peter Washington, *Madame Blavatsky's Baboon: Theosophy and the Emergence of the Western Guru* (1993) and Alison Winter, *Mesmerized: Powers of Mind in Victorian Britain* (1998). The boost to Spiritualism provided by the First World War is covered in chapter 3 of Jay Winter's *Sites of Mourning, Sites of Memory* (1993) and David Cannadine, 'War and death, grief and mourning in modern Britain', in Joachim Whaley (ed.), *Mirrors of Mortality* (1981). Eric and Andro Linklater, *The Black Watch* (1977) enabled me to imagine Henry Duncan's war service; and Gena Brealey's *The Two Worlds of*

Helen Duncan, the *People's Journal* articles and various genealogical records supplied details for the remainder of his life as a young man. Service records belonging to Henry's father can be consulted at PRO, WO 364/1072. To understand Sir Oliver Lodge's reaction to the loss of his son, one need look no further than his own *Raymond Revised* (1922).

3. RADIANT EFFECTS: 'Albert' and the Spectacle of the Seances

Helen Duncan's granddaughters, Sheila Downie and Ann Pooey, told me the story with which the chapter begins. Copies of Ellis T. Powell, *Psychic Science and Barbaric Legislation*, 3rd edn (1917) and *The Medium: a Journal Devoted to Mediumship* (September 1926) were found in the Loseby collection on Guernsey (classmark: AQ 197/1) and in the CUL respectively. J. Arthur Findlay's study of John Sloan was expanded and became a best-seller, *On the Edge of the Etheric* (1931). The story of Henry's astral journey is taken from the *People's Journal* (14 October 1933), subsequent events from other editions and Brealey's *Two Worlds of Helen Duncan*. Information about William Eglinton comes from his SPR Mediums File. On Crookes, see Trevor H. Hall, *The Spiritualists: the Story of Florence Cook and William Crookes* (1962). The investigations by Sidgwick, Lodge, Richet, Myers *et al.* are retold engagingly in Alan Gauld, *The Founders of Psychical Research* (1968), a book from which I learned a great deal. On Schrenck-Notzing, there is no substitute for his illustrated 1913 book, translated as *Phenomena of Materialization* (1920). For the Golighers, see W. J. Crawford, *Psychic Structures of the Goligher Circle* (1921); his obituary, by W. Whatley Smith, is in *Proceedings of the SPR* (November 1920). Jenny Hazelgrove, *Spiritualism and British Society between the Wars* (2000) surveys physical mediumship in the post-1918 period (a work published too late for me to exploit fully), as does John Beloff's *Parapsychology: a Concise History* (1993). For briefer, more credulous guides, see Linda Williamson, *Mediums and the Afterlife* (1992) and Alan Crossley, *A Journey of Psychic Discovery* (1993). In *Science and Parascience* (1977), Brian Inglis continues his history of the paranormal up to 1939; his discussion of the work of Kathleen Goligher, Mina Crandon ('Margery'), 'Eva C.' and others I exploited thoroughly. The Margery mediumship is well documented in the SPR archives and deserves a new book of its own, and there are Mediums Files on the other key figures. Essential was Fodor's *Encyclopaedia of Psychic Science* and more particularly the 1966 edition with its valuable introduction by Leslie Shepard. Gena Brealey's autobiography, and Harry Duncan's letter referred to above, give the child's perspective of Helen Duncan's seances at Dundee in the later 1920s. The report from 1930 was found in the Harry Price Library (HPL) at the University of London Library. Harvey Metcalfe's photographs are reproduced in Crossley, *The Story of Helen Duncan*.

4. DARKNESS AND LIGHT: Research and the Search for Respectability

Ena Bügg's story is told in an autobiographical booklet – Georgina Brake, *My Spiritual Quest* (1999) – and I also interviewed Mrs Brake (née Bügg) and her husband Bob. The observation about Binyon belongs to David Cannadine and on the Armistice see Charles Drayton Thomas, *Life Beyond Death with Evidence* (1928), chapter 34. C. E. Bechhofer Roberts, *The Truth about Spiritualism* (1932) is a fine guide to inter-war Spiritualism, likewise W. K. Lowther Clarke, *Spiritualism and Psychical Research* (1941) and G. W. Butterworth, *Spiritualism and*

Religion (1944). Montague Summers, *The History of Witchcraft and Demonology* (1926) puts the Catholic case. F. W. Fitzsimons, *Opening the Psychic Door* (1933) is worth a read, if only for the creepy pictures. On the early history of the SPR, Alan Gauld is stylish, W. H. Salter, *The Society for Psychical Research: an Outline of its History* (1948) and Renée Haynes, *The Society for Psychical Research, 1882–1982* (1982) less so but still informative. For work being done elsewhere, see Muriel Hankey, *J. Hewat McKenzie: Pioneer of Psychical Research* (1963). The story of Helen Duncan's London tests is told in various reports published in *Light* – the journal of the London Spiritualist Alliance – in 1931–2; and the medium's grim adventures can be picked up in Harry Price, *Regurgitation and the Duncan Mediumship*, published by the National Laboratory of Psychical Research in 1931. The 'Materials Relating to Helen Duncan' in the LSA's archives at the College of Psychic Studies in London and the 'Helen Duncan Box' in the HPL add colour and depth to events. Price glossed the story in chapter 9 of *Leaves from a Psychist's Casebook* (1933). Price himself has taken some knocks over the years. To Paul Tabori's mistakes in *Harry Price: the Biography of a Ghost-Hunter* (1950), Trevor Hall added vitriol in *Search for Harry Price* (1978); although John Randall, 'Harry Price: the case for the Defence', *Journal of the SPR*, 64 (2000) sets the record straight. To summarize reactions to the 1931 tests, I relied on Helen Duncan's SPR Mediums File. Testaments to her mediumship in the early 1930s crop up in *Psychic News* and *Two Worlds*. The story of Mary McGinlay came from the *Daily Mail* (7 March 1932) and from her declaration (22 February 1932), a copy of which survives in the Helen Duncan box at the HPL. The turning point in Price's thinking sparked by Kanichka the Human Ostrich is also documented there.

5. CHANGING FORTUNES: A Brush with the Law and the Coming of War

The story of the Tomsons comes from the *Sunday Chronicle* (12 February 1928); a letter from Houdini about them is item 766 of Lodge's correspondence in the SPR archives. For prosecutions under the Vagrancy and Witchcraft Acts, I used Owen Davies, *Witchcraft, Magic and Culture, 1736–1951* (1999) and James Hayward, 'Mediums, psychics and the law', *The Criminologist*, 19 (1995). Details of the Metropolitan Police's purges – and Spiritualist reactions – were gleaned from PRO, MEPO 2/1323 and PRO, HO 144/1806; the latter, which contains the royal petition of 1921, remains closed to the public at the time of writing. A letter – CUL, SPR, Lodge 759 – was revealing. Police policy regarding mediums can be studied at PRO, MEPO 2/9158. The 1933 seance and trial in Edinburgh were reconstructed from documents and photographs in the HPL, and a police report (dated 1 February 1944) in PRO, DPP 2/1204. The *People's Journal* articles are at Colindale and the HPL has a selection too. The works of Brealey, Crossley and Cassirer supplied details of the 1930s seances, and letters sent to me helped also. The Treherbert incident is recorded in correspondence in the HPL; Price's other exploits in the mid-1930s are related in his *Confessions of a Ghost-Hunter* (1936). The files of the International Institute for Psychical Research are kept in the SPR archives in CUL. Stories of the male mediums were drawn from Harry Edwards, *The Mediumship of Jack Webber* (1940), Harry Emerson, *Listen my Son* (1984) and the SPR Mediums File on Charles Stewart. A Mediums File also documents extensively the peculiar mediumship of Hylda Lewis. The quotation about mediums and capitalism comes from Harry Boddington, *The University of Spiritualism* (1947), p. 447. Accounts of Helen Duncan's seances from the early 1940s originated in various sources; Arthur Oram describes his experience in *The System in Which We Live* (1998) and expanded upon it to me personally. The Master Temple is described in Bechhofer Roberts (ed.), *The Trial of Mrs Duncan*; PRO, HO 144/22172; and DPP 2/1204. More about wartime beliefs can be learned from Miriam Akhtar and Steve Humphries, *Far Out: the Dawning of New Age Britain* (1999), chapters 2–3. Details of Spiritualism in the armed forces were found in files in the PRO, classmarks ADM 1/23868 and PCOM 9/1482.

6. A KIND OF CONJURATION: Trial and Denial at the Old Bailey

The sinking of HMS *Barham* was reconstructed from Admiralty records in the PRO (class: ADM; pieces 1/11948, 186/801, 223/152) and I owe the point about the Enigma decrypts to volume 2 of F. H. Hinsley (ed.), *British Intelligence in the Second World War*, 5 vols (1979–90) – note on p. 329. The story of the sailor's spirit appears in many places; I used Gena Brealey's account and Mollie Goldney's notes on a paper given by Percy Wilson in 1958. Works I found useful on wartime secrecy include: John Court Curry, *The Security Service, 1908–45* (1999); Nigel West, *MI5* (1983); and Christopher Andrew, *Secret Service* (1985). The Home Defence Executive minutes are in the PRO at CAB 93/2–3 – see also the committee on Overlord preparations: CAB 98/40. For the complaints of Mrs Evans, Mrs Martin and Mrs Gray, see: PRO, DPP 2/1204; CUL, SPR, Helen Duncan file; and the HPL respectively. Abdy Collins's quote comes from *Psychic Science*, 21 (1942), and for Stella Hughes, see *Psychic News*, May–June 1943. *Psychic News* (21 September 1940) was also where Maurice Barbanell reported his warning from Scotland Yard and information about other police activity comes from Edward Smithies, *Crime in Wartime* (1982). Evidence of the involvement of the Magic Circle is in the HPL's Helen Duncan box. The remainder of the chapter was assembled from the sources given above for the prologue, especially the PRO files (HO144/22172, DPP 2/1204) and Bechhofer Roberts (ed.), *The Trial of Mrs Duncan*. Additional material includes: reports in the *Portsmouth Evening News*; W. A. E. Jones writing in the *Daily Herald* (4 April 1944); Barbanell's *The Case of Helen Duncan*; and an interview with Charles Loseby's daughter Diane White. Loseby's service record from the First World War is at PRO, WO 339/14142. Helen Duncan's trial records also survive in the PRO: classmark CRIM; pieces 1/1581, 4/1709, 2/256. For an account of the prediction made at the Bonnington Hotel, see *Psychic News* (29 December 1956).

7. SQUARING THE CIRCLE: Phenomena and Fraud at the Seances

Houdini's copy of the *Atlantic Monthly* is among the SPR's 'Margery' files. On Houdini, see Inglis, *Science and Parascience*, chapter 5 and Milbourne Christopher's *Houdini: the Untold Story* (1969). Among many exposés of trickery, Harry Price and Eric J. Dingwall (eds), *Revelations of a Spirit Medium* (1922) is the best introduction, and Price's *Short-Title Catalogue* (NLPR *Proceedings*, April 1929) lists similar books. Arthur Wilkinson's *Spiritualism on Trial* (1953) is enlightening. The discussion of the *Barham* episode in Edmunds, *Spiritualism* is useful; for McDougall's report, see Price, *Regurgitation*. Price's photographs can be seen in the HPL. Fru Lára Agustsdóttir has an SPR Mediums File. The 'secondary stomach' debate can be sampled in Joad's article in the *Sunday Dispatch* (2 April 1944) and a reaction in the *Psychic Times* (May 1944); see also Barbanell,

The Case of Helen Duncan. Hannen Swaffer's poem is in the HPL. On swallowers in history, see Price, *Regurgitation*. The story of Emma Eckstein is told in Roy Porter, *The Social History of Madness* (1987). Varina Taylor's letter is in the DPP's file (PRO, DPP 2/1204) and Esson Maule's report in the HPL. The story about the sailors' cheesecloth hammock comes from the SPR Helen Duncan file and is summarized in Cassirer, *Medium on Trial.* The Cefn Coed cloth from 1939 is in the CUL; letters relating to its seizure in the HPL. My thinking was shaped by Nicholas Humphrey's *Soul Searching: Human Nature and Supernatural Belief* (1995); see also David Hume, 'Of miracles', in *An Enquiry Concerning Human Understanding* (1748) and C.G. Jung, *Psychology and the Occult* (1978). H. H. Furness's description is quoted in Gauld, *Founders of Psychical Research.* Two works – Theodore Besterman's 'The psychology of testimony in relation to paraphysical phenomena', *Proceedings of the SPR*, 40 (1930–2) and Denys Parsons's 'Testimony and truth', *Horizon*, 9 (1944) – helped to inspire Donald West's 'The trial of Mrs Helen Duncan', *Proceedings of the SPR*, 47 (1942–5). Also valuable are chapters 2–3 of West's *Psychical Research Today* (1954), which discusses the phenomena and psychology of mediumship. David Marks and Richard Kammann offer further insights in this direction in *The Psychology of the Psychic* (1980); and on multiple personalities see Stephen Braude, *First Person Plural* (1991). On the hallucinations of the bereaved, see W. Dewi Rees, 'The hallucinations of widowhood', *British Medical Journal*, 4 (1971) and Sylvia Wright, 'Experiences of psychokinesis after bereavement', *Journal of the SPR*, 62 (1998). For the dialogue between Fodor and Freud, see Shepard's foreword to Fodor's *Encyclopaedia*. Henry's confessions are recorded in Price, *Regurgitation* and *Light* (17 July 1931). For striking parallels with seventeenth-century possession, see James Sharpe,

The Bewitching of Anne Gunter (1999). J. B. McIndoe describes the medium in full flow in 'The phenomena of Mrs Helen Victoria Duncan', *Psychic Science*, 21 (1942).

8. MANY MANSIONS: Public Life and Prominent Men

Bob Brake read his story to me from his unpublished memoirs. Information about W. T. Stead came from Fodor's *Encyclopaedia* and the spirit account of the *Titanic* disaster is in the SPR archives. For W. B. Yeats, see Brenda Maddox, *George's Ghosts* (1999); a letter by Yeats is among Barrett's SPR papers. From here, see David Herbert Donald, *Lincoln* (1995); Elizabeth Longford, *Victoria R. I.* (1964); and for Gladstone, see *Two Worlds* (18 November 1887) and Nandor Fodor in the Glasgow *Sunday Mail* (15 November 1936). Charles Fryer, *Geraldine Cummins: an Appreciation* (1990) speaks for itself. For Shaw Desmond on Roosevelt, see *Psychic News* (29 March 1947); Arnewood Tower can be seen in Ronald Pearsall, *The Table-Rappers* (1972). Details of transfiguration come from SPR Mediums Files. Lodge's dealings with Baldwin are recorded at PRO, HO 45/14235; and with Helen Duncan in Price, *Leaves from a Psychist's Casebook* and the College of Psychic Studies' 'Materials relating to Helen Duncan'. On Lodge in general, see W. P. Jolly, *Sir Oliver Lodge* (1974). Miss Wainwright's letter is in an SPR 'Research File' ('Seances'). The letters from Mackenzie King are at CUL, SPR, Lodge 994–5; see also C. P. Stacey, *A Very Double Life: the Private World of Mackenzie King* (1976). The letter from Conan Doyle is at SPR, Lodge 455. On Conan Doyle, see Kelvin I. Jones, *Conan Doyle and the Spirits* (1989) and Daniel Stashower, *Teller of Tales: the Life of Arthur Conan Doyle* (2000). Details of his campaigning come from: the Churchill Archives, CHAR 22/240; the College of Psychic Studies archives; and PRO, HO 45/11968. The Home Office file on the Spiritualism and Psychical Research (Exemption) Bill is PRO, HO 45/14235. On Lloyd George, see CUL, SPR Lodge 643; on MacDonald, see: PRO, PRO 30/69/834; David Marquand, *Ramsay MacDonald* (1997); and H. Dennis Bradley, *The Wisdom of the Gods* (1925). Hannen Swaffer's *My Greatest Story* (1945) is the key work here; see also Tom Driberg, *'Swaff': the Life and Times of Hannen Swaffer* (1974). Mrs Vernon-Smith's letter is at PRO, HO 144/22172. For Dowding, see Basil Collier, *Leader of the Few* (1957) and Hugh Dowding, *Many Mansions* (1943). For what follows, see: *The Report of the Deputation of the SNU to the Home Office* (1943); PRO, MEPO 2/9158; PRO, HO 144/22172; *Hansard, Commons* (3 May 1945). For prosecutions under the Witchcraft Act, see: Davies, *Witchcraft, Magic and Culture*; Hayward, 'Mediums, psychics and the law'; and Eric Maple, *The Dark World of Witches* (1962). 'Nesta of the Forest' has an SPR Mediums File; see also *Hansard, Commons* (5 June 1934) and PRO, HO 144/20121. The Cardiff case is referred to in PRO, PCOM 9/1482. For the occult and the war effort, see Akhtar and Humphries, *Far Out* and Dion Fortune, *The Magical Battle of Britain* (1993). Peter Brookesmith (ed.), *Cult and Occult* (1985), pp. 156–67 is good on the Nazis and Clifford L. Lindecker, *Psychic Spy: the Story of an Astounding Man* (1976) deals with Ernesto Montgomery. Details of Worth's role come from Mollie Goldney's notes of Wilson's lecture, Loseby's notes in the SPR archive and personal correspondence from Stanley Worth. Other details come from the HPL, the DPP's file and PRO, HO 144/22172. For the chief constables' meeting, see PRO, MEPO 2/9158. Evidence of MI5 activity can also be found in: PRO, WO 283/11; Curry, *Security Service*; and West, *MI5*. The files of the Metropolitan Police's Special Branch (PRO, MEPO 38) were still closed at the time of writing. Maude also features in West, *MI5* and in A. B. Schofield, *Dictionary of Legal Biography* (1998). For Churchill, see Churchill Archives, CHAR 2/123/12–35, 72–96; 2/126/35; 2/71/81; 1/165/34; 2/67/30. David Stafford, *Churchill and the Secret Service* (1997) was helpful here. For Mr Latimer's letter, see PRO, HO 144/22172. Loseby's involvement is recorded in the Guernsey archives (files AQ 196/7, 10, 19, 27). The Hinchcliffe incident is recorded in the Churchill Archives, CHAR 1/200/59, 60, 61, 63–82. The query put to Morrison is in the Prime Minister's Personal Minutes, April 1944 (copy in the Churchill Archives), and the original correspondence in PRO, HO 144/22172. For other Cabinet business, see PRO, CAB 65/42. On the Boer War escape, Churchill is quoted in *Psychic News* (29 March 1947). The Tennant letter is at Churchill Archives, CHAR 1/43/13; the Hickling correspondence at CHAR 2/53, 57, 62; 13/47, 49, 51. The memories of 'W. T. P.' come from Elizabeth Gaythorpe (ed.), *My Dear Alexias: Letters from Wellesley Tudor Pole to Rosamond Lehmann* (1979). Brooks's story is in the *Report of the SNU* (1943).

9. NELLIE, KEEP YOUR CHIN UP!: The Path to Liberty

To reconstruct Helen's incarceration in 1944, I used Kathleen Lonsdale *et al.*, *Some Account of Life in Holloway Prison for Women* (1943) and John Camp, *Holloway Prison* (1974). A key source for the appeal is another recently declassified Director of Public Prosecutions file (PRO, DPP 2/1234); see also: Bechhofer Roberts (ed.), *The Trial of Mrs Duncan*; Barbanell, *The Case of Helen Duncan*; and Brealey, *The Two Worlds of Helen Duncan*. Details are recorded formally at PRO, CRIM 2/256, and J 81/48. Newspaper clippings came from the HPL and PRO, HO 144/22172; other reactions to trial and appeal can be gauged from the latter, and from the SPR's Helen Duncan file. For the case of the Rector of Stiffkey see A.J.P. Taylor, *English History, 1914–1945* (1965), which is rich in the flavour of the period. Also helpful was Stephen Inwood, *A History of London* (1998). Legal outcomes are detailed in the *Law Quarterly Review*, 61 (1945) and *Halsbury's Laws of England* (1990), volume 11 (2). Loseby's papers in the SPR archive and on Guernsey expand the story, and the latter contains his introduction to McIndoe's book (AQ 196/25). For Henry Duncan's letters, see PRO, HO 144/22172, which also contains the medical report. Jane Yorke's file is at PRO, CRIM 1/1617. On Redhill Spiritualist church, see Nelson, *Spiritualism and Society*, p. 166. Price's prediction to Mollie Goldney was made in a letter (4 April 1944): SPR Mediums File 'Schneider, Rudi'. Mrs Osborne Leonard's prediction is in Box One of the Bosanquet material in the SPR archive. The stories of June Moore and Denise Iredell (née Hankey) were told to me personally; the Lingwoods sent e-mails. Mrs Goldney's letter to Lady Balfour is in the SPR Helen Duncan file, as are papers relating to Donald West; statements made by S. M. Gardiner and Leah Longman are there too. Family details here come from Gena Brealey's accounts and from her daughters. On Minnie Harrison, see Tom Harrison, *Visits by our Friends from the Other Side* (1989). The Mass-Observation study is *A Puzzled People* (1947); and for the history of Spiritualism in these years see: Edmunds, *Spiritualism*; and Cannadine, 'War, death, grief and mourning'. Ivy Northage's recollections are in her *While I Remember* (1998). Brealey, *The Two Worlds of Helen Duncan* is the main source for Helen Duncan's later life. Tony Cornell, Chris Newberry, Jean Frost and Alan Crossley told me their stories; other accounts come from Mr Crossley's book, the SPR archives and Cassirer, *Medium on Trial*. For the Glover Botham case, see Hayward, 'Mediums, psychics and the law', and his SPR

Mediums File. The letter from Percy Wilson is in file AQ 196/27 in the Guernsey archives. The story of the Fraudulent Mediums Act is told in: *Hansard, Commons* (1 December 1950); *Hansard, Lords* (3 May 1951); and Davies, *Witchcraft, Magic and Culture*, pp. 73–5. For police reactions, see PRO, MEPO 2/9158. Bill Neech's quote comes from Edmunds, *Spiritualism*, p. 99.

EPILOGUE: Beyond the Veil

Chapters 1, 2 and 22 of Gena Brealey's *The Two Worlds of Helen Duncan* are the principal source for Helen Duncan's final months. Drawing on *Psychic News* reports, chapter 4 of Crossley's *The Story of Helen Duncan* is also informative. Various articles supplemented the story of the police raid at Nottingham, including those in *Psychic News* (15 December 1956); and *Two Worlds* (8 and 15 December 1956). Mollie Goldney's notes from Percy Wilson also contained relevant information. Details of the funeral came from Sheila Downie and from *Two Worlds* (15 December 1956). For the aftermath, see *Two Worlds* (5–12 January 1957) and *Psychic News* (29 December 1956 and 2 February 1957). Maurice Barbanell's memory of spirit writing can be found in his *This is Spiritualism* (1959); the words of the Stockport housewife are quoted in Manfred Cassirer, 'Helen Victoria Duncan: a reassessment', *Journal of the SPR*, 53 (1985); and for the Yorkshire miner, see Crossley, *The Story of Helen Duncan* (pp. 57–8). For Ena and Bob Brake, see Brake, *My Spiritual Quest*. The supposed spirit of Swaffer is quoted in Edmunds, *Spiritualism*, p. 92. Alistair Hendry told me about the bronze bust. For Helen's return, see *Two Worlds* (15 December 1956 and 5 January 1957). Alan Cleaver and Alan Crossley told me about Rita Goold; see also Andrew Collins, *The Circlemakers* (1992), pp. 224–5. The communications at Scole are respectively valorized, vilified and vindicated in Robin Foy, *In Pursuit of Physical Mediumship* (1996); Bryan Appleyard in the *Sunday Times Magazine* (27 Jun. 1999); and Montague Keen *et al.*, *The Scole Report, Proceedings of the SPR*, 58 (1999). The cartoon of Helen Duncan at the stake can be found in Terry Deary, *Horrible Histories: the Twentieth Century* (1996).

INDEX

* *Figures in italics indicate captions.*

Abbott, Agnes 171–2, 255, 336
Abbott, David Phelps: *Behind the Scenes with the Mediums* 226
'Abdul' (Arabian physician) 330, 341
Abdy Collins, B. 177, 187, 210, 251, 295, 311, 321, 330
Aberfoyle 29
Abstainers' Union 27
Adair, James 159
Adare, Lord 87
Adhyar, India 116
Admiralty 183, 184, 185, 292–5, 301, 333
Adventism 49
Agustsdóttir, Fru Lára 234–5
Ahlefeldt Lauring, Countess 128
'Ahmed, Darak' (a spirit guide) 281
Air Ministry 294
Alabaster, Bertha 235

'Albert' *see* 'Stewart, Albert'
Albert, Prince Consort 266
Allen, Mrs (seance-goer) 235
Altrincham 324–5
Ancram, Rt. Hon., Michael, MP 365
angels 29, 50, 73, 79, 167, 273, 312, 361
'Angels of Mons' 60, 228
Anglo-American Bio-Tableau Cinematograph 38
'animal magnetism' 49, 270
animism 363–4
Anne of Denmark 20
anti-Darwinism 79
apportation 82, 111, 142, 166, 172, 251, 336, 341, 361–2
Arbroath 74, 289
Archbold's *Criminal Pleading, Evidence and Practice* 314
Ark Royal, HMS 182, 230
Arnold, Matthew 52

Asquith, Herbert Henry 296, 301, 308
Astor, Philip: *A Séance with the Lights Up* 226
astrology/astrologers 187, 188, 266, 288–9
Atlantic Charter (1941) 282, 297
Atlantic Monthly 223, 238, 254
Attlee, Clement 343
Attorney-General 293–4, 295, 320, 321, 322, 343
'Audrey' (spirit girl) 192
automatic writing 49, 56, 111, 255, 277, 283, 357
Ayer, A. J.: *Language, Truth and Logic* 169

Bailey, Lilian (medium) 210, 300
Bailey, Nathaniel 318
Baker, Jean 176–7
Baldwin, Stanley 270, 274
Balfour, A. J. 115–16, 151, 277
Balfour, Lord Gerald 267–8, 277
Balfour, Lady Ruth 329–30
Balmer, Edith (transfiguration medium) 269
Band of Hope, Callander 27
Bank Street Register Office, Edinburgh 63
banshees 29, 67, 75
Barbanell, Maurice 127, 143, 152, 153, 163, 183, 188, 235, 236, 280, 285, 287, 313, 315, 317, 318, 320, 336, 343, 345, 354, 357, 358, 360
Barham, HMS 181–2, 197, 229, 230, 295
Barker, Elsa: *Letters from a Living Dead Man* 61
Barnes, Captain 192
Barnes, Shirley 192
Barnum, Phineas T. 48
Barrett, Sir William 56, 151, 238, 265
Battle of Britain 282, 290
Baylis, Mrs (medium) 109, 110
Beatson, Jean 164, 311
Beaumont, John: *Treatise of Spirits, Apparitions, Witchcrafts and Other Magical Practices* 250
Bechhofer Roberts, C. E. 248, 315, 336, 344
Beenham, Ethel *109*, 137, 141
Belfast 93, 95, 236
Bell, John (of Callander) 22
Ben Ledi, Callander 28
Ben Ledi Masonic Lodge, Callander 27
Bennett, Sir Ernest 278–9

Béraud, Marthe *see* 'Carrière, Eva' ('Eva C.')
Berovsky-Petrovo-Slovovo, Count 139
Besterman, Theodore 248, 249
Bettison, Mrs (Portsmouth Spiritualist) 178
Bevan, Aneurin 285
Bible, the 50, 77, 80, 111, 317
'Bien Boa' (a spirit guide) 85, 86, 249
Binyon, Lawrence: 'For the Fallen' 110
Birch, Bessy (a gypsy) 288
Birkenhead 188
Birkenhead, Lord 312
Birkett, Mr Justice 316, 317
Birmingham 188
Bismarck 184
Bisson, Juliette 91, 331
Black Watch 40, 41, 58, 60, 61–2, 168
Blackburn, Charles 83
Blackpool 329
Blair, Tony 365
Blake, Rev. Frank 142
Blavatsky, Madame Helena 116, 134, 232
Bond, Rev. Frederick Bligh 61
Borley Rectory 168
Boston Herald 97
Boswell, James 29
Bournemouth 167, 286–7
Bournemouth Spiritualist church 142
Bow Street Police Court 149
Brackenbury, Eve 139, 233
Brake, Bob 263, 264, 357, 358
Brake, Georgina, *see* Bügg, Ena
Braunau-am-Inn 95
Brealey, Ann (later Pooey; HD's grand-daughter) 335, 360
Brealey, Gena (née Duncan; HD's daughter) 44, 45, 46, 63, 64, 69, 72, 79, 99–100, 103–4, 132, 137–8, 142, 143, 153, 154, 162–3, 164, 166, 173, 174, 179, 217, 218, 219, 257, 311, 321, 326, 327, 328, 335, 350, 352–6, 361
Brealey, George (HD's son-in-law) 328
Brealey, Sandra (HD's granddaughter) 335
Brealey, Sheila (later Downie; HD's grand-daughter) 43, 44, 46, 72, 335, 354, 360
Bredalbane 30
Bristol 143
Britain, Rev. S. B. 52–3, 54
British Broadcasting Company (later Corporation; BBC) 73, 82, 170, 194, 280, 292, 337, 343; *Brains Trust* 175

INDEX

British College of Psychic Science 115,
151n, 252
British Expeditionary Force 60
British Intelligence 182
British National Association of Spiritualists
83
British Spiritualists' Propaganda Hymn Book
110
Brockway, Almira (US medium) 151n
Bronco (a parrot) 8, 215
Brooks, Thomas 283, 284, 302, 345
Brown, Frances 193, 215, 339; on trial 4;
at a seance 7; sees invisible spirits 192;
summons 198; criminal history 202;
spirit photographs 206; her sentence
216; in Holloway Prison 306, 307, 316;
appeal 316, 317, 320
Brown, John (Queen Victoria's ghillie) 266
Brown, Dr William 132, 237–8
Browning, Elizabeth Barrett 55, 88
Browning, Robert 55, 87–8; 'Mr Sludge,
the Medium' vii, 88, 160, 215
Buckingham, Duke of 312
Bügg, Ena (later Hill, then Brake) 109–10,
174, 263, *349*, 357–8
Bullock, Mrs (transfiguration medium)
170, 276
Burrell, Charles 189, 291
Bux, Kuda 171
Byron, George Gordon, Lord 47, 269

Caldecote, Viscount 316, 319–20
Callander 201, 210, 355, 357, 360;
described 23–4; local economy 24,
25–6; emigration 27, 45; religion in
27–8; public lectures 28, 30, 38; First
World War 40, 41; HD banished 46
Callander Advertiser 26, 32, 40
Callander Community Council 360
Callander Literary Society 28, 30
Callander Recreation Company 26
Cambridge 56, 88, 115, 226, 232
Cambridge University Library 94, 243, 249
Cambridge University Union Society 131
Cameron, John (of Callander) 41
Cardiff 188, 287
'Carrière, Eva' ('Eva C.'; Marthe Béraud)
85, 89, 91–3, 96, 97, 126, 135, 225,
265, 331
Case, Lieutenant G. R. A. 57
Cassirer, Manfred 262

Catholic Apostolic Church 49
Catholic Church/Catholics 27, 53, 111
cave paintings 50
Cefn Coed, Merthyr Tydfil 242
Cenotaph, London 274
Chamberlain, Joseph 269
Champion de Crespigny, Mrs Philip 275
Charing Cross Hospital Medical School
126
Charles II, King 50
charms 286
Chenevix-Trench, Mrs (of Callander) 27
childbirth, history of 259–60
Christian Age 102
Christian Church, early 50
Church of England 84, 111
Church of Scotland 27, 354
Churchill, Sir Winston 150, 182, 185, 280,
295–303, 318, 322, 362, 366
Chuter Ede, James 343, 344, 345–6
clairaudience 82, 111, 328
clairvoyance/clairvoyants 77, 82, 110, 111,
112, 117–18, 125, 129, 151, 163, 164,
165, 189–90, 227–8, 325, 336
Clive-Holmes, A. H. 287
Clynes, J. R. 275, 276
Cockhill Fair, Callander 38
Code, Grant 98
Colburn, Nettie: *Was Abraham Lincoln a
Spiritualist?* 266
Cole, Rose (seance-goer) 208, 235
College of Psychic Science 292, 336
College of Psychic Studies 240, 355
Colley, Thomas 84–5
Colmer, Michael 365
complementary and congruent fantasies
254
Conan Doyle, Sir Arthur 39, 53, 57, 97,
147–8, 151, 184, 209, 213, 224, 228,
244–5, 274–7, 280, 284, 296, 299, 323,
324, 347
Confessions of a Medium 226
conjuration 4, 21, 22, 111, 287, 310, 315,
317, 324
Conservative Party 275
controls *see* spirit guides
Cook, Florence (Victorian medium) 86, 87,
90
Cooke, Grace (a medium) 276, 277, 289
Coombe Tennant, Winifred 267
Cooper, Hon. Mrs 128

389

Cooper-Key, Rt. Hon. Sir Astley 275
Corelli, Marie: *The Romance of Two Worlds* 270
Cornell, Tony 340
Courageous, HMS 230
Court of Criminal Appeal 316, 324, 365
Craggs, Douglas 188, 292–3
Craigleith Military Hospital, Edinburgh 62
Crandon, Dr L. R. G. 96–9, 129, 232, 254, 256
Crandon, Mina ('Margery') 96–9, 101, 105, 129, 130, 135, 210, 223, 228, 232, 239, 243, 254, 255, 256, 268, 270, 271
Cranshaw, Dorothy Stella ('Stella C.') 124
Crawford, Dr William J. 92–4, 96, 100, 115, 232, 255
Criminal Appeals Office 219
Criminal Cases Review Commission 364–5
Criminal Justice Act (1948) 344, 347
Crookes, Sir William, OM 86, 87, 94, 177, 247
Cross, War Reserve Constable Rupert 7, 192, 200, 204, 206, 241, 293, 359
'Cross of Light' campaign 289–90
Crossley, Alan 268–9, 341, 355, 357, 358, 361, 365, 366
Crossman, Richard 185
Crowley, Aleister 289
crystal-gazing, *147*
Culme Seymour, Lady 128
Cumming, Alexander 30, 36, 38, 210
Cummins, Geraldine 267, 268, 273, 289, 301; *The Scripts of Cleophas* 267; *A Swan on a Black Sea* 267
cunning folk 22, 286
Curzon, Lord 277

D-Day (Normandy Landings) 6, 185, 199, 285, 288, 294–5, 315, 318, 324, 356, 366
Daily Express 151, 218, 354
Daily Herald 198, 205
Daily Mail 144–5, 152, 218, 282, 313, 361–2
Daily Mirror 185, 308
Daily Sketch 98, 184
Daily Telegraph 185
Daily Worker 218
Dalry 17, 22
Dalton, Michael: *Countrey Justice* 318
Dane, Victor 237
Daniel, Book of 111

Darwin, Charles 55, 149, 267
Daulby Hall, Liverpool 331
Davidson, Harold 316
Davies, Trefor (materialization medium) 171
de Wohl, Louis 289
Deane, Ada (spirit photographer) 274
Decca 171
Dee, Dr John 50, 265
deism 50
demonology 19, 22
Descartes, René 51
Desmond, Shaw 268
Destrees, Madame 128
Devant, David 233
devil's mark 20, 29, 130
Dewar, Sir James 362
diabolic possession 21, 47, 258–9
Dickens, Charles 55; *Worse Witches than Macbeth's* 225
Dickin, Mrs, OBE 128
Dickson, Ian 159, 160–61
Dingwall, Dr Eric 96–8, 188, 225, 227, 238, 330
Director of Public Prosecutions (DPP) 185, 186, 197, 200, 202, 219, 251, 293, 309, 310, 321, 324, 344, 346, 347, 352, 353
dissociative identity disorder 260–61
Dodd, Alfred 9, 210, 211, 312
Dodson, Sir Gerald, Recorder of London 3, 10, 204–11, 213, 214, 216, 217, 280, 281, 297, 314, 317, 319, 324, 344, 358
'Donald' (a spirit guide) 81, 82
Donegall, Marquis of 309
Donkin, Dr Horatio 149
dopplegängers 79, 86
Double Chance (a horse) 72, 355
Douglas, Angus (HD's son-in-law) 174, 176
Douglas, Dawn (HD's granddaughter) 176, 328
Douglas, Joan (HD's granddaughter) 176
Douglas, Lilian (née Duncan; HD's daughter) 65, 162, 174, 176, 217, 218, 257, 321, 326, 331, 355
'Douglas, Matthew' (a spirit guide) 81
Doune Castle, Scotland 33
Dowding, Air Chief Marshal Sir Hugh 282–3, 289–90, 345, 346; *Many Mansions* 283

Dr Faustus 79

Dr Finlay's Casebook (BBC television series) 24

Drayton Thomas, Rev. Charles 110, 275; Life Beyond Death with Evidence 273

Dreadnought Hotel, Callander 25, 28

Drysdale, Mrs (of Glasgow) 154

du Maurier, George: Trilby 253

Duncan, Alex (HD's son) 65, 76, 114, 353

Duncan, Anna (Henry's second wife) 43, 44, 359–60

Duncan, Annie (née Mearns; HD's mother-in-law) 59, 62, 68

Duncan, Geillie (executed for witchcraft) 20

Duncan, Gena see Brealey, Gena

Duncan, Harry (HD's son) 44, 64, 104, 176, 219, 326–7, 353

Duncan, Helen (née MacFarlane; 'Hellish Nell'): birth (25 November 1897) 32, 44; nickname xi, 33, 360; childhood xi, 17, 32–9; campaign to clear her name xii, 312–13, 364–5; the trial (1944) 1–13, 51, 200–217, 280–82, 287, 294, 295, 302, 364; appearance 1, 4, 17, 32–3, 43, 106, 113, 147, 186, 305, 331, 354; fined in Edinburgh (1933) 11; predicts the sinking of a warship 11, 216, 292; background 31; starts to see strange things 34, 35; education 36–7; personality 37; predictions about the First World War 40–41; birth of Isabella 45–6; in the First World War 46, 47; meets and marries Henry 62–3; health 63, 64, 66, 76, 114, 126, 134–5, 136, 154, 165–6, 176, 193, 216, 217, 259, 306, 307, 322–3, 339–40, 350, 352, 353; childbirth 64–5, 103–4; gives clairvoyant readings at home 67; starts to usher back the dead in physical form 69, 83; psychometry 74, 82, 165; aptitude for healing 77; and the ape-spirit 77–80; payment for seances 106, 152, 153, 155, 158, 168, 186, 199, 333; contract with the LSA 127, 136; X-rayed 132–4, 235; SNU diploma 141–2, 153, 164, 244, 329, 331; Maule affair and fine (1933) 154–61, 198, 199, 210–11; in Holloway Prison 193, 197, 217, 299, 303, 305–7, 311–12, 313–14, 316, 318–19, 322–3, 325–6; at the magistrates' court 198–200; fights Miles for material 242–3; regressive tendencies 256; and Churchill 299–300, 303; appeal against conviction 303, 310, 313–23; freed from prison 326; train crash 328; death of Nan 340; achievements 346–7; the Nottingham incident 350–54; death 353–5; bust controversy 360; communications after death 360–62; importance of her story 366–7

Duncan, Henrietta (Etta; HD's daughter) 64, 65, 76, 353

Duncan, Henry (HD's husband) 43, 114, 119, 126, 144, 153, 289, 326, 327, 339, 353, 355; and HD's death 43, 353–4; remarries 43; HD writes to 47; in the Black Watch 58, 60–62; background 59; meets and marries HD 62–3; army pension 64, 128; his business 64, 65; health 64, 65, 66, 76, 166, 311; reads paranormal literature 67, 72, 73, 74; records HD's communication with spirits 69, 75, 165; and Albert 120, 121, 122, 262, 271–2; the NLPR Council interrogation 135–6; Price offers a second deal 137; blamed by the LSA 139; and Miss Maule 154; police investigations 197–8; and Nan's prediction 217; newspaper interview 218–19; his role 252–3, 254; adept at hypnotism 253; petitions 321–2; vision of HD 349–50; and the Nottingham incident 350, 352–3; Gena looks after 356; HD appears to after her death 360–61; death 44, 359–60

Duncan, Henry, Snr (HD's father-in-law) 59, 61n, 67, 68, 75, 80

Duncan, Jean (HD's sister-in-law) 46, 47, 62, 63, 74

Duncan, Nan (HD's daughter) 142, 166, 326, 353, 360; in court 6, 11, 217–18; in charge of her siblings 65, 166; infirmity 153–4, 217, 218; loss of son Thomas 174; her Guardsman husband 176; death 340

Duncan, Peter (HD's son) 65, 166, 219, 327

Duncan, Robert (HD's brother-in-law) 104

Dundee 45, 46, 58, 62, 64, 66, 71, 74, 79, 81, 100, 106, 113, 124, 140, 161, 234, 236

Hellish Nell

Dundee *Daily Record and Mail* 161
Dundee Maternity Hospital 46
Dundee Royal Infirmary 46, 115
Dunfermline 331, 333, 342
Dunmore Fort, Callander 33

'E. M.' *see* Maule, Miss Esson
'earth electricity' creation theory 288
Eckstein, Emma 238
ectoplasm 6, 7, 9, 89–95, 97–101, 104,
  105, 115, 116, 119–24, 126, 127,
  129–31, 135–7, 139–42, 144, 167, 170,
  171, 202, 209, 212, 229, 231, 232, 235,
  237–40, 243, 244, 264, 271, 281, 284,
  311, 321, 327, 331, 332, 336, 338, 340,
  342, 350, 355, 360
Edinburgh 18, 63, 74, 142, 145, 153, 154,
  159, 179, 197, 199, 277, 326, 327
Edinburgh CID 198
Edinburgh City Police 219
Edinburgh Psychic College and Library
  101, 112, 153, 165, 209, 321, 332, 354
Edinburgh Evening News 67
Edinburgh Royal Infirmary 339
Eglinton, William 83–4, 85, 89, 267
Egyptian Hall, Piccadilly 84
Einstein, Albert 85
Elam, Henry 4, 201, 202, 204, 205, 208,
  210, 211, 214, 241, 281, 315, 324, 358
electricity 52, 81–2, 270
Eliot, George 55, 56
Elizabeth, Queen, the Queen Mother 299
Elizabeth I, Queen 19, 50, 265, 317
Elkin, Godfrey 194, 198, 314
Elliott, Rev. G. Maurice: *Psychic Life of
  Jesus* 111
Enigma code 182, 183
Episcopalians 27
Esslingen, Germany 259
Estelle, Madame 151
Eugénie, Empress 87
Evans, Dorothy 178, 186, 199
Evans, Timothy 365
Everett, Mrs (transfiguration medium) 170
evil eye 286
Exodus, Book of 19, 21
exorcism 77, 87
Ezekiel, Book of 111

Faces of the Living Dead 274
fairies 164, 311, 331, 341

Falconer brothers (spirit photographers) 152
Fay, Mr (escapologist) 84
'Feda' (a spirit guide) 256
Ferguson, William (of Callander) 41
Ferriar, Dr John: *Essay Towards a Theory of
  Apparitions* 249–50
Fielding-Ould, Dr Robert 118, 119, 121,
  122, 123, 136–7, 139, 261
Fiery Cross Lodge, Callander 27
Findlay, J. Arthur 73, 140; *On the Edge of
  the Etheric* 270
Firebrace, Brigadier Roy 184, 230, 276, 290
First World War 39–41, 46, 47–8, 56–7, 58,
  60–61, 150, 174, 258, 260, 296, 301–2,
  335
Fitzsimons, F. W. 112, 113
Fleming, Alice (sister of Rudyard Kipling)
  265
Fliess, Wilhelm 238
Fodor, Dr Nandor 131, 171, 252, 336–7;
  Encyclopaedia of Psychic Science 169–70
folk tradition 22, 50
Ford, Detective Inspector Frederick 7, 189,
  191, 193, 197–200, 219, 220, 239, 241,
  243, 292
Formidable, HMS 219, 327
fortune telling 5, 149, 150, 173, 187, 286,
  299, 323
Fortune Telling Act (USA) 148
Foster Turner, Mrs (an Australian
  medium) 39, 40, 41
Fournier d'Albe, Dr E. E. 94–5
Fowler, Surgeon Lieutenant Elijah 190,
  206, 234
Fox, J. D. 48
Fox sisters 48–9, 51, 52, 54, 76, 98, 364;
  Kate Fox, 265
Frame's Vaudeville Company 38
Franklin, Benjamin 268
Fraser-Harris, Professor David 132, 133–4,
  237
Fraudulent Mediums Act (1951) 346–7,
  352, 356, 365
Frazer, Sir James 34; *The Golden Bough* 30,
  164
Free Kirk School, Callander 27
Freud, Sigmund 238, 252, 256–7, 269–70,
  274
Frost, Jean 342
Fry, Rev. E. B. 167
Fulton, Mr (teacher in Callander) 38n

392

INDEX

Furness, Professor Horace 247

Gardiner, S. M. 332–3, 334
Garrett, Eileen 125, 154, 276, 299
Garrett, Julia E.: *Mediums Unmasked* 226
Gauld, Alan 268
Gaulle, General Charles de 299
'Gef', the talking mongoose 169
George, Frederick: *A Disciple* 101
George II, King 5, 317, 319
George Walpole & Co. 316
Gill, Harold 208, 284
Gillies, Robert Pearse 25
Gladstone, William Ewart 115–16, 266–7, 269, 277
Glanvill, Joseph 245, 250; *Sadducismus Triumphatus* 301; *The Vanity of Dogmatizing* 50–51, 300
Glasgow 22, 102, 112, 154, 160, 166, 262, 328
Glasgow Herald 309
Glover Botham, Charles 175, 183, 344, 345
Goethe Centenary Committee 169
Goldney, Mollie 2, 3, 10–13, 130–34, 137, 139, 141, 171, 172, 193, 201, 227, 234, 237, 241, 243, 247, 255, 292, 295, 308, 311, 315, 326, 329–30, 332, 334, 341, 344, 359
Goldston, Will 143, 152, 168, 281
Goldzier, Hans 288
Goligher, Kathleen 93, 94, 95, 100, 115, 232
Goligher family 93, 94, 96, 129
Gone with the Wind 2
Gonne, Maud 255
Goold, Rita (physical medium) 361
Graham-Harrison, Francis 197, 293, 309–10, 322
Gray, Marion 186–7
Greig, Lily (medium) 327
Grey, Sir Edward 273, 300, 301–2
Grey, Lady Pamela 273, 277, 300–301
Grey family 300–301
Guardian 365
Gunning, Maud 341
Gurney, Edmund 56, 336
gypsy 39, 59, 149, 174, 286, 288, 347

hallucinations 116, 249
Hamilton, Gert (Auntie Gert) 339–42, 350–52, 354

Hammerton, Mrs (physical medium) 170
Hankey (later Iredell), Denise 332, 340
Hankey, Muriel 332, 340
Hardinge Britten, Emma 53–4
Harris, Lady 128
Harrison, Minnie 335–6, 338
Harvard University 96–7, 223, 238, 256
Hatcher, Austin (materialization medium) 287–8, 311
Hayden, Mrs (an American medium) 53
Haylock, Arthur (stage swallower) 237
Hazeldine, Lena 82, 102
Hazeldine, Peggy (a spirit guide) 82, 101–2, 122, 127, 132, 143, 156, 157, 166, 168, 191, 206, 233, 331, 357
healing 54, 77, 178
Henderson, Dorothy (physical medium) 172
Henry VIII, King 317
Herbert, C. V. C. 232
Herries, Sir James 213
Hesiod 50
Hewart, Lord, LCJ 287
Hickling, R. G. (astrologer) 301, 302
Hickok, Wild Bill 266
Hill, Ronald *349*, 357–8
Himmler, Heinrich 288
Hinchcliffe, Mrs 299
Hinchcliffe, Captain Walter 125, 299
Hiroshima 327
Hitler, Adolf 92, 95, 125, 173, 288, 289, 300
Hoagland, Dr Hudson 223–4, 238, 254, 255
Hoare, Sir Samuel 287
Hobbes, Thomas 24
Hogarth, William 2
Hogg, Quintin (later Lord Hailsham) 287
Holland Street Spiritualist church, Glasgow 154
Hollander, Dr Bernard 99
Holloway Prison 193, 197, 217, 258, 299, 303, 305–7, 313–14, 316, 318–19, 322, 325–6, 359
Home, Daniel Dunglas 87–8, 105, 113, 149, 225, 266, 267
Home Defence Executive 185
Home Office 150, 185, 187, 194, 196, 199, 270, 275, 276, 282, 283, 284, 287, 290, 293, 297, 309, 310, 313, 320–23, 325, 343–7, 352, 365; 'C' Division (Criminal Matters) 197, 219; library 345

Home Secretary 197, 275, 282, 284, 299, 322, 354
Homer 268
Homer, Christine 193, 206
Homer, Elizabeth Anne (Elizabeth Jones) 198–9, 200, 207, 231, 232, 259, 308, 330; on trial 4, 208; involvement in seances 6, 7, 178, 189, 190, 192; bound over 12, 216; summons 198
Homer, Ernest Edward Hartland 200, 204, 231, 232; on trial 4, 207, 208; seances held above his shop 6, 178, 189, 192; bound over 12, 216; summons 198
Hood, HMS 182, 184, 229, 230, 290
Hope, Elizabeth ('Madame d'Espérance') 35, 90, 240
Hopi Indians 249
Hopkins, Matthew 78–9
Horizon (arts magazine) 248
horoscopes 175, 188, 276, 289
Hotspur, HMS 182
Houdini, Bess 269
Houdini, Harry (Erich Weiss) 92, 94, 96, 98, 118, 130, 148, 164, 223–6, 238, 244–5, 254, 269, 270; *A Magician Among the Spirits* 96
House of Commons, London 182, 276, 287, 298, 299, 302, 325, 345, 346
House of Lords, London 313, 320, 321
Hove, Sussex 363
Howe, Richard 168
Hughes, Stella (medium) 187, 280
Hughes, Susie (medium) 331
Hume, David vii, 245–6
Humphrey, Nicholas 254, 257, 362
Hungarian uprising 342
Hutchinson, James, minister of Kilallan 21, 22
Huxley, T. H. 267
Hydesville, New York 48, 75, 87
hypnosis 49, 253–4, 270
hysteria 260

ideoplasts 92
Ile Roubard, South of France 88, 272
Illustrious, HMS 178
immortality 50
Ineson, Taylor (medium) 190, 191
Intelligence Corps 294, 295
Inter-Services Security Board 294
International Institute for Psychical Research (IIPR) 170, 171, 177, 184, 210, 234, 252, 255, 287
Inverleny (Callander Military Extension Hospital) 40
Irtzl, Maria 34–5
Irwin, Flight-Lieutenant H. C. 125
Isle of Man 169

Jacobs (a naval instructor) 241
James I, King 19–20, 21, 201, 265, 310, 317; *Daemonologie* 20, 21, 345
Jefferson, Thomas 268
Jeffrey, Rev. Thomas 354
Jehovah's Witnesses 185
Jencken, H. D. 265
Jennings, Kitty 206
Jesus Christ 110–11, 163, 179, 193, 254, 262, 288, 296
Joad, Professor C. E. M. 169, 235, 248, 249
Joan of Arc 76, 354
'Joe' (a spirit guide) 264
'Johansen, Dr' (a spirit physician) 166, 335
John the Baptist 111
John Bull magazine 227, 287
Johnson, Effie 277
Johnson, Dr Samuel 29, 51–2, 317
Jones, W. A. E. 198, 205
Joyce, William (alias Lord Haw-Haw) 294
Jung, Carl 139, 256, 262
Justice of the Peace 151

Kanichka the Human Ostrich 145, 162, 239
Kardec, Allen 49
Keats, John 25
Keighley, Yorkshire 53
Kelley, Edward 50
Kelly, William 275
Kelso 142
Kerrick 18; the minister of 21–2
Kilmahog 31, 41, 355
'King, Katie' (a spirit guide) 86, 177, 247
Kingston Cross police station 193
Kipling, Rudyard 48, 59, 265
Kirk, Robert 29–30, 35, 36, 79; *The Secret Common-wealth and a Short Treatise of Charms and Spells* vii, 164
Kirkby, Basil 209
Kirkcaldy 176

INDEX

Kirkcudbright 18, 21, 285, 363
Knatchbull, Lady Doreen 128
Knollys, Lady 287
Koons family (of Ohio) 49
Korean War 273, 346

Labour Party 275, 277, 343, 359
Lambe, Dr John 312
Lane, Sir Hugh 264–5
Lang, Cosmo, Archbishop of Canterbury 167
Lankester, Edwin Ray 149
Larkin, Philip 40
'Latif, Abduhl' (a spirit guide) 154
Latimer, Mr (of Alloa) 297, 338
Lavradio, Countess de 128
The Law Quarterly Review 314
Lawrence of Arabia (T. E. Lawrence) 184
Lecky, W. E. H.: History of the Rise and Influence of the Spirit of Rationalism 300
Lehmann, Rosamond 302
Leigh-Mallory, Air Chief Marshal Sir Trafford 175, 282, 344
Leigh-on-Sea 143
'Letari, Dr' (a spirit guide) 324
levitation 49, 54, 80, 82, 88, 93, 97, 113, 141, 166, 170, 223, 336, 361
Lewis, Angelo: Modern Magic 236
Lewis, Rev. C. G. R. 167–8
Lewis, Hylda ('the flower medium') 172, 240
Lewis, Nesta ('Nesta of the Forest') 287
Liberal Party 275
Light (a Spiritualist weekly) 73, 92, 101, 126, 139, 154, 170, 336
Lilley, Mr (of Portsmouth City Police) 208
Linck-Hutchinson, Marguerite 160
Lincoln, Abraham 54, 266, 269
Lindsay, Lord 87
Lingwood, Eileen 331, 339
Lingwood, Harvey 331, 342
Lingwood, Mr and Mrs 331
Linklater, Eric 61–2
Little, Emily (medium) 287
Liverpool Post 139
Lloyd George, David 277
Lloyd George, Gwilym 356
Lobb, John 102
Lock, Bessie 206, 291
Lock, John 291

Lock, William 206, 291
Lodge, Lady 57
Lodge, Sir Oliver 56, 57, 78, 88, 96, 98, 116–17, 148, 150–51, 152, 209, 269, 270–72, 274, 276, 277, 279, 280, 284, 364; Raymond 57, 61, 283, 335
Lodge, Raymond 56–7, 87, 269, 270, 272, 274, 276, 336, 361, 364
logical positivism 169
London: the 'Little Blitz' 1; HD visits 106, 115, 116, 143, 145; fortune telling in 150; V-1 flying bombs 318–19
London Evening News 218
London Psychical Laboratory 127, 129, 261
London Spiritualist Alliance (LSA) 73, 83, 115, 124, 171, 177, 251, 253, 254, 341; HD's seances 117–24, 126, 127–8, 131, 136, 160; the Duncans' house in Thornton Heath 126–7; contract with HD 127, 136; publishes reports on the Duncans 129; the Duncans' repatriation to Scotland 137; and Price's book 138, 139; blames Henry 139; ectoplasm 240; renamed 336
Longman, Leah 333
Loseby, Charles 8–12, 51, 194–7, 199, 202–13, 215, 216–17, 233, 256, 281, 283, 295, 296, 308, 311, 314–18, 320, 321, 345, 354, 358
Luce e Ombre journal 140, 365
Ludendorff, Erich 92
Ludwig, King of Bavaria 95
Luftwaffe 2, 178
Lusitania 264
Lyon, Margaret 360

Macbeth, Mrs (of Perth) 168
MacCarthy, Desmond 248–9, 344
McDiarmid, Dr (lectures in Callander) 30
MacDonald, Margaret 277, 278, 359
MacDonald, Ramsay 275, 276–8, 359
Macdonald, Sheriff, KC 159, 161
McDougall, Professor William 96, 130, 140, 223, 231, 255
McEwen, Elspeth (executed for witchcraft) 17, 18, 19, 22, 37, 83, 285, 363
MacFarlane, Archibald (HD's father) 31, 32, 40–41
MacFarlane, Florence 218
MacFarlane, Isabella (HD's daughter)

62–3, 68, 128, 142; birth 45–6; attacked by a ferret 65, 77; marriage 166; her husband reported missing 176
MacFarlane, Isabella (HD's mother) 31, 32, 34, 35, 46, 201
MacFarlane, John 31, 36
MacFarlane, Mary 41
MacFarlane, Nell *see* Duncan, Helen
MacFarlane, Norman 31
MacFarlane, Peter (HD's brother) 33, 46
MacFarlane clan 31, 32, 41, 45, 355, 360
McGinlay, Mary 126, 128, 132, 136, 142–5, 202, 204, 334
McGonagall, William 67
MacGregor, Robert (Rob Roy) 28, 29
MacHattie, Mrs (gypsy medium) 174
McIndoe, J. B. 102, 112, 134n, 140, 145, 153, 160, 177, 187, 197, 260, 321
Mackay, Charles 30; *Extraordinary Popular Delusions and the Madness of Crowds* vii, 23
MacKay, Elizabeth 156, 157
Mackenzie King, W. L. 272–3, 299, 301
Mackie, George 207
Mackie family 18, 22, 79
MacLain, David 68
MacLain, Mrs (Auntie Mac) 67, 67–8, 76, 81
McLaren Trust 27–8
McNab family 28
McNib (of *Edinburgh Evening News*) 67
Maggie (HD's house guest) 334–5
Magic Circle 189, 244, 292, 295, 359; Occult Committee 188, 274
'Magical Battle of Britain' 289
Magicians' Club 143
magnetism 52
Malmesbury, Susan, Countess of 128
Maltby, Colonel 289
Manchester 54
Manchester *Empire News* 139, 141
Mann, Thomas 95
Margate 150
'Margery' *see* Crandon, Mina
Martin, Mrs (in Torquay) 186
Martin, William 118
Mary, Queen of Scots 19, 50, 210
Marylebone Spiritualist Association 211, 275
Maskelyne, Captain Clive 99
Maskelyne, J. N. 84, 226, 232, 233; *Modern Spiritualism* 226

Maskelyne and Cook, illusionists 84
Mass-Observation 175, 336
Master Temple Psychic Centre, 301 Copnor Road, Portsmouth 6, 178, 179, *181*, 186, 189–90, 198, 231, 241, 284, 291, 308, 359
materialism 53, 89, 91
materialization 83, 85, 86, 87, 89, 102–3, 109, 111, 119, 125, 128, 136, 143, 145, 147, 154, 168, 207, 230, 232–4, 245–51, 264, 276, 284, 291, 300, 317, 327, 332, 333, 336, 341, 342, 352, 357
Mathew, Theo 283, 297–8, 309–10, 313, 347
Maude, John, KC 4–9, 12, 200–206, 208, 211, 214, 215, *263*, 294–5, 302, 317, 319, 358
Maugham, W. Somerset 173
Maule, Esson ('E. M.') 145, 153–9, 162, 233, 239, 240, 245, 328
Maxim, Sir Hiram 84
Maxwell, Jean 285–6
Maxwell, Sir John 18
Mead, Gunner T. A. 313
The Medium (a periodical) 73
mediums: fined 5; in the First World War 47–8; and the Fox sisters 49; standard repertoire 49; condemned by the Catholic Church 53; women as 54; jealousies among 73; fraudulent 84–5, 134, 145, 148, 152, 227–9, 232, 338; mental instability 85; advertising by 105, 142; Victorian 112; inter-war 112; prosecution of 148–52, 186; air-raid forecasting 175
Melrose, Daniel (of Callander) 31
Menteith Hills 31
Mercier, Charles 269
Mesmer, Friedrich 49
mesmerism 49, 55, 116, 270
Metcalfe, Harvey 100
Methodists 75
Methuen & Co. 61
Metropolitan Police 150, 152, 284, 290, 291, 299; Special Branch 185
MI5 184, 185, 197, 289, 290, 294, 295, 302; B19 (renamed B1K, later absorbed into SLB2) 186, 295; 'D' Division (Counter-Espionage) 184, 294; SLB 185–6; SLB2 186, 295
MI6 185, 289

INDEX

Miles, A. J. (of Cefn Coed) 242–3, 245
millenarianism 75
Milton, John 50
Ministry of Information 188
Le Miroir 92
Misell, Benjamin (medium) 187
Mission Hall, Callander 27
Monck, Francis Ward 84–5, 89, 150, 286
Monmouth, Bishop of 167
Monslow, Walter 345
Montagu Scott, Mr 123, 126, 240
Montgomery, Ernesto 289
Moore, June 328–9
Mormonism/Mormons 49, 75
Morning Post 125, 138, 151
Morris, Louise Meurig 152
Morrison, Herbert 199, 279, 282, 283–4,
    297, 298, 302, 322, 325, 343, 358
Morrison, Rev. William 35–6
multiple personality disorder 260–61
Munich 95
Murray, Frank 76, 80
Murray, Jim 75, 76, 80
Mussolini, Benito 173
Myers, Frederick 56, 57, 86, 88, 253, 336

Nagasaki 327
National Bible Society of Scotland 60
National Laboratory of Psychical Research
    (NLPR) 116–17, 125, 126, 130–35,
    144, 161, 162, 168, 187, 231, 237, 253;
    International Research Council 152
Nature (journal) 98
Nazis 288, 289; Occult Bureau 288
Neech, Bill 347
Needleman, Jacob 362
Nephi (an angel) 75
New Age paganism xi, 363
New Statesman 309, 310
New York Police Department 148
Newberry, Chris 340
Newman, Cardinal 269
News of the World 218, 257, 308–9
Newsam, Sir Frank 293
Newton, Sir Isaac 51, 52, 87
Nicholson, Major (MI5 officer) 294
Nita, Madame 150
Noah's Ark Society 362
Noël, General 85
Noël, Madame 85, 91
Noël, Maurice 85

Norman's Pool, Callander 31, 34, 46
North Berwick church 20
Northage, Ivy (medium) 338
Northcliffe, Lord 269, 280
Nottingham 351–2
Nottingham police 350–53, 356

Oaten, Ernest 95, 102, 139, 140, 141, 161,
    196, 345
Occult Review 61, 268
'odic force' 288
oesophageal diverticulum 237, 238
O'Hara, Sadie 166
Old Bailey (Central Criminal Court),
    London 2, 51, 102, 200, 203, 204, 231,
    235, 241, 244, 257, 280, 290, 291, 294,
    308, 309, 317, 323, 324, 344, 358, 360
Old Bailey Trial Series 248, 315
Old Moore's Almanac 40
Oliver, Mr Justice 316
'Operation Cone of Power' 289
'Operation Mistletoe' 289
Oram, Arthur 177
Osborne Leonard, Gladys 57, 116, 256,
    272, 273, 277, 327
Ouija boards 272, 363
Owen, Robert 53
Oxford University 172

Paignton 186–7
Paisley 18, 21, 23
Palladino, Eusapia 88, 91, 96, 116, 226,
    232, 240, 272, 340
Pankhurst, Emmeline 306
parapsychology 362
Parsons, Denys 241, 269; 'Testimony and
    truth' 248
Passchendaele 95
Peake, Sir Osbert 199, 283
Pedler, Simpson 204
Peedle and Cozbie: *The Fallacie of the Great
    Water-Drinker Discovered* 236
People's Journal 165, 219n
Perth 168
Pharmacy and Poisons Act (1933) 200
Phillimore, Mercy 117, 119, 121, 122, 123,
    127, 129, 137, 145, 254, 299
Pickett, Able Seaman Peter 192, 241–2
Piper, Alta 56
Piper, Leonora (American medium) 56,
    116, 258, 265, 268, 272

Podmore, Frank 256; *Modern Spiritualism* 226
Poe, Edgar Allan 268
Pohl, Baron von 128
Police Review 310
Portsmouth 177–9, 189, 204, 215–16, 284, 288, 291, 292, 293
Portsmouth Brotherhood 272
Portsmouth City Police 186, 189, 193, 196–7, 208, 239, 243, 291
Portsmouth Evening News 189, 194
Portsmouth Magistrates Court 196–7, 288, 290
Pound, Ezra 47
Powell, Dr Ellis T.: *Psychic Science and Barbaric Legislation* 72–3, 196, 314
Presbyterianism/Presbyterians 27, 30–31, 80
Preston 209, 263–4, 357
Price, Professor H. H. 172, 261
Price, Harry 13, *109*, 141, 142, 145–6, 148, 164, 168–9, 188, 224, 228, 268, 279, 292, 326, 329, 332, 334; at Willi Schneider's seances 96; and the National Laboratory of Psychical Research 116, 117, 125–6; reviled by Spiritualists and psychical researchers 124; disposal of his library 124–5; letter to Miss Phillimore 129–30; flash photographs of a Duncan seance 131; HD's anguish 132; X-ray photograph of HD 132–3; offers Henry a second deal 137; and the cheesecloth issue 140; and Mary McGinlay 143–5; in Edinburgh 145; the Barbanell-Goldston alliance 152; accused of entrapment 161–2; debunking lectures 168; on HD 187, 252; and HD's Old Bailey trial 201, 209; on ectoplasm 235, 240; and stage swallowing 236–7; and Miles 242–3; and Conan Doyle 276; HD's appeal 314; and Donald West 330; and cinematographically recorded seances 338; recording of Albert's voice 355; death 358–9; *Regurgitation and the Duncan Mediumship* 138–40, 202, 220, 293; *Leaves from a Psychist's Casebook* 163, 167
Prison Commission 311
Privy Council 18
Proceedings of the Archaeological Society of Scotland 29

Protestantism 27
Psychic Book Shop and Library, London 274
Psychic News 12, 143, 152, 167, 183, 199, 287, 313, 326, 336, 347, 352, 357, 361
'Psychic Research Centre', Edinburgh 159–60
Psychic Science 177
psychometry 74, 82, 104, 165, 187, 227, 325
Public Record Office 290
Punch 116

Queen Charlotte's Midwifery Hospital, London 130
Queen Elizabeth, HMS 181
Quinlan, Mrs (of Manchester) 341–2

R-101 airship 125, 154, 276–7
Radford, E. A. 287
radio 337
railway, social impact of 25, 112
Rathbone, Eleanor 199
Rayleigh, Lord 115
Redhill Spiritualist church 325
Reichenbach, Karl, Baron von 288
Reid, Dr E. S. 128
reincarnation 49
Renfrewshire 22
Revelations of a Spirit Medium 226, 227
Rhondda, Lady 175
Ribbentrop, Joachim von 269
Richet, Dr Charles 85–9, 91, 92, 247, 249; *Thirty Years of Psychical Research* 86
Rob Roy Visitor Centre 360
Roberts, Estelle (medium) 264, 357; *Red Cloud Speaks* 263; *see also* Stead, Estelle
Robertson, Colonel (of Callander) 27
Robertson, Rev. Dr James 25, 29
Robey, George 3, 120, 199
Robey, J. E. 3, 198, 199–200, 293, 309, 358
Robinson, James 241
Roosevelt, Franklin D. 268, 301
'Rosalie' (a spirit girl) 168
Ross, Hannah (Bostonian medium) 249
Rosser, Llewellyn 178, 186
Rothermere, Lord 131
Royal Air Force (RAF) 176, 199
Royal Courts of Justice, Strand, London 316, 319

Royal Navy 175, 230
Royal Oak HMS 230
Royal Society 51, 86, 87
Russell, Superintendent L. R. 313
Rust, Dr Montague 102, 105, 112, 115, 117–20, 140–41, 251, 260
Rust, Jane 193

Saints: Augustine 50; Paul 83, 250
St Thomas's Hospital, London 134, 136
Salem witch trials 79, 250
Salter, W. H. 311, 314–15, 330, 336
Sampson, Agnes (executed for witchcraft) 20, 29
Saul 48, 111
Schneider, Rudi 95, 96, 124, 125, 135, 143, 188
Schneider, Willi 95, 96, 124
Schrenck-Notzing, Baron Albert von 91, 92, 94, 95, 96, 125, 126, 225; *Materialisationsphänomene* 91
science/religion 49, 52
Scientific American 96, 223
Scoffern, John: *Explosive Spiders and How to Make Them* 228; *Firework Pie for a Picnic* 228
Scoggins, Annie (transfiguration medium) 170
Scole Circle, Norfolk 362
Scot, Reginald: *Discoverie of Witchcraft* 125, 236
Scotch Girls Friendly Society 33
Scotland Yard, London 188, 219, 290, 291, 292
Scott, W. M. (Dundee photographer) 153, 162
Scott, Sir Walter 28, 45, 268; *The Lady of the Lake* 25
Scott-Horscroft, Reginald 178
Scottish Office 322
'Scratching Fanny' 51
seances: HD's 6–8, 78–82, 102–5, 113, 115, 117–26, 130–34, 136, 140–41, 143, 154, 155–6, 163–4, 167, 168, 177, 186–7, 190–93, 212–13, 229, 242, 245, 261–4, 271–2, 280–81, 291, 312, 327–9, 331–3, 338, 340–42, 349, 350, 351, 354, 357; held in darkness 6–7, 54, 81; Mesmer's 49; and the educated élite 55–6; Eglinton's 83–4; Home's 87–8; Palladino's 88; Schneider's 95;

Gena attends her first 104; the Catholic Church and 111; Madame Blavatsky's 116; LSA rules 117
second sight 34, 41, 51, 67, 68, 87, 201
Second World War 1, 2, 3, 6, 11, 13, 61, 69, 173–6, 181–6, 199, 229–30, 285, 288, 289, 290, 302, 315–16, 318–19, 323, 325, 327, 335
Sefton-Cohen, Arthur 198
Segrave, Sir Henry 357
Seton-Karr, H. W. 83, 84
Shakers 49
Shakespeare, William 57–8; *Macbeth* 20–21, 125, 286
shamanism 50
Shatford, Sarah Taylor (American medium) 57
Shaw, George Bernard 112–13, 265, 269, 280
Sheargold, Richard 342
Shelley, Percy Bysshe 215, 268; 'A Song of Italy' 296
Sheridan, Clare 300n
Sheridan, Wilfred 300n
Sheriff Summary Court of the Lothians and Peebles, Edinburgh 159
Sidgwick, Eleanor 115, 116, 225, 257, 265
Sidgwick, Henry 56, 86, 88, 115, 265, 336
Sidney, Sir Philip 45, 269
Sitting Bull, Chief 299
Sitwell, Sir George 86
Slade, Henry (American medium) 149–50
Sladen, Midshipman A. E. H. 182
Sloan, John (physical medium) 73
Smith, Lady Eleanor 312–13
Smith, Frank 163–4
Smith, Joseph (founder of Mormonism) 75
Smith, Mrs (wife of Frank) 164
Smith, Sir Thomas 60
Smyth, J. P.: *The Men Who Died in Battle* 61
socialism 53, 185, 195, 280, 282, 359
Society for Psychical Research (SPR) 2, 10, 12, 124, 177, 242, 248, 261, 311, 333–4, 341, 359, 362; founded (1882) 56; 'Eva Carrière''s seances 92; archives 94, 115, 169, 289; the American SPR 96, 140, 237; and the Crandons 99; Gladstone and 115–16, 266; break-away members 116, 125–6; Price's library 125; overtures to HD 127; and Price's

book 139; 'The Probe' 172, 188;
museum *223*; Stead abhors 264; Salter's
history 336; *Proceedings* 94, 330
Society of Communion 72, 110
Society of the Inner Light 289
The Solicitor 343
Somervell, Sir Donald 322
Souter, James 101, 126
Southend Society of Spiritualists 142
Sowden, Hilda 154, 155, 157
Spare, Austin 280
speaking in tongues 49
Spearman, Gladys (medium) 187
Spencer, William 291, 292
Spenser, Edmund 19
'spirit depots' 48
spirit guides 76, 94, 189, 209; *see also*
individual guides' names
spirit hands 111, 243, 244
spirit photography 48, 102, 152, 206, 264,
274
'spiritism' 49
spirits: communication with 4, 9, 41,
49–52, 67–8; Swedenborg and 49–50;
HD's ability to summon in physical
form 69, 83, 102–3; *see also* materialization
Spiritualism: the principles of 47; origins
48; the 'father' of 49; Victorian 52; and
materialism 53, 89; and socialism 53;
the first English Spiritualist church 53;
Darwin and 55; flourishes in the
trenches 60–61; HD ceases being sceptical 68; outlawed 73; and Christian
millenarianism 75; and the Church of
England 84; Browning condemns 88;
popularity in Braunau-am-Inn 95;
churches 110, 175, 328; investigated
111; in the Second World War 175; a
turning point in its history 201;
Houdini's war against 224; a 'violent
hobby' 255; and political life 278; as a
religion in prison 311–12; declines in
vitality as a religion 335; the 'kiss of
death' 347
Spiritualism and Psychical Research
(Exemption) Bill 276
Spiritualists: at HD's trial 2, 8, 9; 'credulity'
of 5; view of Christ 110–11; legal prosecution of 150
Spiritualists' National Union (SNU) 8, 12,

72, 73, 95, 102, 110, 112, 140, 163,
199, 284, 343, 344–5; HD's diploma
141–2, 153, 164, 244, 329, 331;
Freedom Fund 187, 194, 208, 326;
London District Council 194; defence
of HD 194, 196, 197, 201;
Parliamentary Committee 275;
deputation (1930) 275, 280;
deputation (1943) 283, 287, 293, 343;
and Hatcher 287–8, 311; and HD's
appeal 313; claim for number of
Spiritualist members 336; loss of
prestige 359
stage swallowing 236–7
Stainton Moses, Rev. William 73, 84
Stavely Bulford, Mr and Mrs 128
Stead, Estelle (later Roberts) 264, 274,
275, 299
Stead, W. T. 264, 266, 274, 279, 299
Stein, Dr Walter 288
Stephenson, Charles and Martha (fortune
tellers) 286
Stevenson, J. A. 123, 126
'Stewart, Albert' (a spirit guide) 82, 83,
100–103, 105, 113, 119–23, 128,
130–35, 142, 145, 154–6, 163, 166,
167, 170, 173–4, 177, 187, 190, 191,
204, 208, 212, 217, 218, 229–31, 233,
235, 240, 251, 257, 261–3, 271–2, 280,
312, 314, 327, 328, 331–3, 339–41,
351, 352, 353, 355–6, 358, 360
Stewart, Charles (physical medium) 171
Stewart, Major 128
Stirling District Tourism Limited 360
Straw, Rt. Hon. Jack, MP 365
Suez Crisis (1956) 350, 356
Summers, Montague 111
Sunday Dispatch 235, 309
Sunday Pictorial 283
Sunday Times 152, 248
Swaffer, Hannen 99, 235–6, 275, 279–82,
302–3, 312, 325, 345, 347, 358
Swayne, Major and Mrs J. S. 128
Swedenborg, Emanuel 49–50, 73

table turning 76, 96
Taylor, Varina (of Southport) 239
Teddington, Middlesex 40
telegraphy 269, 270
telekinesis 95
telepathy 269–70, 362

INDEX

television 337
Temple, Shirley 102
Tennyson, Alfred Lord 55, 269
Terrington, Lady 252
Thackeray, William Makepeace 55
Theosophical Society 116
Thomson, J. J. 115
Thomson, Lord 125, 276
Thornton Heath, Surrey 126–7, 128
thought transference 52
Thouless, Robert 248
Tiesenhausen, Kapitänleutnant Hans-
    Diedrich von 181, 182, 183
Tillyard, Professor R. J., FRS 98
The Times 308, 365
Timmins, Mr (chiropodist and healer)
    351, 356
Tindal Atkinson, Sir Edward 197, 200,
    293, 309
Titanic, sinking of 150, 244, 264
Todd, Dr 35, 38
Toft, Mary 259–60
Tomson, Eva and Willie 147, 148
Torquay 186
trance 49, 75, 81, 83, 95, 97, 99, 111, 121,
    135, 154, 167, 174, 256, 300, 328
Treherbert, Rhondda Valley 167–8
Trollope, Anthony 55
Trossachs 23, 24
Truth 309
Tudor Pole, Wellesley 283, 302
Two Worlds newspaper 54, 139, 142, 161,
    194, 345, 353, 356, 357
Two Worlds Publishing Company 208

U-331 submarine 181, 182
University Ghost Club, Cambridge 56
University of London 125; Library 202,
    220, 240

V-weapons 318–19, 323, 325, 327
Vagrancy Act (1824) 5, 73, 85, 149, 150,
    151n, 187, 188, 193, 197, 284, 285,
    286, 290, 299, 323, 344, 345, 346
Valiant, HMS 181, 182
veridical dreams 111
Vernon-Smith, Mrs (of Folkestone) 282
Verrall, Margaret 265
Victoria, Queen 22, 27, 31, 32, 266, 269,
    323, 324
Villiers, Major Oliver 125

Vivian, Dr Margaret 127, 142, 235, 251

W. T. P. *see* Tudor Pole, Wellesley
Wainwright, Miss (of St Leonards-on-Sea)
    272
Wallace, Alfred Russel 149, 267
Wallis, E. W. and M. H.: *How to Develop
    Mediumship* 64
Walter (brother and spirit guide of Mina
    Crandon) 96, 97, 99, 101, 237, 243n,
    261
Walther, Dr Gerda 152
War Cabinet 295, 298, 303
War Office 175, 288–9, 294, 295, 301, 302
Warriston Crematorium, Edinburgh 354
Waymark, Mrs (medium) 184
Webber, Jack (physical medium) 170–71,
    210, 240
Weekly Intelligence Reports 183
Wellington, Arthur Wellesley, 1st Duke of 5,
    112
Wembley, London 106
Wesley, John 75
West, Chief Constable Arthur 11, 193, 197,
    199, 201, 202, 215–16, 220, 234, 239,
    291, 292, 293, 309, 310, 358
West, Donald 1–5, 7, 10, 13, *223*, 234,
    241, 243, 246–7, 248, 261, 262, 292,
    310–11, 315, 329, 330, 332, 334, 359
Western General Hospital, Edinburgh 350
Western Morning News 84
White Brotherhood 174
White Eagle Lodge 276, 289–90
White Rose Fellowship 360
Wicca 363
Wild, Hon. Mrs 128
Wilde, Oscar 265, 268, 305
Wilhelm I, Kaiser 39–40
Wilkinson, Arthur 227, 228
Willey, Dr Florence 238, 239
'Williams, Dr' (a spirit guide) 75, 76, 78,
    81, 83, 99–100
Williamson, Cecil 289
Wilson, Geoffrey 212, 359
Wilson, Lady 344
Wilson, Laurence 212, 251
Wilson, Percy 183, 194, 211–12, 230, 281,
    291–2, 321, 356, 359
Wilson, Richard 291
Wingate, Orde 298
Winning, Dr John 212, 251, 311, 329–30

401

Wireless for the Blind Fund 208
Witch of Endor 48, 111, 317
witch-hunts and trials 5, 19, 20–3, 29, 282, 288, 308, 346, 363
Witchcraft Act (1542) 314
Witchcraft Act (1604) 21; amended (1607) 265
Witchcraft Act (1735) xi, 4, 5, 11, 22, 73, 149, 188, 201, 203, 214, 241, 279, 284–8, 293, 294, 297, 298, 303, 309–10, 312–15, 320, 321, 324, 325, 343–6
Witchcraft Acts 317
Witchcraft Research Centre 289
Wittgenstein, Ludwig 45
'Woo Fang' (a Chinese spirit) 170
Woodcock, Vincent 213, 358
Woodward, Mr (physical medium) 170
Wordsworth, Dorothy 25, 29
Wordsworth, William 25, 29, 131
World's Pictorial News 173
Wormwood Scrubbs 287

Worth, Chief Constable Percy (of Scotland Yard) 291
Worth, Lieutenant Stanley 234, 241, 245, 259, 291, 292; attends seances 6, 7, 189–93; at the Old Bailey trial 203, 205–6, 231, 315; at the Portsmouth hearing 204; emigrates 359
Wren, Sir Christopher 268
Wriedt, Etta (American medium) 264, 266, 272, 273, 301
Wright, Mrs (of St Albans) 165
Wydenbruck, Countess Nora 172

Yarmouth 188
Yeats, W. B. 264, 265; *A Vision* 255
YMCA, Callander 8, 31, 38
'Yolande' (a spirit guide) 90
York, Duke of 302
Yorke, Jane (medium) 323–4
Yorkshire Post 321
YWCA, Callander 27